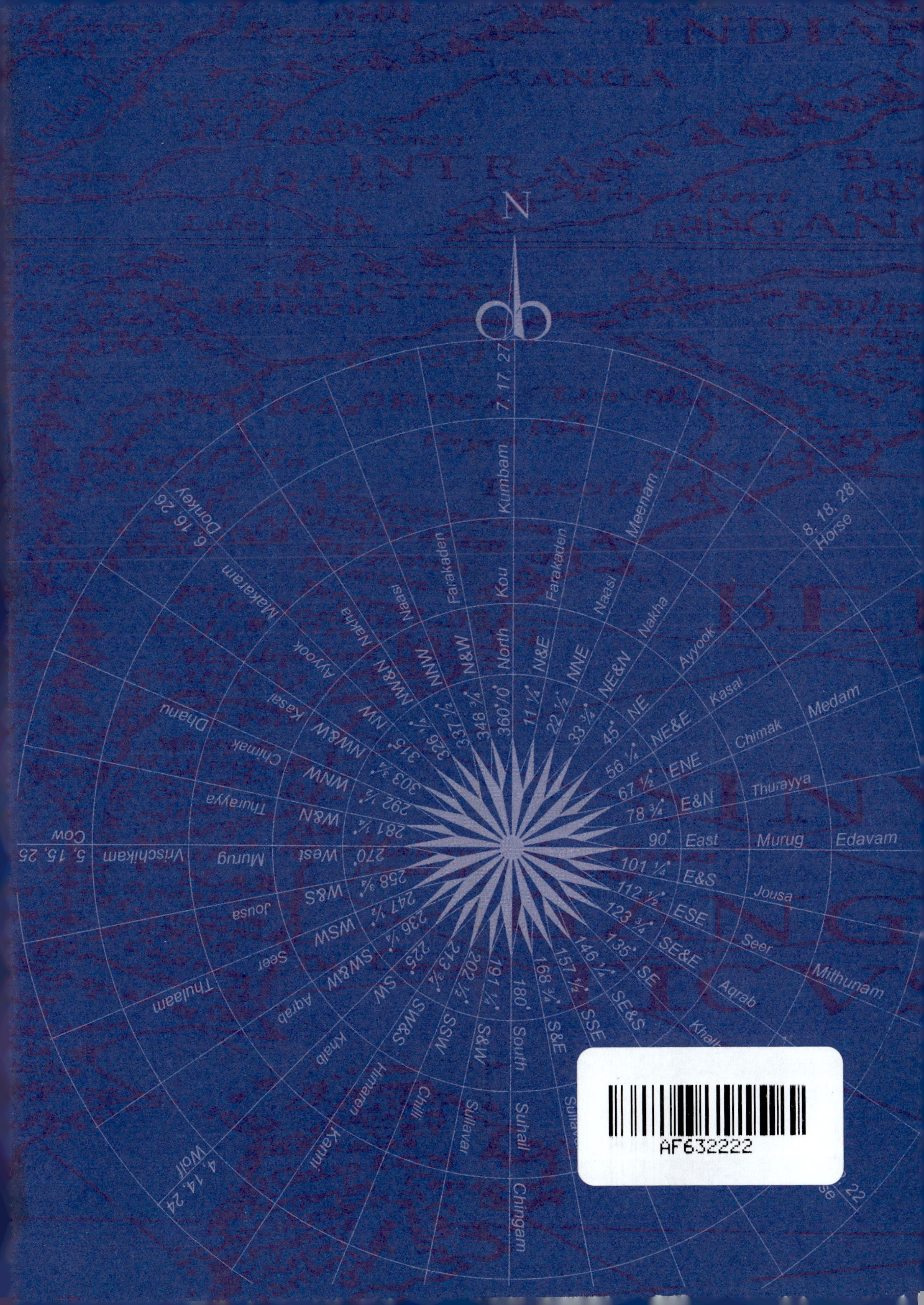
N
North
Kou
Kumbam
7, 17, 27
360°/0
N&E
Farakaden
11 ¼°
NNE
Naasi
22 ½°
NE&N
Nakha
Meenam
33 ¾°
NE
Ayyook
45°
NE&E
Kasal
56 ¼°
ENE
Chimak
Medam
8, 18, 28
Horse
67 ½°
E&N
Thurayya
78 ¾°
East
Murug
Edavam
90°
E&S
Jousa
101 ¼°
ESE
Seer
112 ½°
SE&E
Aqrab
Mithunam
123 ¾°
SE
135°
SE&S
146 ¼°
SSE
157 ½°
S&E
168 ¾°
South
Suhail
Chingam
180°
S&W
Sullavar
191 ¼°
SSW
Chilli
202 ½°
SW&S
Himaren
213 ¾°
SW
Kanni
225°
SW&W
Khalb
4, 14, 24
Wolf
236 ¼°
WSW
Aqrab
Thulaam
247 ½°
W&S
Seer
258 ¾°
West
Jousa
270°
W&N
Murug
Vrischikam
5, 15, 25
Cow
281 ¼°
WNW
Thurayya
292 ½°
NW&W
Chimak
303 ¾°
NW
Kasal
Dhanu
315°
NW&N
Ayyook
326 ¼°
NNW
Nakha
Makaram
6, 16, 26
Donkey
337 ½°
N&W
Naasi
348 ¾°
Farakaden

The *Rahmani* of
M.P. KUNHIKUNHI MALMI
of Kavaratti

The *Rahmani* of M.P. KUNHIKUNHI MALMI of Kavaratti

A Sailing Manual of Lakshadweep

Edited by
Lotika Varadarajan

MANOHAR
2004

First published 2004

ISBN 81-7304-287-X

Published by
Ajay Kumar Jain
for Manohar Publishers & Distributors
4753/23 Ansari Road, Daryaganj
New Delhi 110 002

The study and publication have been
jointly sponsored by NISTADS & INSA

Design
Sophie Gaur

Printed at
Lordson Publishers Pvt Ltd
Delhi 110007

CONTENTS

ILLUSTRATIONS

FOREWORD

The Council of Scientific and Industrial Research from its inception six decades ago and with the dawn of national independence (with the Prime Minister as the President), has been entrusted with wide ranging missions to outline the National Wealth of India and harness these together with the rich knowledge and skills of its people for enhancing their economic and social well being. The Council has taken uncommon and bold initiatives, from time to time, to specially nurture research into outlining the diverse mechanisms combining science, technology, social and economic systems among the self-reliant communities and groups. These have raised the aspirations of highly motivated experts and institutions. The Union of India has a large marine coast and islands in the Arabian Sea, Bay of Bengal and the Indian Ocean. There has been a wide comprehension of astronomy, planetary movements, calendars, winds, rainfall, seasons and of design and construction of sailing boats and ships from local renewable resources unique to each area. Travel, trade, rich crafts have thus flourished.

CSIR provided support for a Research Project on Indigenous Traditions of Indian Navigation (ITIN), from 1987 at the Heras Institute of Indian History and Culture of St. Xavier's College, Bombay and the Department of Geography, University of Bombay. Dr. Lotika Varadarajan, a Fellow of the Heras Institute and Professor B. Arunachalam, functioned as the Co-Investigators respectively in those institutions. The Islands of Lakshadweep and Minicoy were among those studied. Excellent original results emerged and were presented in reports of CSIR in 1990 and in seminars and publications.

Encouraged by these, National Institute of Science Technology and Development Studies of CSIR extended further studies, focusing on the Islands of Lakshadweep in a Project supported by the Department of Culture of the Government of India after 1990. Dr. Lotika Varadarajan was nominated as Honorary Project Investigator. Through visits and interactions with the different groups in the inhabited Islands, the traditions of science, technology and socio-economic aspects of the choice of materials, design and construction of boats and of navigation have been investigated and recorded during 1991-1995. An illustrated publication, *The Sewn Boats of Lakshadweep*, by Dr. Lotika Varadarajan was prepared by the National Institute of Oceanography (NIO), Goa jointly with NISTADS, which are institutions in the family of CSIR. I had the pleasure of recording a Foreword and releasing it at the CSIR Pavilion in the Exhibition at Lisbon in July 1998.

A major book of Navigation and associated subjects, compiled in a manual, the *Rahmani*, by M.P. Kunhikunhi Malmi of Kavaratti, in old Malayalam from notes and oral traditional knowledge imparted by teachers was identified by Lotika Varadarajan. A preliminary translation has been arranged by her with the support of NISTADS. Extensive studies have resulted in an annotated and illustrated presentation in English with footnotes, references, explanatory, statements in English by her in association with experts and advisers of the Indian National Commission for the History of Science of the Indian National Science Academy. The publication edited by Lotika Varadarajan thus provides a valuable compendium of the richness of the knowledge of sailing in Lakshadweep. My congratulations to the Editor and her colleagues on the sustained effort which was coordinated in early stages by Dr. Ashok Jain, Director, NISTADS. The work on the publication has received assistance from the Indian National Science Academy. I am sure it will invite wide interest of scholars internationally and will stimulate further studies

Director General R.A. MASHELKAR
Council of Scientific and Industrial Research
New Delhi
April 2004

PREFACE

The Council of Scientific and Industrial Research has been committed to assist the nation in deriving enhanced and sustainable value from the entire system of endogenous resource base. This includes the rich diversity of natural resources as well as of human resources such as occupational skills that span modern and traditional knowledge systems.

Since the 1980s a coordinated project undertaken by CSIR on "Indigenous Traditions of Indian Navigation (ITIN)" brought out very valuable material on the subject and generated a number of research publications.

National Institute of Science Technology and Development Studies (NISTADS) which carries out research on similar interdisciplinary studies in science, technology and culture, also took up follow-up work on the subject in Lakshadweep in a project sponsored by Department of Culture. It was as a result of such a programme that the *Rahmani* of Kunhikunhi Malmi was identified as a document meriting in-depth analysis, particularly as there are no known publications of Indian rutters. This publication reflects how, seemingly isolated communities in fact, constitute components of mainstream tradition. Although, information on the Indian astronomical traditions of antiquity, Arab seafaring and boat building technologies has yielded a rich atlas of amalgamated traditional knowledge systems, a big lacuna is found in terms of literature on Indian nautical tradition and instrumentation. This material, put together by Kunhikunhi Malmi in this century compiled from the instructional components he obtained from three Malmi *ustads* who taught him, helps fill in those gaps.

This annotated translation into English has highlighted the contribution of the subcontinent in the development of navigation. It reveals the overlap in this area between empirical seafaring and the academic tradition of Indian mathematics and astronomy as also the role of instrumentation in navigation. It has brought out the belief that astronomical skills required of a navigator are also essential in the scheme by which daily life is governed. The *Rahmani* therefore has many sections devoted to household affairs and healing. The language is mixed; the original text has portions based on Arabi-Malayalam, Malayalam and Arabic founts. This is important as it shows it is a rare compilation of seafaring and nautical traditions derived from many sources. It contains several parallels with Arab sailing manuals while aspects of pre-Muslim Indian heritage, including its Greeco-Indian past have been incorporated.

The preparation of this publication has involved complex interdisciplinary teamwork between experts in diverse fields. The very fact that there are several persons in Lakshadweep who have a living memory of these practices invests this document with added importance.

I have to thank Dr. Lotika Varadarajan without whose zest this work would have never been accomplished. M.P. Kunhikunhi Malmi is the author of the original document. The translation was initially done by Dr. M. Mulla Koya. Mr. E.P. Atta Koya Thangal, with his vast personal knowledge of the subject, not only coordinated the preliminary translation but also provided valuable insights in the preparation of the final document. Ms. Saharunnisa from Lakshadweep gave typing support for the first copy.

Dr. A.K. Bag has used his classical learning to interpret the astronomical material found in the manual and Professor S.R. Sarma has worked diligently on the aspects of instrumentation and astrological inputs. Captain R.B. Jayaram (Indian Navy) provided pointers for interpretation based on his perspectives as sailor and hydrographer. Professor S.M.R. Ansari has been generous enough to lend his knowledge of astronomy during the Islamic period. To Ms. Sophie Gaur goes the credit of designing and preparing the final copy for publication. From NISTADS, Dr. S. Mohan has helped in comparing contentious translations against the original Malayalam text and has explained literal meanings of technical words. Mr. A. Wahid has provided technical assistance in computerisation of the project. Dr. S.R. Ali has helped in cartography. Mr. S.A. Nabi has kept accounts for the project. Ms. Veena Kautilya has painstakingly typed the document while the coordination merits go to Ms. Asha Uberoy.

We wish to record our sincere appreciation to Manohar Publishers & Distributors for bringing out this publication. Finally, we must express our gratitude to The Indian National Science Academy for sponsoring the publication.

Director, NISTADS — ASHOK JAIN
November 1998

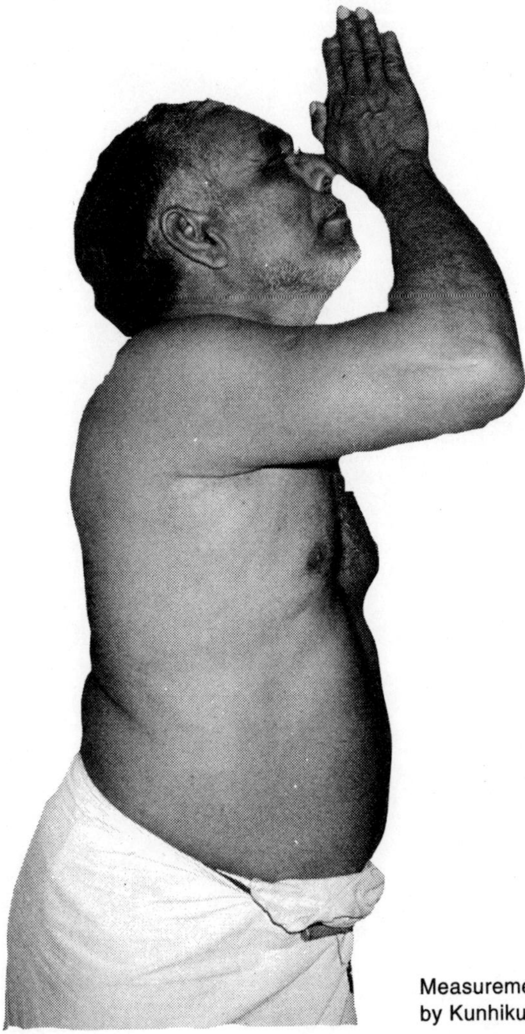

Measurement of Sun at noon
by Kunhikunhi Malmi

INTRODUCTION

The *Rahmani* of Kunhikunhi Malmi enjoys a special position in the maritime history of India. It is a late text. Nevertheless it testifies to the vitality of an oral tradition through which many past practices have been absorbed to flow within the confines of ethnological time.

The strength of Indian astronomy is very aptly brought out by Dr. A.K. Bag in Appendix I. Ancient Indian traditions in astronomy combine systems of observation and measurement with an appropriate range of instruments, supplemented by tables in selected areas. However, since Sanskrit texts are either very brief and succinct or many-layered, they are difficult to deconstruct. In this context, the Lakshadweep tradition, as mirrored in the present text, provides convincing indicators to suggest that the empirical traditions of modern times had overlaps with a theoretical substratum in the past.

In the period, circa 12th to 15th century AD, three sets of maritime tradition may be observed: Indian, Arab and European. The vitality in the Indian sector derived its strength from several sources. The sub-continent was virtually self-sufficient in the prerequisites necessary to service a shipping industry based essentially on the coir-sewn boat, viz., timber, sail cloth and Lakshadweep-Maldives sea-retted coir. The tropical latitudes within which major maritime trade routes were set made recourse to stellar maps for position-finding at sea both feasible and possible.

Luciano Pereira da Silva (1943, 421-422) describes very well the particular circumstances which favoured the evolution of a star compass in the tropics. An observer situated in the terrestrial north pole would have the celestial north pole at his zenith and the celestial equator would correspond with the horizon. Stars observed from this point would appear to rotate in a circular fashion along a horizontal plane. The succession of rising and setting stars as seen in the tropical firmament would be missing.

Inhabitants living near the equator have a much better view of the celestial sphere. There the stars remain above the horizon for twelve hours and below for twelve hours. The stars situated below the horizon rise on the east at nightfall and after the lapse of twelve sidereal hours they appear to sink in the west. From a point on the equator, therefore, it would be possible to see in one night all the constellations, both of the northern as well as those of the southern hemisphere.

The turbulence of the Atlantic Ocean and the dangers associated with the passage around the Cape of Good Hope were distant echoes amidst the waters of the Arabian Sea fanned by the northeast monsoons with tranquil regularity.

Centred as India is between West and Southeast Asia, the sub-continent has both given to and received much from its surrounding neighbours. Communications have not been hindered either by the Himalayas or by the seas surrounding peninsular India. The invasion of Alexander of Macedon led to other kinds of interaction. This is evident in the Siddhantic astronomical repertoire.

The rise of Islam coalesced with the expanding Arab empire. The empire itself absorbed much from its constituent entities. The necessity of marking times of prayer for the Muslim brotherhood and the primacy accorded to the Kaaba as a direction marker (*qibla*) throughout the Islamic world generated much activity in areas such as horology and physical geography. Arab traders extended trade routes opened by the Persians, and journeyed by sea through Southeast Asia to the southern ports of China. By the beginning of the Christian era, Indonesians had travelled to Madagascar, sailing in the opposite direction, in their fragile outriggers (Varadarajan, 1987, 92-103). However, very little is known about their navigational practices, although there are stray references in Arab texts.

The Arabs had developed a 32-point sidereal azimuthal compass rose, which has been much discussed (Ferrand, 1928; Tibbetts, 1971). The place of origin of this wind rose is unknown, although Ferrand places it circa 8th century AD at some point around 10° N latitude (de Morais, 1960, 23-24). Tolmacheva (1977, 33) points out that the Arab azimuthal compass rose, *da'ira*, must have taken centuries to develop. The *Rahmani* of Kunhikunhi Malmi is of considerable interest in this context as it could throw light on what could constitute the zero point in tables of Pole Star elevation.

With regard to the development of European tradition, Mediterranean rather than Viking prescription held sway. Within the Mediterranean, the legacy centred around tidal movement, dead reckoning, wind rose and *portolan* charts. The latter did not have parallels and meridians. After the 15th century the coastline was indicated in terms of thirty-two rhumb lines. Circa AD1200, sailors of Amalfi introduced the innovation of a magnetised needle in the existing thirty-two rhumb wind rose. The navigator would now plan the course with the help of the compass. The chart had central and peripheral roses, each having its own set of distance-measuring rhumbs (da Mota, 1966, 61). While navigating its course, the ship could deviate from the set direction because of currents or the exigencies of tacking against an adverse wind. The *Toleta de Marteloio* provided tables with the help of which such deviations could be taken into account. Taylor (1971, 117-118) dates the *Toleta* to between AD 1286 and 1295, while Albuquerque (1988, 82-83) prefers to situate it in the 15th century. With the top of the chart facing east, for each quarter of wind direction, the chart would show deviations for a trajectory of 100 miles in relation to rhumb lines (Cortesão, 1975, 294; Taylor, 1971, 117-121). With the advent of Atlantic navigation in the first decades of the 14th century, astronomical navigation developed. Circa AD 1480-85 nautical charts began to show parallels of latitude in addition to rhumb lines. Gerhardt Kremer, called Mercator (AD 1512-94) made the next advance circa AD 1569. He drew a distinction between measurements along the great circles and rhumb lines, demonstrating that this difference increased proportionatly to the distance from the equator (Maddison, 1969, 22; Clos-Arceduc, 1960, 143, 146).

Dead reckoning was also a constituent in the Arab sailing repertoire, but there was no direct ancillary computational guide as was the case in Europe. This element is reflected in Section 35 of this *Rahmani*. In their quest for access to the Spice Islands in Indonesia, Europeans began to chart their way eastwards around the Cape of Good Hope and westwards across the Atlantic. The aids which kept pace with these navigational endeavours were not mnemonic devices and creative application of oral tradition, but a complex amalgam of charts, tables and navigational instruments.

The Lakshadweep tradition, as exemplied in this *Rahmani*, is a composite work. It can be linked to early Indian, no less than to Arab tradition. Arab tradition itself had been shaped by Greek and Indian knowledge systems through the efforts of the Abbasid Caliphs. It is inevitable that in an empire as complex and diversified as that of the Arabs, that regional culture-specific variants should have arisen. R. Morelon, in a personal communication to the Editor, has stressed that the durations given for the individual months of the solar calendar in Section 38, and the explanation offered by E.P. Attakoya Thangal for Section 32 are unknown in Arabic and Persian calendrical computation. Elements from the European stream were also absorbed. It can be debated as to whether the process could be described as one of synthesis or syncretic adjustment. Since this is the first among the several existing *Rahmanis* to be studied, it is hoped that the doors will have been opened for further investigation.

The Islands

The set of coral islands in the Arabian Sea situated between north latitudes 8° and 12°31', and east longitudes 70° and 74°, was constituted into a Union Territory on 10 November 1956, the name Lakshadweep being conferred on it in 1973. There are ten inhabited and twenty-six uninhabited islands. The inhabited islands fall into three entities: (i) Amini, Kadmat, Chetlat, Kiltan, Bitra (formerly known as Amindivi); (ii) Kavaratti, Agatti, Kalpeni, Andrott (formerly known as Laccadives); and (iii) Minicoy.[1]

The Indian Ocean has been the the stage of much unrecorded activity. Flora, fauna and material remains bear mute witness to this. The first peopling of the islands of Lakshadweep also forms part of this silent saga. Robinson (1846, 10) noted that in the centre of Amini there was a patch of about fifty acres where the crust of the coral layer had been removed. This made limited agriculture possible in the area. Such an enterprise needed a great deal of labour, but nothing was known about the people who had achieved the task. To this day knowledge has not advanced relating to the identification of the performers of this feat, although Muthukoya (1986, 34-36) postulates that the people may have been of Austronesian origin. Hindu and Buddhist remains have also been found. Islam reportedly reached the islands circa 7th century AD. Today the indigenous population is wholly Muslim. While there are close ties with Kerala, there is also pride in linkages with the Arab heartland.

The Muslim population of Lakshadweep has close traditional links at the social level with the Mappila community of Kerala. This community had its genesis in the Arab system of *mut'ah* marriage which legalised matrimony between the itinerant Arab traders and local women. It is, therefore, curious that the term Mappila is absent on the Islands. Among the Mappilas of the mainland, the titles *koya* and *thangal* denote high standing. Although hierarchical divisions on the Islands are not as sharp as those prevailing on the mainland, Koyas and Thangals enjoy significant status within the Island context.

Professor T. Abdul Aziz (Department of Arabic, Calicut University), in an oral communication, has pointed out that the title *Thangal*, denoting "illustrious achievement", was bestowed on Nambudris. With the advent of Islam, rulers conferred titles such as *Mappila* and *Thangal* on the nascent Arab-Malayali community in Kerala. This was done in order to fix their status within the community. Thangals, both in Kerala as well as in Lakshadweep, are practitioners of traditional medicine in which there is an overlap with esoteric Islam. It is noteworthy that while Malmi *Ustads* (navigator-teachers) in Lakshadweep hearken back to Kerala for published sources of navigational literature, Thangals from Kerala, until three generations ago, would go to the Islands to study medicine as the tradition was on the wane on the mainland (oral communication, Thurab Thangal, Chunkan, District Kozhikode).

Maritime Heritage

Until the 1970's there was an absence of a strong material base to support the literary and inscriptional evidence pointing to the existence of vigorous maritime relations between India and its neighbouring countries. Despite literary references to navigators of the past and to recorded voyages (Varadarajan, 1980, 1983a, 1991), the image was that of a caste-bound Hindu society in which the elite was prohibited from sailing across the black waters. This was enunciated through the concept of *Kalivarjya* (Varadarajan, 1983b). This image is now being eroded. The first evidence came to light as a result of a lead provided by the late Dr. U.P. Shah, Baroda. This led to the location of a set of sailing manuals in

Jamnagar in the possession of Sri Dushyanta Pandya. These have since been acquired by the National Museum, New Delhi. Since that time Dr. Kalpana Desai (Prince of Wales Museum, Bombay) and Professor B. Arunachalam (University of Bombay) have located many more such documents from coastal communities. The present document forms part of this valuable corpus.

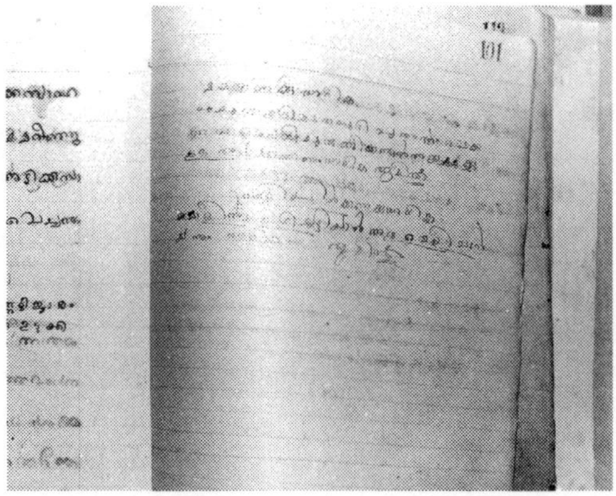

Fig. 1. *Rahmani* with colophon: Collection of K.B. Aboobacker, Kavaratti.

Such texts are called *Rahmani* in Lakshadweep. Several *Rahmanis* are to be found on the Islands. As pointed out by F. Kidave Malmi, Agatti, when a *Rahmani* became old, it would be recopied. Since the *Rahmani* was a practical manual, importance was given to the contents rather than to the orginal source. If at all there is a colophon, it would, more often than not, indicate the owner of the current manuscript and its copyist. For example, K.B. Aboobacker, Kavaratti, has in his possession the *Rahmani* which belonged to his father. On the first page is written "Book belongs to Ahmed Malmi, Malai Illam, Kavaratti, and no unnecessary things to be written to this. This (is) written (by) Kunhi Koya of Agatti dated 22.12.54." On the other hand, the present *Rahmani* does not contain any such writing at the beginning or the end. The only information which is provided is the name and address of the author on the first page.

The question of the origin of the word *rahmani* remains open ended. Ferrand (1924, 211, 212, 214) traces the modern Persian word *rah-nameh*, "book of the route", from the Middle Persian *rah-namag*, which itself was derived from *rahmanag*. The *Rahmanag* was a "Book of the Route" comprising nautical instructions in prose form. Ferrand surmises that the terms *rahmani* and *ramani* are Arabic variations of the original Persian loan word *rahnamag*. Tibbetts (1971, 2) states that by circa AD 850, the traditions of navigational literature current in the Indian Ocean since the time of *The Periplus of the Erythraean Sea* (1st to 2nd century AD) were available in Persian for Arabic speaking specialists to peruse. While the *Rahmanag* contained nautical instructions, there was also the *dafatir* cited by al-Maqdisi, circa AD 985, which could be taken in the sense of a nautical directory serving the needs of ship-masters, agents and merchants, apart from pilots (Fatimi, 1960, 74). The Lakshadweep *Rahmanis* can be taken as additional variants within the genre. Similar navigational manuals attributed to Ibn Majid, Sulaiman Mahri and Sidi Reis have been studied, translated and published by G. Ferrand (1928), G.R. Tibbetts (1971), Baron Joseph von Hammer-Purgstall (1835, 1836).

K.I. Abdul Kader, Malmi, Chetlat, offered another explanation for the origin of the word *rahmani*. According to him, the entire nautical tradition in oral form is to be traced to Abu Bakr and Ali. A man by the name of Rahman had journeyed from Malapuram in Kerala to Shamshir in Arabia to trace this tradition. Having studied navigation at Shamshir, he returned to Malapuram and wrote a book on the subject. This is how the word *rahmani* came into common parlance. This explanation, however, cannot be verified and circumstantial evidence militates against its validity.

The range of subjects covered in the *Rahmani* of Kunhikunhi Malmi is similar to that in the text of Ibn Majid as published by Tibbetts (1971) and Ferrand (1928). However, whereas Ibn Majid tries to relate lunar dates to those of the solar year in terms of *Nairuz* dates (Tibbetts, 1971, 360-364), the *Rahmani* makes use of solar months with Arabic and /or Malayalam names in Sections 38, 39 (cf. Appendix II). The *bashi* measurement, so integral to Ibn Majid (Tibbetts, 1971, 30-31) is not easily recognizable in the Malayalam text. The preoccupation with the monsoon evinced by Ibn Majid (Tibbetts, 1971, 360-382) is found missing in the *Rahmani*. However, local terms for the monsoon may be found. While the Southwest monsoon was called *Aqrab* after its direction point, the Northeast monsoon was given the name *Karakkad*, meaning "coming from the direction of the mainland" (Kerala). Unlike the Arabic sailing manuals, the astrological contents constitute a significant proportion of Lakshadweep *Rahmanis*. The reason given by E.P. Atta Koya Thangal, Kavaratti, is that when individuals proceed on a sea voyage, at all times pregnant with danger, every recourse is taken to prevent mishap.

Determination of the auspicious moment, the *muhurtham*, is be done on the basis of the positions of the heavenly bodies. For example, the auspicious moment for launching a new boat is determined by the planetary position at the time of the birth of the owner. Knowledge was a privileged one open only to the Koyas, Thangals and Malmis, the three upper groups in Lakshadweep. From the occupational angle, Koyas were boat owners, Thangals were medical practitioners and Malmis were navigators. According to Kunhikunhi Malmi, in earlier times navigation was taught by Malmis rather than Thangals. This was because for the latter, knowledge of heavenly bodies was important for determining the auspicious moment. For the Malmi, however, this knowledge would be required for more practical purposes because the steering was done by means of an azimuthal compass rose incorporating wind direction.

Apart from this it should also be remembered that for an isolated island community prognostication could play a psychological and therapeutic role. An island environment is much more circumscribed than similar terrain on the mainland. Dominated by the potency of a localised belief system, auto-suggestion can be of an intense order. It is, therefore, not surprising to find many different subjects included in what appears to be an arbitrary order in the *Rahmani* (see Appendix V).

Unlike the sea, the land had paucity in animal life on the Islands. Rats, associated with nocturnal habits, could wreak dire damage on coconuts nestling among the tree tops. For a rat to bite a human in the daytime was an unusual event and its astrological significance was noted (Section 76). References to kings and nobility (Section 68), slaves (Section 89), thieves (Section 63), no less than the reference point of the temple in house construction (Section 60) are suggestive that these segments may have been absorbed from the mainland. The absence of religious bigotry in Malabar which allowed the conferment of the honorific title of *mappila*, son-in-law, on members of the Muslim Mappila community, may explain the inclusion of the temple as a direction marker in house construction on the mainland.

The navigational information contained in the *Rahmani* is essentially applicable to the routes indicated in the text. Much of this information is encapsulated in Section 2, Composite Circular Compass. Since actual sailings had a strong empirical orientation, the textual material contained in the *Rahmanis* was meaningful only in the context of a sustained system of apprenticeship. Buttressed by oral tradition, field data collected in Lakshadweep supports the view that in conformity with Arab navigational tradition, a large number of stellar indicators have been used for purposes of direction finding at sea.

Navigational contents of *Rahmani* can be accommodated within two broad divisions. One grouping comprises *Kou Kanakku,*[2] and includes the names of *nakshatras, raasis,* and *mujiras* (directions). These had to be learnt by heart and recited in a typical sing-song fashion. Shapes of star clusters, distances between stars, movements of the sun and the moon, occurrences of the equinox and solstice were memorised in this way. For the mariner, it was imperative to have instant recall of the co-relation between the positions of the heavenly bodies, seasonal variations and directional bearings. (Informants: the late Saiyid Shaikh Koya, Andrott; A. Kojan Koya, Chetlat). Directional bearings necessarily had a connotation of longitude. If the sailing was along the same latitude, longitudinal distance was measured in terms of linear distance (Section 6). If it involved North to South or South to North distances it was measured in terms of Pole Star elevation, *Kou Nila* (Section 7). The collective term for these longitudinal bearings was *Anavetti Kanakku* (cf. Section 10). Guidelines on how calculations were to be made were included (Sections 14, 34, 36, 37, 41, 45-48). Some stars were directional guides (Sections 7-10) while others were used for prognostication (Sections 23, 42, 50, 53, 58, 63).

The second kind of knowledge was categorised as *Nuri*, and it took its birth circa AD. 1840. This appears to have been integrated within *Kau Kanakku* as may

Fig. 2. *Kuppi*, hourglass, used for assessing speed. Courtesy: K.B. Aboobacker, Kavaratti.

be seen in the quadrennial tables of declinations of the sun (Section 3) the section on port locations in terms of latitude and longitude (Section 4) and Section 35 which describes how such traverse tables were used in a journey from Kavaratti to Mangalore. *Nuri* was based on the work of J. W. Norie, of which the 18th edition was published in 1864 (see Norie, 1864). The continuity in the *Nuri* tradition is shown in a *Rahmani* in the possession of Parthama Seedi Koya, Amini. In this text, tables of declination of the sun are shown. He classifies this as a *Nuri* component. However, these tables are not derived from J. W. Norie but from a book entitled *Useful Tables from the American Practical Navigator*, No. 9, Part II, Revised edition of 1938 edition, Washington, 1940. This book was salvaged from an American shipwreck in Lakshadweep in 1940. It is to be noted that Lakshadweep mariners also utilised the hour glass (Fig. 2). The illustration shows an instrument of European origin. However S.R.Sarma has traced pre-European references to this object (Appendix III).

While *Kau Kanakku* was learnt by heart, copies of *Rahmani* were taken on board for the consultation of *Nuri* tables. The last component which was added was the body of nautical information derived from the work, *Navika Shastram (Otta Kanakka)* by P.I. Koya Kidave, published by Naduvilaketh Hameed, Cannanore, 1939. It was written on the basis of the recommendation of R.H. Ellis. This information is given in "Memorandum to the Presidency Port Officer, No. 649 D/23-2, dated 11 April 1923," on pages 1-3 of the publication. The *Navika Shastram* combines aspects of sailing with navigation and improved instrumentation. It provides yet another input from the west into the prevailing Lakshadweep repertoire.

The knowledge contained in the *Rahmanis* and the technique of using the various instruments are handed down from teacher to pupil. Whereas no overt schools of navigation have been identified in the Islands, there was a well recognised system of nautical training and apprenticeship. Malmi *Ustads* provided instruction both in the home environment and at sea. Apprenticeship started at about the age of fifteen. Each *Ustad* would take about ten students, but only one or two would complete their education (informant: Pandel Attakoya Malmi, Andrott). In Minicoy the period of training continued for about ten years. During this time the student was called Kuda Malmi (informant: Kasimagothi Husain, Malmi, Minicoy). This compendium of knowledge was intimately linked with the tradition of the *odam*, the sail boat of the Islands (see Varadarajan, 1998a). The total emasculation of this tradition is demonstrated by the fact that in Amini, the most outstanding centre for *odam* construction, the late Atta Koya Puthiyapura and Nalla Koya (Akka) built the last *odam* in 1965 (informant: K.P. Pookoya, Kunnipoovaka, Kalpeni).

The following chart incorporates some details about *Ustads* and their pupils.

Ustad	Place	Student	Specialisation
Kunhi Koya Cheeniyoda (contemporary of Uvva) - he learnt from a mainland *musliyar* based at Kadmat	Agatti		*Kau Kanakku, Rapalagai, Kolpalagai.* Reference point for *Bandar Darja* was Beypore.
Panthinoda, circa 1920 son of Cheeniyoda	Agatti	Haji Abu Sala, Kadmat	
Ustad Ahmed Haji Bathada	Agatti	Muqrioda Mohammed Koya Haji, Agatti	
Mythannappura Ahmed Kunhi, also called Uvva, died circa 1975	Amini	P. Seedi Koya Amini	*Bandar Darja, Navika, Shastram, Balisti.* Reference point for *Kau Kanakku* was east-west line from Amini, Vellimakallu (East) Perumal Reef (West).
Saiyid Bukhari, Kanamkulam Muthu Koya Thangal	Andrott	Saiyid Sheikh Koya, Andrott	
Haji Abu Sala	Kadmat	Pandel Attakoya Malmi, Kadmat	
Pathada Suleiman, circa1920	Kadmat	Haji Abu Sala Kadmat	
Ahmed Malmi	Kadmat	C.N. Badar (nephew), Kadmat	
Koya Kidave, died 1975	Kalpeni		

Ustad	Place	Student	Specialisation
Punoda Kunhi Koya, died circa 1985	Kalpeni		Taught use of sextant and compass, reading of maps with the help of divider.
Kunhika Kunhipuvakada, died 1940	Kalpeni		
Yusuf Waliullah, son of Shaikh Mohammed Kasim (grave of latter in Hujra Mosque, Kavaratti)	Kavaratti	Saiyid Bukhari Muthu Koya Thangal, Andrott	
Sheikh Koya	Kiltan	Uvva	
Thekkila-illam Mohammed Musliyar	Kiltan	K.I. Abdul Kadar Malmi, Chetlat. Circa 1954, Kadar's *Ustad* came to Chetlat.	
Ali Manikfan, contemporary of Uvva	Minicoy		*Nuri* position fixing
Kandamathugothi Ibrahim Mali	Minicoy	Kasimkagothi Husain Mali, Minicoy (age 84 in 1995)	

There was thus a rich tradition of transmission of knowledge. A degree of specialisation among Malmi *Ustads* also appears to have existed. When a particular area is mentioned as a reference point, what is meant is that navigation from this point received special emphasis (cf. Section 8, n. 26).

Instruments

Ethnological evidence in Lakshadweep links methods of measuring star elevation through *viral*, finger units, with a set of instruments. This is suggestive of some connections *inter se*. The table of *Kou Kannaku*, Position of the Pole Star, Section 6, mentions finger measurements which reach a maximum of fourteen units. In present times this memory of finger measurements has shrunk to a maximum of four fingers. G. de Almeida (1995, 58), however, demonstrates how single and multiple fingers along with a clenched fist can be read in terms of stellar angles ranging from 2° to 22°. Knowledge of how these finger measurements were taken, no less than how instruments were used is available among some of the Malmi of Lakshadweep.

K.I. Abdul Kader, Malmi, Chetlat, and Pathada Abossala Haji, Kadmat, can demonstrate how finger measurements were taken with bent arm with the nose as the point of reference (Figs. 11-13). Kunhikunhi Malmi, Kavaratti is aware of how the outstretched arm could be used for the same purpose. He also demonstrated how the moment of noon could be assessed by another set of body measurements (Figs. 22-24). Carpentry measures which can be related to astral calculations are shown in Figures 40-43.

Apart from these finger measurements, instruments have also been used. These comprise the *Rub^c^a al-mujayyab* (Quadrant), the *Kolpalagai* (Davis Quadrant), the *Rapalagai* (*Kamal*) and *Kaukutty* (the *Balisti*, or Cross Staff). These instruments are not only mutually compatible, but in the case of the Quadrant, *Rapalagai* and *Kolpalagai,* parallels with pre-Islamic tradition can be drawn (Appendix I, 8.2, 13.4, explanation for Table III). The case for giving the *Kaukutty* an Arab provenance will be made below.

The Quadrant was known in India, at least from the seventh century AD, when Brahmagupta gave a detailed account of its construction and use. Since that time, nearly every astronomical treatise included the Quadrant in its repertoire of instruments. In Europe, although the Quadrant was known to the Greeks, this knowledge was lost and resurfaced only in the 11th century (Dos Reis, 1989, 247). The Quadrant can be used in the day to measure the altitude of the sun and at night to measure that of any bright star. In Fig. 13 (Appendix I),

Fig. 3. *Rub^c^a al-mujayyab* held by Muqrioda Mohammed Koya Haji, Agatti. According to him the weighted string shows declination of sun and time. The placement of the moveable knot on the string is related to the reticulated background to calculate position.

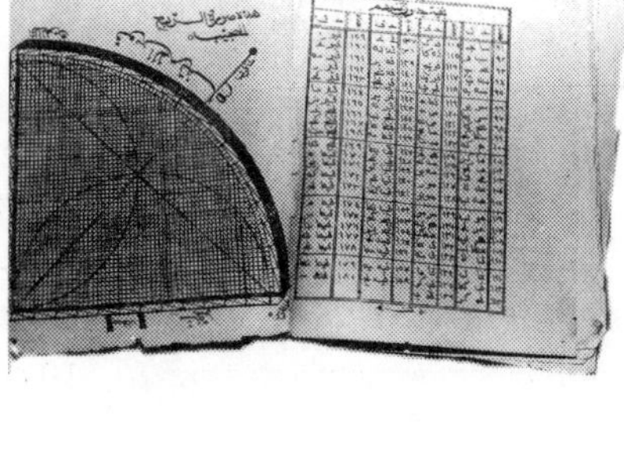

Fig. 4. Tables to accompany usage of *Rub^c^a al-mujayyab.* Courtesy: K.P. Abdul Jabbar Musliyar, Bandwel.

Fig. 5. *Risala*, by Maradim. Printed at Tirurangadi, Kerala. The work describes four ways in which the *ruba*ᶜ *al-mujayyab* can be used. Courtesy: K.P. Abdul Jabbar Musliyar, Bandwel.

the altitude is measured directly on the arc AD. It is used for ascertaining latitude as well as for time fixation. In Lakshadweep it has yet another function– to determine the height of a coconut tree. According to Kunhikunhi Malmi, the Quadrant was used for measuring time and distance from the equator as well as for determining the direction of Mecca in relation to Kavaratti. Muqrioda Mohammed Koya Haji, Agatti, has a set of tables to be used in conjunction with the quadrant (cf. Appendix IV).

Although the whole process cannot be traced, there appears to be a degree of evolutionary linkage between the Quadrant and the *Kolpalagai* (cf. Appendix I, Figs. 13,15). The Lakshadweep *Kolpalagai* is called Davis Quadrant by the English and the Double Arc Quadrant by the Portuguese (see Dos Reis, Sousa Machado, 1992, 93). D.W. Waters ascribes the development of this instrument to Captain John Davis in the year 1595 (Waters, 1958, Figs. LIV-LV, 205-206; cf. Maddison, 1969, Fig. 52). The *Kolpalagai* has two separate arcs, both measuring 90°. However, one is smaller and the other is larger. The ray of the sun is caught on the smaller arc but the altitude is measured on the larger arc. It could, therefore, be suggested that the *Kolpalagai* is a much more refined instrument than the Quadrant. A. Haji Kidave, Mammer, Agatti has a *Rahmani* in his possession in which calculations to be used along with the *Kolpalagai* are to be found. The text is written in Arabi-Malayalam and the manuscript is ascribed to the last century. Calculations are based on an Almanac and are called *falakiya*. A. Haji Kidave, Agatti, and K.P. Pookoya, Kalpeni, own copies of a work, *Bijanul Falag*, written by Zainuddin Mahal Divi Thangal, printed in 1976 and 1978 respectively. Apart from calculations and other topics, this astrological work describes inauspicious directions which are to be avoided (cf. Sections 23, 90).

Fig. 6. *Kolpalagai*

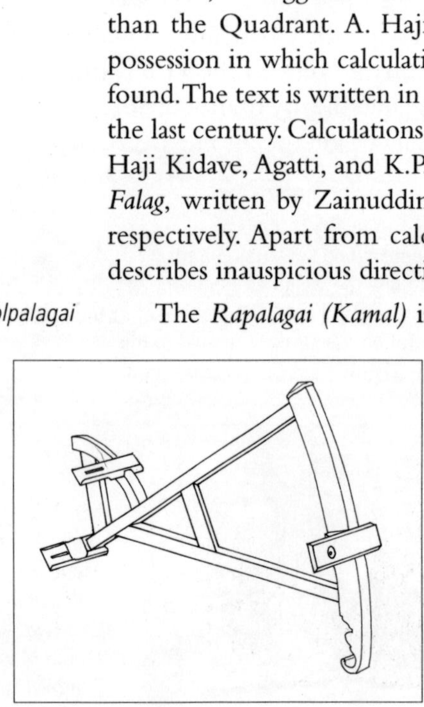

The *Rapalagai (Kamal)* is described in detail in Appendix I, 13.4 and n.8. This instrument to which Vasco da Gama was introduced in Malindi, has been very well described by Sidi Celebi in the mid-sixteenth century. According to Celebi, the instrument had nine graduated boards. However, the one utilised by Ibn Majid, the pilot of Vasco da Gama, appears to have comprised three boards (Ferrand, 1928, 12-16; Pereira da Silva, 1946, 31). S.Q. Fatimi traces the root of *kamal*, a term taken from Tamil-Maldivian sailor's vocabulary, to Arabic *qaws*, meaning to measure a thing by

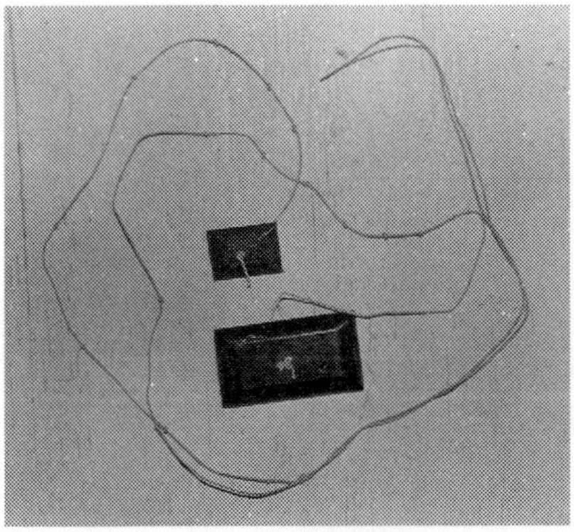
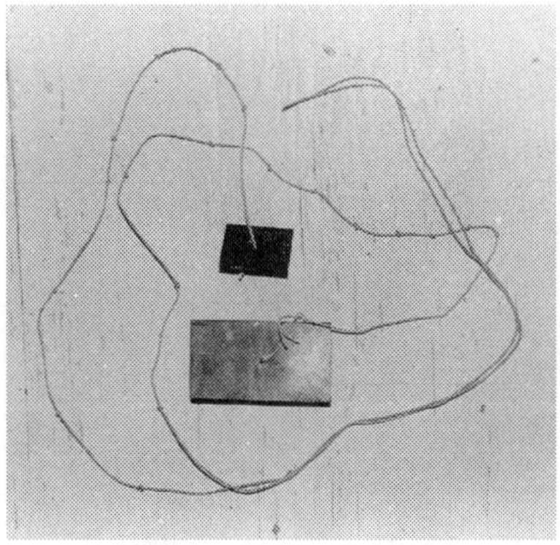

Figs. 7 & 8.
Rapalagai/Kamal.
Tortoise shell.
Front and rear view.
Courtesy:
K.B. Aboobacker,
Kavaratti.

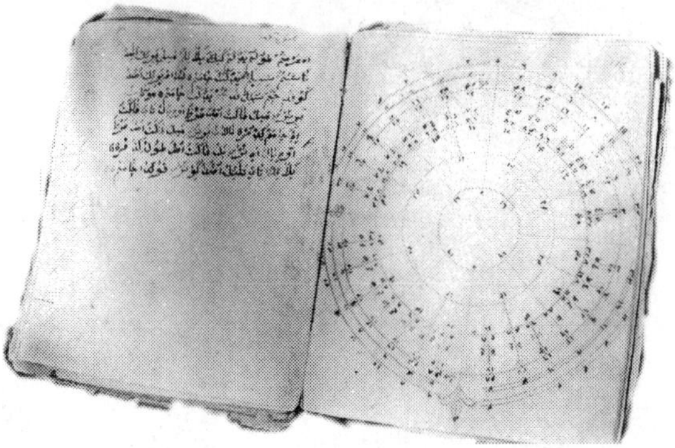

Fig. 9.
Sailing Manual.
Calculations for measurements taken by *Rapalagai.*
Courtesy: A Haji Kidave, Mammer, Agatti.

another thing. Ibn Majid referred to it as *qiyas*, plural of *qaws*, because of the multiplicity of tablets, while an alternative term was *al-khashabat*, the wooden tablets (Fatimi, 1996, 285-288). With the use of the graduated knotted string it was possible to measure Pole Star altitudes within the range of 14 to 5 *isbas*, that is to say, from 24° to 8°4'7". This covered the region from Muscat to the mouth of the Indus, and to the 9° Channel (Maldives). It could also be used in the Bay of Bengal in the same latitudes between Calcutta and the Nicobars. The *isba* was translated by the Portuguese as *dedo* (finger) or *polegada* (thumb) (Pereira da Silva, 1946, 39). Lakshadweep usage shows that *finger* could not be taken synonymously with the thumb as a unit of measurement (Fig. 10). De Almeida (1995, Fig. 32) gives a value of 2° to the forefinger and 2°30' to the thumb. Apart from the two-unit *Rapalagai* in the possession of K.B. Aboobacker, Kavaratti (Figs. 7, 8), K.P. Pookoya, Kalpeni, also has a memory of a two unit *Rapalagai*.

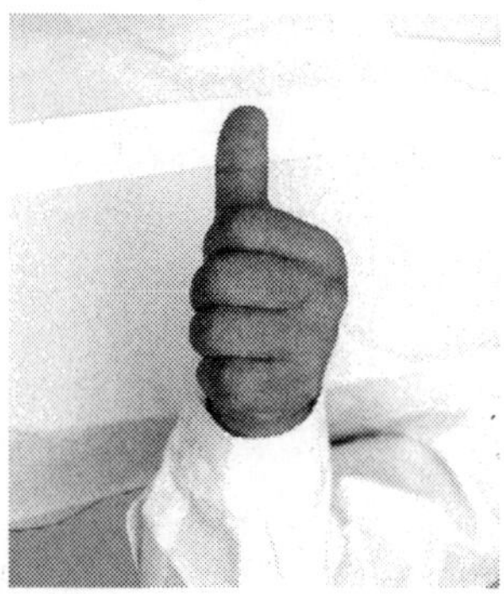

Fig. 10.
Thumb (*polegada*) as unit of measurement.

Fig. 11

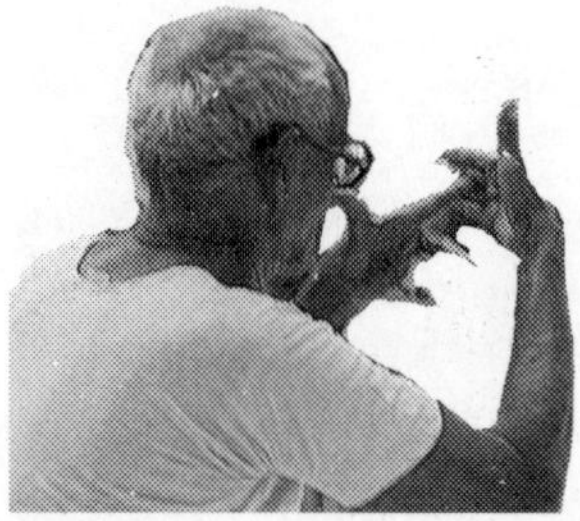

Fig. 12

Fig. 13

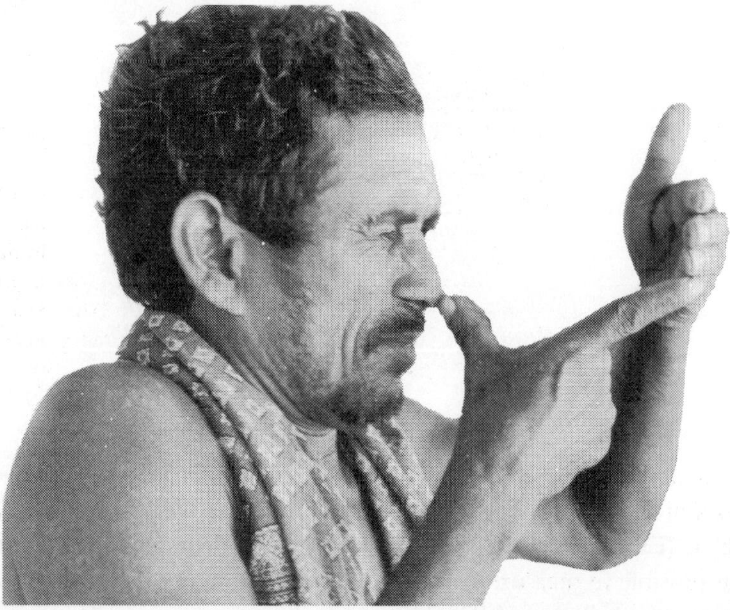

Figs. 11,12,13.
The Portuguese referred to angular measurement of Pole Star altitude in terms of *Polegada*, thumb or finger width measurements. They were introduced to this system by mariners of the Indian Ocean. In Fig. 11 Pandel Pathada Abossala Haji, Kadmat, aligns himself in relation to the Pole Star. In Fig. 12 the altitude of the Pole Star is to be taken. In Fig. 13 K.I. Abdul Kadar Malmi, Chetlat, demonstrates the same practice. In this case also the nose is taken as the central point of focus. Star altitude is measured with the laterally placed finger above the forefinger.

Latif Banglapura, Kadmat, claims ability to handle both the *Kamal* and the *Kaukutty*. Kunhi Koya Cheeniyoda, Agatti, taught the use of the *Rapalagai* as well as the *Kolpalagai*.

In the mid-fifteenth century, Sulayman al Mahri improved the *Kamal* by substituting the cords[3] with a measuring stick called *jaz*. Unlike the *Kamal* which is used only at night for measuring the elevation of stars, the new device can be used also in the daytime for taking solar altitudes (Figs. 14-16). This new device is called *al-Balisti* in Arabic, from which the Portuguese derived the term *balestilha*. In Lakshadweep and Maldives, however, this instrument is known respectively as *Kaukutty* and *Dighu Fila* (Figs. 14-16). Adopted from the Orient in the 15th century, it was called Cross Staff by the English, and was progressively improved in Europe between 1606 and 1712 (Albuquerque, 1988, 11-12, 24-26; Maddison,

1969, 47; Waters, 1958, Fig. LIII, 201-205). C.A. Moura Braz has emphasised that the Portuguese term *balestilha* was derived from Arabic *al-balisti*, meaning "Altitude" and not from Latin *balista* (Moura Braz, 1962, 32). The *Kamal*, however, remained in use in its earlier form despite the development of the *al-balisti*.

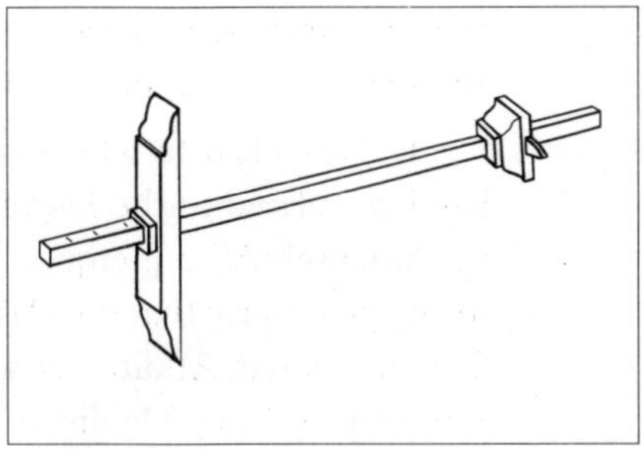

Fig. 14. *Balisti.*

Prinsep, in describing a *balisti* used by a Maldivian navigator circa 1836, states that the instrument was an improvement on the *kamal*. A wooden glider, at right angles to this rod, could slide along the rod. The rod was marked on each of its four surfaces and four gliders could be used for different angular measurements. The scale of the marks had its commencement at the end held up near the eye. It was used particularly at night to mark the altitude of a star and was well suited to measuring the angular distance between stars (cf. Section 9). During the day, when used to measure the altitude of the sun the instrument would be held from the opposite end with the user having the sun at the rear (Prinsep 1928, 5-6; Albuquerque, 1988, 21, Malhão Pereira, 1994,168).

Albuquerque notes the possibility that the Cross Staff may not have been used in Europe prior to 1518, but by the second half of the 16th century its use had become general. The first description on how the Cross Staff was to be made is found in a Spanish source by Martin Cortez in 1551. By 1581, the Cross Staff with three gliders had emerged. An early innovation, which has not been dated, was the cutting of different sets of graduations on two sides of the staff. One was used for measuring the altitude of the stars, the other for zenith distance of solar observations taken at noon. This was done with the help of the table *Regiment of the Altitude of the Pole* (cf. Sections 12, 13; Albuquerque, 1988, 10-28). It would

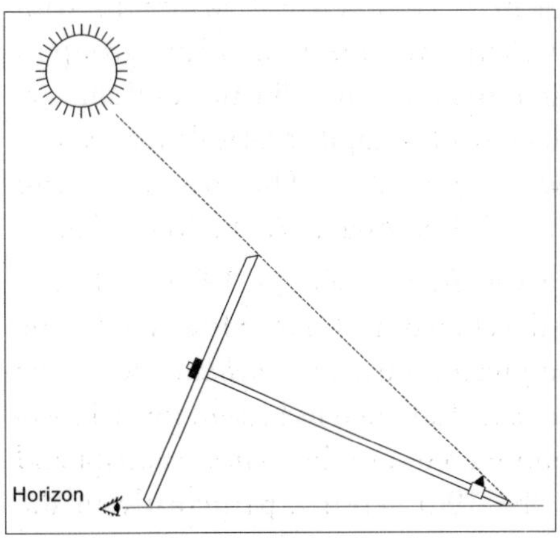

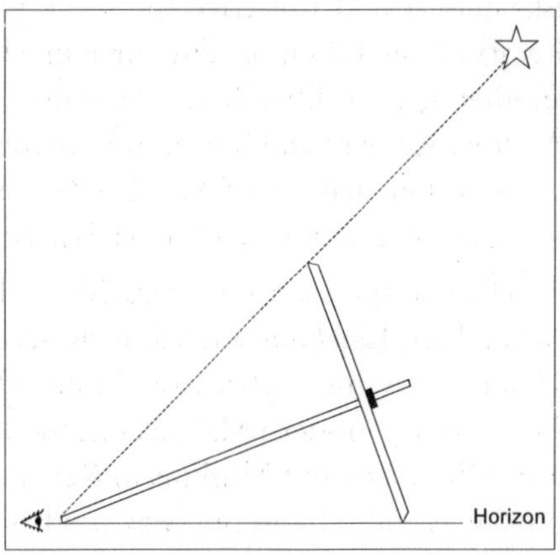

Figs. 15, 16. Drawing to illustrate positioning of *Balisti* for calculation of sun altitude during the day and star altitude at night.

appear that there was a variation in the parts used for taking star altitude at night and that of the sun during the day.

It is not clear to what extent the *Balisti* described by Prinsep can, on the one hand, be related to the *Dighu Fila* and, on the other, to the descriptions provided by Pimentel (Albuquerque, 1969, 74-76) and Waters (1958, 204-205). There is a strong possibility that the *Balisti* was taken to Europe from the Indian Ocean and further refined. Additional studies have to be undertaken of the Lakshadweep *Kaukutty* and the Maldivian *Dighu Fila* before any definite conclusions can be drawn. While this is outside the scope of the present work, it is of interest to note that Pathini Oda Kojan Koya, Malmi, Agatti, has used the *Kaukutty*. His comments would throw much light on the use of this instrument.

Fig. 17. *Rahmani.* Arabic script. Courtesy: A Haji Kidave, Mammer, Agatti.

Language

In the context of Lakshadweep a distinction has to be maintained between spoken language and its written form. The script may be recognized but ethnicity is provided by the language. In view of the fact that Islam was the prevailing religion since the medieval period, Arabic, the language of the Quran was known. At the same time, the structure of society showed a close relationship with Malabar. The language spoken on the islands has been called *Jaziri* (informants: N. Koya Haji, Kilton; Joy Joseph, Department of Linguistics, University of Poona). It was a variant of Malayalam and differed from the language spoken by the Mappilas of Kerala. When islanders spoke among themselves, a Malayali from Kerala would find it difficult to follow the speech. Islanders would not have the same problem as commercial transactions with Kerala obliged them to discourse in Malayalam. Even from one island group to another dialects differ. In the Amindivi islands there was an influence of Kannada. Andrott, Kalpeni and Kavaratti bore the shadow of Mappila Malayalam as well as of the other dialects of Malabar (Andrewskutty, 1973, 7). The advent of Islam gave rise to a new variety of Malayalam, which is known as Arabi-Malayalam.

The script used for Arabi-Malayalam was Arabic (Kunju, 1979, 100). For Malayalam, *Vatteluttu* was the early script developed in Kerala. However, by the 16th century, the higher caste Hindus had given up use of *Vatteluttu* and by the 17th century modern Malayalam, *Aryaneluttu*, had attained its present form. However, Christians and Muslims in Kerala continued to use the *Vatteluttu* script and on the Islands this script was used into the 19th century, particularly in the

Rahmanis. In the present times, the modern Malayalam script has totally displaced the usage of *Vattelettu* script in Lakshadweep.

These developments did not touch Minicoy. *Mahl*, the language and script of Minicoy, was derived from 17th century *Divehi*, the language and script of the Maldives. The reason why *Mahl* is akin to 17th century *Divehi* is because it was in this century that Minicoy was detached from the Maldives and brought within the jurisdiction of the Arakkals of Cannanore. It was thus cut off from later linguistic developments in the Maldives.

M.P. Kunhikunhi Malmi

M.P. Kunhikunhi Malmi was born in Lakshadweep in 1934. His father, Janab Yusuf Malmi, was a well-known navigator and Malmi *Ustad*. Each year batches of seven to ten students would be accepted and taught navigational precepts in the home surroundings. From a very young age, therefore, Kunhikunhi was exposed to navigational lore. He recalls that it was in this way, by listening to the lessons, that, much before his formal initiation, he was able to familiarise himself with the names of stars, the *saayaths* and other related subjects. According to local convention, Yusuf Malmi did not handle the education of his child himself. Normally fathers did not initiate their own children as it was felt that someone outside the family would be more impartial. Only when the educational process was complete would the father accept the role of providing clarifications as and when required.

Yusuf Malmi, himself, had been taught by Saiyid Kasimussani, popularly known as Koliyala Koya Thangal. Saiyid Kasimussani headed the three Sufi orders of Rifai, Qadiriyah and Chisti. He was well known not only on the Islands but also among Islamic communities in South India for his knowledge in navigation and astronomy. The son of Saiyid Kassimussani, Saiyid Mohammed Koya Thangal, had set up a school of navigation at Kavaratti, and it was to this school that Kunhikunhi Malmi was sent.

It was a common practice for teachers to ask students to write down what they had been taught. These notes were then corrected by the *Ustad* and returned to the student. Kunhikunhi Malmi has utilised these notes in the preparation of his *Rahmani*. Saiyid Mohammed Koya Thangal practiced medicine while heading a religious sect. He, therefore, discoursed on many different subjects. Kunhikunhi Malmi preferred to retain those notes which were of a predominantly navigational nature. This explains why the *Rahmani* of Kunhikunhi Malmi contains navigational data in a more concentrated form than is the case with several other *Rahmanis* available on the Islands. It was for this reason that the present Rahmani was selected for study and publication in the first instance.

Circa 1960 to 1970 Kunhikunhi Malmi came in touch with another famous Malmi, Ali Manikfan of Minicoy. Ali Manikfan, at the time, had become stranded at Kavaratti because the monsoon had set in earlier than expected. This *Ustad* from Minicoy taught Kunhikunhi Malmi *Nuri* components of navigation. At this point it is of interest to take note of the fact that, whereas developments in the Amindivi and Laccadive group of islands were controlled by the coir-rice exchange, Minicoy was able to generate other sources for its requirements (Varadarajan 1998a, 11, 29). Sailors from Minicoy not only took service in British ships but also conducted their own sailing-vessel trade in the Bay of Bengal. They switched over to western methods of navigation much earlier than others on the Islands and their navigators became known for their mastery over *Nuri*. The knowledge acquired from Manikfan is integrated in Sections 1, 3 and 4.

When Kunhikunhi Malmi began preparing his manuscript, he enriched his corrected notes with additional information derived from his own experiences and information culled from other skilful navigators. At some point, the original manuscript appears to have got damaged. The manuscript was transcribed afresh by Kunhikunhi Malmi, P.K. Mohammed of Kavaratti, and two other persons. This explains why, at least, four sets of writing are in evidence in the Malayalam manuscript.

Kunhikunhi Malmi has recollections of a primary school which he attended during the British regime. Later he worked as carpenter (*maistri*) in the Public Works Department, Kavaratti. Here he was able to learn modern techniques in house construction.

Kunhikunhi Malmi has been a teacher of navigation since about 1970. He has also made several sailings from the Islands to the mainland. This provided

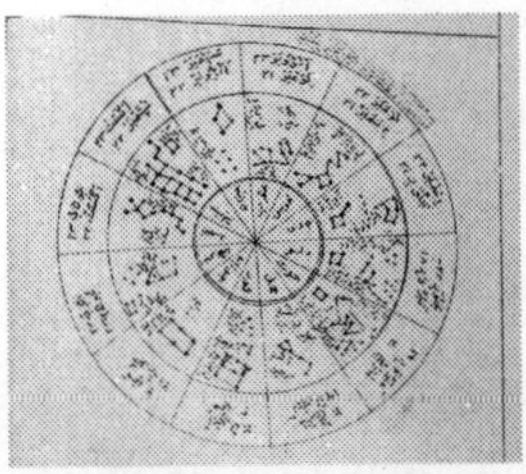

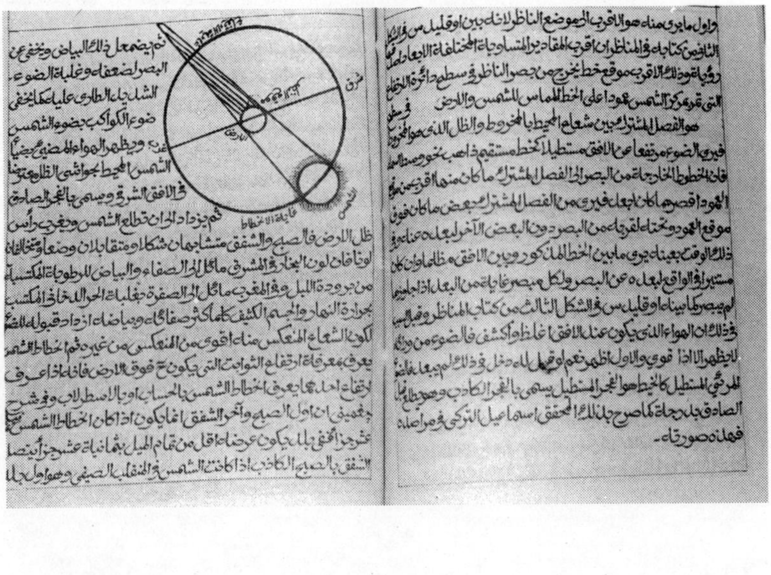

Figs. 18, 19. Pages from *Har Risayatal Mardiniyalu wal habi yatu al Mukubilath wal Aufatu al Islamiya mal Hawashi al Bayani yatu wal burham yatu*, by Ismail Ahmed Nalkat, Malapuram, Kerala. Courtesy: Kunhikunhi Malmi, Kavaratti.

opportunities for his students to obtain practical instruction from him on the high seas. Apart from the present text, he has many other items of navigational literature with him. This includes the Arabic work, *Har Risalatal Mardiniyalu wal habi yatu al Mukubilatu wal Aufatu al Islamiya mal Hawashi al Bayani yatu wal Buharni yatu* by Ismail Ahmed Nalkat, Malapuram, Kerala. Despite his many other preoccupations he has always made himself available and the present translation has been greatly enriched and facilitated by his unfailing cooperation.[4] Had there been no constraint of time he could have explained the text in much greater detail.

Manuscript of the *Rahmani*

The manuscript is written in an ordinary hard-bound copy book, measuring 18.2 × 16.5 cm. There is a water mark on the paper in which only the letters CONQU can be deciphered. From page 1 to page 42, each page is numbered in serial order. From page 43 onwards, every alternate page on the left is numbered in serial order. The last page number is 70 even though one face of the next page is inscribed. The last twelve pages are left blank. On each inscribed page, lines are drawn in pencil for writing the text, and the writing is enclosed in a double border drawn in ink. Although the Malayalam script has been used for the text, the numbers are written in modern numerals. This follows the common convention of South India. The entire manuscript of this *Rahmani* is reproduced in facsimile in Part I of the present work.

The subject matter in the manuscript has been organized under specific headings except in six cases. To facilitate cross-referencing, the headings have been serially numbered by us. Subject-headings have been introduced in Sections 1, 2, 13, 61-63. Twenty-nine Sections deal with *Kanakku*. *Kanakku* is a Tamil word, taken over into Malayalam. According to the *Tamil Lexicon, Kanakku, s.v.*, the range of meanings include number, account, reckoning, calculation, computation, account book, ledger. According to Hermann Gundert, *A Malayalam and English Dictionary*, 1st edition, 1872, reprint, Kottayam 1992, *Kanakku s.v.*, the word, both in Tamil and Malayalam, means 1. Computation, account; 2. estimation, manner, way. The *NBS Malayalam-English Dictionary* by C. Madhavan Pillai (1st edition 1976), reprint, Kottayam 1985, *Kanakku s.v.*, gives: arithmetic, computation, estimation, estimate, account. In the *Rahmani*, the word seems to have much wider connotations denoting, computation, enumeration, numerical list and information in tabular form.

The Malayalam used in this manuscript is somewhat archaic. Out of a total of 92 sections, 53 are marked by the concluding word *Ameen*. According to Atta Koya Thangal, the term *Ameen* carries the meaning, "may god bless us for having arrived at a correct conclusion". It would appear that the author offers this thanksgiving at the conclusion of sections dealing with subject such as calculations, *raasi, nakshatra,* movements of the sun, *saayaths* and related topics.

Similar *Rahmanis* may be found among other navigators of the islands. K.B. Aboobacker of Kavaratti has a *Rahmani* which is written by hand partly in Arabic and partly in Malayalam. The author was Kunhi Koya, the Malmi Ustad of Agatti, who had taught the father of the owner. The colophon is dated 22.12.54. The contents are similar to those of the present *Rahmani.* As in Section 6 of the present work, the altitudes of the Pole Star *(Kou Kanakku)* are given for places along the west coast from Cape Comorin to Porbandar. The same principle holds for the east coast. The first part of the book is written in Arabic and deals with the determination of the *muhurtham.* This is followed by more pages in Arabic in a different hand. The Malayalam script then takes over. Subjects include *nakshatras,* auspicious and inauspicious periods in each month and each day, tidal movements, navigation, *kou nila, mujira,* the azimuthal star compass, use of *Rapalagai,* astrological forecasting, Arabic names of stars, a circular chart in which sailing to the north and south are correlated to stars (cf. Section 7), *Hamal* (cf. Section 86), domestic illness, curing of spirit possession, *raasi nila,* how to deal with rat menace, agricultural operations, seasonal winds and their relation to stars, auspicious times for bloodletting, identification of currents according to compass points, *kol nila* or wind and weather conditions for sailing and the date of *Muharram.* Although the core remains the same, there is much complementary and supplementary data in the individual *Rahmani* such as this one.

Transliteration of Malayalam and Arabic Terms

S.R. Sarma has taken in hand the problem of standardisation of spelling. He notes that the document contains a large number of astronomical and astrological terms. Some of these are Malayalam variants of Sanskrit words, others Arabic terms as pronounced in Lakshadweep. In transliterating these terms in Roman script, attempts have been made to remain faithful to the local pronunciation and local method of transliterating Indian words in Roman script. In this system of popular transliteration, the long Indian vowel sound is represented by two Roman alphabet vowels (*aa* means long *a*; *oo* means long *u*); soft dental *t* is represented by *th*; and palatal *s* by simple *s* (thus *raasi* instead of *rashi* as it written in the North). This will, it is hoped, retain the local flavour in this version although, at times, the transliteration may seem somewhat awkward. However, in Appendices I-IV, Abbreviations and Bibliography, Sanskrit and Arabic words are transliterated with the standard diacritical marks.

Interpolations

In order to provide greater clarity to the text a number of interpolations have been made. These have been placed in parenthesis wherever these have been inserted. Other changes have been duly noted as and when these have occurred.

Translation and Annotation

This study had its genesis in a project "Indigenous Traditions of Indian Navigation", conducted by Professor B. Arunachalam and Dr. Lotika Varadarajan in Lakshadweep between 1987 and 1990. This project had been sponsored by the Council of Scientific and Industrial Research, New Delhi. During the field investigations undertaken for this project, the two researchers were introduced to the manuscript through the good offices of Mr. E.P. Attakoya Thangal, Assistant Director (Planning), Secretariat, Kavaratti. On completion of the project, Dr. Ashok Jain, Director, National Institute of Science, Technology and Development Studies (NISTADS), New Delhi, realising the signficance of this manuscript, provided facilities for its study and publication. The Malayalam text was initially translated into English by Dr. M. Mulla Koya (MM), then Lecturer in Malayalam at M.G. College, Andrott. After this initial translation the first set of verifications had to be made. The process has been repeated on at least two occasions. Mr. E.P. Atta Koya Thangal (AKT) has played a key role not only in coordinating the process of translation but also in maintaining a constant liaison with the author, Kunhikunhi Malmi. Several terms used in the text have become abstruse in modern times and it is singularly fortunate that the author himself could provide many explanatory details through so meticulous an intermediary as Mr. Atta Koya Thangal. Some gaps, however, could not be filled. The task of annotation has involved close team-work between Dr. A.K. Bag, Indian National Science Academy, New Delhi, Professor S.R. Sarma, Aligarh, and the Editor. Dr. S. Mohan (Mohan), NISTADS, New Delhi, readily helped whenever his language expertise in Malayalam was needed. It was he who provided a possible explanation for the term *Marma* in Section 84 of the Malayalam text. This was based on his knowledge of the *Vadakkan Pattukal*, the Northern Ballads of Kerala.[5] However, the relevance of the term *Marma* to the text remains unresolved. The Kunhikunhi Malmi document thus, not only highlights the importance of the oral tradition in India, but also provides a glimpise of the richness of the data encapsulated in the sailing traditions of Lakshadweep.

The Editor is particularly grateful to S.R. Sarma (SRS in the text) for the meticulous manner in which he has gone through the present work and for his help in shaping the introduction. Dr. A.K. Bag (AKB) has readily spared time for fruitful discussion. He has re-oriented his expertise in the history of mathematics and astronomy and helped clarify many aspects of astronomical navigation. We had the benefit of discussing certain aspects of navigation with Captain R.B. Jayaram (RBJ) of the Indian Navy, for which we are deeply grateful to him. We would also like to thank Professor S.M.R. Ansari, Aligarh, for his unfailing help and support with regard to Islamic sources. Thanks are also due to Ms. Sophie Gaur who has painstakingly plotted the maps and prepared the numerous illustrations including photographs so that these can serve as valuable adjuncts to the text.

Editor

NOTES

[1] *When the word* ***Lakshadweep*** *is used in the text, unless it is otherwise stated, Minicoy is excluded from the ambit of this word for purposes of working clarity.*

[2] *The table in* ***Section 6****, taken in terms of Pole Star altitudes, could be called* ***Kou Kanakku****. In Andrott such tables were called* ***Kou Nelli*** *while in Kavaratti the term was* ***Padyam****. Informants: Saiyid Sheikh Koya, Andrott; Kunhikunhi Malmi, Kavaratti.*

[3] *This reading of Fatimi contradicts the statement of Tibbetts that the system of knotting the rope was a mid-sixteenth century innovation of Sidi Celebi. Fatimi, 1996, 290; Tibbetts, 1969, 9.*

[4] *Biographical details have been culled by AKT and MM.*

[5] *Since medieval times the Nair community in Kerala has performed the functions of the warrior class. Training in warfare was imparted through* ***kalarippayyat****, a physical regimen providing both gymnastic training and techniques of the martial arts. Other groups such as* ***chekors*** *(a segment of the* ***Ilava*** *caste, traditional coconut gatherers and toddy tappers), Christians and Muslims also practiced* ***kalarippayyat*** *in their own* ***kalaris*** *or gymnasiums. Warriors trained in* ***kalarippayyat*** *not only served as military retainers but could also be hired to fight in duels (****ankam****) to solve conflicts between opposing parties. This gave rise to heroic ballads, the* ***Vadakkar Pattukal*** *of North Kerala (Zarrilli, 1993, 98).*

PART I

MALAYALAM TEXT IN FACSIMILE

M. P. Kunhikunhi MALMI

Mashaetnapura House.

Kavaratti

Island

(1)

കോഴിക്കോട്.	സുഹേലി.	കല്പേനി	കവരത്തി	അന്ത്രോത്ത്	പിട്ടി	സുത്താന്ത	ബങ്ങാരം
210 / 72 253							
143 / 62 242	76 / 271 11						
187 / 78 258	29 / 218 38	67 / 115 295					
123 / 78 282	89 / 241 81	38 / 182 2	64 / 256 76				
195 / 82 262	41 / 199 19	78 / 121 301	14 / 155 335	67 / 87 267			
207 / 84 264	41 / 171 351	96 / 118 298	31 / 121 301	85 / 91 271	21 / 104 284		
207 / 85 265	48 / 178 358	94 / 123 303	30 / 136 316	82 / 95 275	17 / 122 302	7 / 226 46	
175 / 87 267	62 / 203 23	81 / 138 318	35 / 189 9	58 / 106 286	24 / 210 30	33 / 245 45	29 / 248 68
220 / 89 269	62 / 168 348	111 / 123 303	48 / 134 214	95 / 101 281	39 / 128 308	19 / 154 334	18 / 133 313
180 / 90 270	70 / 202 22	84 / 143 323	37 / 192 12	57 / 144 324	29 / 208 29	42 / 236 56	34 / 238 58
160 / 94 274	91 / 206 26	95 / 166 336	62 / 201 21	55 / 135 315	51 / 212 32	60 / 233 53	54 / 231 51
207 / 95 275	82 / 175 355	121 / 135 315	62 / 154 334	98 / 115 295	49 / 154 334	38 / 188 [illegible]	34 / 169 349
178 / 98 278	96 / 194 14	110 / 150 530	66 / 183 3	76 / 132 312	55 / 190 10	57 / 211 31	51 / 208 28
243 / 99 279	106 / 164 344	150 / 134 314	88 / 148 328	125 / 120 300	78 / 165 45	63 / 159 339	61 / 153 333
240 / 106 285	131 / 169 349	169 / 142 322	112 / 157 337	138 / 130 310	115 / 145 325	112 / 169 249	84 / 165 345

[illegible]

39														
93	273	[illegible]												
6		41												
200	20	269	85	[illegible]										
32		56		19										
215	35	252	72	[illegible]	41	[illegible]								
43		17		40		48								
126	306	197	17	116	296	92	272	[illegible]						
35		45		27		20		30						
176	356	231	51	170	350	126	306	255	75	[illegible]				
70		42		68		74		25		53				
130	310	161	341	124	304	87	275	135	315	101	281	[illegible]		
88		66		82		81		45		60		23		
115	325	172	352	142	322	129	309	162	342	130	310	194	14	

(2)

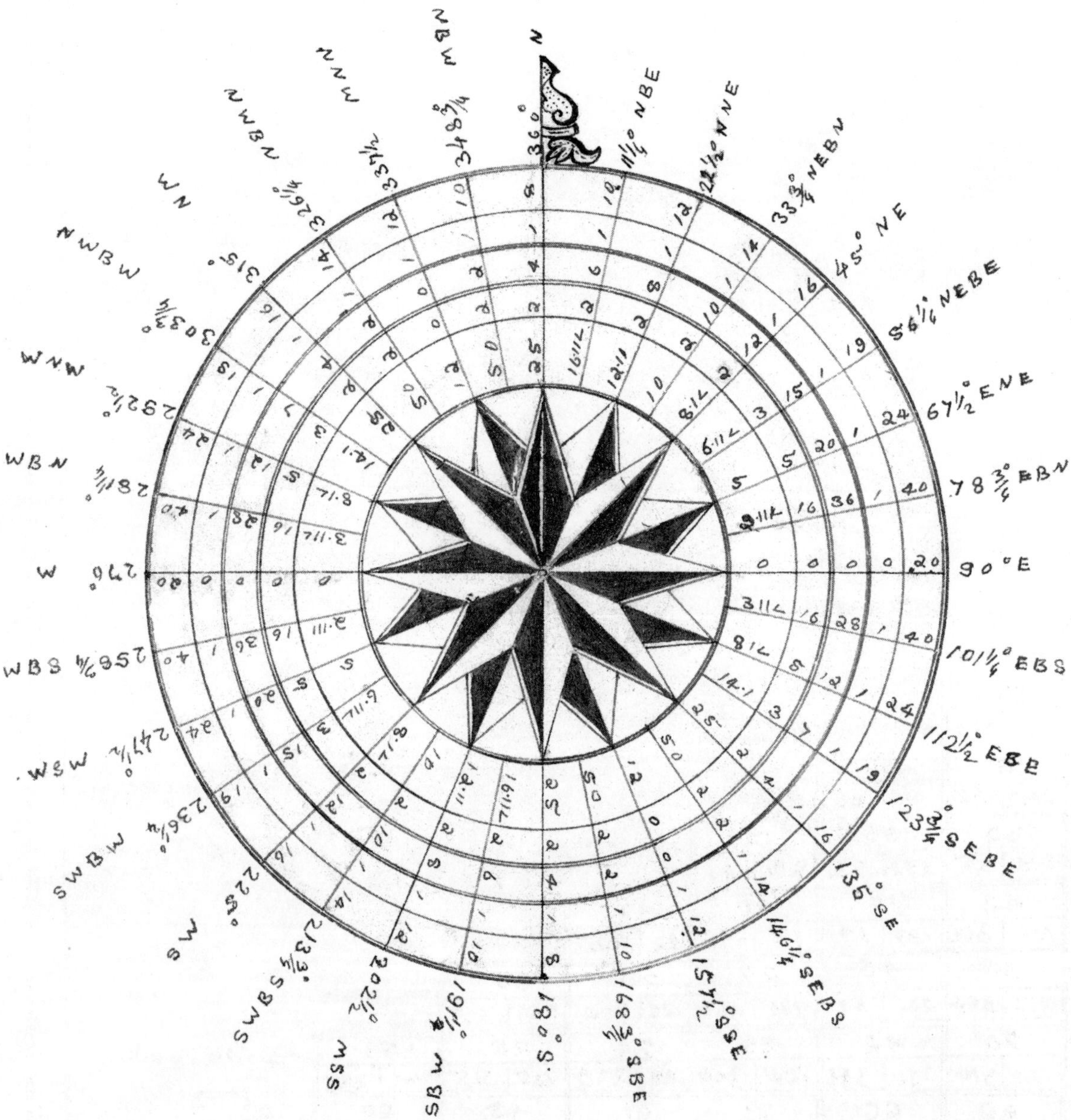
N
360°
NBE
NNE
NEBN
NE
45° NE
NEBE
ENE
EBN
90° E
EBS
EBE
SEBE
135° SE
SEBS
SSE
SBE
180° S
SBW
SSW
SWBS
SW
225°
SWBW
WSW
WBS
W
270°
WBN
WNW
NWBW
315°
NW
NWBN
NNW
NBW

(3)

ജനുവരി			ഫെബ്രുവ			മാർച്ച്			ഏപ്രിൽ			മെയി.			ജൂൺ		
ദി	ഭാ	ല	ദി	ഭാ	ല	ദി	ഭാ	ല	ദി	ഭാ	ല	ദി	ഭാ	ല	ദി	ഭാ	ല
1	23	2	1	17	10	1	7	40	1	4	27	1	15	.	1	22	2
2	22	57	2	16	53	2	7	17	2	4	50	2	15	18	2	22	10
3	22	51	3	16	35	3	6	54	3	5	13	3	15	36	3	22	18
4	22	45	4	16	17	4	6	31	4	5	36	4	15	54	4	22	25
5	22	39	5	15	59	5	6	8	5	5	59	5	16	11	5	22	32
6	22	32	6	15	41	6	5	54	6	6	22	6	16	28	6	22	36
7	22	25	7	15	22	7	5	22	7	6	44	7	16	45	7	22	44
8	22	17	8	15	3	8	4	58	8	7	7	8	17	1	8	22	50
9	22	9	9	14	44	9	4	35	9	7	29	9	17	13	9	22	55
10	22	-	10	14	25	10	4	11	10	7	52	10	17	33	10	23	
11	21	51	11	14	5	11	3	48	11	8	44	11	17	46	11	23	5
12	21	41	12	13	46	12	3	24	12	8	36	12	18	4	12	23	9
13	21	31	13	13	26	13	3	1	13	8	58	13	18	19	13	23	13
14	21	21	14	13	5	14	2	37	14	9	19	14	18	34	14	23	16
15	21	10	15	12	45	15	2	13	15	9	41	15	18	49	15	23	19
16	20	59	16	12	24	16	1	50	16	10	2	16	19	3	16	23	21
17	20	47	17	12	3	17	1	26	17	10	23	17	19	16	17	23	23
18	20	35	18	11	42	18	1	2	18	10	44	18	19	30	18	23	25
19	20	23	19	11	21	19	..	39	19	11	5	19	19	43	19	23	26
20	20	10	20	11	-	20	S	15	20	11	26	20	19	56	20	23	27
21	19	57	21	10	38	21	N	9	21	11	46	21	20	8	21	23	28
22	19	44	22	10	16	22	..	32	22	12	7	22	20	20	22	23	28
23	19	30	23	9	54	23	..	56	23	12	27	23	20	32	23	23	27
24	19	19	24	9	32	24	1	20	24	12	47	24	20	44	24	23	26
25	19	1	25	9	10	25	1	43	25	13	7	25	20	55	25	23	25
26	18	49	26	8	48	26	2	7	26	13	26	26	21	5	26	23	23
27	18	31	27	8	25	27	2	30	27	13	45	27	21	15	27	23	21
28	18	16	28	8	3	28	2	54	28	14	4	28	21	26	28	23	19
29	17	51				29	3	17	29	14	23	29	21	35	29	23	16
30	17	43				30	3	41	30	14	42	30	21	44	30	23	13
31	17	27				31	4	4				31	21	53			

ജൂലായി			ആഗസ്റ്റ്			സെപ്തംബ്ര			ഒക്ടോബ്ര			നവമ്പ്ര			ഡിസമ്പർ.		
ദി	നാ	ന	ദി	നാ	ന	ദി	നാ	ന	ദി	നാ	ന	ദി	നാ	ന	ദി	നാ	ന
1	23	9	1	18	7	1	8	24	1	3	5	1	14	22	1	21	47
2	23	5	2	17	52	2	8	2	2	3	28	2	14	41	2	21	57
3	23	"	3	17	36	3	7	40	3	3	42	3	15	..	3	22	5
4	22	55	4	17	20	4	7	18	4	4	15	4	15	19	4	22	14
5	22	50	5	17	4	5	6	56	5	4	38	5	15	37	5	22	22
6	22	44	6	16	48	6	6	33	6	5	1	6	15	55	6	22	29
7	22	39	7	16	31	7	6	11	7	5	24	7	16	13	7	22	36
8	22	25	8	16	15	8	5	48	8	5	47	8	16	31	8	22	43
9	22	25	9	15	57	9	5	26	9	6	10	9	16	48	9	22	49
10	22	18	10	15	40	10	5	3	10	6	33	10	17	5	10	22	55
11	22	10	11	15	22	11	4	40	11	6	56	11	17	22	11	23	..
12	22	2	12	15	5	12	4	18	12	7	18	12	17	39	12	23	5
13	21	54	13	14	47	13	3	55	13	7	41	13	17	55	13	23	9
14	21	45	14	14	28	14	3	32	14	8	3	14	18	11	14	23	13
15	21	36	15	14	10	15	3	9	15	8	26	15	18	26	15	23	17
16	21	26	16	13	51	16	2	45	16	8	48	16	18	42	16	23	20
17	21	16	17	13	32	17	2	22	17	9	10	17	18	57	17	23	22
18	21	6	18	13	13	18	1	59	18	9	38	18	19	11	18	23	24
19	20	55	19	12	53	19	1	36	19	9	45	19	19	25	19	23	26
20	20	44	20	12	34	20	1	12	20	10	15	20	19	39	20	23	27
21	20	33	21	12	14	21	..	49	21	10	37	21	19	53	21	23	27
22	20	21	22	11	54	22	..	26	22	10	58	22	20	6	22	23	28
23	20	9	23	11	33	23	N	2	23	11	19	23	20	19	23	23	27
24	19	57	24	11	13	24	S	21	24	11	40	24	20	31	24	23	26
25	19	44	25	10	52	25	..	45	25	12	1	25	20	43	25	23	25
26	19	31	26	10	32	26	1	8	26	12	22	26	20	55	26	23	23
27	19	18	27	10	11	27	1	13	27	12	43	27	21	6	27	23	21
28	19	4	28	9	50	28	1	55	28	13	3	28	21	17	28	23	19
29	18	50	29	9	28	29	2	18	29	13	22	29	21	28	29	23	15
30	18	36	30	9	7	30	2	41	30	13	43	30	21	38	30	23	12
31	18	22	31	8	45				31	14	2				31	23	8

ജനവരി			ഫെബ്രുവ			മാൎച്ച്			ഏപ്രിൽ			മെയി.			ജൂൺ.		
ദി	മി	സ	ദി	മി	സ	ദി	മി	സ	ദി	മി	സ	ദി	മി	സ	ദി	മി	സ
1	23	3	1	17	14	1	7	23	1	4	45	1	15	14	1	22	8
2	22	58	2	16	57	2	7	..	2	5	8	2	15	32	2	22	16
3	22	53	3	16	39	3	6	37	3	5	31	3	15	49	3	22	23
4	22	47	4	16	22	4	6	14	4	5	53	4	16	7	4	22	30
5	22	41	5	16	4	5	5	51	5	6	16	5	16	24	5	22	37
6	22	34	6	15	45	6	5	27	6	6	39	6	16	41	6	22	43
7	22	27	7	15	27	7	5	4	7	7	1	7	16	57	7	22	49
8	22	19	8	15	8	8	4	41	8	7	24	8	17	14	8	22	54
9	22	11	9	14	49	9	4	17	9	7	46	9	17	30	9	22	59
10	22	2	10	14	30	10	3	51	10	8	8	10	17	45	10	23	4
11	21	53	11	14	10	11	3	30	11	8	30	11	18	1	11	23	8
12	21	44	12	13	51	12	3	6	12	8	52	12	18	16	12	23	12
13	21	34	13	13	31	13	2	43	13	9	14	13	18	31	13	23	15
14	21	24	14	13	10	14	2	19	14	9	36	14	18	45	14	23	18
15	21	13	15	12	50	15	1	56	15	9	57	15	18	59	15	23	21
16	21	2	16	12	29	16	1	32	16	10	18	16	19	13	16	23	23
17	20	50	17	12	8	17	1	8	17	10	39	17	19	27	17	23	25
18	20	38	18	11	47	18	..	44	18	11	..	18	19	40	18	23	26
19	20	26	19	11	26	19	5	21	19	11	21.	19	19	53	19	23	27
20	20	14	20	11	5	20	N	3	20	11	42	20	20	5	20	23	27
21	20		21	10	43	21	..	27	21	12	2	21	20	17	21	23	28
22	19	47	22	10	22	22	..	50	22	12	22	22	20	29	22	23	27
23	19	33	23	10	..	23	1	14	23	12	42	23	20	41	23	23	26
24	19	19	24	9	38	24	1	38	24	13	2	24	20	52	24	23	25
25	19	5	25	9	15	25	2	1	25	13	21	25	21	3	25	23	24
26	18	50	26	8	53	26	2	25	26	13	41	26	21	13	26	23	22
27	18	35	27	8	31	27	2	48	27	14	..	27	21	23	27	23	19
28	18	19	28	8	8	28	3	12	28	14	19	28	21	33	28	23	17
29	18	3	29	7	45	29	3	35	29	14	37	29	21	42	29	23	13
30	17	47				30	3	58	30	14	56	30	21	51	30	23	10
31	17	31				31	4	21				31	22	..			

ജൂലായി			ആഗസ്റ്റ്			സെപ്റ്റംബർ			ഒക്ടോബർ			നവംബർ			ഡിസംബർ		
തി	ദ്	ദ	തി	ദ്	ദ	തി	ദ്	ദ	തി	ദ്	ദ	തി	ദ്	ദ	തി	ദ്	ദ
1	23	6	1	17	55	1	8	7	1	3	23	1	14	30	1	21	54
2	23	1	2	17	40	2	7	45	2	3	46	2	14	55	2	22	8
3	22	57	3	17	24	3	7	23	3	4	9	3	16	14	3	22	12
4	22	51	4	17	8	4	7	1	4	4	22	4	16	33	4	22	20
5	22	46	5	16	52	5	6	39	5	4	55	5	15	57	5	22	27
6	22	40	6	16	35	6	6	16	6	5	19	6	16	9	6	22	35
7	22	33	7	16	19	7	5	54	7	5	24	7	16	27	7	22	41
8	22	27	8	16	2	8	5	39	8	6	4	8	16	44	8	22	48
9	22	19	9	15	44	9	5	9	9	6	27	9	17	1	9	22	53
10	22	12	10	15	27	10	4	46	10	6	50	10	17	18	10	22	56
11	22	4	11	15	9	11	4	23	11	7	13	11	17	35	11	23	4
12	21	56	12	14	51	12	4	..	12	7	35	12	17	51	12	23	8
13	21	47	13	14	33	13	3	37	13	7	58	13	18	7	13	23	12
14	21	38	14	14	14	14	3	14	14	8	20	14	18	21	14	23	16
15	21	29	15	13	55	15	2	51	15	8	42	15	18	38	15	23	19
16	21	19	16	13	36	16	2	28	16	9	5	16	18	53	16	23	21
17	21	8	17	13	17	17	2	5	17	9	27	17	19	8	17	23	24
18	20	58	18	12	58	18	1	41	18	9	48	18	19	22	18	23	25
19	20	47	19	12	38	19	1	18	19	10	10	19	19	36	19	23	26
20	20	36	20	12	18	20	..	55	20	10	32	20	19	50	20	23	27
21	20	24	21	11	58	21	..	31	21	10	53	21	20	3	21	23	27
22	20	12	22	11	38	22	N	8	22	11	14	22	20	16	22	23	27
23	20	..	23	11	18	23	S	16	23	11	25	23	20	28	23	23	27
24	19	47	24	10	57	24	..	39	24	11	56	24	20	40	24	23	25
25	19	35	25	10	37	25	1	2	25	12	17	25	20	52	25	23	24
26	19	21	26	10	16	26	1	26	26	12	38	28	21	4	26	23	22
27	19	8	27	9	55	27	1	49	27	12	58	27	21	14	27	23	19
28	18	54	28	9	34	28	2	13	28	13	18	28	21	25	28	23	16
29	18	40	29	9	12	29	2	36	29	13	38	29	21	36	29	23	13
30	18	25	30	8	51	30	2	59	30	13	58	30	21	45	30	23	9
31	18	10	31	8	29				31	14	18				31	23	4

ജനുവരി			ഫെബ്രുവരി			മാർച്ച്			ഏപ്രിൽ			മെയ്			ജൂൺ		
ദി	നാ	വി	ദി	നാ	വി	ദി	നാ	വി	ദി	നാ	വി	ദി	നാ	വി	ദി	നാ	വി
1	22	59	1	17	1	1	7	28	1	4	39	1	15	9	1	22	6
2	22	54	2	16	43	2	7	5	2	5	2	2	15	27	2	22	14
3	22	48	3	16	26	3	6	42	3	5	25	3	15	45	3	22	21
4	22	42	4	16	8	4	6	19	4	5	48	4	16	3	4	22	28
5	22	35	5	15	50	5	5	56	5	6	11	5	16	20	5	22	35
6	22	28	6	15	31	6	5	33	6	6	33	6	16	37	6	22	41
7	22	21	7	15	13	7	5	10	7	6	56	7	16	53	7	22	47
8	22	13	8	14	50	8	4	46	8	7	18	8	17	10	8	22	53
9	22	4	9	14	30	9	4	23	9	7	41	9	17	26	9	22	58
10	21	55	10	14	15	10	3	59	10	8	3	10	17	41	10	23	3
11	21	46	11	13	55	11	3	36	11	8	25	11	17	57	11	23	7
12	21	36	12	13	35	12	3	12	12	8	47	12	18	12	12	23	11
13	21	26	13	13	15	13	2	48	13	9	9	13	18	27	13	23	14
14	21	15	14	12	55	14	2	25	14	9	30	14	18	42	14	23	17
15	21	4	15	12	34	15	2	1	15	9	52	15	18	56	15	23	20
16	20	53	16	12	13	16	1	37	16	10	13	16	19	10	16	23	22
17	20	41	17	11	52	17	1	14	17	10	34	17	19	23	17	23	24
18	20	29	18	11	31	18	..	50	18	10	55	18	19	37	18	23	26
19	20	16	19	11	10	19	..	26	19	11	16	19	19	50	19	23	27
20	20	4	20	10	48	20	[illegible]	3	20	11	37	20	20	2	20	23	27
21	19	50	21	10	17	21	[illegible]	21	21	11	57	21	20	14	21	23	27
22	19	37	22	10	5	22	..	45	22	12	17	22	20	26	22	23	27
23	19	22	23	9	43	23	1	8	23	12	37	23	20	38	23	23	27
24	19	8	24	9	21	24	1	32	24	12	57	24	20	49	24	23	26
25	18	53	25	8	59	25	1	56	25	13	17	25	21	..	25	23	24
26	18	38	26	8	36	26	2	19	26	13	36	26	21	11	26	23	22
27	18	23	27	8	14	27	2	43	27	13	55	27	21	21	27	23	20
28	18	7	28	7	51	28	3	5	28	14	14	28	21	30	28	23	17
29	17	51	29	7	28	29	3	29	29	14	33	29	21	40	29	23	14
30	17	35				30	3	53	30	14	51	30	21	49	30	23	11
31	17	18				31	4	16				31	21	58			

ജൂലായ്			ആഗസ്റ്റ്			സെപ്റ്റംബർ			ഒക്ടോബർ			നവംബർ			ഡിസംബർ		
ദി	മ	മി	ദി	മ	മി	ദി	മ	മി	ദി	മ	മി	ദി	മ	മി	ദി	മ	മി
1	23	7	1	17	59	1	8	13	1	3	17	1	14	32	1	21	52
2	23	3	2	17	44	2	7	51	2	3	40	2	14	51	2	22	1
3	22	58	3	17	28	3	7	29	3	4	4	3	15	10	3	22	10
4	22	53	4	17	12	4	7	7	4	4	27	4	15	28	4	22	18
5	22	47	5	16	56	5	6	~~44~~	5	4	50	5	15	47	5	22	25
6	22	41	6	16	39	6	6	22	6	5	17	6	16	5	6	22	33
7	22	35	7	16	23	7	5	58	7	5	36	7	16	22	7	22	40
8	22	28	8	16	6	8	5	39	8	5	59	8	16	40	8	22	46
9	22	21	9	15	49	9	5	14	9	6	22	9	16	57	9	22	52
10	22	14	10	15	31	10	4	51	10	6	45	10	17	14	10	22	57
11	22	6	11	15	14	11	4	29	11	7	7	11	17	31	11	23	2
12	21	58	12	14	55	12	4	6	12	7	30	12	17	47	12	23	7
13	21	49	13	14	37	13	3	43	13	7	52	13	18	3	13	23	11
14	21	40	14	14	14	14	3	20	14	8	15	14	18	19	14	23	15
15	21	31	15	14	..	15	2	57	15	8	37	15	18	34	15	23	18
16	21	21	16	13	41	16	2	33	16	8	59	16	18	48	16	23	21
17	21	11	17	13	22	17	2	10	17	9	21	17	19	4	17	23	23
18	21	..	18	13	3	18	1	47	18	9	43	18	19	19	18	23	25
19	20	50	19	12	43	19	1	24	19	10	5	19	19	33	19	23	26
20	20	39	20	12	23	20	1	..	20	10	26	20	19	40	20	23	27
21	20	27	21	12	3	21	..	37	21	10	48	21	20	.	21	23	27
22	20	15	22	11	43	22	N	14	22	11	9	22	20	13	22	23	27
23	20	3	23	11	23	23	S	10	23	11	30	23	20	25	23	23	27
24	19	51	24	11	2	24	..	33	24	11	51	24	20	37	24	23	26
25	19	38	25	10	42	25	..	57	25	12	12	25	20	49	25	23	24
26	19	25	26	10	21	26	1	20	26	12	33	26	21	1	26	23	22
27	19	11	27	10	--	27	1	43	27	12	53	27	21	12	27	23	20
28	18	57	28	9	39	28	2	7	28	13	13	28	21	22	28	23	17
29	18	43	29	9	17	29	2	30	29	13	33	29	21	33	29	28	14
30	18	27	30	8	56	30	2	54	30	13	53	30	21	43	30	23	10
31	18	14	31	8	34				31	14	12				31	23	5

ജനുവരി			ഫെബ്രുവരി			മാർച്ച്			ഏപ്രിൽ			മെയ്			ജൂൺ		
ദി	നാ	വി	ദി	നാ	വി	ദി	നാ	വി	ദി	നാ	വി	ദി	നാ	വി	ദി	നാ	വി
1	23	1	1	17	5	1	7	34	1	4	33	1	15	5	1	22	4
2	22	55	2	16	48	2	7	11	2	4	50	2	15	23	2	22	12
3	22	50	3	16	30	3	6	48	3	5	19	3	15	41	3	22	19
4	22	44	4	16	12	4	6	25	4	5	42	4	15	58	4	22	27
5	22	37	5	15	54	5	6	2	5	6	5	5	16	16	5	22	33
6	22	30	6	15	36	6	5	38	6	6	28	6	16	33	6	22	40
7	22	22	7	15	19	7	5	15	7	6	50	7	16	49	7	22	46
8	22	15	8	14	58	8	4	52	8	7	13	8	17	6	8	22	51
9	22	6	9	14	39	9	4	28	9	7	35	9	17	22	9	22	57
10	21	57	10	14	20	10	4	5	10	7	58	10	17	39	10	23	1
11	21	48	11	14	..	11	3	41	11	8	20	11	17	53	11	23	6
12	21	38	12	13	40	12	3	28	12	8	42	12	18	8	12	23	10
13	21	28	13	13	20	13	2	45	13	9	3	13	18	23	13	23	13
14	21	18	14	13	..	14	2	31	14	9	25	14	18	38	14	23	17
15	21	7	15	12	39	15	2	7	15	9	47	15	18	52	15	23	19
16	20	56	16	12	19	16	1	43	16	10	8	16	19	6	16	23	22
17	20	44	17	11	58	17	1	20	17	10	29	17	19	20	17	23	24
18	20	32	18	11	36	18	..	56	18	10	50	18	19	33	18	23	25
19	20	20	19	11	16	19	..	32	19	11	..	19	19	46	19	23	26
20	20	7	20	10	54	20		9	20	11	32	20	19	59	20	23	27
21	19	54	21	10	32	21		15	21	11	52	21	20	11	21	23	27
22	19	40	22	10	10	22	..	39	22	12	12	22	20	24	22	23	27
23	19	26	23	9	40	23	1	3	23	12	32	23	20	35	23	23	27
24	19	12	24	9	26	24	1	26	24	12	52	24	20	46	24	23	26
25	18	57	25	9	4	25	1	50	25	13	12	25	20	57	25	23	24
26	18	42	26	8	42	26	2	13	26	13	31	26	21	8	26	23	23
27	18	27	27	8	19	27	2	37	27	13	50	27	21	18	27	23	21
28	18	11	28	7	56	28	3	..	28	14	9	28	21	28	28	23	18
29	17	55	2			29	3	24	29	14	23	29	21	38	29	23	15
30	17	39				30	3	49	30	14	47	30	21	47	30	23	12
31	17	22				31	4	10				31	21	55			

ജൂലായി			ആഗസ്റ്റ്			സെപ്റ്റംബർ			ഒക്ടോബർ			നവംബർ			ഡിസംബർ		
തി	മ	ന	തി	മ	ന	തി	മ	ന	തി	മ	ന	തി	മ	ന	തി	മ	ന
1	23	8	1	18	2	1	8	18	1	3	11	1	14	24	1	21	50
2	23	3	2	17	47	2	7	56	2	3	35	2	14	46	2	21	59
3	22	59	3	17	32	3	7	34	3	3	58	3	15	5	3	22	8
4	22	54	4	17	16	4	7	12	4	4	21	4	15	24	4	22	16
5	22	48	5	17	'	5	6	49	5	4	44	5	15	42	5	22	24
6	22	43	6	16	43	6	6	27	6	5	7	6	16	..	6	22	31
7	22	36	7	16	27	7	6	5	7	5	30	7	16	18	7	22	38
8	22	30	8	16	10	8	5	45	8	5	53	8	16	36	8	22	44
9	22	23	9	15	53	9	5	20	9	6	16	9	16	53	9	22	50
10	22	15	10	15	35	10	4	57	10	6	39	10	17	10	10	22	56
11	22	8	11	15	19	11	4	33	11	7	2	11	17	28	11	23	1
12	22	..	12	15	..	12	4	11	12	7	24	12	17	43	12	23	6
13	21	51	13	14	44	13	3	48	13	7	47	13	17	59	13	23	10
14	21	42	14	14	23	14	3	25	14	8	9	14	18	15	14	23	14
15	21	33	15	14	4	15	3	2	15	8	32	15	18	31	15	23	17
16	21	23	16	13	46	16	2	39	16	8	54	16	18	46	16	23	20
17	21	13	17	13	26	17	2	16	17	9	16	17	19	1	17	23	22
18	21	3	18	13	7	18	1	52	18	9	38	18	19	15	18	23	24
19	20	52	19	12	47	19	1	25	19	10	..	19	19	29	19	23	26
20	20	40	20	12	28	20	1	6	20	10	21	20	19	43	20	23	27
21	20	29	21	12	8	21	..	42	21	10	43	21	19	56	21	23	27
22	20	18	22	11	48	22	..	19	22	11	4	22	20	10	22	23	27
23	20	6	23	11	28	23	[illegible]	4	23	11	25	23	20	22	23	23	27
24	19	53	24	11	7	24	[illegible]	28	24	11	45	24	20	35	24	23	26
25	19	41	25	10	47	25	..	51	25	12	7	25	20	46	25	23	25
26	19	28	26	10	26	26	1	15	26	12	28	26	20	58	26	23	23
27	19	14	27	10	5	27	1	38	27	12	48	27	21	9	27	23	20
28	19	..	28	9	44	28	2	1	28	13	8	28	21	20	28	23	18
29	18	46	29	9	22	29	2	25	29	13	28	29	21	30	29	23	14
30	18	32	30	9	1	30	2	48	30	13	48	30	21	40	30	23	11
31	18	17	31	8	39				31	14	8				31	23	8

(4)

ദ്വീപ് നാമം	അക്ഷം		രേഖ			ദ്വീപ് പേര്	അക്ഷം		രേഖ	
മലിക്കു	8	17	73	18		പെരുമുളപാറ്	11	9	72	"
സുഹേലി തെക്കേ	10	"	72	15		ബിത്തിര പാ	11	35	72	9
" വടക്കേ	10	6	72	15		ചെത്തിലാം	11	42	72	42
കല്പേനി	10	7	73	35		ചെറിയപാണിയം വടക്കേ	11	58	71	46
ചെറിയം	10	10	73	33		" തെക്കേ	11	48	71	43
കവരത്തി	10	32	72	57		വലിയപാണിയം	12	23	72	5
അന്ത്രോത്ത്	10	47	73	39		വടക്കേ " തെക്കേ	12	17	71	53
അഗെട്ടി	10	45	72	31		മഞ്ഞാച്ചാര് വട	13	37	72	32
[illegible]	10	51	72	11		" തെക്കേ	12	31	72	42
ബങ്ങാരം	10	55	72	35		ഹ്ലോറ ദ്വീപ്	13	51	72	13
അമേനി	11	6	72	42		ജിദ്ദ പട്ടണം	21	29	39	15
കൊടിക്കല്ലേരി	11	15	73	57		മക്കാ പട്ടണം	21	"	40	"
കടമത്ത്	11	14	72	44		മദീന പട്ടണം	24	50	39	51
കില്ത്താന്	11	28	72	58		**ബന്തര്**	~	~	~	~
ബന്തര്	~	~	~	~		അഞ്ചെങ്ങി	8	40	76	
കന്യാകുമാരി	8	5	77	32		കൊല്ലം	8	53	76	35
തിരുവനന്തപുരം	8	31	76	57		പുറക്കാട്ടി	9	12	76	26
തൂത്തുക്കുടി	8	48	78	10		ആലപ്പുഴ	9	30	76	18

ബന്നാര്	അര്ള്		തൂല്	
	ദറജ	ദഖീ	ദറജ	ദഖീ
കൊച്ചി	9	58	76	14
കൊടുങ്ങല്ലൂര്	10	8	76	18
[illegible]	10	10	76	8
[illegible]	10	12	76	5
ചേറ്റുവായി	10	28	76	2
ചാവക്കാട്	10	33	76	3
പൊന്നാനി	10	48	75	53
താനൂര്	10	58	75	52
പരപ്പനങ്ങാടി	10	50	75	47
ചാലിയം	11	"	75	45
ബേപ്പൂര്	11	10	75	47
[illegible]	11	12	75	46
കോഴിക്കോട്	11	15	75	45
പുതിയങ്ങാടി	11	18	75	44
എലത്തൂര്	11	21	75	42
കൊയിലാണ്ടി	11	28	75	40
കോട്ടക്കൽ	11	29	75	36

ബന്നാര്	അര്ള്		തൂല്	
	ദറജ	ദഖീ	ദറജ	ദഖീ
വെള്ളിയാങ്കൽ	11	30	75	31
വടകര	11	37	75	33
മയ്യഴി	11	40	75	32
തലശ്ശേരി	11	44	75	28
[illegible]	11	46	75	27
ധര്മ്മടം	11	45	75	27
കണ്ണൂര്	11	52	75	21
അഴീക്കോട്	11	54	75	19
ഏഴിമല	12	1	75	15
നീലേശ്വരം	12	10	75	9
കാട്ടുകച്ചേരി	12	11	75	7
പടന്നാക്കാട്	12	15	75	6
[illegible]	12	23	75	2
[illegible]	12	28	75	.
കുമ്പള	12	35	74	50
മഞ്ചേശ്വരം	12	42	74	49
[illegible]	12	45	74	48

ബന്തര്	അക്ഷാംശം		രേഖാംശം		ബന്തര്	അക്ഷാംശം		രേഖാംശം	
	ഭാഗ	കല	ഭാഗ	കല		ഭാ	കല	ഭാ	കല
കുഡ്ഡാങ്ങ്	12	48	74	47	ചൊന്നാപുറം	14	17	74	25
ഉംഗപാച്ചുറം	12	52	74	50	ഗൊകോൺ	14	35	74	17
കതിര വള്ളി	13	"	74	48	ഭൈന്താകൂത്ത്	14	56	74	14
കാറനാട്ടു	13	6	74	40	ഗോവ	15	28	73	55
ചക്രായ	13	12	74	30	ഒരെക്കോൽ	15	35	73	50
കോട്ടംപുടുയ	13	15	74	28	വങ്ങോർളാ	15	53	73	23
കുന്ദാപ്പൊ	13	30	75	4	ഇസിറാത്തു വാശി	15	55	73	27
ബാർക്കൂർ	13	20	74	55	ത്രൈവാശക്കൽ	15	58	73	10
കണ്ടാപുറം	13	34	74	33	മാൽവാ	16	10	73	12
ഗങ്ങൂ	13	45	74	"	ബന്തർ തനം	16	20	73	2
ബൈന്ദൂർ	13	52	74	36	രൈചാപൂർ	16	37	73	"
ശിരവെച്ചൂർ	13	55	74	34	ജിഞ്ഞ്ഗിരിയാകര	16	39	71	58
ബട്കളെ	13	57	74	33	ചാവൂർ	16	47	73	28
മഞ്ചിരിയാ	14	6	74	30	കാടിച്ചൂർ	16	38	73	27
ഹൊന്നവർ	14	20	74	23	വലയങ്കാശിഞ്ഞു	18	4	73	20
കുമ്ടി	14	25	74	23	രത്നഗിരി	16	59	73	16
ജൻസിറാനദ്ധി റിവാ	14	15	74	24	രാജാപുർ	18	18	72	57

(5)

[illegible]	[illegible]		[illegible]	
	[illegible]	[illegible]	[illegible]	[illegible]
[illegible]	18	42	72	48
[illegible]	19	54	72	48
[illegible]	19	10	72	40
നക്ഷത്രപേര്				
	[illegible]	[illegible]		
[illegible]	34	24	,,	,,
തിരുഓണം ,,	24	,,	,,	,,
,, [illegible]	13	6	,,	,,
[illegible]	13	6	,,	,,
കാറന്നിക.	15	11	,,	,,
രോഹിണി	13	16	,,	,,
[illegible] വ:	52	45	,,	,,
പുണർത്തം	29	28	,,	,,
[illegible]	36	52	,,	,,
[illegible]	31	16	,,	,,

[illegible]	[illegible]		[illegible]	
	[illegible]	[illegible]	[illegible]	[illegible]
[illegible]	21	29	39	15
[illegible]	21	-	40	,,
[illegible]	24	50	39	51
നക്ഷത്രപേര്				
	[illegible]	[illegible]		
[illegible]	11	32	,,	,,
[illegible] വട: [illegible]	19	22	,,	,,
,, [illegible]	38	58	,,	,,
മഹം	21	15	,,	,,
[illegible]	8	26	,,	,,
അത്തം	24	28	,,	,,
തിരുഓണം	17	1	,,	,,
[illegible]	11	20	,,	,,
ഉത്രാടം	15	49	,,	,,
ചോദി	44	19	,,	,,
[illegible]	19	22	,,	,,

(6)

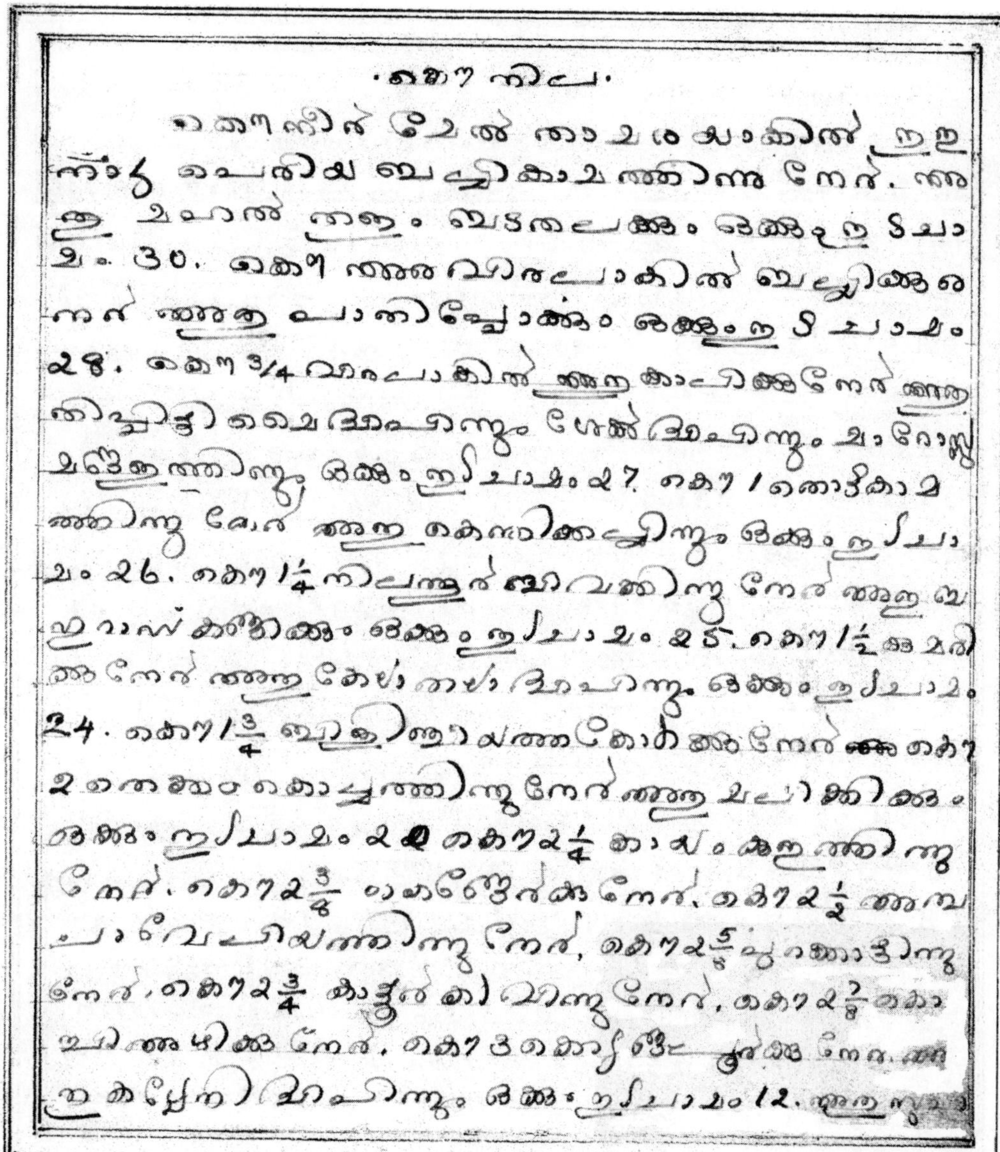

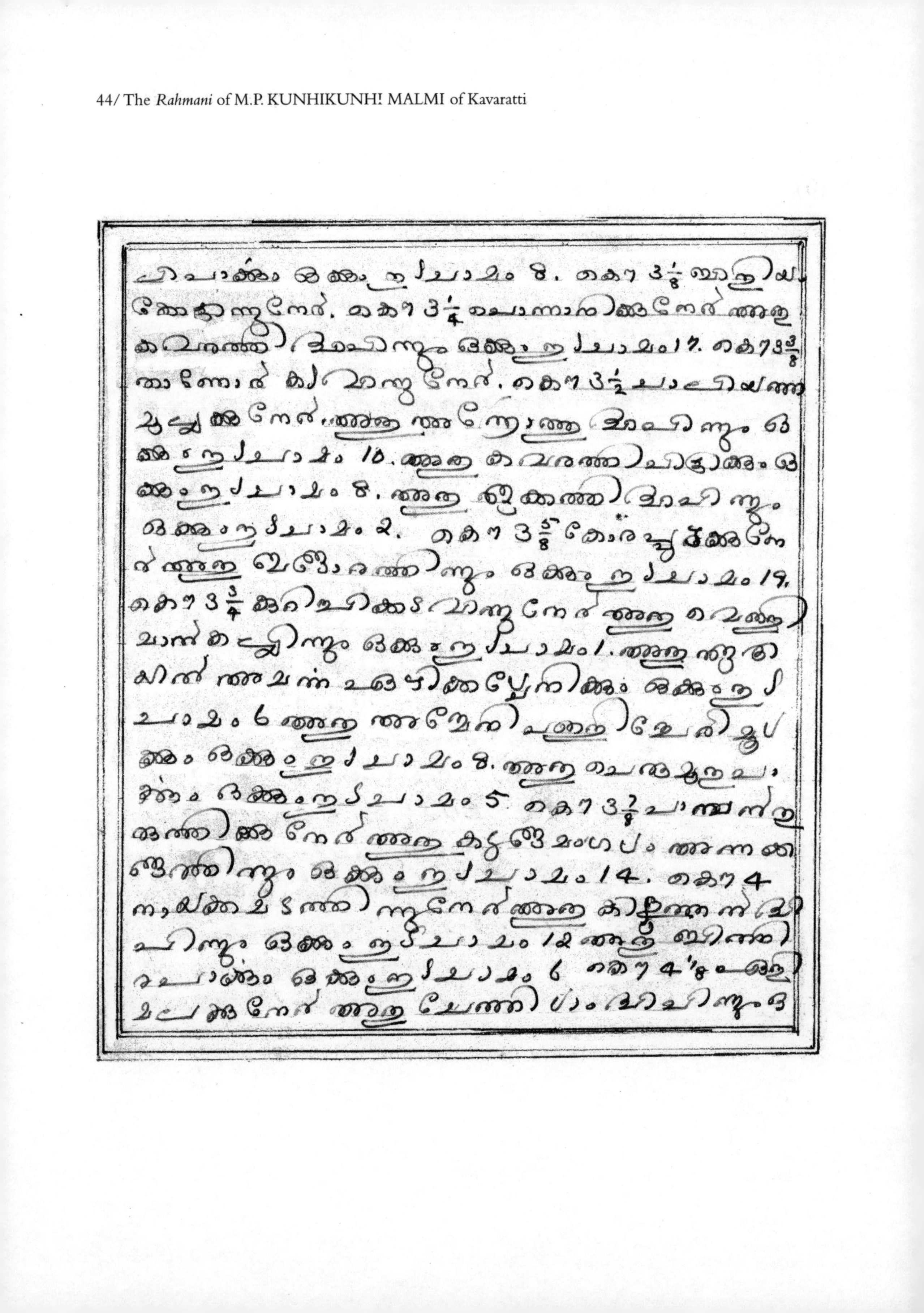

[illegible]

ക്കം ഇടപാടം 14. ആറു ചെറിയ പനിയം പാറ
തെക്കെപക്കം ഒക്കം ഇടപാടം 6. കൊൽ 4¼ നീർ
പുരം നിടിയ മരത്തിനു നേർ. കൊൽ 4⅜ കാഞ്ഞി
രക്കോട്ടിനു നേർ. കൊൽ 4½ കമ്പിളി വൈരത്തി
നു നേർ കൊൽ 4⅝ വാഗപാലപുരം വെത്തക്കു നേർ.
കൊൽ 4¾ ആറു മാൻചക്രയായിക്കു നേർ. കൊൽ 4⅞
കള്ളപ്പാടി ന്നെക്കു നേർ. കൊൽ 5 ചൊക്കത്തുക്കു നേ
ർ. ആറു വലിയ പനിയം പാറ വടക്കെ പക്കം ഒ
ക്കം ഇടപാടം 20. കൊൽ 5⅛ വൈനാപുരത്തി
നു നേർ. കൊൽ 5¼ വൈത്തൂർ മലക്കു നേർ. കൊ
5⅜ ചെട്ടക്കുറത്തിനു നേർ. കൊൽ 5½ കായക്കുളത്തി
ക്കു നേർ. ആറു ചെറിയ നിന്നാലിപ്പാലിക്കം ഒക്കം
ഇടപാടം 2. ആറു [illegible]
[illegible]
[illegible]
[illegible]
[illegible]
[illegible]
[illegible]
[illegible]

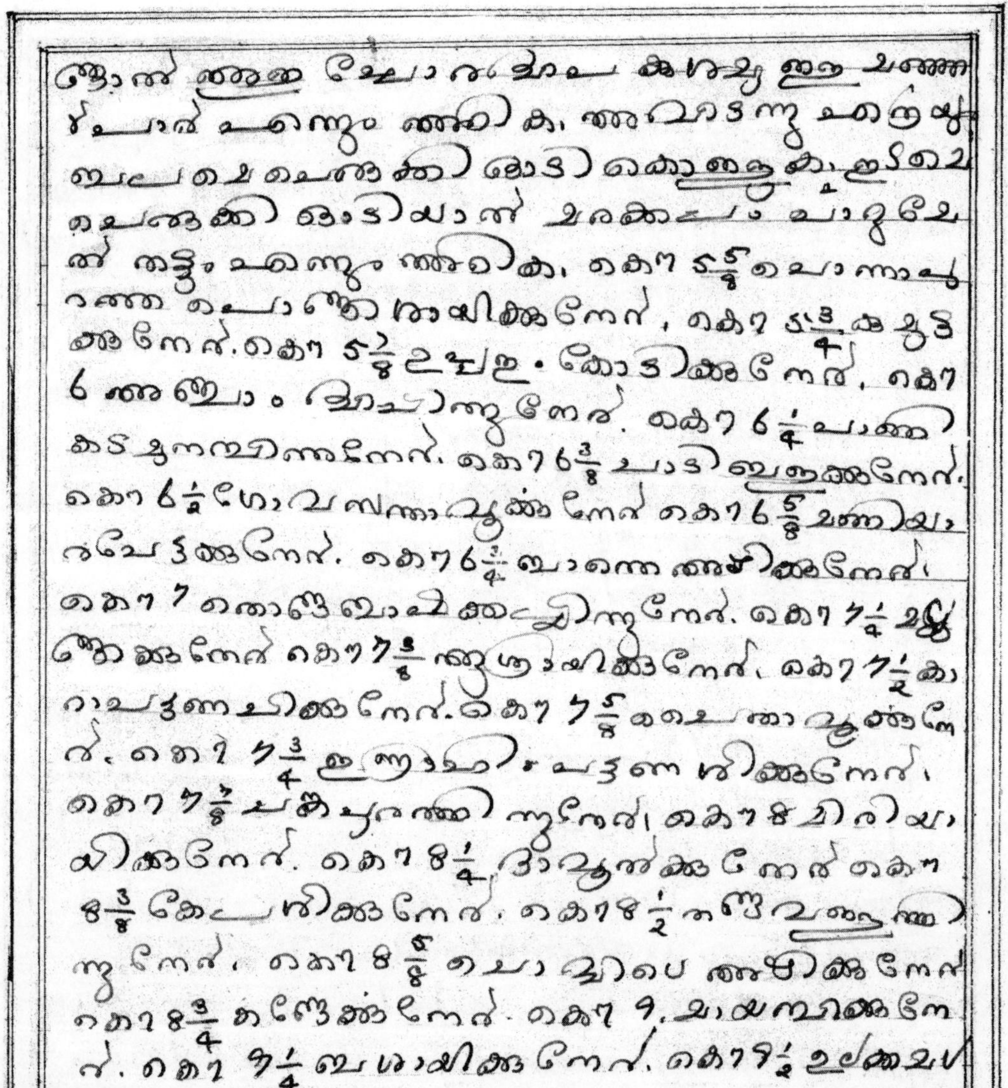

ക്കനേര്. കൊ 10 ദക്ഷിണത്തിക്കനേര്. ഇതു ബഹ-
റടിച്ച്ചായിക്കു ഒക്കു നടപ്പാച്ചം 2. ഇതു ചടപ്പാട്ടു-
ന്നും ഒക്കു നടപ്പാച്ചം 6. കൊ 10¼ ഇതു ശാട്ടിക്ക-
ത്തിൽ മെച്ചിന്നു നേര്. കൊ 10½ ബന്നാണ്സ്റത്തിക്ക
നേര്. കൊ 10¾ കോബാരിക്കനേര്, കൊ 11 കബാ-
യത്തിക്കനേര് കൊ 11¼ കറാച്ചി ബന്തക്കനേര്.
കൊ 10½ ചാബായിക്കനേര് കൊ 10¼ സചന്നപട്ട-
ണത്തിക്കനേര് കൊ 10⅛ മൈസൂര് ആനാരത്തിന്നു
നേര് കൊ 10¼ ചൊറട്ടു ചംഗലൂർപട്ടണത്തിന്നു
നേര് കൊ 10½ കുർമിയായിക്കനേര്. കൊ 11 ക്കു-
ഹത്തിന്നു നേര് ഇതു സിർണ്ണത്തമലക്കു ഒക്കും
നടപ്പാച്ചം 40 ഇതു കാത്തബത്തിന്നും ഒക്കും നട-
പ്പാച്ചം 72. കൊ 12 സിന്ധിന്നു നേര് കൊ 12½ ബ-
ഷക്കനേര്. കൊ 13 ശര്ശാച്ചിക്കനേര് കൊ
13½ കൊച്ചബാറക്കിന്നു നേര് കൊ 14 ഉറുമ്പ്സ്ബെ-
ത്തു നേര് ഇതു കൽബ്യൂത്ത് ബഹാനേതിക്കും ഒ-
ക്കും ഇതു രണ്ടു കരെക്കും ന്യൂബേചെരിയ മേപ്പാ-
ഴിരിക്കും. ക്ലവിസ്.

(7) . കരവസല .

ഇരട്ടുവാട്ടു കമരി ഇരുവും 1½ നില. ക-
ബാന്തിയെ തിടക്കം. കമരിവാട്ടു നെഞ്ചം കൊച്ചു.
ഇരുവും ½ നിലം കാബത്ത് ഇരുമ്പാനം വാട്ടു ഒരുച

(8)

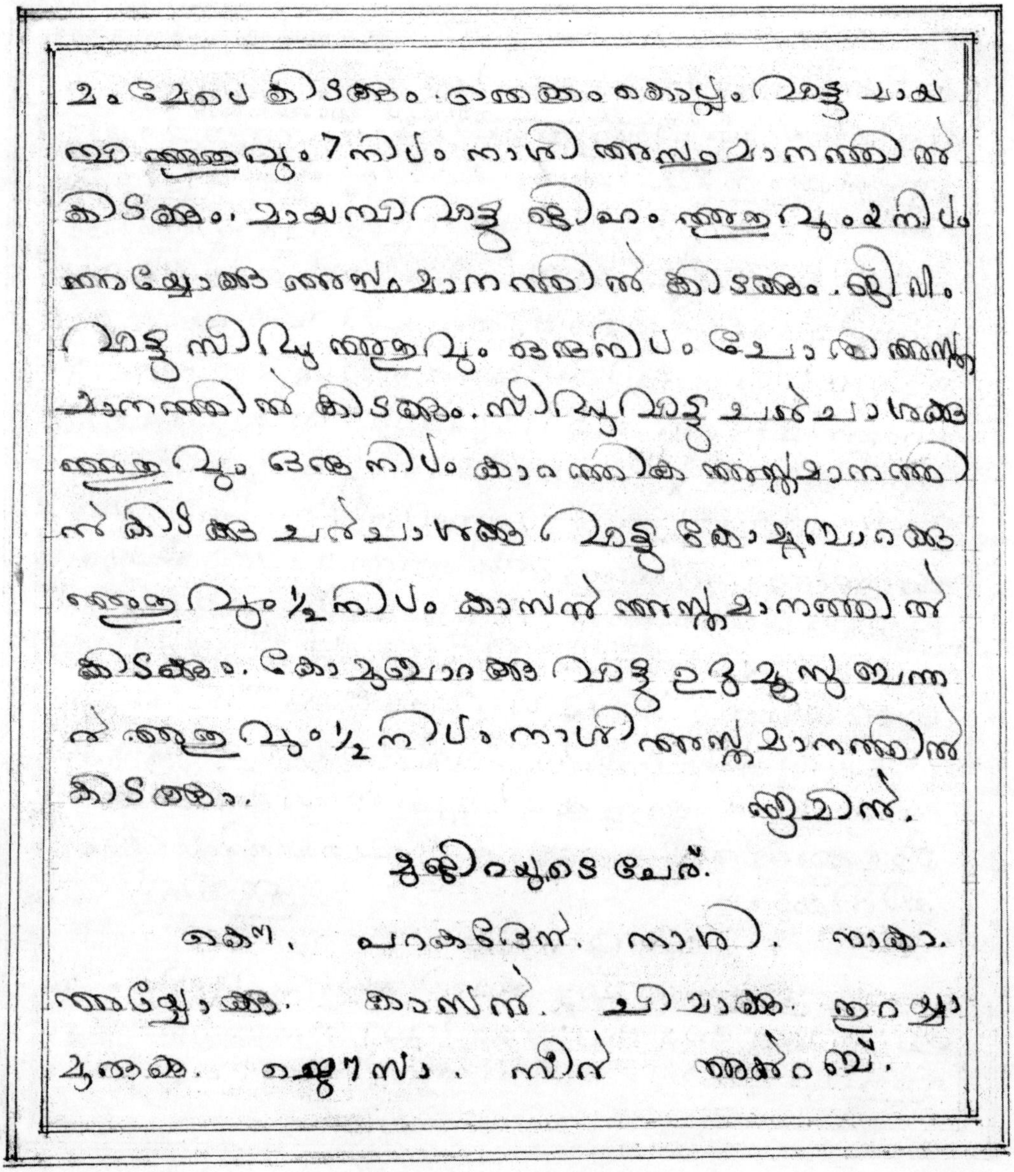

കൽബ്യു. ഹാചാറിൻ. ചപ്പി. ...

ജൊ.ദ. സ്സൈൻ ...

(9) കന്നിട ചാവക്കാണങ്ങൾ. (നം. തായ്യോളു)

നാശിവാട്ടു പറകുരേശൻ 2. പറകുരേശൻ
വാട്ടു ഒകറ 2. ഒകറ വാട്ടു നാശിഷ. നാശിവാ
ട്ടു നാകാ. 2 നാകാ വാട്ടു അയ്യോക്ക 2. അ
യ്യോക്ക വാട്ടു കാസൻ 3. കാസൻ വാട്ടു ചാവ
ക്ക 5. ചാവക്ക വാട്ടു ഉറായ്യ 16. ഉറായ്യായിന്നു
ചുങ്കിന്നും നുവെ 32. ചുങ്കാൻ കന്നിൽ 64
ചുങ്കാവെ അങ്ങാൻ കന്നിൽ 128. ചുങ്കാവെ
അങ്ങാവെ ചാകാണി കന്നിൽ 256. ചുങ്ങ
കുഞ്ഞ ചാകാണി കന്നിൽ 512.

നാ. ചേയ്യോളു.

നാശിവാട്ടു നാകാ 2 നാകാ വാട്ടു അ
യ്യോക്ക 2. അയ്യോക്ക വാട്ടു കാസൻ 3. കാസൻ
വാട്ടു ചാവാക്ക 5 ചാവക്ക വാട്ടു ഉറായ്യ 16. ഉ
റായ്യായിന്നും ചുങ്കിന്നും നുവെ. 32. 64. 128.

256. 512.

ഛാ. മേപോട്ടു.

ഛാച്ചി വാട്ടു സുബ്ബറാർ 2. സുബ്ബറാർവാ
ട്ടു സുതൈബർ 2. സുതൈബർ വാട്ടു സുബ്ബറാർ 2
സുബ്ബറാർ വാട്ടു ഛാച്ചി 2. ഛാച്ചി വാട്ടു ഹി
മാറേൻ 2. ഹിമാറേൻ വാട്ടു കൻബു 2. ക
ൻബു വാട്ടു ഞണ്ടെറബു 3. ഞണ്ടെറബു വാട്ടു സി
ർ 5. സിർ വാട്ടു ജൈനസാ 16. ജൈനസായിന്നു.
മുങ്ങികിന്നും. നുവെ 32. 64. 128. 256. 512.

ഛാ. താഴോട്ടു.

ഛാച്ചി വാട്ടു ഹിമാറേൻ 2. ഹിമാറേ
ൻ വാട്ടു കൻബു 2 ക. ൻബു വാട്ടു ഞണ്ടെറബു
3. ഞണ്ടെറബു വാട്ടു സിർ 5. സിർവാട്ടു ജൈന
സാ 16. ജൈനസായിന്നു. മുങ്ങികിന്നു. നുവെ 32
64. 128. 256. 512 ളുമൻ

(10) ഞണ്ടവേറ്റെ ഞണ്ടങ്ങ.

ഞെ ഗ്ഗപെ 8 ചാചത്തിൽ ഓടി
നാൽ ഒക്കെ 1 പെരുക്കം. 4 ചാചം. കരക്കൊ

ങ്ങളാകും. കർക്കടത്തിന്ന് 7 രാശിയിൽ 10 ചാ
ചത്തിൽ ഓടിനാൽ കൈ 1 ചെല്ലും. 6 ചാ
ചം കരങ്ങളാകും. സിംഹത്തിന്ന് 7 രാശിയിൽ 12
ചാചത്തിൽ ഓടിനാൽ കൈ 1 ചെല്ലും 8
ചാചം കരങ്ങളാകും. കന്നിക്ക് 7 രാശി
യിൽ 14 ചാചത്തിൽ ഓടിനാൽ കൈ 1
ചെല്ലും 10 ചാചം കരങ്ങളാകും. തു
ലാമിന്ന് 7 രാശിയിൽ 16 ചാചത്തിൽ ഓ
ടിനാൽ കൈ 1 ചെല്ലും 12 ചാചം കര
ങ്ങളാകും. വൃശ്ചികത്തിന്ന് 7 രാശിയിൽ 19
ചാചത്തിൽ ഓടിനാൽ കൈ 1 ചെല്ലു
ം 15 ചാചം കരങ്ങളാകും. ധനുവി
ന്ന് 7 രാശിയിൽ 24 ചാചത്തിൽ ഓടിനാ
ൽ കൈ 1 ചെല്ലും 20 ചാചം കരങ്ങ
ങ്ങളാകും. മകരത്തിന്ന് രാശിയിൽ 40 ചാ
ചത്തിൽ ഓടിനാൽ കൈ 1 ചെല്ലു
ം 36 ചാചം കരങ്ങളാകും. കു
ംഭത്തിന്ന് 7 രാശിയിൽ 20 ചാചത്തിൽ ഓ

ടിനാൽ കെ1 ഉരുക്കായ ഓടിയുരു
ണ്ടു വായരിക്കും. ഒജ്ജ സ്വാഇറാനി
ലെ 40 ചാമത്തിൽ ഓടിനാൽ കെ7
1 ചുരുങ്ങും. 28 ചാമം. കരക്കണ്ണണയും.
സിൽ ഇറാനിലെ 24 ചാമത്തിൽ
ഓടിനാൽ കെ7 1 ചുരുങ്ങും. 12 ചാമം.
കരക്കണ്ണണയും. അക്റബു ഇറാനി
ലെ 19 ചാമത്തിൽ ഓടിനാൽ കെ7
1 ചുരുങ്ങും. 7 ചാമം. കരക്കണ്ണണയും.
കൽബു ഇറാനിലെ 16 ചാമത്തി
ൽ ഓടിനാൽ കെ7 1 ചുരുങ്ങും. 4 ചാമം.
കരക്കണ്ണണയും. ഹിമാറൈൻ ഇറാ
നിലെ 14 ചാമത്തിൽ ഓടിനാൽ
കെ7 1 ചുരുങ്ങും. 2 ചാമം. കരക്കണ്ണണ
യും. ഉപ്ലി ഇറാനിലെ 12 ചാമത്തിൽ
ഓടിനാൽ കെ7 ചുരുങ്ങും. കരക്കണ്ണണ
യാത്തകപ്പാ ഓടിയതുണ്ടു വായരിക്കും.

സ്പ്രെബൻ ഇഗ്രാനിലെ 10 ചാമത്തി
ൽ ഓടിനാൽ കൊ൭ 1 ചുങ്കങ്ങളും 2 ചാവം
കരവാട്ടങ്ങളും. സ്സൈബെൻ ഇഗ്രാ
നിലെ 8 ചാമത്തിൽ ഓടിനാൽ കൊ൭
1 ചുങ്കങ്ങളും 4 ചാവം. കരവാട്ടങ്ങളും.
സ്പ്രെബൻ ഓങ്ങ്രാനിലെ 10 ചാമത്തി
ൽ ഓടിനാൽ കൊ൭ 1 ചുങ്കങ്ങളും 6 ചാവം.
കരവാട്ടങ്ങളും. ചെപ്പി ഓങ്ങ്രാനിലെ
12 ചാമത്തിൽ ഓടിനാൽ കൊ൭ 1 ചുങ്കങ്ങളും 8
ചാവം കരവാട്ടങ്ങളും. ചരിചാറെന്ന് ഓങ്ങ്രാ
നിലെ 14 ചാമത്തിൽ ഓടിനാൽ കൊ൭ 1 ചുങ്ക
ങ്ങളും 10 ചാവം കരവാട്ടങ്ങളും. കാൽബു ഓങ്ങ്
രാനിലെ 16 ചാമത്തിൽ ഓടിനാൽ കൊ൭ 1
ചുങ്കങ്ങളും 12 ചാവം കരവാട്ടങ്ങളും. അക്കറബ്ബു
ഓങ്ങ്രാനിലെ 19 ചാമത്തിൽ ഓടിനാൽ
കൊ൭ 1 ചുങ്കങ്ങളും 15 ചാവം കരവാട്ടങ്ങളും.
ജിൽ ഓങ്ങ്രാനിലെ 24 ചാമത്തിൽ ഓടിനാൽ
കൊ൭ 1 ചുങ്കങ്ങളും 20 ചാവം കരവാട്ടങ്ങളും.
ഞ്ജാസ്സ് ഓങ്ങ്രാനിലെ 40 ചാമത്തിൽ ഓടിനാ

(11)

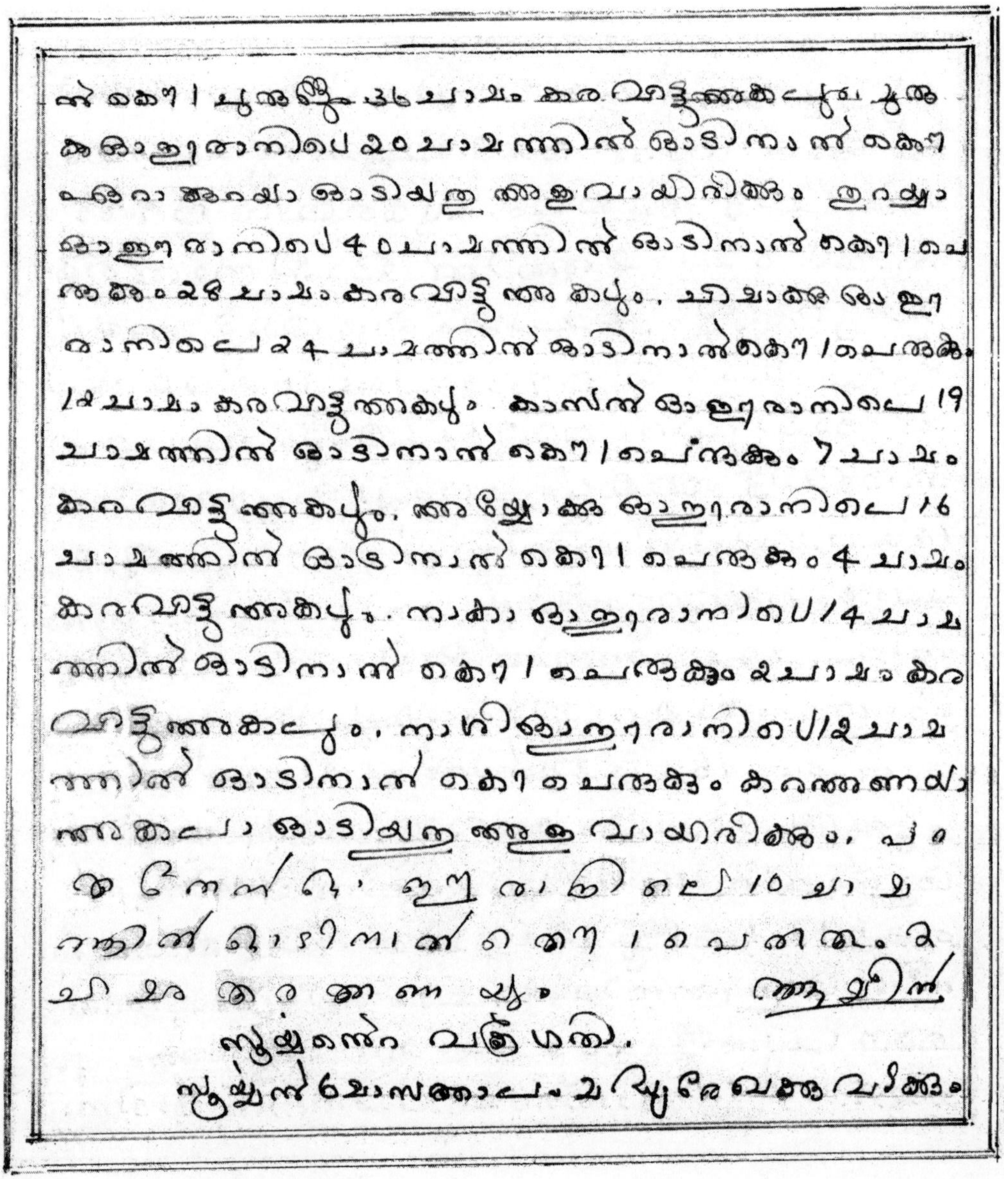

ഭാഗത്തായും 6 മാസക്കാലം തെക്കുഭാഗത്തായുമാണ
ക്കാണും. ഭൂമിയും സഞ്ചരിക്കാറുള്ളത്. ഇതു ഏപ്രി
ൽ, മെയി, ജൂൺ, ജൂലായി, ആഗസ്റ്റ, സെപ്തമ്പർ എന്നീ
6 മാസം വടക്കായും ഒക്ടോബർ, നവമ്പ്ര, ഡിസമ്പ്ര, ജ
നവരി, ഫെബ്രുവരി, മാർച്ച എന്നീ 6 മാസങ്ങളിൽ
തെക്കായു മാറ്റമുണ്ടാവുക.

കൊല്ലത്തിൽ 2 പ്രാവശ്യം സൂര്യൻ മദ്ധ്യ
രേഖക്കുനേരെ ഉച്ചിക്കു കാണപ്പെടുന്നു. അതു മാ
ർച്ച് 21-ാം൹യും സെപ്തമ്പർ 21-ാം൹യുമാണ്.
മാർച്ച് മാസം 21-ാം൹ മുതൽ സൂര്യൻ മദ്ധ്യരേഖയി
ൽനിന്നു വടക്കോട്ടുള്ള ചലനം ആരംഭിക്കയും
ജൂൺ 21-ാം൹ പൂർണ്ണ ഉത്തരായനം (മദ്ധ്യരേഖയിൽ
നിന്നു 23½ ഡിഗ്രി വടക്ക) എത്തുകയും പിന്നെ തെക്കോ
ട്ടുള്ള ചലനം തുടങ്ങി സെപ്തമ്പർ 21-ാം൹ മദ്ധ്യരേഖ
യിൽ എത്തി അവിടന്നു പിന്നെ തെക്കോട്ടുള്ള ച
ലനം ആരംഭിക്കുന്നു. ഡിസമ്പർ 21-ാം൹ ദക്ഷിണാ
യനത്തിൽ മദ്ധ്യരേഖയിൽനിന്നു 23½ ഡിഗ്രി തെക്ക
എത്തുകയും അവിടന്നു വീണ്ടും വടക്കോട്ടു മാറി
മാർച്ച് 21-ാം൹ മദ്ധ്യരേഖയിൽ എത്തുന്നു

ജോമാൻ.

(12)

സൂര്യഗതി.

ഹമൽ മേടം മുതൽ തൗറ് ഇടവം കാ
ണിക്ക. ജൗസാ മിഥുനം ചോതി. സറത്താൻ ക
ർക്കടകം ചിങ്ങം ചോതി. അസദു ചിങ്ങം. കാറത്തി
സുമ്പുൽ കന്നി മുതൽ മീസാൻ തുലാം ചക്രം.
അക്റബു വൃശ്ചികം സിദ്ദ്. കൗസു ധനുവും അൽ
ജൈ. ജദിൻ മകരം ചിങ്ങി അക്റബ്. ദൽവു കും
ഭം. സിദ്ദ്. ഹൂത്ത് മീനം ചക്രം. അപ്പോൾ സൂര്യൻ ക
ള്ളൻ ത്സ്സ് വായിലായിരിക്കും. ശുഭമസ്.

(13)

മാസത്തിന്റെ പേര്	[illegible]	[illegible]	[illegible]	ഭാഗം.	മാസത്തിന്റെ പേര്	മൂന്നാം ദിവസം	രണ്ടാം ദിവസം	ഒന്നാം ദിവസം	ഭാഗം.
	തൈ	തൈ	തൈ			തൈ	തൈ	തൈ	
ഹമൽ	24	23	22	$11\frac{1}{2}$	മീസാൻ	24	23	22	$11\frac{1}{2}$
തൗറാ	18	17	16	$8\frac{1}{2}$	അക്റബ്	18	17	16	$8\frac{1}{2}$
ജൗസാ	8	7	6	$3\frac{1}{2}$	കൗസ്	8	7	6	$3\frac{1}{2}$
	ഞെ	ഞെ	ഞെ			വ	വ	വ	
സറത്താൻ	6	7	8	$3\frac{1}{2}$	ജദിൻ	6	7	8	$3\frac{1}{2}$
അസദ്	16	17	18	$8\frac{1}{2}$	ദൽവ്	16	17	18	$8\frac{1}{2}$
സുമ്പുൽ	22	23	24	$11\frac{1}{2}$	ഹൂത്ത്.	22	23	24	$11\frac{1}{2}$

(14)

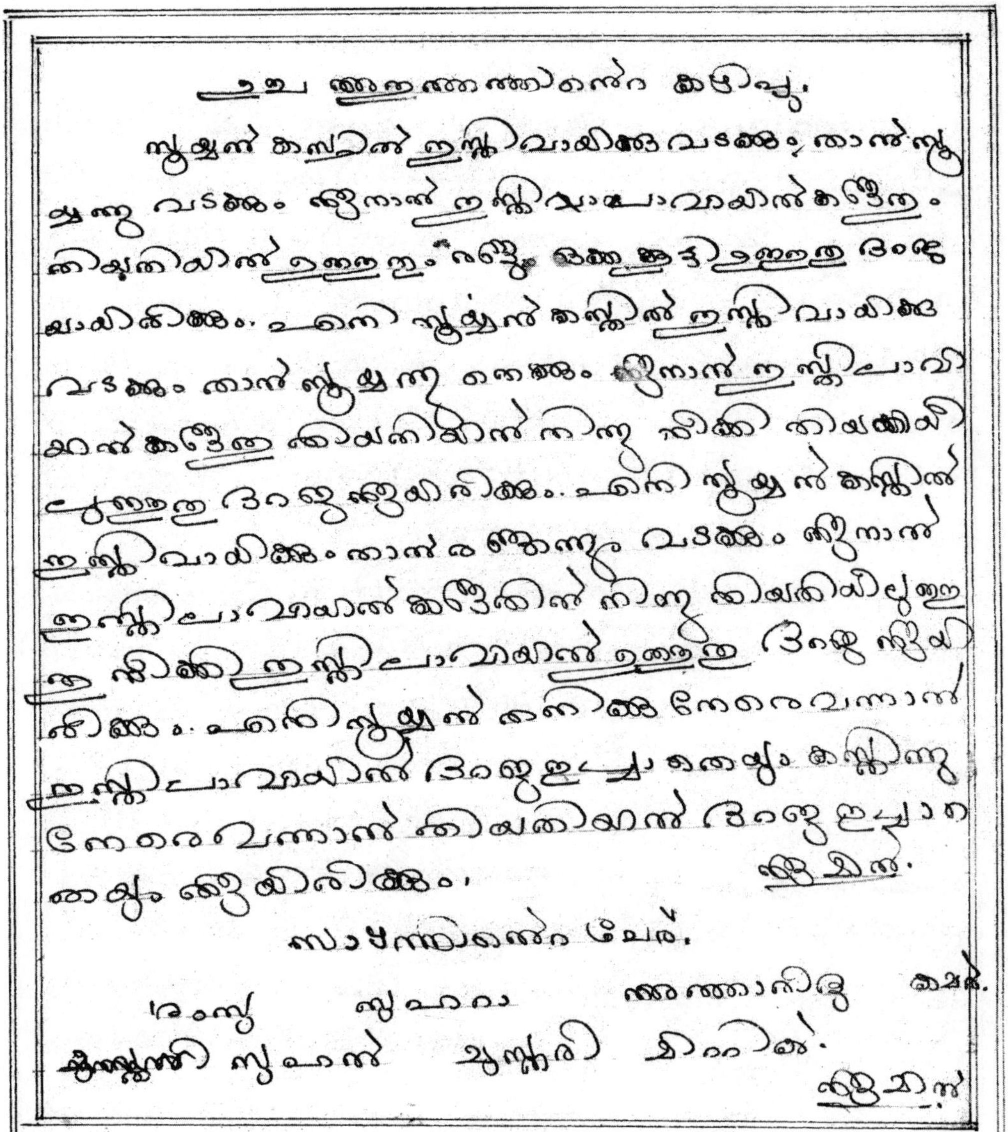

(15)

(16) നക്ഷത്രങ്ങളുടെ പേര്.
അശ്വതി. ഭരണി കാർത്തിക. രോഹിണി
മകീരം. തിരുവാതിര. പുണർതം. പൂയം. ആ
യില്യം. മകം. പൂരം. ഉത്രം. അത്തം
ചിത്തിര. ചോതി. വിശാഖം. അനിഴം. തൃ
ക്കേട്ട. മൂലം. പൂരാടം. ഉത്രാടം. തിരുവോ
ണം. അവിട്ടം. ചതയം. പൂരുരുട്ടാതി. ഉ
ത്രട്ടാതി. രേവതി. തമാമ്

(17) നക്ഷത്രപ്പോലിമം
ഇന്നാൾ അറിവാൻ തക്ക വണ്ണം
ഇന്ന കടകങ്ങൾ നക്ഷത്രങ്ങളെല്ലാം ഭരണി
മൂന്നും അടുപ്പു വെച്ചപോലെ കാർത്തിക പ
തിനൊന്ന് ഒറ്റക്ക രോഹിണി ഉരുളായി
ൽ പോലെ. മകീരം മൂന്നു. മാൻതല പോ
ലെ. [illegible] മൂന്നു. നേർകൊണ്ടപോലെ.
[illegible] [illegible] [illegible] [illegible]
[illegible] [illegible] ഒന്ന [illegible]
[illegible] [illegible] പൂയം [illegible] [illegible]

ലെപാലെ. ജ്യേഷ്ഠ്യം നാരിന്റെ ഞെമ്പി പോലെ. ഉ
ത്രമത്തി നാരകം കന്നിയ പോലെ പൂരവും ഉത്രവും
പതിനൊന്നാമത്തിൽ പോലെ. അത്തം ചെമ്പിൻ്റെ ക
ഷ്ണം പോലെ ഉന്നത്തിര. ഒന്നാമത്തിൽ ചന്ദ്രരിൽ
ൽ മേൽ മൂന്നുക പോതി വിശാഖം വലവന്നി
പോലെ അനിഴം അന്ന്യം കാഞ്ഞനപോലെ. തൃക്കേ
ട്ടം മൂന്നും അരവിന്ദു പോലെ. പൂരം കാണം. പോ
ലെ. ഉത്രാടം പൂത്ത വാഹിനി പോലെ. ഉത്രാടം
തൃത്തി പോലെ. തിരുവോണം മൂന്നും പൂർക്കോൺ
പോലെ. അവിട്ടം. ചതയം. ചക്രം പോലെ. പ
നകം. പേർത്തും. പോലെ, പൂരുരുട്ടാതിയും ഉ
ത്തൃട്ടാതിയും. ചെക്കതിപോലെ, ഇരവതി
ന്ന് ഒന്നൊന്നാമത്തിൽ പോലെ. ഇടിക്ക.

(18) അവസ്ഥാ യന്ത്രം

ഞായറ്.	പകല്	ശനി.	രാത്രി.	ഞാറിദ.
തിങ്കള്.	"	കുജൻ	"	ചൊവ്വ.
ചൊവ്വ.	"	ബുധൻ	"	ശുക്രൻ.
ബുധന്	"	ഞാറിദ.	"	ശുക്രൻ
വ്യാഴം	"	ചൊവ്വ.	"	ശനി.

വെള്ളി പകൽ സുബ്ഹിന് രാത്രി [illegible]
ശനി. " സുബ്ഹിന് " മഗ്‌രിബ്.

(19) [illegible]

[illegible] വെള്ളി [illegible]
[illegible]
[illegible]
[illegible]
[illegible]
[illegible]

(20) [illegible]

[illegible] 98 നാടി, 28 നാടി
[illegible] 1. 14 നാടിക്കു സായുന്ന 2. 7. നാടി
ക്കു സായുന്ന 3. $3\frac{1}{2}$ നാടിക്കു സായുന്ന 4. $1\frac{3}{4}$ നാടി
ക്കു സായുന്ന 5. [illegible] നാടിക്കു സായുന്ന 6. [illegible]
[illegible] $1\frac{3}{4}$ നാടിക്കു സായുന്ന 7. $3\frac{1}{2}$ നാടി
ക്കു സായുന്ന 8. 7. നാടിക്കു സായുന്ന 9. 14 നാടി

ക്കു സായനം 10. 28 നാടിക്കു സായനം 11. 78 നാടിക്കു
സായനം. 12. ശുഭം.

(21) രാഹുവുടെ ഉദയങ്ങൾ.

ബുധനാഴ്ച ഉദിച്ചു 2½ നാഴികക്കു ശേഷം 2½ നാഴിക നില്ക്കും

ചൊവ്വാഴ്ച	„	6	„	„	2½	„ „
തിങ്കളാഴ്ച	„	10	„	„	2½	„ „
ഞായറാഴ്ച	„	14	„	„	2½	„ „
ശനിയാഴ്ച	„	18	„	„	2½	„ „
വെള്ളിയാഴ്ച	„	24	„	„	2½	„ „
വ്യാഴം	„	26	„	„	2½	„ „

ചെറു ചെക്കിയം തന്നെ ഒരു കാര്യങ്ങളും തൊടങ്ങുകയും യാത്രയും ആരംഭവും അരുത്
തായെ.
ശുഭം.

(22) ഉല്പാതങ്ങൾ

ചന്ദ്രനെ വെൺ പൂർണ്ണനാഴിക ഭേദിക്കും ഉൽപത്തിക്കു ചന്ദ്രനെ കാണാ. ചൊവ്വ, ഉത്തരാടം ... ചൊവ്വ ബുധൻ ... ചൊൻ ... പോൽ വെള്ളിക്കു പൂരാടം ...

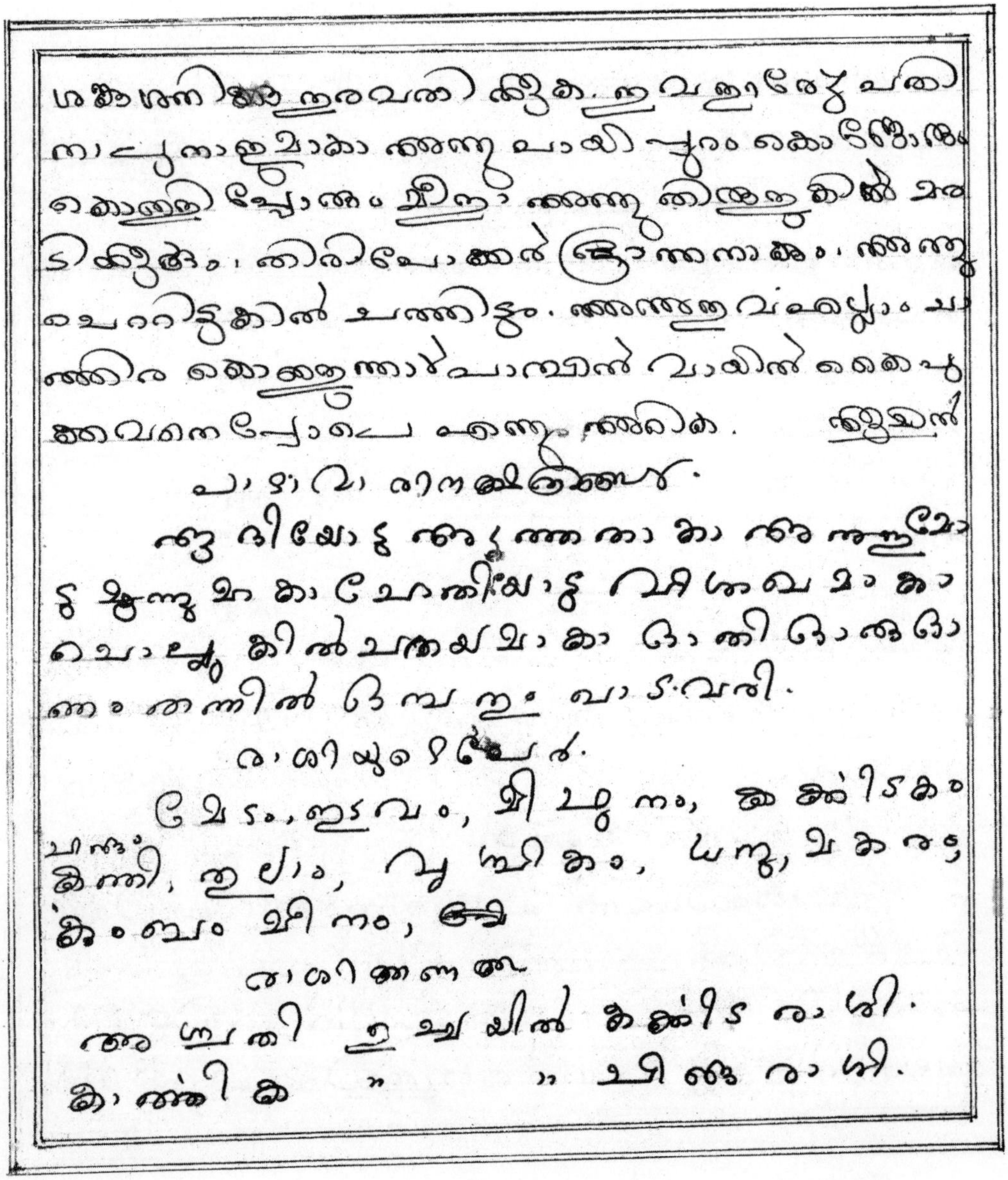

(23)

(24)

(25)

മകയിരം ഉദയമിൽ കന്നിരാശി.
പുണർതം ,, ,, തുലാരാശി.
ആയില്യം ,, ,, വൃശ്ചികരാശി.
അത്തം ,, ,, ധനുരാശി
ചോതി ,, ,, മകരരാശി.
അനിഴം ,, ,, കുംഭരാശി.
പൂരാടം ,, ,, മീനരാശി.
തിരുവോണം ,, ,, മേടരാശി.
ചതയം ,, ,, ഇടവരാശി.
പൂരുരുട്ടാതിയിൽ ഉത്രട്ടാതിയിൽ
ക്കും നല്ലവ മിഥുനരാശി. ...
~~മേടരാശി.~~

(26) രാശിയുടെ നില.
മേടരാശി മേടത്തിൽ ഉദയത്തിൽ നില്ക്കും
ഇടവരാശി (ഇടവം) ന്നേ ,, ,,
മിഥുനരാശി മിഥുനഉദയം ,, ,,
കർക്കിടകം ഉദയത്തിന്നേ ,, ,,
ചിങ്ങരാശി ചിങ്ങത്തിന്നേ ,, ,,
കന്നി രാശിയിൽ ഇരുന്നേ ,, ,,

തുലാരാശി. [illegible] സ്ഥാനത്തിൽ
വൃശ്ചികരാശി. [illegible] ന്ന്.
ധനുവെരാശി [illegible] സ്ഥാനം.
മകരരാശി [illegible] ന്ന്.
കുംഭരാശി [illegible] ന്ന്.
മീനരാശി [illegible] ന്ന് [illegible]
(27) രാശിയിൽ ചെല്ലുമ്പോൾ [illegible]
മേടത്തിൽ [illegible] നിന്നു [illegible] വാൻ
[illegible] ഇടവത്തിൽ [illegible] ൻ ന
ന്നു [illegible]. [illegible] മിഥു
നത്തിൽ [illegible] ൻ നന്നു [illegible]
വാൻ. [illegible] കർക്കിടത്തിൽ [illegible]
[illegible] ൻ നന്നു [illegible] വാൻ [illegible]. ചി
ങ്ങത്തിൽ [illegible] വാൻ നന്നു [illegible]
[illegible] കന്നിയിൽ [illegible]
[illegible] വിട്ടു [illegible]
[illegible] നന്നു [illegible]
തുലാത്തിൽ [illegible] നന്നു [illegible]
[illegible] വൃശ്ചികത്തിൽ [illegible]

(28)

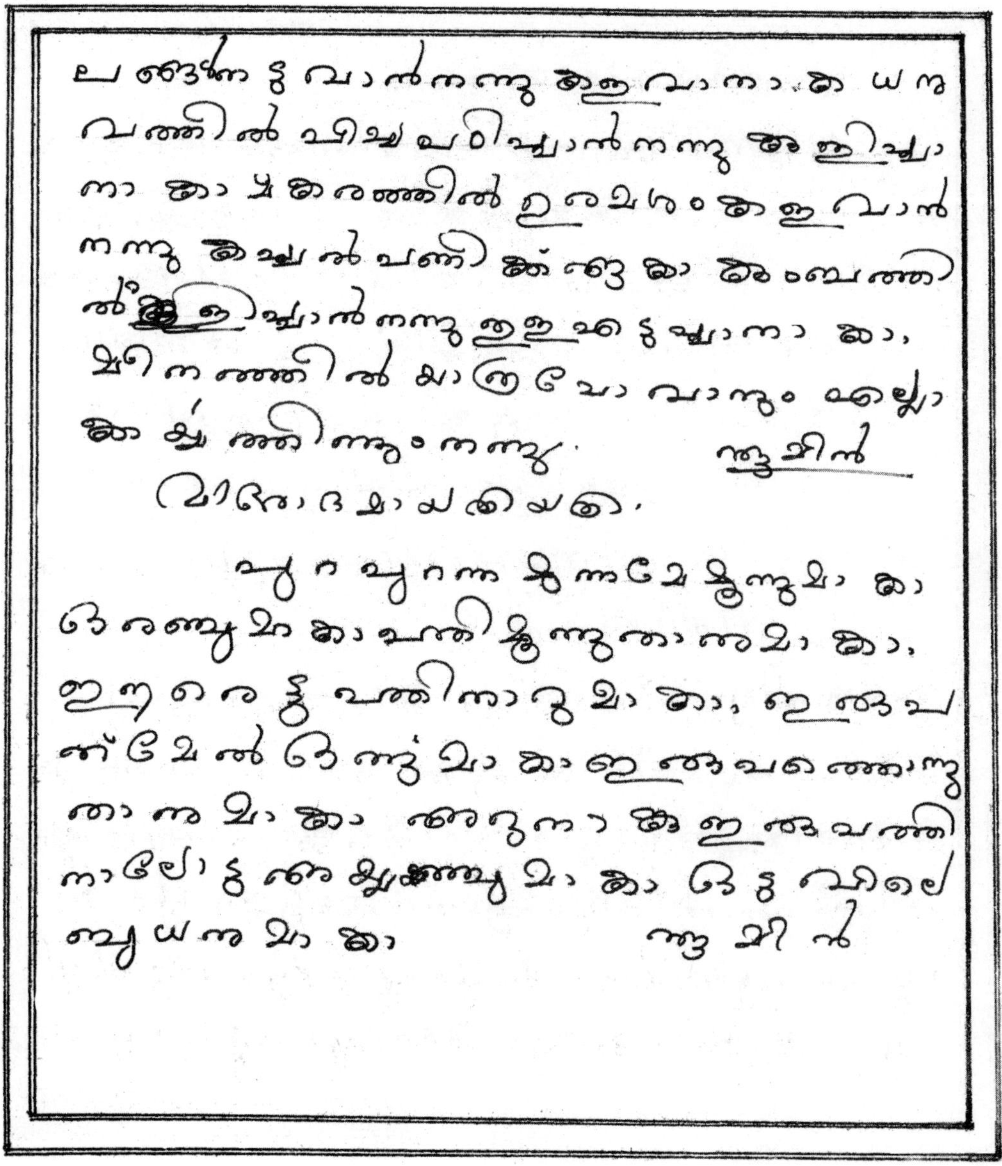

(29) മാസത്തിൽ വാല്യക്കാര്യ.

മാസം ... ത്തൽ ഞായറു വന്നുകിൽ ആമാസം തിങ്കളാകാ

" " തിങ്കൾ വന്നുകിൽ " " വെള്ളിയാകാ

" " ചൊവ്വ വന്നുകിൽ " " ചൊവ്വാകാ

" " ബുധൻ വന്നുകിൽ " " ശനിയാകാ

" " വ്യാഴം വന്നുകിൽ " " ബുധനാകാ

" " വെള്ളി വന്നുകിൽ " " ഞായർ

" " ശനി വന്നുകിൽ " " വ്യാഴമാകാ

(30) രാശിലെ.

അശ്വതിയും ഭരണിയും കാർത്തികാലും
മേടം. കാർത്തിക മുക്കാലും രോഹിണിയും
മകയിരം അരയും ഇടവം. മകയിരം അരയും
തിരുവാതിരയും പുണർതം മുക്കാലും മി
ഥുനം. പുണർതം കാലും പൂയവും ആയില്യ
വും കർക്കിടകവും. മകവും പൂരവും.

ഉത്രം കാല്യം ചിങ്ങം. ഉത്രം മുക്കാല്യം അത്ത
വും ചിത്തിര അരയും കന്നി. ചിത്തിര അ
രയും ചോതിയും വിശാഖം മുക്കാല്യം തുലാം. വി
ശാഖത്തുകാല്യം അനിഴവും തൃക്കേട്ടയും
വൃശ്ചികം മൂലവും പൂരാടവും ഉത്രാടം
കാല്യം ധനു. ഉത്രാടം മുക്കാല്യം തിരു
വോണവും അവിട്ടം അരയും മകരം. അ
വിട്ടം അരയും ചതയവും പൂരുരുട്ടാതി
മുക്കാല്യം കുംഭം. പൂരുരുട്ടാതി കാല്യം
ഉത്രട്ടാതിയും രേവതിയും മീനം. ഇതിൽ
(31) രാശികൾക്കു ഗ്രഹങ്ങളെ വാഴ്ക.

12 ചെന്ന ഞായറാക 11 ചെന്ന തിങ്കളാക
10 ചെന്ന ചൊവ്വാക 9 ചെന്ന ബുധനാ
ക 8 ചെന്ന വ്യാഴമാക 7 ചെന്ന വെള്ളി
യാക 6 ചെന്ന ശനിയാക ......

(32) മാസങ്ങൾവാഴുന്നതിനെ.

അൽമുഹർറം 12 വരില്ക്ക് സഫർ 10 വ
രില്ക്ക് റബീഉൽ അവ്വൽ 4 വരില്ക്ക് റബീഉ
ൽ ആഖിർ 18 വരില്ക്ക് ജമാദുൽ അവ്വൽ 28
വരില്ക്ക് ജമാദുൽ ആഖിർ 28 വരില്ക്ക് റജ
ബ് 12 വരില്ക്ക് ശഅ്ബാൻ 26 വരില്ക്ക് റമളാ
ൻ 27 വരില്ക്ക് ശവ്വാൽ 20 വരില്ക്ക് ദുൽ
ഖഅ്ദ്. 18 വരില്ക്ക് ദുൽഹജ്ജ 8 വരില്ക്ക്
ഇന്ന വരില്ക്ക് നാളുകളിൽ സഫർ പോവെ
ലും പലതർ ഉണ്ടാക്കലും കാട്ടാക്കാനാങ്ങ
ടെ തൊലിക്കട്ടാക്കല്യാണങ്ങ് ളുമിൽ

(33) സമയങ്ങൾ അറിയുന്നത.

നാൾ ഒന്നുക്ക് നാഴിക 60 പകൽ 30 രാത്രി 30
ഒരു നാൾക്ക് രാശി 12 പകൽ 6 രാത്രി 6
" " സാമത്ത് 24 " " 12 " " 12

" " യാമം 8 ചേർന്നാൽ 4 നാഴിക - 4

യാമം ഒന്നിന്ന് രാശി 1½ സാമാന്യം 3 നാഴി

ക 7½ രാശി ഒന്നിന്ന് സാമാന്യം 2 നാഴി

ക 5. സാമാന്യത്തിൽ ഒന്നിന്നു നാഴിക 2½ നാ

ഴിക ഒന്നിന്നു വിനാഴിക 60 മിനുട്ട് 24

കൊല്ലം ഒന്നിന്ന് ദിവസം 360 (365¼)

" " മാസം 12.

" " ആഴ്ച 52

മാസം ഒന്നിന്ന് ദിവസം 30 (31)

ആഴ്ച ഒന്നിന്ന് " ദിവസം 7

(34) ഉദ്ദേശ്യത്തിന്ന ചെറുതു ആണെന്നുവെച്ചു 100 യാമം എന്നുവെച്ചു 12

മാസം പന്ത്രണ്ടിന്റെ പേരറിഞ്ഞു

ഞായറാഴ്ച തുടങ്ങി ഏഴു ദിവസങ്ങളുടെ

പേരും ഓർത്തിരിക്കുന്ന പ്രകാരം

[illegible]

[illegible]

[illegible]

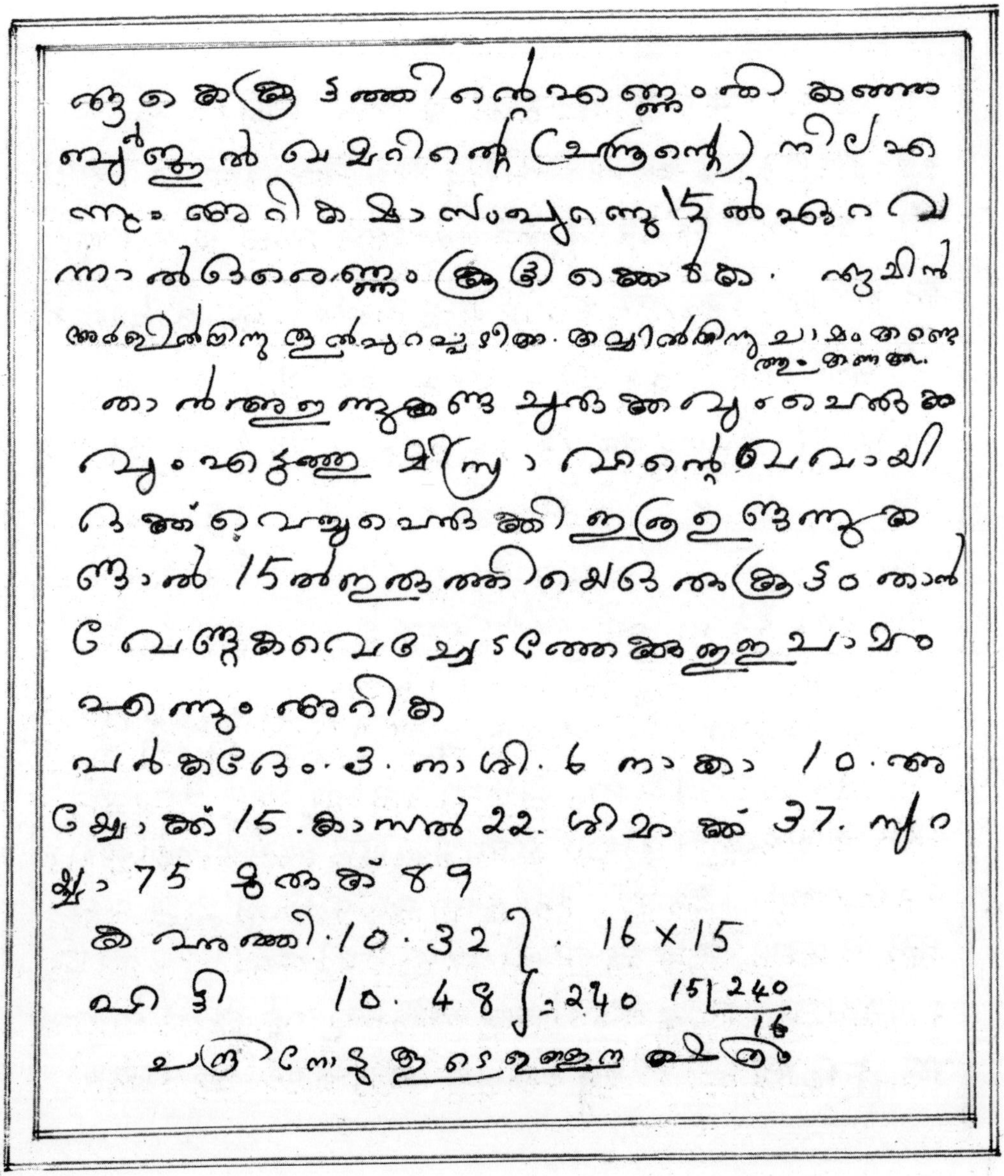

(35)

(36)

മേടം പിടിച്ചു നാൾനിന്ന മാസം വരെ
മൊട്ടുഞ്ഞ ഞതിനെഞ്ചിച്ചു ഉത്രമെന്നി
ഞ്ഞാൽ അശ്വതി പിടിച്ചു മണ്ണിഞ്ഞഴിക്ക
ഒടുവിൽ വന്ന നക്ഷത്രത്തിന്റെ കൂടെ [illegible]
മാസം ചുറ്റുമെന്നു അറിക ഒാരോ
ദിവസത്തിന്നും ഒാരോ ന നക്ഷത്രം മ
ണ്ണിക്കൊൾക മാസം വക്കത്തി കഴിഞ്ഞാ
ൽ ഒന്നു അധികം കൂട്ടിക്കൊൾകയും
വേണം. [illegible]

(37) കയമത്ത് അറിയും [illegible]

മേടം പിടിച്ചു നാൾനിന്ന നാൾ വരെ
എട്ടുഞ്ഞ പത്തിനട്ടും കൂട്ടി വന്ന മണ്ണും ഉത്ര
മെന്നു അറിഞ്ഞു ഹമൽ പിടിച്ചു മണ്ണിഞ്ഞഴി
ക്ക ഒടുവിൽ വന്നമണ്ണോം നാൾ അറിവാൻ
വേണ്ടുക വൈചിത്ര്യത്തിമെന്നും അറിക

(38) കയമൊഴ്ക.

ഹമൽ 31 തൗർ 31 ജൗസാ 32 സർത്താൻ
31 അസദ് 31 സുമ്പുൽ 31 മീസാൻ 30 ..

ശഅ്ബാൻ 30 റമളാൻ 29. ശവ്വാൽ 29
ദുൽഖഅ്ദ് 30 ഹജ്ജ് 30

(39) ഞായർമാസം

മേടം 31 ഇടവം 31 മിഥുനം 32
കർക്കടകം 31 ചിങ്ങം 31 കന്നി 31
തുലാം 30 വൃശ്ചികം 29 ധനു 30
മകരം 29 കുംഭം 30 മീനം 30

(40) നക്ഷത്രം. ഇടനാഴിക.

അശ്വതിമുതൽ ഭരണിക്കിടനാഴി . 3.
ഭരണിമുതൽ കാർത്തികക്കുള്ള വെനാഴിക 1 1/8
കാർത്തികമുതൽ രോഹിണിക്കും ,, ,, 2
രോഹിണിമുതൽ മകയിരത്തിന്നും ,, ,, 2
മകയിരത്തിന്നും തിരുവാതിരക്കും ,, ,, 1 1/8
തിരുവാതിരക്കും പുണർതത്തിന്നും ,, ,, 2 1/8
പുണർതത്തിന്നും പൂയത്തിന്നും ,, ,, 2.
പൂയത്തിന്നും ആയില്യത്തിന്നും ,, ,, 1 1/8
ആയില്യത്തിന്നും മകത്തിന്നും ,, ,, 1 1/8
മകത്തിന്നും പൂരത്തിന്നും ,, ,, 1

പൂരത്തിന്നും ഉത്തരത്തിന്നും നടുവെ നാഴിക 1/8
ഉത്തരത്തിന്നും അത്തത്തിന്നും „ „ 1/8
അത്തത്തിന്നും ചിത്തിരക്കും ചോതിക്കും
നടുവെ . . . . നാഴിക 2 1/8
ചോതിക്കും വിശാഖത്തിന്നും നടുവെ നാ 2 1/8
വിശാഖത്തിന്നും അനിഴത്തിന്നും ന. നാ 1/8
അനിഴത്തിന്നും തൃക്കേട്ടത്തിന്നും ന. നാ 2
തൃക്കേട്ടത്തിന്നും മൂലത്തിന്നും ന. നാ 2
മൂലത്തിന്നും പൂരാടത്തിന്നും ന. നാ 1/4
പൂരാടത്തിന്നും ഉത്രാടത്തിന്നും ന. നാ 2.
ഉത്രാടത്തിന്നും തിരുവോണത്തിന്നും ന. നാ 3 1/8
തിരുവോണത്തിന്നും അവിട്ടത്തിന്നും ന. നാ 2 1/8
അവിട്ടത്തിന്നും ചതയത്തിന്നും ന. നാ 4
ചതയത്തിന്നും പൂരുരുട്ടാതിക്കും ന. നാ 3
പൂരുരുട്ടാതിക്കും ഉത്രട്ടാതിക്കും ന. നാ 7

[illegible]

(41) ശുക്രാംശുരത്തെംതെണ്ടെ.

ശുക്രൻ ക്രൂരന്മാരായവർ വരുകിൽ

ഞ്ഞു ഞ്ഞു ഞ്ഞിൽ ടെ ക്ഷീണം വൃഷണ്ണിയിരിക്കും

ഉഷ്ണപിത്തിയും ദുഷ്ടമൃഗങ്ങളിലും ഭയിക്കുമാകും

6ഉം തിങ്കൾ വരുകിൽ

ഞാനാലും വെളുപ്പായതായിരിക്കും മ

ഴയും പഴവർഗ്ഗങ്ങളും വെള്ളപ്പൂണ്ടോ[illegible]

ൽ [illegible]യിക്കും [illegible]ിക്കും -

6ഉം ചൊവ്വ വരുകിൽ

ദീനം വെളുപ്പുണ്ടാകും [illegible]യും [illegible]

[illegible]ണ്ടാകും. വെണ്ണും [illegible]ങ്ങും [illegible]

കും [illegible]ിക്കും. [illegible] [illegible]ടെ [illegible]

വേറാകും. -

6ഉം ബുധൻ വരുകിൽ

വെളുപ്പും [illegible]ങ്ങും [illegible]ങ്ങും [illegible]

[illegible]ങ്ങും [illegible]യിരിക്കും [illegible]യും.

കുടിനീരും വെളുപ്പുന്നോം കാം.

6 വ്യാഴം വരുകിൽ

അധികം വെടുപ്പാക്കപ്പെടുന്നോം ധിനിക്കം
എവിടെയെങ്കിലും പോകുന്നോം കാം.

6 വെള്ളി വരുകിൽ

രുചിരുഗന്ധങ്ങൾക്കും മനസ്സിൽക്കും വെ
ള്ളഞ്ഞൊഴിഞ്ഞന്നോം കാം.

6 ശനി വരുകിൽ

മഴ വെള്ളക്കും ഐശ്വര്യവാന്മാർ
അധികം മരിക്കും ഫല ...
ഉണ്ടാകുന്നോം കാം.

(42) ഉച്ചക്കു പിറക്കും ഫലം.

പൂരം ഉച്ചയിൽ പിറക്കും മക്കൾ ഉടനെ മരിക്കും.
ഉത്തിര ഉച്ചയിൽ പിറക്കും വെള്ളത്തിൽ ചാകും.
അത്തം ഉച്ചയിൽ പിറക്കും മക്കൾ ....
ചിത്തിര ഉച്ചയിൽ പിറക്കും മക്കൾ [illegible].
ചോതി ഉച്ചയിൽ പിറക്കും മക്കൾ ഇരന്നു നടക്കും.

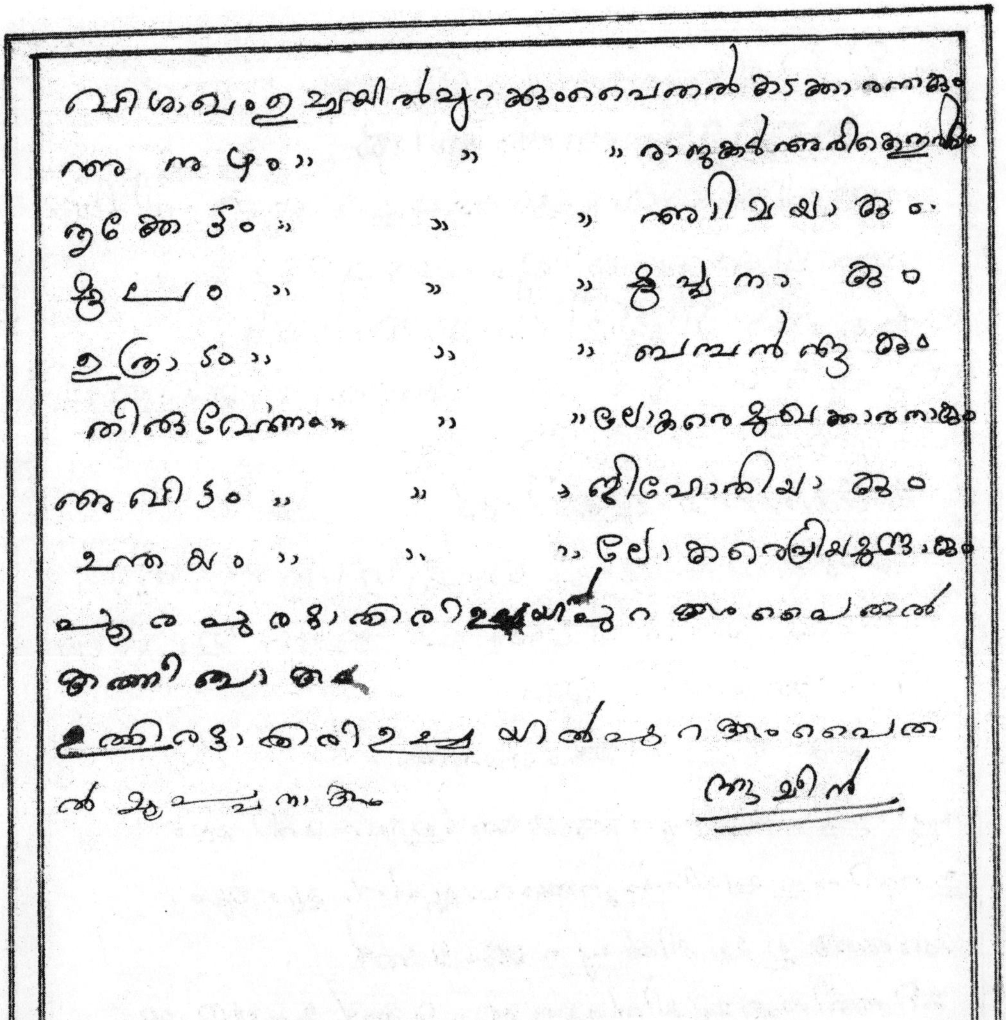

വിശാഖം ഉച്ചയിൽ പുറക്കംവെച്ചാൽ മടക്കാരനാകും
അനിഴം ,, ,, ,, രാജാക്കൾക്കിഷ്ടനാകും
തൃക്കേട്ടം ,, ,, ,, അറിവയാകും.
മൂലം ,, ,, ,, മൂപ്പനാകും
പൂരാടം ,, ,, ,, ബെമ്പൻണ്ടാകും
തിരുവോണം ,, ,, ലോകരെ മുവെക്കാരനാകും
അവിട്ടം ,, ,, ,, ജീവോതിയാകും
ഉതയം ,, ,, ,, ലോകരെപ്രിയമുണ്ടാകും
പൂരുരുട്ടാതിയിൽ ഉച്ചയിൽ പുറക്കം വെച്ചാൽ
കാണിപോകൻ
ഉത്തൃട്ടാതിയിൽ ഉച്ചയിൽ പുറക്കം വെച്ചാ
ൽ മൂപ്പനാകും
അനുമിൻ

(43) ചന്ദ്രൻചെരിയുംകണക്ക്.

മീനഞ്ഞാററിലും മേടഞ്ഞാററിലും മാസം
പിറക്കുമ്പോൾ തെക്കെ തലെ ഉയർന്നിരിക്കും. ഇടവ
ഞ്ഞാറിലും മിഥുനഞ്ഞാറിലും മാസം പിറക്കുമ്പോൾ രണ്ടു
തലയും ഒത്തിരിക്കും. കർക്കടകം, ചിങ്ങം, കന്നി, തു
ലാം, വൃശ്ചികം, ധനുവം, മകരം എന്നീരാശികളി
ൽ പിറക്കുമ്പോൾ വടക്കെ തലെ ഉയർന്നിരിക്കും.

(44) ചന്ദ്രഗ്രഹണങ്ങളെദോഷം.

മേഷത്തിൽ ചന്ദ്രഗ്രഹണമുണ്ടായാൽ ജന
ങ്ങൾക്കു ദെണ്ണം. സിംഹത്തിൽ മഴ ഇല്ലായ്കയും. രെവതിഇൽ
അശ്വതിയിൽ വാതുകൾക്കു ദെണ്ണം. ദുഃഖം പിറക്കും. രെവ
തിഇൽ ഭരണിയിൽ കുഞ്ഞുങ്ങൾക്കു ദെണ്ണം. സിംഹാസനം ഒഴിയും.
ഇടവത്തിൽ അശ്വതിയിൽ ബന്ധുജനങ്ങൾക്കു മ
ഹാഭയവുമുണ്ടാകും. മിഥുനത്തിൽ ഭരണിയിൽ വേല ദെണ്ണം.
കർക്കടകത്തിൽ മഴ ദെണ്ണം. രെവതിയിൽ ജനങ്ങളുടെ
ഉടയിൽ ക്ഷേമമുണ്ടാകും. ദശമത്തിൽ മെഘങ്ങൾ ദെണ്ണം.
ഭൂമിയിൽ ധാന്യമായവർക്ക് ദുഃഖമുണ്ടാകും. ധനുവിൽ ബ്രാഹ്മ
ണർക്കു ദുഃഖം. മകരത്തിൽ ബന്ധുക്കൾക്ക് മഹാഭയവുമുണ്ടാകും.

ദെമകിൽ---

(45) ദുഹ്റാം വിറക്കും കണക്ക്:

ഹിജ്റത്തു എന്നറിഞ്ഞാൽ അതിൽ നിന്ന
930 കഴിച്ചു ശേഷിച്ചുള്ള തുകയെ ഒട്ടുഞ്ഞ് 4-ൽ വെട്ടി
വന്ന കണക്ക് അസ്സൽ എന്ന വേറെ വെക്കുക. പിന്നെയും
~~93ൽ~~ 930ൽ വരം തുകയെട്ടുഞ്ഞ് 11ൽ വെട്ടി വന്ന
തിന്റെ ഇരട്ടിഞ്ഞ് 30 മേൽ വരുന്ന് 30 കളികയായി വന്ന
ന്നതു വന്നതാവന്നതെ ഒന്നിലും. അതിലും. അധിക
മെങ്കിലും ഒന്നു കൂട്ടിക്കൊള്ളുക. 19 കുറഞ്ഞ
വന്നാൽ അതിനെ തള്ളിക്കളയുക. 30 മേൽവ
രുന്ന വന്നതും ഇതു എന്നറിഞ്ഞാൽ അത്
നാട്ടിൽ വെട്ടി അസ്ലിനോടു കൂട്ടുക. പിന്നെ
7ൽ തള്ളുക. 7ൽ തള്ളിയതിൽ ഞായറാഴ്ച വിട്ട
ഴ്ച എണ്ണിക്കൊണ്ട് വന്ന എണ്ണം (തുല്യ) ആന്നേ
ത്തെ ദുഹ്റാം പുറന്നതു എന്നറിക.

അതുമല് — — — — —

(46) മാസം വിറക്കും കണക്ക്:

ദുഹ്റം മുതൽ താഴെ നിന്നവരെ എണ്ണിയ

ജ്യമാസക്ഷയവും കൂട്ടിരണ്ടുമാസത്തില്‍ 3ദിവസം
എടുത്തുകളയുക. ഒററവന്നമാസങ്ങളില്‍നിന്ന്
ഒരുദിവസം എടുത്തു. എണ്ണീട്ടു ഇത്ര എന്നുകണ്ടാല്‍
7ല്‍ ഇരുത്തുക. ബാക്കിവന്നതിനെക്കൊണ്ട് ഞായറാം ആ
ഴ്ചമുതല്‍ എണ്ണി ഒടുവാല്‍വന്ന ആഴ്ച മേടുക്കു 87
മാസപ്പിറവം എന്നറിക.

ആയതില്‍— — — —

(47) കന്നിഞ്ഞായര്‍ എണ്ണിയ ആഴ്ച

കന്നിപിറച്ചുതാല്‍ നിന്ന നാളോളമു
ള്ള ഏകാംശം എടുത്ത് ഇത്ര എന്നുകണ്ടാല്‍ അതു
7ല്‍ ഇരുത്തുക. ശേഷിച്ചതിനാല്‍ ഇത്ര എന്നുകണ്ട്
അത്ര ഞായറ്‍നിന്ന ആഴ്ച പിടിച്ചു പറഞ്ഞാല്‍ എണ്ണി
യാല്‍ ഒടുക്കം ഒന്ന ആഴ്ച കന്നിഞ്ഞായര്‍ എണ്ണിയ ആ
ഴ്ച എന്നറിക.

ആയതില്‍— —

(48) മാസംപിറവം ~~[illegible]~~ ന [illegible]

മുമ്പിലെ നിന്റെ ... നാളോ
ടുകൂടി 15ഉം കൂട്ടി ഇത്ര എന്നുകണ്ടാല്‍ അതു നാലു
എന്നതില്‍നിന്നും പിടിച്ചു എണ്ണിയാല്‍ ഒടുക്കം വ

ന നക്ഷത്രത്തിന്റെ(ദേഹ ഫലം പറഞ്ഞു ഒന്നാക
ആമീന് ----

(49) <u>മൃത്യും അറിവാൻ കണക്ക്.</u>

സിറാജുഹിയ്യിന്നും മുത്തന്നിന്നും ഇ 8 ചാ
മ. 92 അതുതൊട്ടു ന്യൂഹൂസ് (മുന്നാൽ ഒന്ന്) കുറയ
അമ്പു ചാമം വെച്ചു കണ്ട് വന്ന് മുന്നുറിന്റെ കഴിച്ചു
ശേഷം ഇരുപത്തെന്നുകണ്ടാൽ അവർ നന്നെ
നന്നേ രോഗിവരകേൾ അമ്പും വായിലാക്കാൽ
അവരെ മത്തെ വന്ന അറിയുവിൻ. മറ്റ ചാമവും
2 ന്യൂഹൂസും താഴെയുള്ളയാവരന്റെ മൃത്യും തൈബത്ത
ൽ 2. കഴിയോന്ന് ഒന്നും. അറിക. (പോയാ മത്ത ഇരിവ
ന്റെ നല്ലൊ) ആമീന് ----

(50) <u>നക്ഷത്രം നല്ലതും ചീത്തയും - ലാവാരും.</u>

രോഹിണി, മകേരം, പുണർതം, പൂയം, ഉത്രം
അത്തം, അവിട്ടം, ഉത്രാടം, ഉത്രട്ടാതി ഇവ ഒമ്പതും
നല്ലത്:
അശ്വതി, കാർത്തിക, ചോതി വിശാഖം ചേർ 8

വരിനക്ഷത്രമാണ്. ആദിയോട് അടുത്താക. അവഴ
മോട്ട് മൂന്നമാക. ഓ ചോതിയും വിശാകവും ആകാ. ചൊ
ല്ലുകിൽ ചതയമാകാ. ഓണിയോടു ഓണംത്തിൽ
ഒമ്പതുവാടവാരി.

ഉപവാസ്നക്ഷത്രങ്ങൾ:— കാർത്തികയു
മാതിര ആയില്യം മകം പൂരം ചിത്തിര, പൂ
രാടം, പൂരുരുട്ടാതി രേവതി ഇവ ചൊന്നഷിന
ക്ഷത്രങ്ങളും കളിവച്ചായിനിക്കും.

ഗുണമായ നക്ഷത്രങ്ങൾ:— രോഹിണി
മകേരം, പുണർതം, പൂശം, ഉത്രം, അത്തം, ഉത്രാടം
അവിട്ടം ഉത്രട്ടാതി ഇവ ഒമ്പതും നല്ലത്:

(51) ആഴ്ചകളിൽ വിലക്കിയ നക്ഷത്രങ്ങൾ:—
ആദരഭരണി ആരാൻ ആയില്യം മൂലം
കേട്ടത്തിൽ ചിത്തിര, വിശാകം, ചോതി മകം ഇരാറ്റം.
മത്താനം കൊണ്ടാൽ താരാൽ വായിട്ടം പെട്ടാൽ
വിളാർ വായിട്ടം കൊണ്ടാൽ ചാവാൻ വാങ്ങൽ
വായിൽത്തിരാർ

(52) ആഴ്ചയിലെ നല്ല നക്ഷത്രം

ഞായർ:— അശ്വതി, രോഹിണി, മകീരം, പുണർതം, പൂശം, അത്തം, മൂലം ഉത്രാടം രേവതി നല്ലത്

തിങ്കൾ:— മകീരം, പൂശം, ആയില്യം പൂരം ഉത്രം, അനിഴം തിരിഓണം ചതയം രോഹിണി.

ചൊവ്വ:— ആയില്യം ഉത്രം, അത്തം, ചോതി വിശാഖം ഉത്രാടം, ഉത്രട്ടാതി അശ്വതി പൂശം.

ബുധൻ:— അത്തം വിശാഖം അനിഴം, മൂലം, പൂരാടം, ചതയം, കാർത്തിക, മകീരം ഉത്രം.

വ്യാഴം:— അനിഴം പൂരാടം, ഉത്രാടം, തിരുവോണം അവിട്ടം, അശ്വതി, പുണർതം ആയില്യം വിശാഖം.

വെള്ളി:— ഉത്രാടം അവിട്ടം, ചതയം, ഉത്രട്ടാതി, രേവതി, മകീരം, പൂരം, അത്തം, പൂരാടം.

ശനി:— രേവതി, അശ്വതി, കാർത്തിക, രോഹിണി, ആയില്യം, ചോതി, അനിഴം അവിട്ടം നല്ലത്

(53)

ഗ്രഹങ്ങളുടെ പേര്.	നല്ല നക്ഷത്രം.	വാടക നക്ഷത്രം
ഞായര്.	മൂലം.	വിശാകം.
തിങ്കള്.	തൃക്കേട്ടം.	കാർത്തിക.
ചൊവ്വ.	മകം.	അവിട്ടം.
ബുധന്.	ഉത്രം.	ചോതി.
വ്യാഴം.	പൂരാടം.	ഉത്രാടം.
വെള്ളി.	പൂശം.	പൂ[illegible]ം.
ശനി—.	മക്കേരം.	രേവതി.

മേൽവറഞ്ഞ ഗ്രഹങ്ങളും നക്ഷത്രങ്ങളും ഒത്തുവരുന്നാൾ മംഗല്യാവങ്ങളും ചെയ്‌വാൻ നല്ലത്. ഫലമുണ്ടാകും.

(54) കാറ്റടിയങ്കം നക്ഷത്രം

രോഹിണി, പൂശം, ഉത്രം, വിശാകം, ചോതി, പൂരാടം, ചതയം ഇവകളെഴും കാറ്റ് അധികരിച്ചു അകവെയുണ്ട്.

രേവതി, കാർത്തിക, തൃക്കേട്ടം, മൂലം ചോതി,

വിശാഖം, ചതയം, തിരുവോണം ഇവകളും കൊള്ളു
ന്നാകുന്നവ. ശംസിന്റെ കൂടെ വന്നാൽ അധികതി
കന്നഹ്സാകുന്നു.

(55) കോഴിഇടുകളും കണക്ക്:

വെള്ളി കോഴിഇടുകളിൽ ഇന്ന ഞങ്ങളോട് ഇഷ്ട
മുണ്ടാകും. ശനി:— രോഗം പിടിക്കും ദുഃഖമുണ്ടാകും.
ഞായർ:— മുസീബത്തുണ്ടാകും. തിങ്കൾ:— അൽപം
മുണ്ടാകും. മുത്തും അധികമുണ്ടാകും. ചൊവ്വ:—
സ്നായും ഫസിലത്തും വെന്തുപോകും. ബുധൻ:—
ഫൈളാകാത്തതിനാനെന്ന് വശത്തുണ്ടാകും.
വ്യാഴം:— ബുദ്ധിയും വാദ്യവും ഉണ്ടാകും. ആമീൻ.

(56) വീട്ടിന്നതിരയിടും കണക്ക്.

ഇടവരാശിയിൽ വീട്ടിന്നതിരയിടുക മി
ഥുനത്തിൽ മോന്തായം കയറ്റുക. ചിങ്ങരാശിയി
ലും ഔലിയാക്കളുടെ മുഖം വീട്ടിന്റെ ഭാഗം തൊട്ടു
പറക്കാതെയും നെ, നെല്ല കവുങ്ങ് മുതലായ
മരങ്ങൾ കൂടാതെയും വീടെടുപ്പിൽ താഴെ പറയു

വഴുതല മുതലായവയുടെ തൈകൾ എല്ലാം മീനം ഞാറ്റുവ ന്ന അപ്പോൾ തന്നെ പറിച്ചു ഒരു ലിയാത്തുടെ ദിവസം വിടിന്നതല്ലാം വെള്ളം തളിച്ചു വിട്ടന്നു ഞങ്ങൾ കൊള്ളുക.

(57) വിത്തിടും നക്ഷത്രങ്ങൾ :—

അശ്വതി — എല്ലാ വിത്തുകളും നടാം.
ഭരണി. — എല്ലാ വിത്തുകളും നടാം.
കാർത്തിക. — കവുങ്ങു നടാം.
രോഹിണി. — എല്ലാ വിത്തുകളും നടാം.
മകീരം. — വിത്തുകൾ നട്ടാൽ കള്ളും പുഴുവും ഏറും വിത്തു നശിക്കും
തിരുവാതിര. — വിത്തുകൾ നടുക.
പുണർതം. — വിത്തുകൾ നടുക.
പൂയം. — ,, ,, ,,
ആയില്യം — ,, ,, ,,
മകം. — ,, ,, ,,
പൂരം — വിത്തുകൾ നട്ടാൽ എലി കടിക്കും.
ഉത്രം. — വിത്തു വിതക്കുക.

അത്തം	വിത്തുവിതെയ്ക്കുക.		
ചിത്തിര	വെള്ളംനനെയ്ക്കുക.		
ചോതി	മുത്തിര കൃഷിചെയ്യുക.		
വിശാഖം	എല്ലാവിത്തും നടുക.		
അനുഴം	,,	,,	,,
തൃക്കേട്ട	,,	,,	,,
മൂലം.	,,	,,	,,
പൂരാടം	,,	,,	,,
ഉത്രാടം.	,,	,,	,,
തിരുവോണം.	,,	,,	,,
അവിട്ടം.	,,	,,	,,
ചതയം.	,,	,,	,,
പൂരുരുട്ടാതി.	,,	,,	,,
ഉത്രട്ടാതി.	,,	,,	,,
രേവതി.	,,	,,	,,

(58) കോടിവസ്ത്രം ധരിക്കും കണക്ക്.

അശ്വതി മേൽനാൾക്ക കോടി ഉടുത്തിൽ ഐശ്വര്യം ഉടലുണ്ടാകും.

ഭരണി കോടി കുഴുകുന്നതിന്നു ചാവുണ്ടാകും.

കാർത്തിക, രോഹിണി അക്ഷ്മമുണ്ടാകും.

മകേരം. – „ എലികടിക്കും.
തിരുവാതിര – „ ഐശ്വര്യം.
പുണർതം. – „ ഇഷ്ടമുള്ളസ്ത്രീയെകിട്ടും.
പൂയം – „ ആയുസ്സുമൈശ്വര്യം.
ആയില്യം. – „ പാമ്പുകടിക്കും.
മകം. പൂരം – „ ചാവുണ്ടാകും.
ഉത്രം – „ നന്മഉണ്ടാകും.
അത്തം – „ ലാഭമുണ്ടാകും. ചന്നിവ്യാധിഉണ്ടാകും
ചിത്തിര – „ ചന്നിവ്യാധിഉണ്ടാകും.
വിശാഖം – „ താന്താൻആഗ്രഹിച്ചവസ്തുകിട്ടും.
അനിഴം – „ [illegible].
തൃക്കേട്ട – „ [illegible].
മൂലം – „ ചാവുണ്ടാകും.
പൂരാടം – „ [illegible].
ഉത്രാടം – „ വ്യാധിഉണ്ടാകും.
തിരുവോണം – „ കൺകാച്ചഉണ്ടാകും.
അവിട്ടം – „ ദുഃഖ[illegible]ണ്ടാകും.
ചതയം – „ [illegible].
പൂരുരുട്ടാതി „ [illegible]ണ്ടാകും.

ഉണ്ടിരിക്കാതിരി --- ദീനമുണ്ടാകും.
രേവതി ഉലാവ്നമുക്കണ്ടാനം ചെയ്യും.

(59) സ്ത്രീ ജനനഫലം അറിവാൻ കണക്ക്.

ഹംല്‌രാശിയിലും ഉത്തരാഷാഢയിലും സാഅത്തിലും
ജനിച്ചവൾ. അവളുടെ മുഖം നല്ലവളും തലയിൽ
ഒരടയാളമുള്ളവളും മുഖത്തുമറവും കണ്ണിന്റെ വെ
ള്ളമേൽ ഒരു പുള്ളിയുള്ളവളും നിലചൊല്ലായവ
ളും വേഗതകൊണ്ടിരിക്കുന്നവളും സ്ത്രീകളിൽ കനത്ത
നല്ലവളുമാകുന്ന്. അവളുടെ മരണത്തിനു മുമ്പു മ
ക്കളെല്ലാം മരിച്ചുപോവുകയും അവൾക്കു വേണ്ട
നവരിൽ നിന്നും [illegible] സ്വഭാവം കാണിക്കുകയും
എപ്പോഴും ദീനമുണ്ടാവുകയും [illegible] കൂട്ടി മരിച്ചു
അനന്തിരവകാശം കിട്ടുകയും ഉത്സാഹമുള്ളവൾ ഉണ്ടാ
കുകയും മക്കൾക്കു നന്നായിരിക്കയും ചെയ്യും

തൌർ രാശിയിലും സുഹ്റാ സായത്തിലും ജനിച്ചവൾ
അവൾ ചിരിച്ചു സംസാരിക്കുന്നവളും നടവടി ഉടയ
[illegible] യും [illegible]
, ഹാജത്തുള്ളവളും ഓർമ്മവെക്കുന്നവളും [illegible]

ഭോഗേച്ഛയുള്ളവരും അവക്കം അനവം ചെ
യ്യുന്നവരും നിഷ്ഠൂരന്മാരുമായവരും ചതിക്കാറായവ
രും മുതൽ വററുകളയുന്നവരും പക്കൽ കുറഞ്ഞവ
രും ഉഷ്ണാംശത്തു [illegible] ബാധിക്കുന്നവരും ഇന്നാൽ
ഒരുവേടിയുള്ളവരും ആയുസ്സ് നടുത്തരമായവരും
ആകുന്നു. [illegible] രാശിയിലും [illegible]
അത്തിലും ജനിച്ചവർ. അവരുടെ മുഖം തെളി
വുള്ളവരും നെഞ്ഞാൽ വാവും പതിക്കുറഞ്ഞവ
രും മുതൽ സമ്പാദിക്കുന്നവരും നല്ല പക്കൽ ഉ
ണ്ടാകുന്നവരും [illegible] കൈ
ക്കുന്നവരും ആയുസ്സ് നടുത്തരമായവരും ആകുന്നു.
ശത്താൽ രാശിയിലും [illegible] സായത്തിലും ജനി
ച്ചവർ. നീളമുള്ളവരും [illegible] ലാക്ക
ന്നവരും ചിരിച്ചു പതിക്കുന്നവരും ബുദ്ധിനല്ലവരും
മുടി വെളുത്തവരും കണ്ണൊന്നൊക്കെ അനുഗ്രഹിക്കുന്നവ
രും കെട്ടുന്നവൻ നിഷ്ഠൂരന്മാരുമാകുന്നു. അവൻ പര
ച്ചു മുതൽ കിട്ടുന്നവരും [illegible] രാശിയിലും [illegible] സാ
യത്തിലും ജനിച്ചവർ. അവർ സംസാരം

കുറഞ്ഞവരും വായിൽ വന്നതു പറയുന്നവരും ഇടംകയ്യി
ൽ ഒരടയാളമുള്ളവരും കെട്ടിയവനെ വെറുത്തിരിക്കു
ന്നവരും ഉടപ്പിറപ്പ് വെറുക്കുന്നവരും മക്കളെക്കൊണ്ട് ഗുണമു
ള്ളവരും ദേഹം തടിച്ചു ആയുസ്സ് കുറെ ഉള്ളവരും മറ്റു
മുള്ളവരുമാകുന്നു. സുമ്പുൽ രാശിയിലും അത്താസിഅ് സാ
യത്തിലും ജനിച്ചവർ. ഇവർ ദേഹം കുറിയവരും മുഖം
നല്ലതും മുടിനീളമുള്ളവരും വിനോദത്താലിൽ ഹരിഷം
ഉള്ളവരും കെട്ടിയവനോടും കുടുംബക്കാരോടും വിരോ
ധമുള്ളവരും മറ്റുമാകുന്നു. മീസാൻ രാശിയിലും സുഹറാ സാ
യത്തിലും ജനിച്ചവർ നടപ്പ് നല്ലവരും ആലോചന
കുറിയവരും മുതൽ സമ്പാദിക്കുന്നവരും ഹലാലും
ഹറാമും തിരിക്കാത്തവരും മാപ്പിളയോട് ഹക്കിനെ
ഉള്ളവരും വേർകുറഞ്ഞവരും മറ്റുമാകുന്നു. അക്
റബ്ബ് രാശിയിലും മിരിക്ക് ~~സാ~~ നക്ഷ യത്തിലും ജനിച്ചവർ ...
സ്വഭാവം നല്ലവരും മാപ്പിളയോടും മക്കളോടും താല്പ
ര്യം കുറഞ്ഞവരും നടപടി പിഴയായവരും പലരോ
ടും വലതും ആവശ്യപ്പെടുന്നവരും ദാരിദ്ര്യം തീരാത്തവരു
ം അറുപതു വയസ്സിനു ശേഷം കഠിനമായ ദീനത്തിൽ
പെടുന്നവരുമാകുന്നു. കൌസ് രാശിയിലും മുശ്തരി സാ
യത്തിലും ജനിക്കുന്നവർ ഗീലത്തുള്ളവരും ഉയരം കു

ന്നവരും പുത്രന്മാരുള്ളവരും മുടിച്ചവരും കലഹം
ചതിവേറിയും കൃത്യവശത്തിൽ താല്പര്യമുള്ളവരും
ചതിക്കുന്നവരുമാകും. കന്നിരാശിയിലും ന്യഗൽ
സായത്തിലും ജനിച്ചവർ ദോഷ്യം ഉള്ളവരും ചതിക്കു
ന്നവരും നെറിക്കേടയാളുമുള്ളവരും വലരോ
ഗം ഹാനിയുള്ളവരും അവമാനവേർ കേൾപ്പിക്കു
ന്നവരും ആകും. രണ്ടാം രാശിയിലും സ്വന്തൽ സാ
യത്തിലും ജനിക്കുന്നവർ ആകണ്ഠ കുറ്റമുള്ളവരും.
വലിയതണ്ണും ചതിയും സത്യകഷ്ടം അഹങ്കരിച്ചവരും
ന ടത്തത്തിൽ ദേഹം കൊള്ളെ നോക്കുന്നവരുമാ
കും. മേഷരാശിയിലും മൂന്നിസായത്തിലും ജനിക്കു
ന്നവർ നിലച്ചാത്തായവരും നമ്പൂരാം. വന്നു. പു 8
പുത്രഞ്ഞകളിൽ ഹാനിയുള്ളവരും വിശ്വാസം നല്ലവ
രും കൃത്രായും ബാധയുള്ള ഇവർക്ക മുമ്പായിറ്റിക്കു
യും മക്കൾ അശികളുണ്ടാകയും ഗുണമുള്ളവരും
------ ആകൻ. ----------

ആമിൻ----

(60) ഭവനം പണിയും കണക്ക.

വീടുനാലു ഭാഗവും തിരിച്ചാൽ വീട്ടിന്റെ
നടുമേശാത്ത, യത്തിന്നു [illegible] പാടിച്ചു[illegible]
ടിങ്ങളെ [illegible]. 40 ൽ പടിച്ചു[illegible]
കാരം തന്നെ ഉട വത്തിൽ [illegible].
വിധനത്തിൽ നിയി [illegible] ത്തിൽ പ
[illegible] ചിത്തിൽ [illegible] ചൊടിൽ
(ഉറൽ) കന്നിയിൽ [illegible] ഉടാത്തി
ൽ വിടി ക. വൃശ്ചികത്തിൽ പള്ളിയ
നുവത്തിൽ [illegible] മകരത്തിൽ
[illegible]. കുംഭത്തിൽ ചാ, വടിമീനത്തി
ൽ കിണർ [illegible] കാരംകിഞ്ഞ

ആമീൻ

(61) [illegible] കളിൽ വീടു പണിതാലുള്ള
ഗുണദോഷം.

ഞായർ – ദുഃഖവും വൈഷമ്യങ്ങളും.
തിങ്കൾ - സൌഖ്യം [illegible] വെള്ളം
ചൊവ്വ - ഭയത്തോടു വ്യസനവുമുണ്ടാകും.
ബുധൻ. സമ്പത്തിന്നും നന്മ വർദ്ധന[illegible]
ർ ആയിരിക്കും.

വ്യാഴം- ബുധശുക്രന്മാർ ദ്വാദശങ്ങളിൽ
വെള്ളി- ധനസന്തോഷങ്ങൾ ഉണ്ടായിരിക്കും.
ശനി- ധന വർദ്ധന ഉണ്ടാകും. ആദിത്യൻ
(62) (മാസത്തിൽ വെളുത്ത പക്ഷത്തിലെ പൂർണ്ണ)
ദോഷം.
ശുഭം - ചുരക്കുളത്തിൽ വെളുത്തപക്ഷ
ത്തിൽ വന്ദനാരിദ്ര്യം ഉണ്ടാകും.
സ്വഭാവം- ജയവും ആരോഗ്യവും
സുഖം ചാരിത്ര്യവും ഉണ്ടാകും.
ഞായറിൽ അമാവാസി- ജയവും ധനവർദ്ധ
നയും ഉണ്ടാകും.
ഞായറിൽ പൗർണ്ണമി- വെളുത്തപക്ഷത്തിൽ
വന്നുവെങ്കിൽ ദോഷമായിരിക്കും.
ശനിയിൽ അമാവാസി = വൈശ്യംവരും
ശനിയിൽ പൗർണ്ണമി = ചൊവ്വ ചൊവ്വ ഇരുവരെ
ജ്ഞാനം ഉണ്ടാകും. ജന്മ- ധനവർദ്ധനയും സു
ഖസന്തോഷവും ഉണ്ടാകും.
ശനിവാരം- അഷ്ടമി രോഗവും നാശവും

(63)

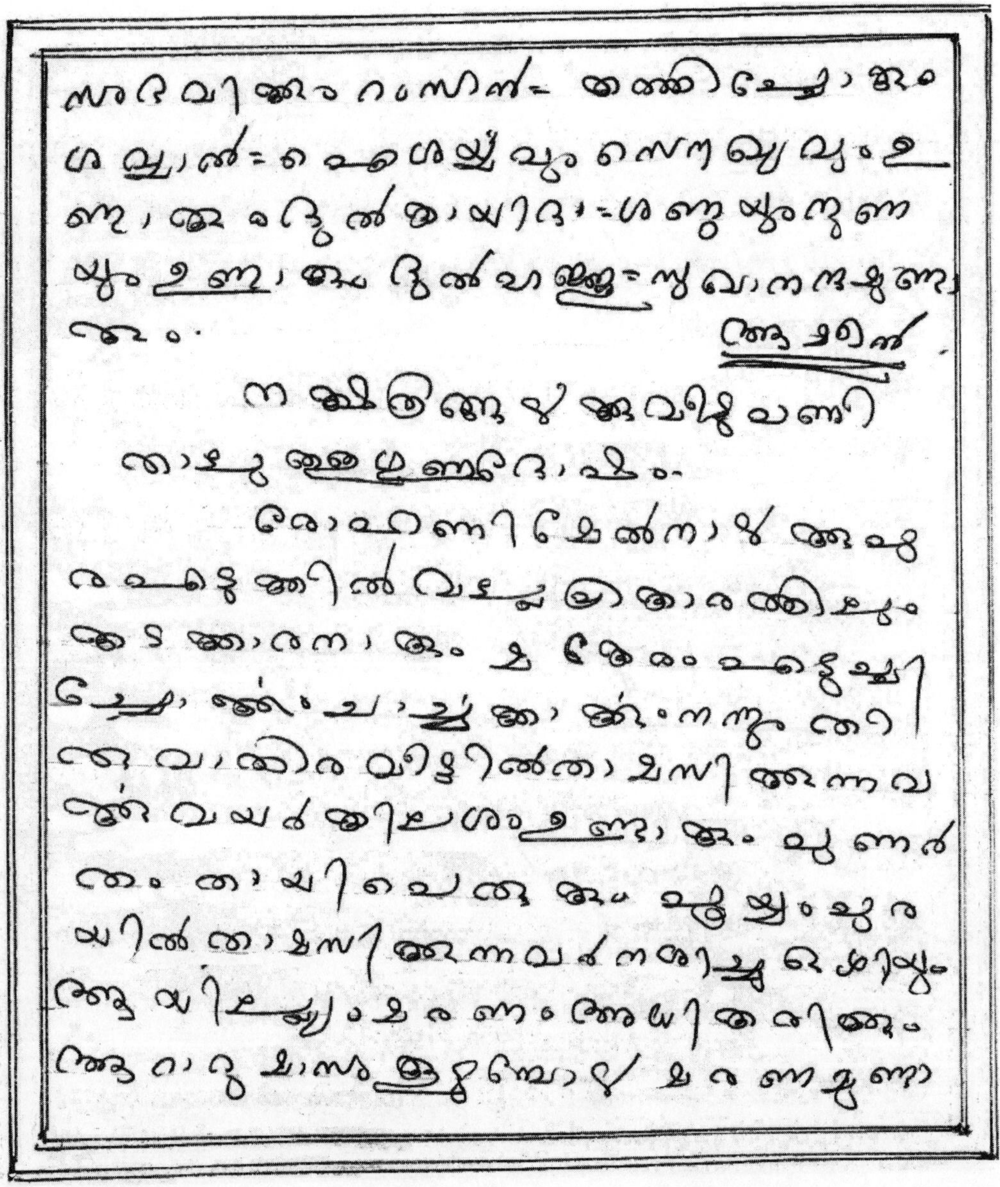

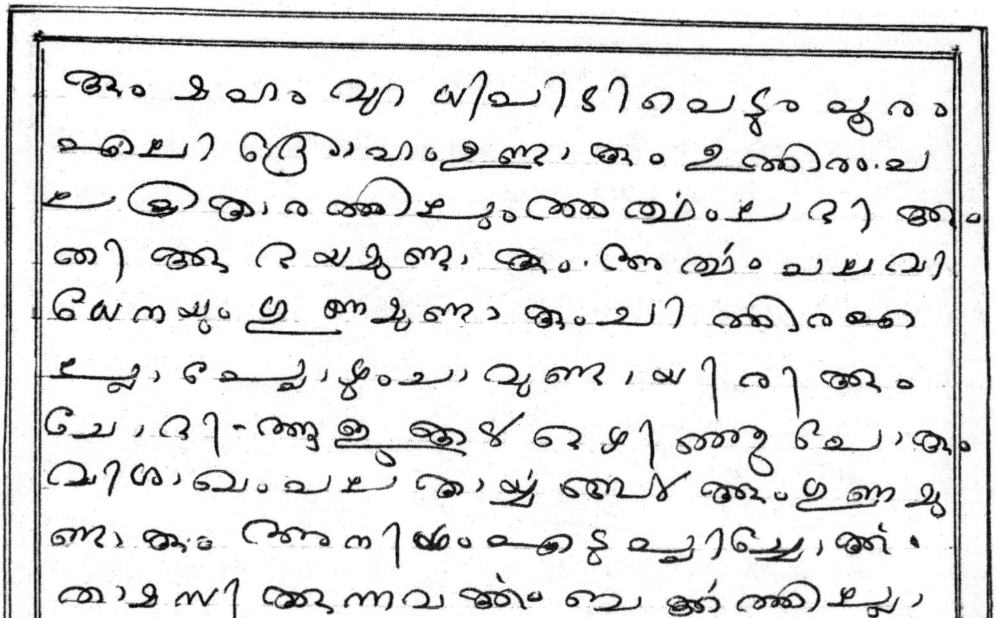

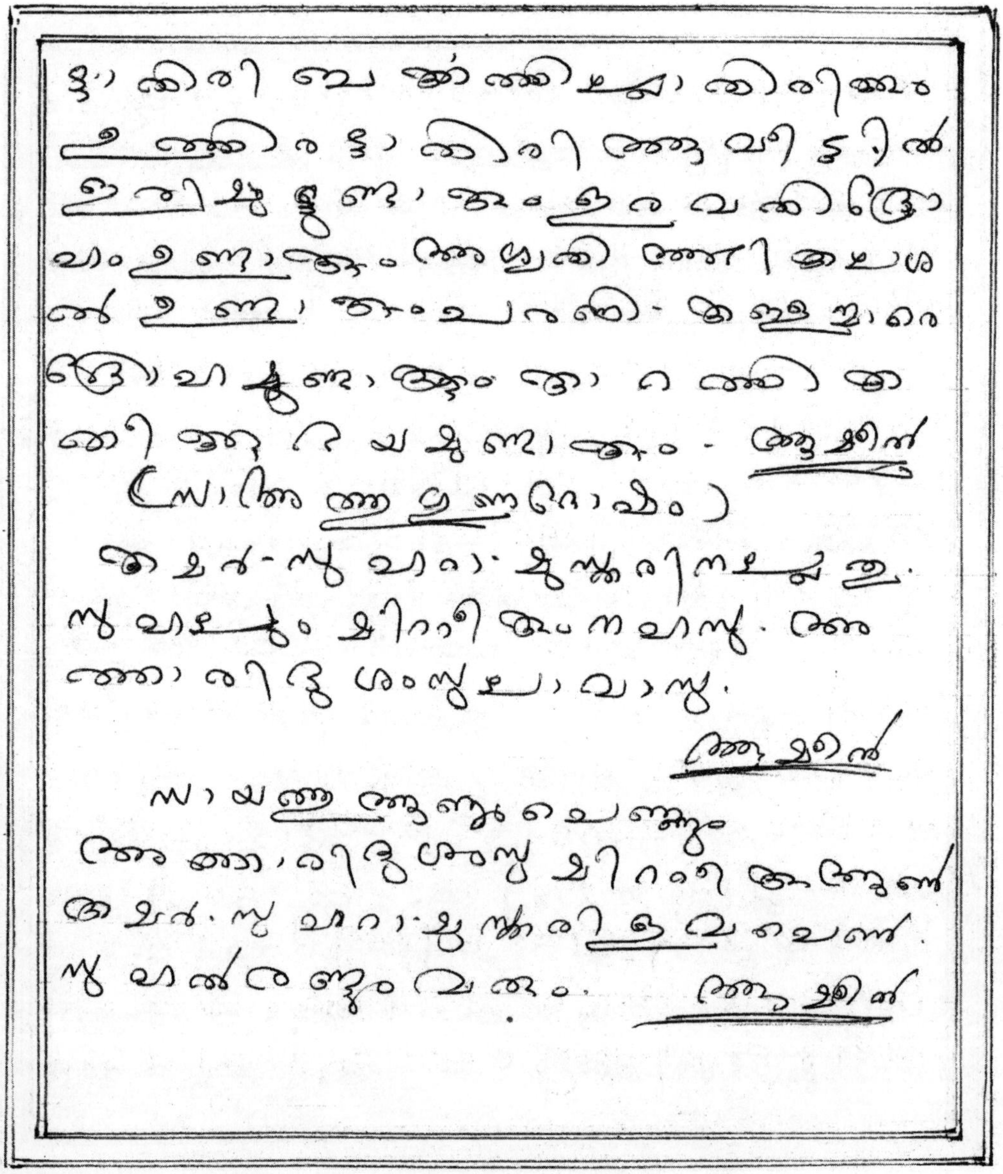

(64)

(65)

(66)

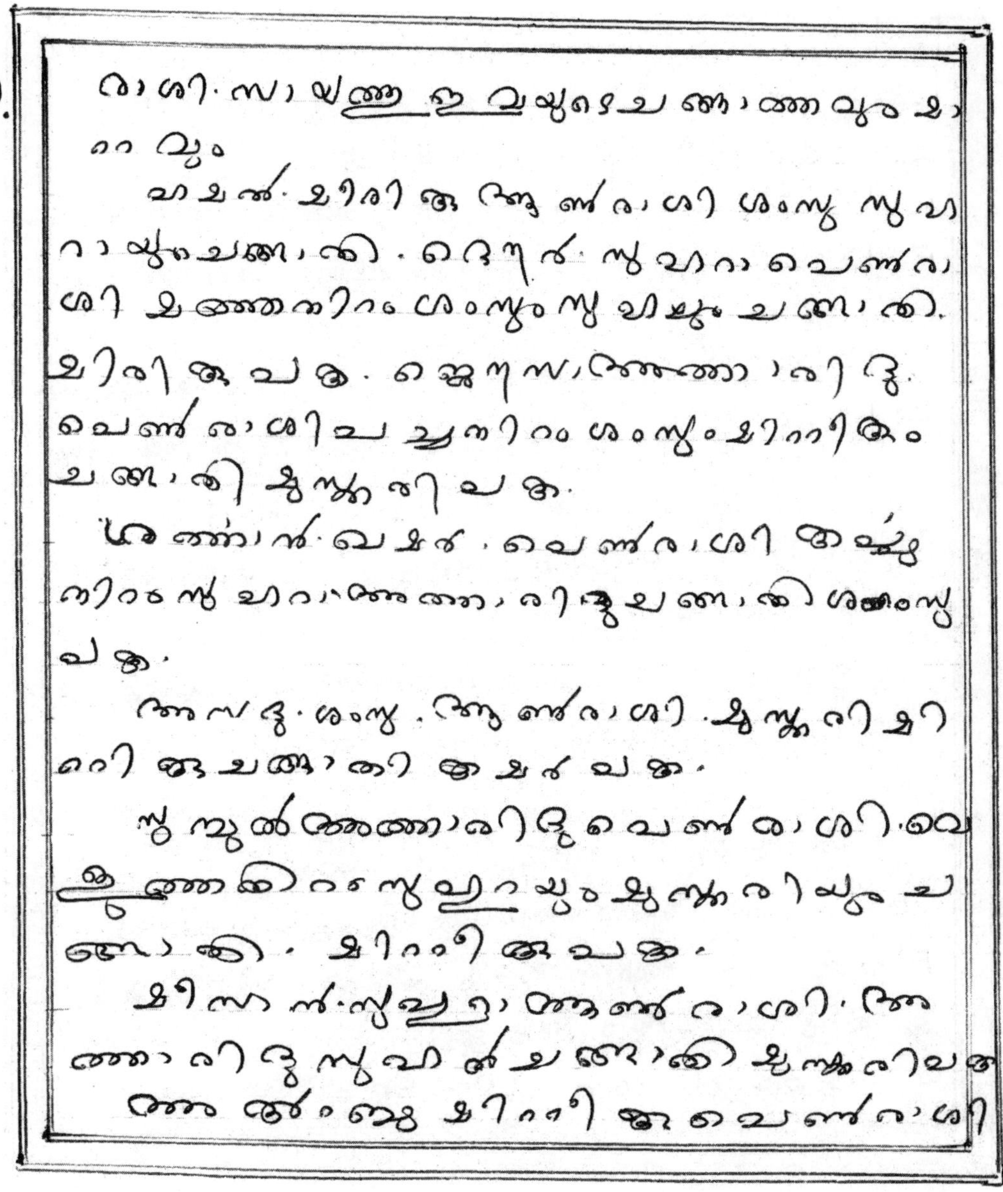

(67)

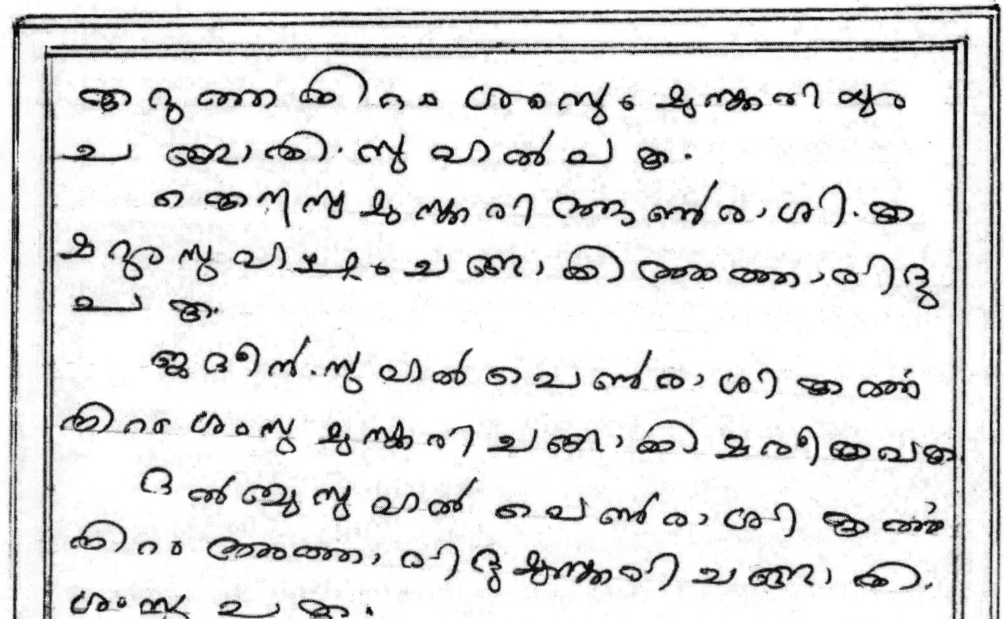

ഞാഞ്ഞാം തെക്കുവാന്നു ഉറൊടപ്പൊറിന്നു
ന്നു.

അഞ്ഞാറിട്ടു= വെൺതെക്കുവാൽനു
ങ്ങടൾ=ഉടപ്പാ ങ്ങാത്തീന്നും നു
ഉടെങ്ങിടുംതെ വ്യസനത്തുണ്ടാം

തുന്നുറി= ഒാളൊാങ്ങാളൊയു ഉങ്ങ
ഷാ ചെയ്യും ഒന്നു ഗറിതത്താചെയ്യാ ഉറ്റും ഒാ
ണ്ടാൽ നന്നു.

ഉിററിങ്ങ= ടെ തെ ങ്ങാ ത്തിന്നു ഉാങ്ങാ
ച ങ്ങ ഉണ്ടാം

നുവാൽ= വങ്ങയും തെക്കുവാക്കും ങ്ങൾ
തുടെപ്പിതവും ഉണ്ടാം.

(ങ്ങാ ഉൾ)

(68) (ശ്വാസത്തിൽ വെൺതെക്കും ഞെഞ്ഞ)

ശ്വാസത്തിൽ= വെൺതെക്കിയാൽ
സന്തൊഷകരമാകാൽ വരിവുക

സവർ= ങ്ങൾ ജ്ജ ങ്ങാ ങ്ങു ഉറ്റ
നാ ങ്ങൾ ചാമ്പിൽ ദിയം ഉണ്ടാം

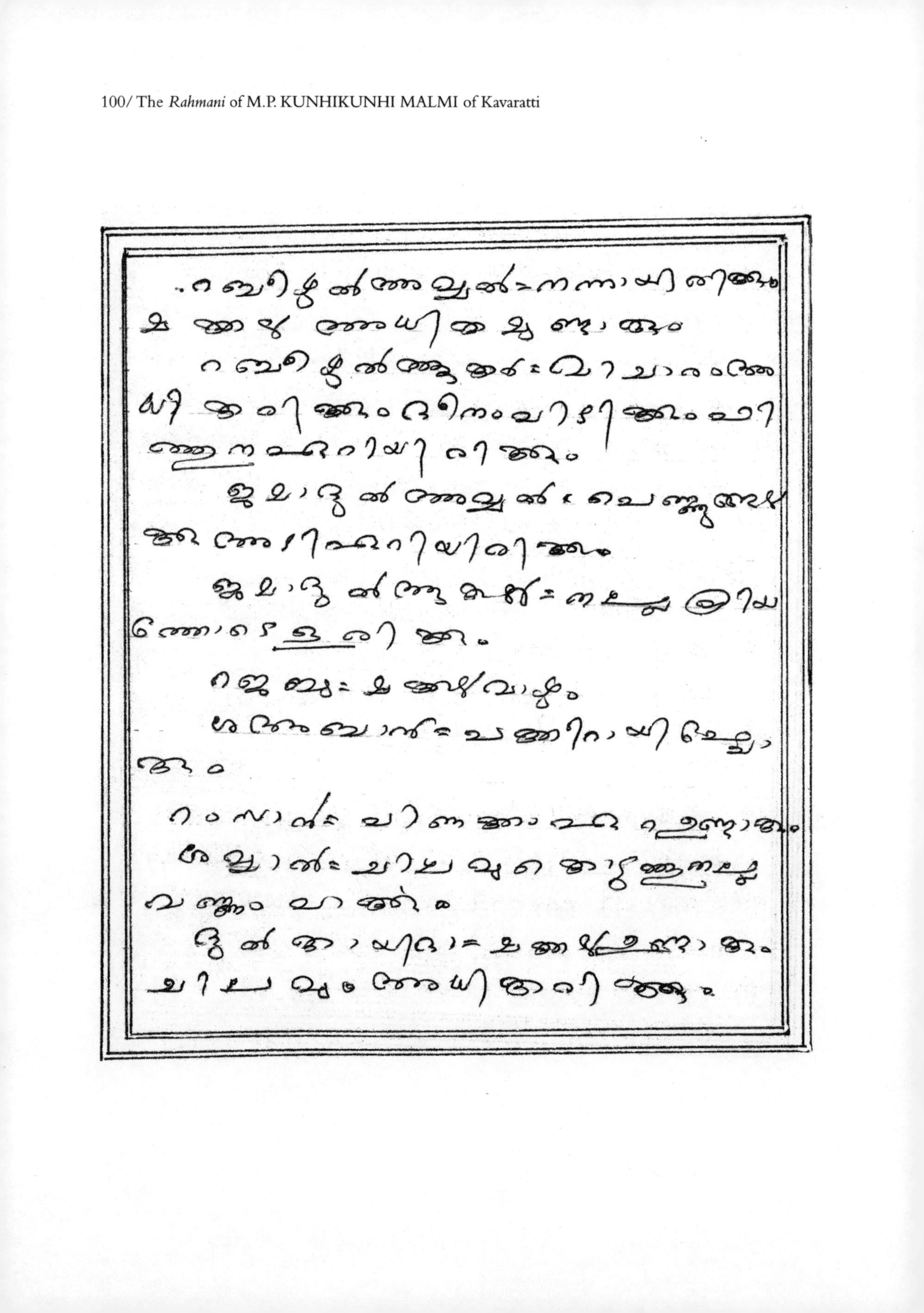

(69) ദിൽവാളു = നല്ല ബെ [illegible] (ങ്ങടി)
ചാ [illegible] [illegible]
(തൊംബു വെ [illegible] [illegible])
1—ാംനമ്പർ തൊമ്പു വെച്ചു റാൽവ്യാറി ഉണ്ടാക്കും
2—ാംന ,, ശരിതൊ [illegible] ഉണ്ടാക്കും
3—ാംന ,, വെളുപ്പു വ്യാറി ഉണ്ടാക്കും
4—ാംന ,, തടി [illegible]
5—ാംന ,, [illegible]
6—ാംന ,, ചു [illegible] ഉണ്ടാക്കും
7—ാംന ,, ദയം ഉണ്ടാക്കും
8—ാംന ,, തൈ [illegible] വിടിക്കാം
9—ാംന ,, തൈലനൊമ്പലം ഉണ്ടാക്കും
10—ാംന ,, വേപ്പുവാസു ഉണ്ടാക്കും
11—ാംന ,, തൈലതിരി ചൂൽ ഉണ്ടാക്കും
12—ാംന ,, ചൊറി ഉണ്ടാക്കും
13—ാംന ,, വെ [illegible] ഉണ്ടാക്കും
14—ാംന ,, [illegible]
15—ാംന ,, മറവി ഉണ്ടാക്കും.

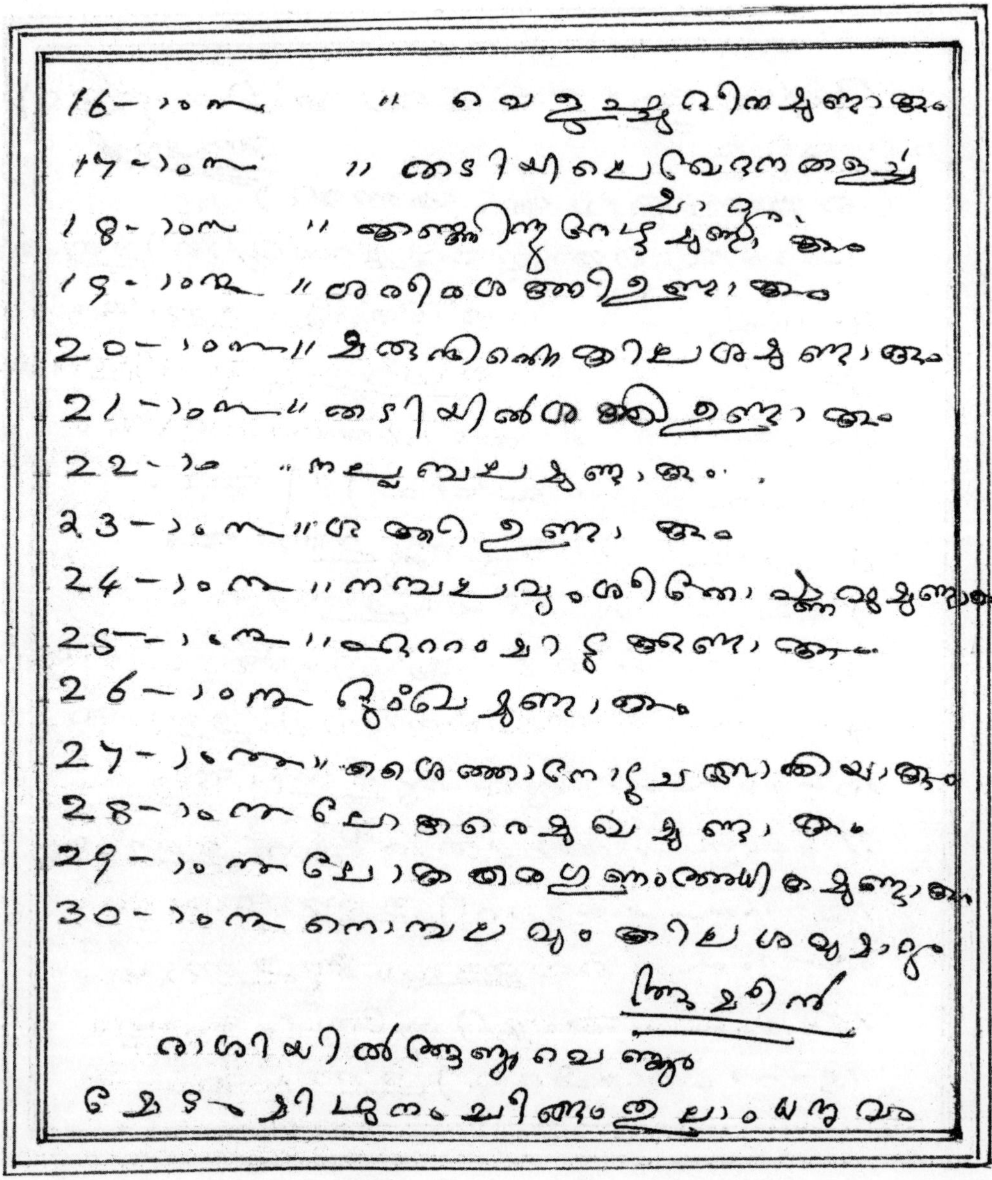

16-10 [illegible]
17-10 [illegible]
18-10 [illegible]
19-10 [illegible]
20-10 [illegible]
21-10 [illegible]
22-10 [illegible]
23-10 [illegible]
24-10 [illegible]
25-10 [illegible]
26-10 [illegible]
27-10 [illegible]
28-10 [illegible]
29-10 [illegible]
30-10 [illegible]
[illegible]
[illegible]
[illegible]

(70)

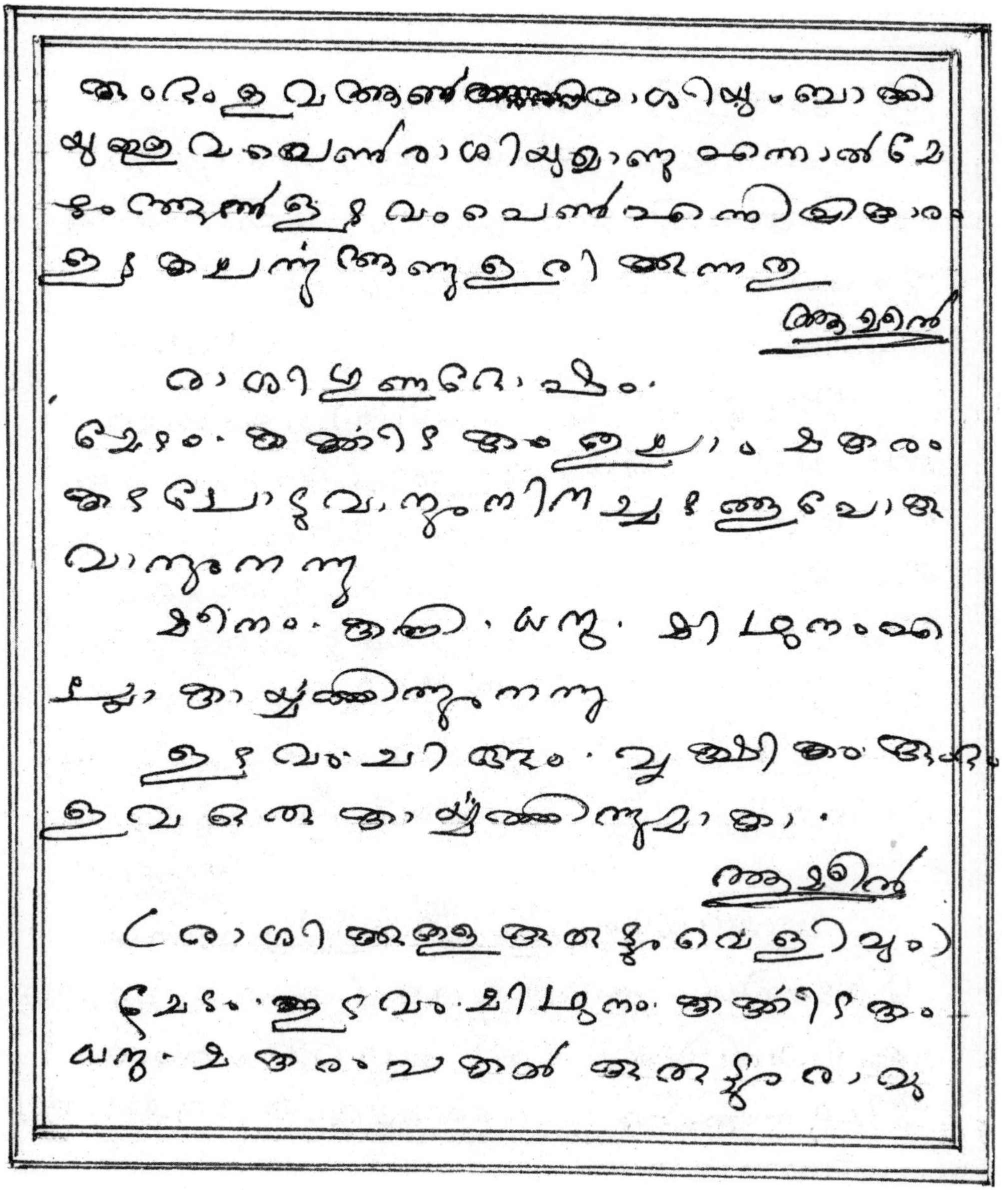

(71)

(72)

നി വെള്ളിവ്യാഴാണ്
ചിങ്ങം· കർക്കടകം· വൃശ്ചി
കം· കുംഭം· മീനം ഇവ നാലിന്നും
ക്കും ഫലം വെള്ളിവ്യാഴാണു.

അമൽ

(73) ആഴ്ചയിലെ നാളുകളിൽ ചൊല്ലേണ്ടും

ഞായർ നാളുകളിൽ· അശ്ശുക്കൂറും
തിങ്കൾ· ,, രിഞ്ഞായം ഒന്നും ഉണ്ടാകും
ചൊവ്വ· ,, ദ്വംവെച്ചുണ്ടാകും
ബുധൻ ,, ഉടൈമ്മക്കളുണ്ടാകും
വ്യാഴം ,, സന്തോഷമുണ്ടാകും
വെള്ളി ,, അഹങ്കാരവുമുണ്ടാകും
ശനി. ,, ചൂരയിൽനാശമുണ്ടാകും

അമൽ

(74) ·രാശിയിലുള്ള നാളുകളിൽ ചൊല്ലേണ്ട.
മേടത്തിൽ· നാളുകളിൽ· അത്ത്വാനിയും
ഇടവത്തിൽ ,, പശുമാനമ്മക്കം
മിഥുനത്തിൽ ,, മൈശൂമും കാശമുമുണ്ടാകും

കർക്കടകത്തിൽ ,, വൈശ്യശൂദ്രന്മാരും

ചിങ്ങം ,, ക്ഷത്രിയ[illegible]ന്മാരും

കന്നി ,, വെട്ടിൽ നാശം സംഭവിക്കും

തുലാം ,, വാചാല[illegible]

വൃശ്ചികം ,, ദീനക്കാരിയായും [illegible]

ധനു ,, [illegible]

മകരം ,, [illegible]

കുംഭം ,, [illegible]

മീനം ,, [illegible]

[illegible]

(75) [illegible]

[illegible]

[illegible]

[illegible]

[illegible]

[illegible]

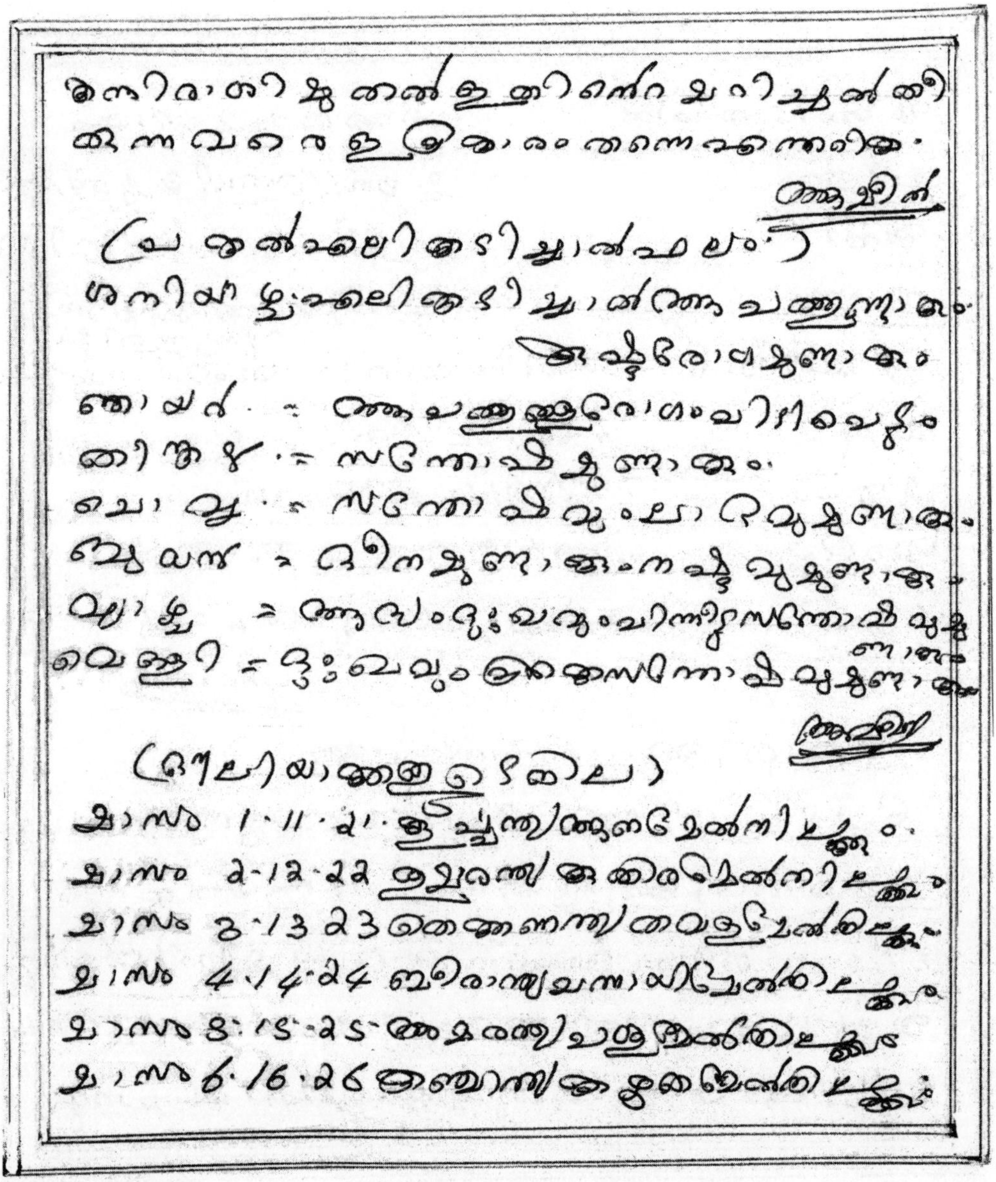

(76)

(77)

മാസം 7· 17·27· [illegible]
മാസം 8· 18·28 [illegible]
മാസം 9·19·29 [illegible]
മാസം 10-20·30 [illegible]

[illegible]

(78) ([illegible])
മീനം 13-ാംന മേടം 1-ാംന.
മേടം 14-ാംന ഇടവം 1-ാംന.
ഇടവം 14-ാംന മിഥുനം 1-ാംന
മിഥുനം 13-ാംന കർക്കടകം 1-ാംന
കർക്കടകം 14-ാംന ചിങ്ങം 1-ാംന
ചിങ്ങം 14-ാംന കന്നി. 1-ാംന
കന്നി 14-ാംന തുലാം 1-ാംന
തുലാം 13-ാംന വൃശ്ചികം 1-ാംന
വൃശ്ചികം 12-ാംന ധനുവം 1-ാംന
ധനുവം 13-ാംന മകരം 1-ാംന
മകരം 12-ാംന കുംഭം 1-ാംന
കുംഭം 13-ാംന മീനം 1-ാംന
(79) ([illegible])
[illegible]

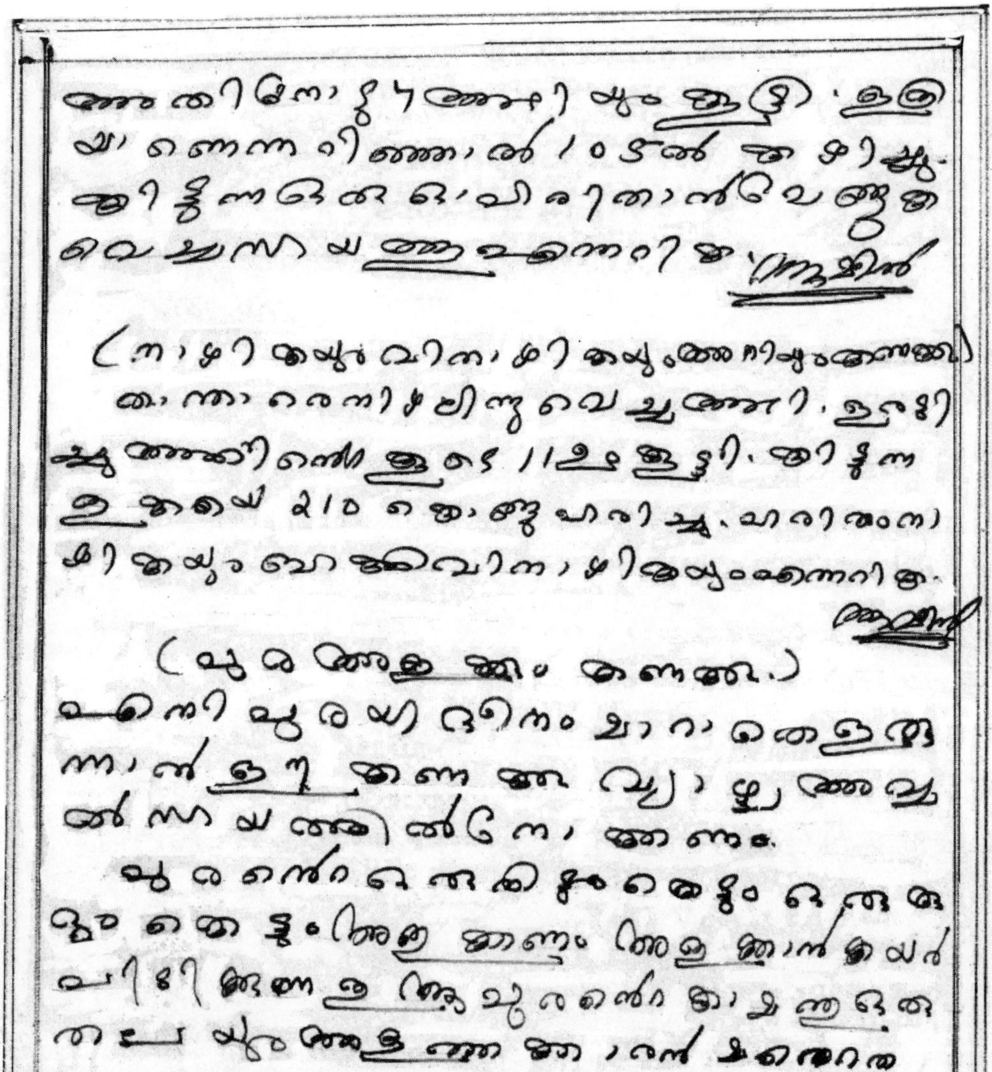

(80)

(81)

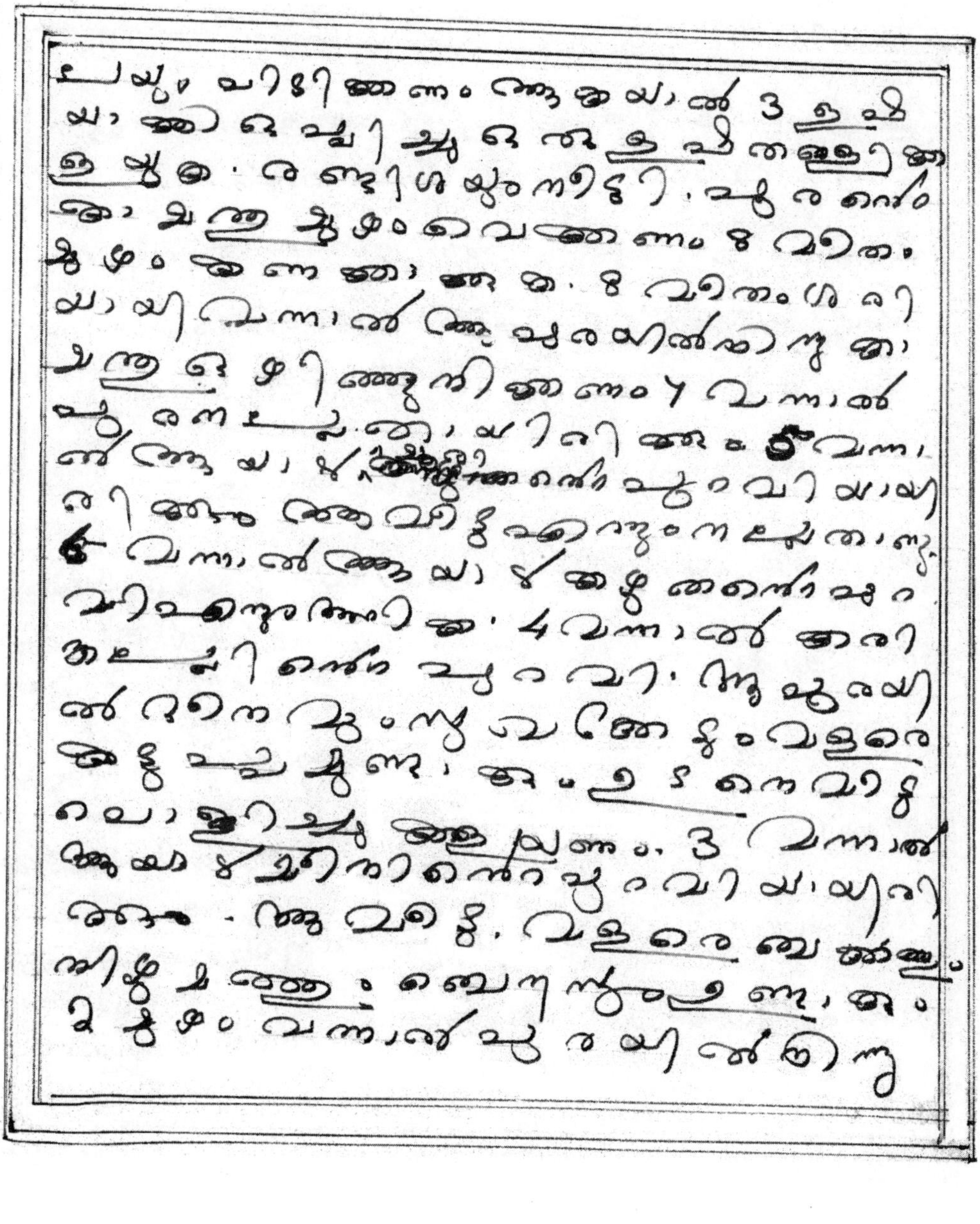

(82)

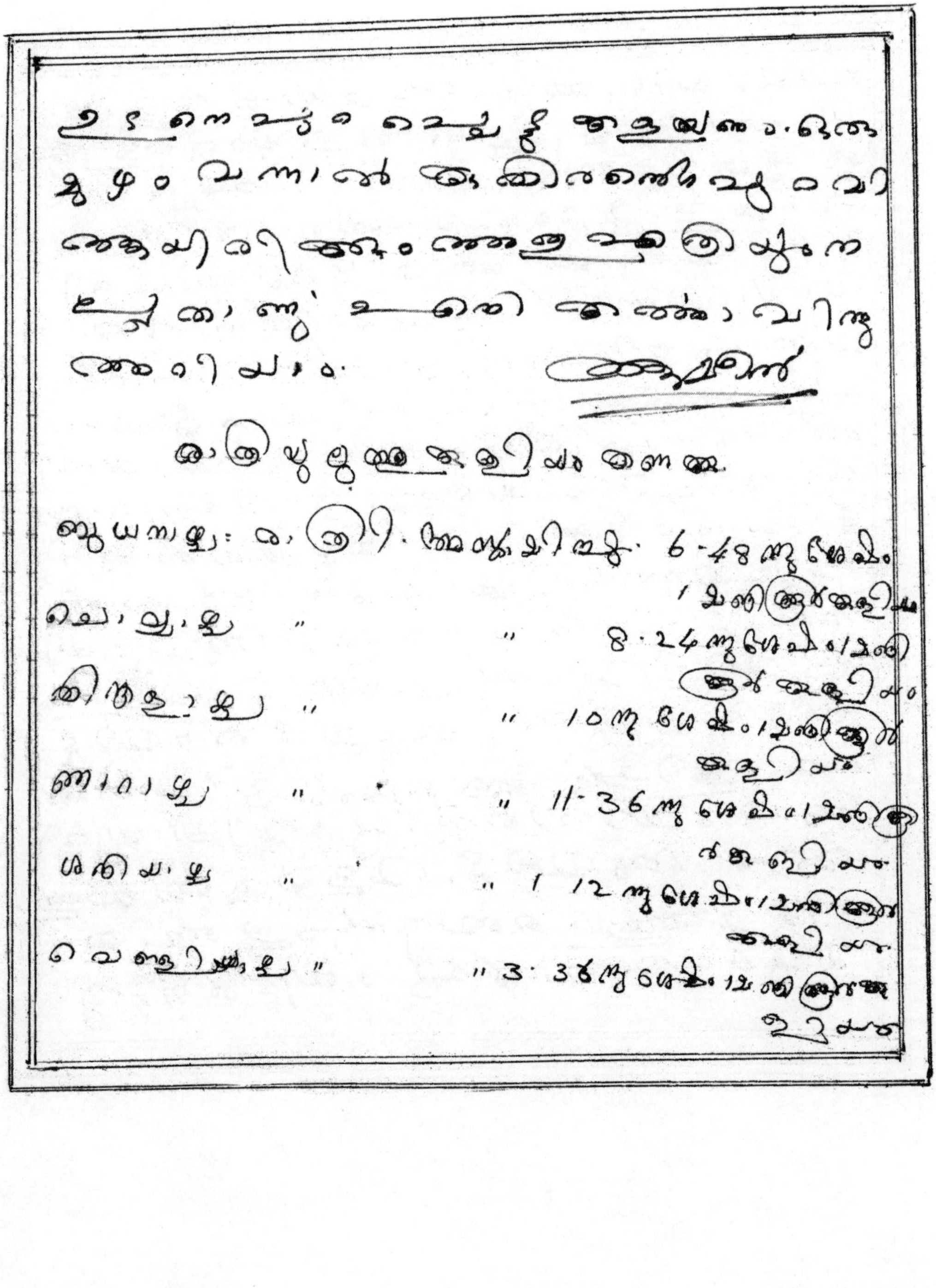

[illegible] 4.24 നു ശേഷം.

[illegible]

(83) [illegible]

(84) [illegible]

ഞായര്	വൈകുന്നേരം	4.30 മുതല് 6 വരെ.
തിങ്കള്	രാവിലെ	7.30 " 9 വരെ
ചൊവ്വ	വൈകുന്നേരം	3 4.30 വരെ
ബുധന്	ഉച്ചക്ക്	12.00 മുതല് 1.30 വരെ
വ്യാഴം	"	1330 " 3 വരെ
വെള്ളി	രാവിലെ	10.30 " 12 വരെ.
ശനി	"	9 മുതല് 10-30 വരെ

(85)

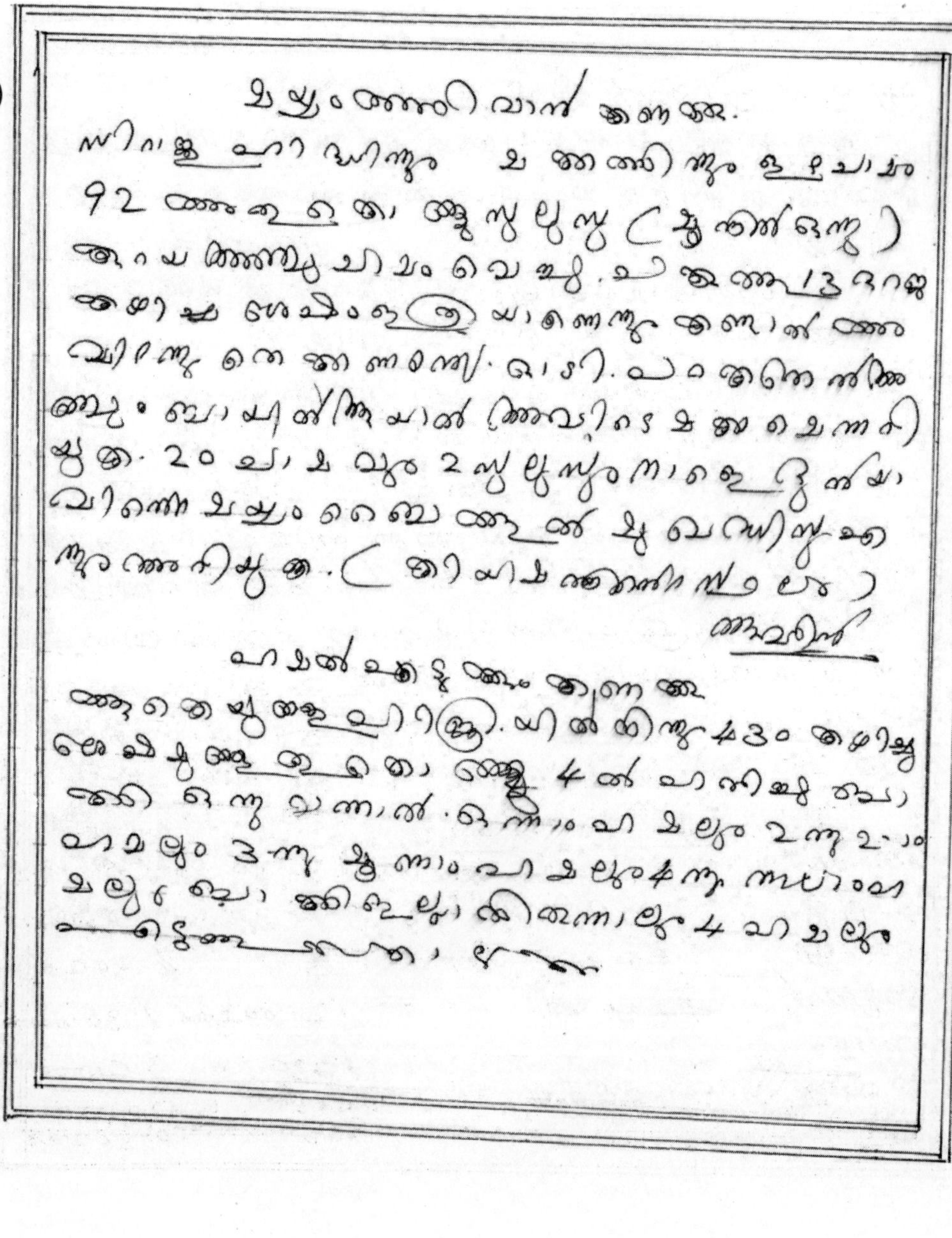

(86)

(87)

(88)

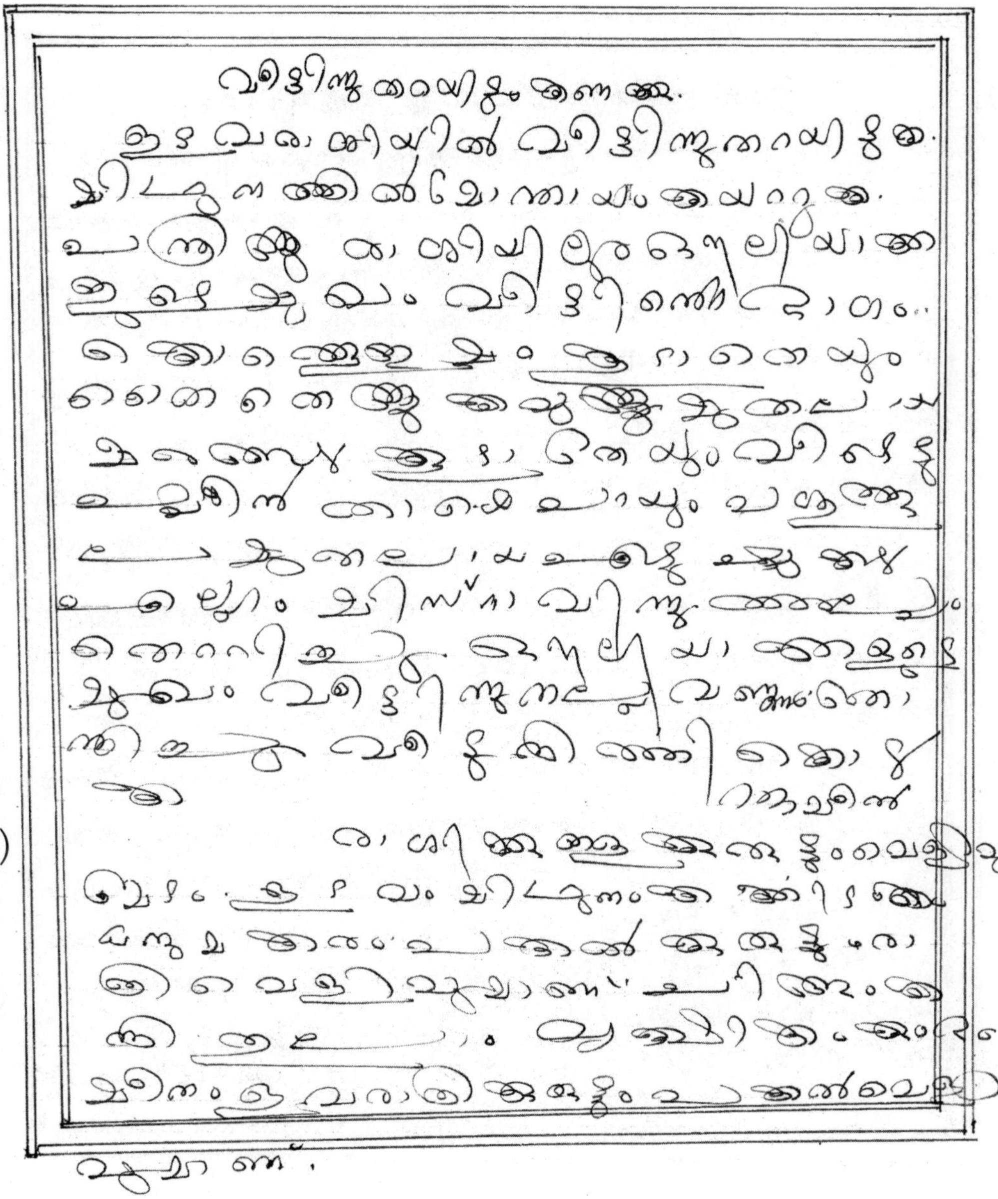

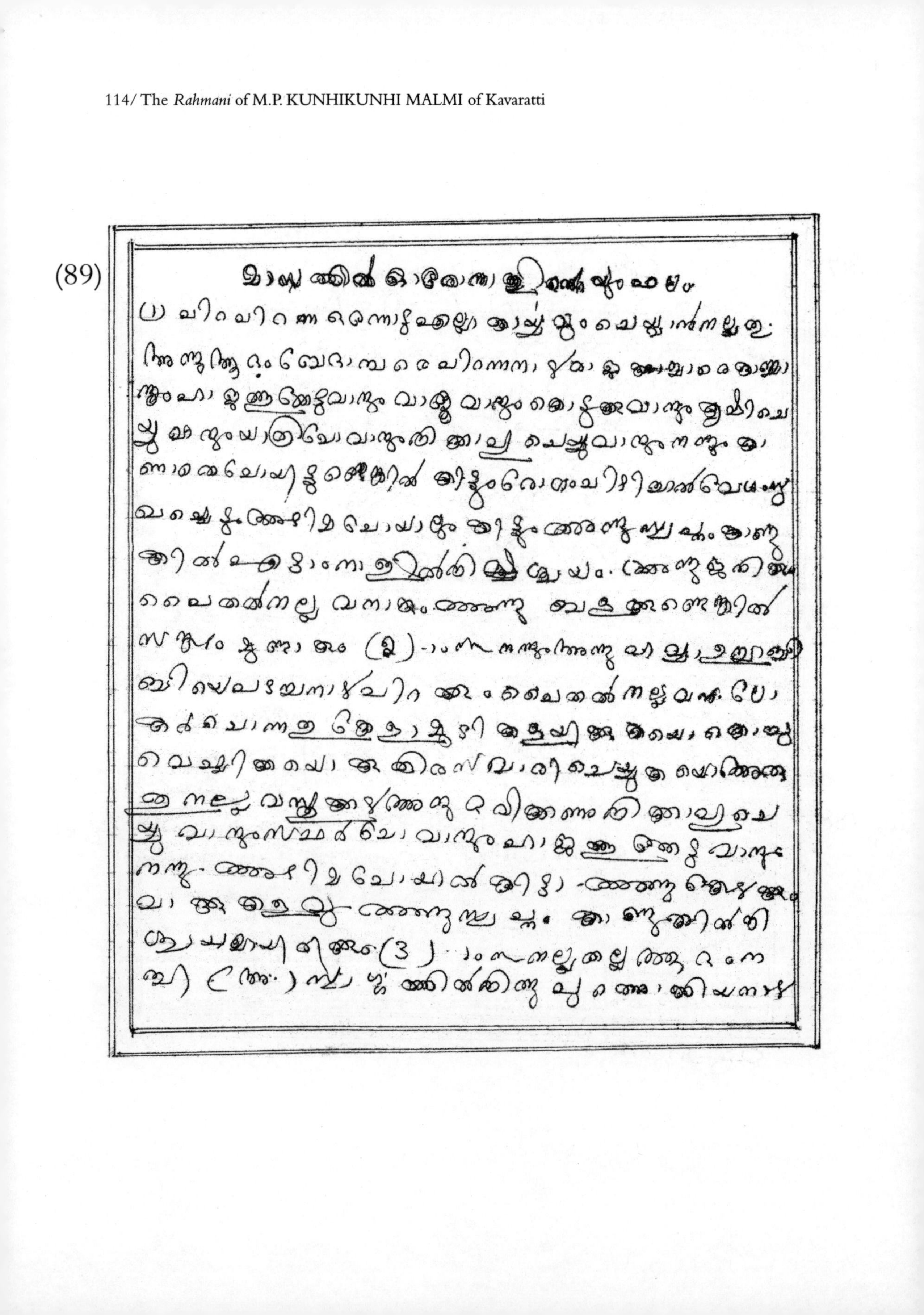

(89) [illegible]

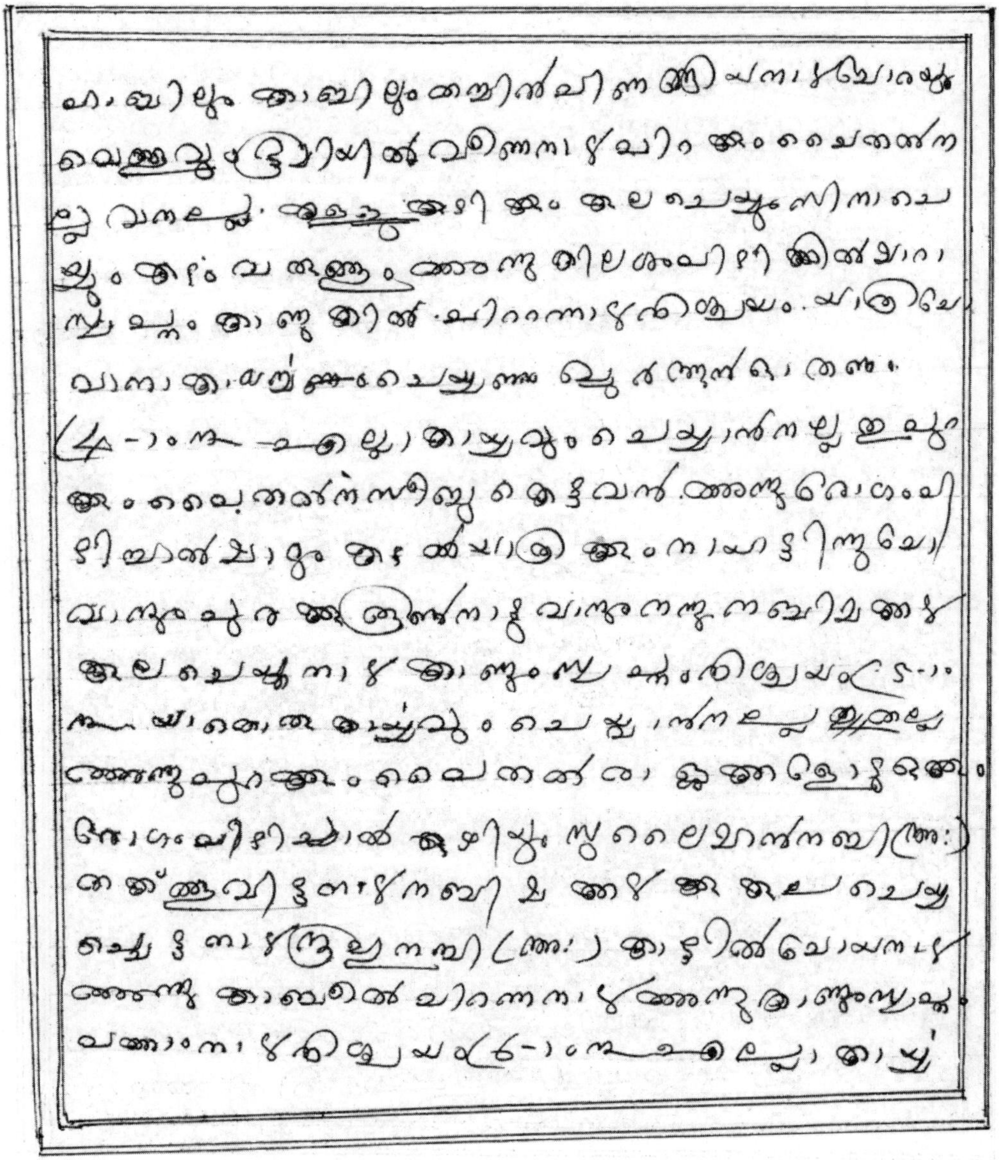

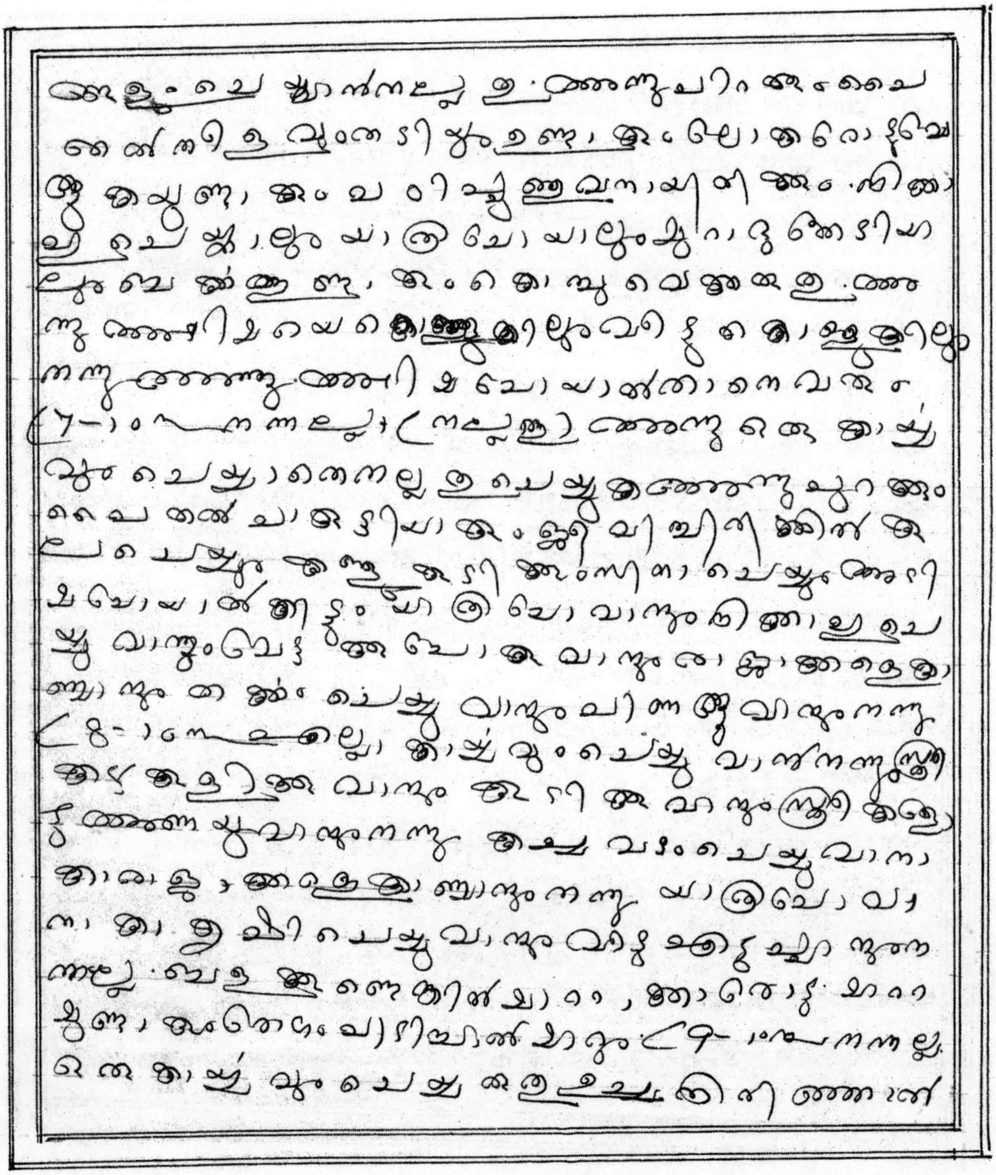

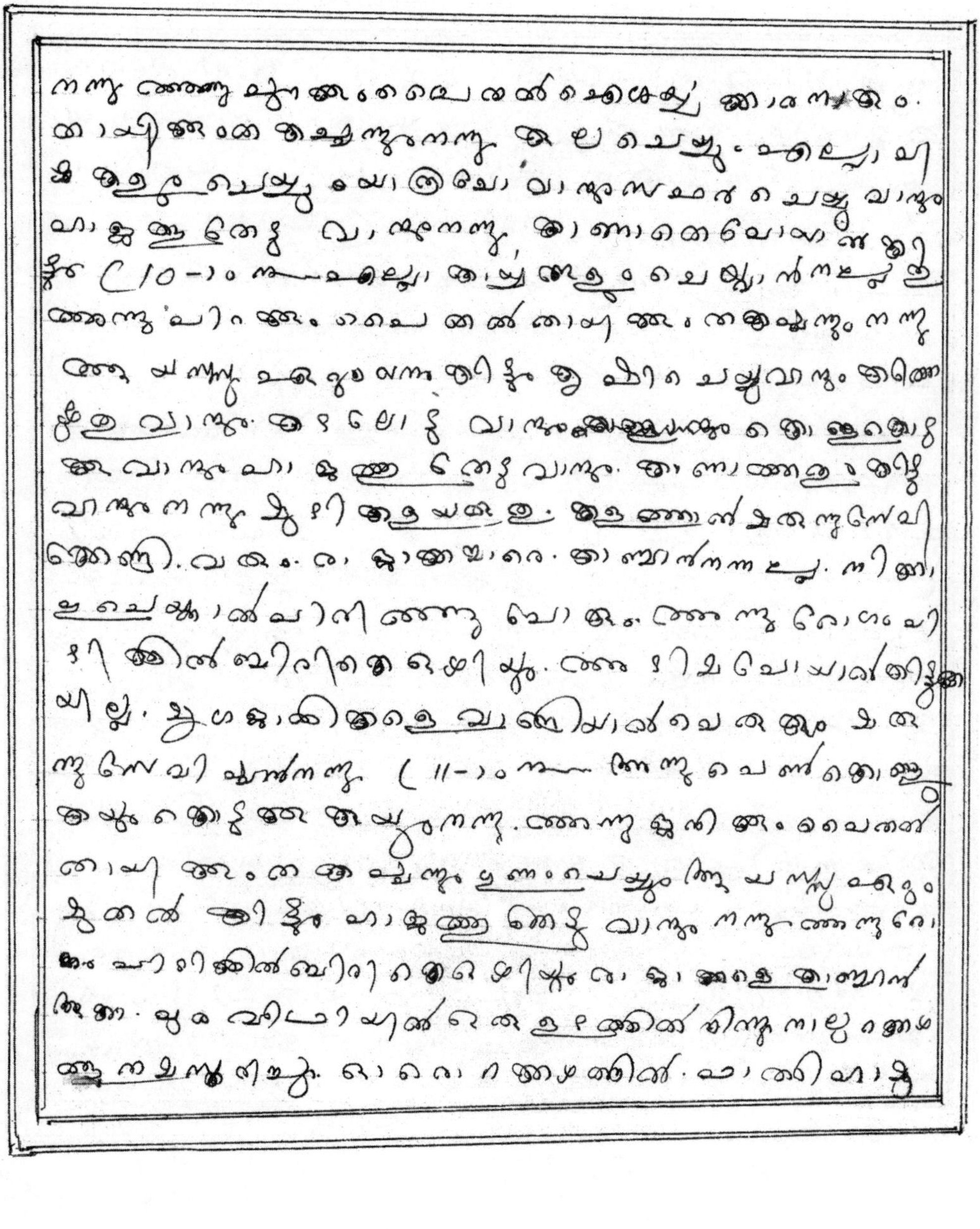

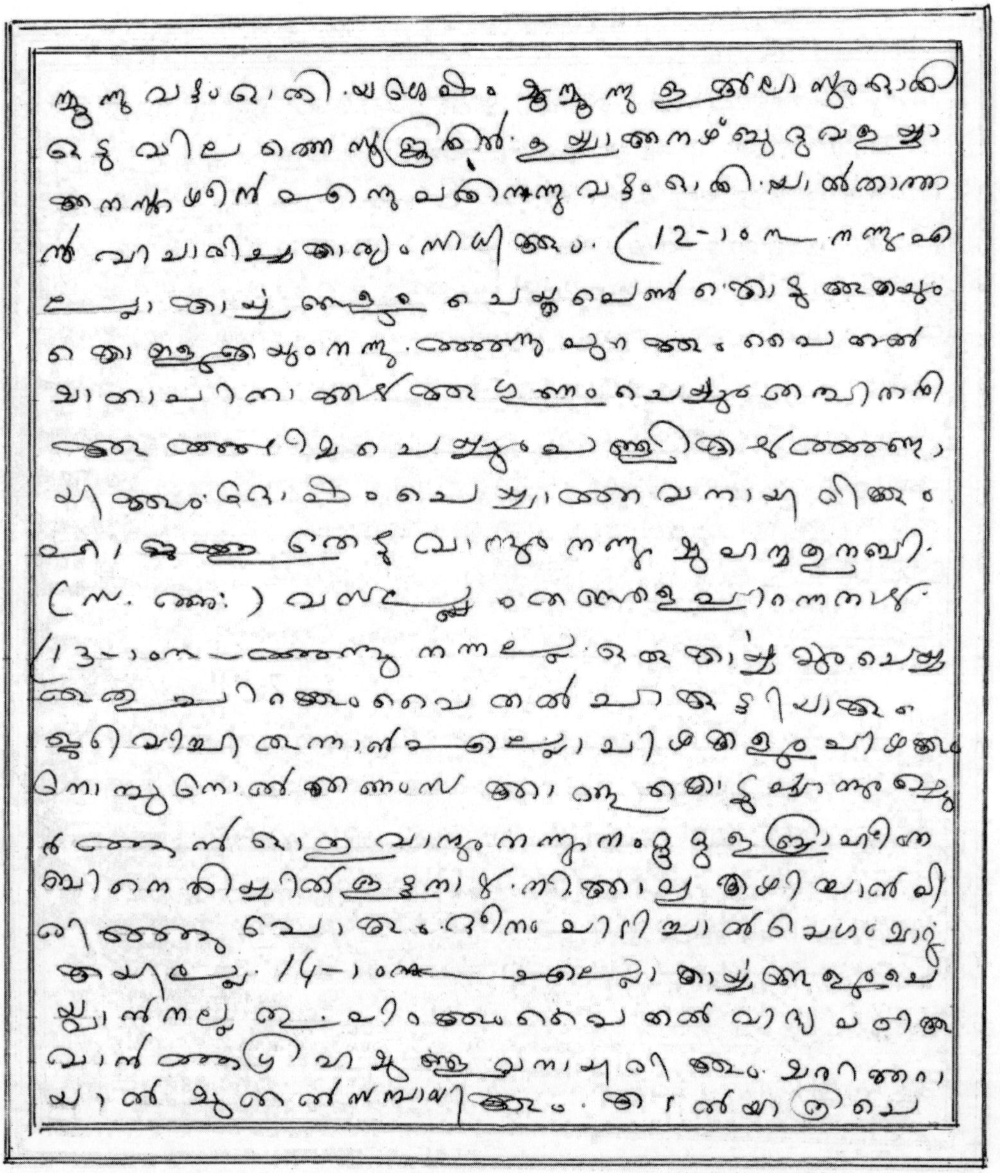

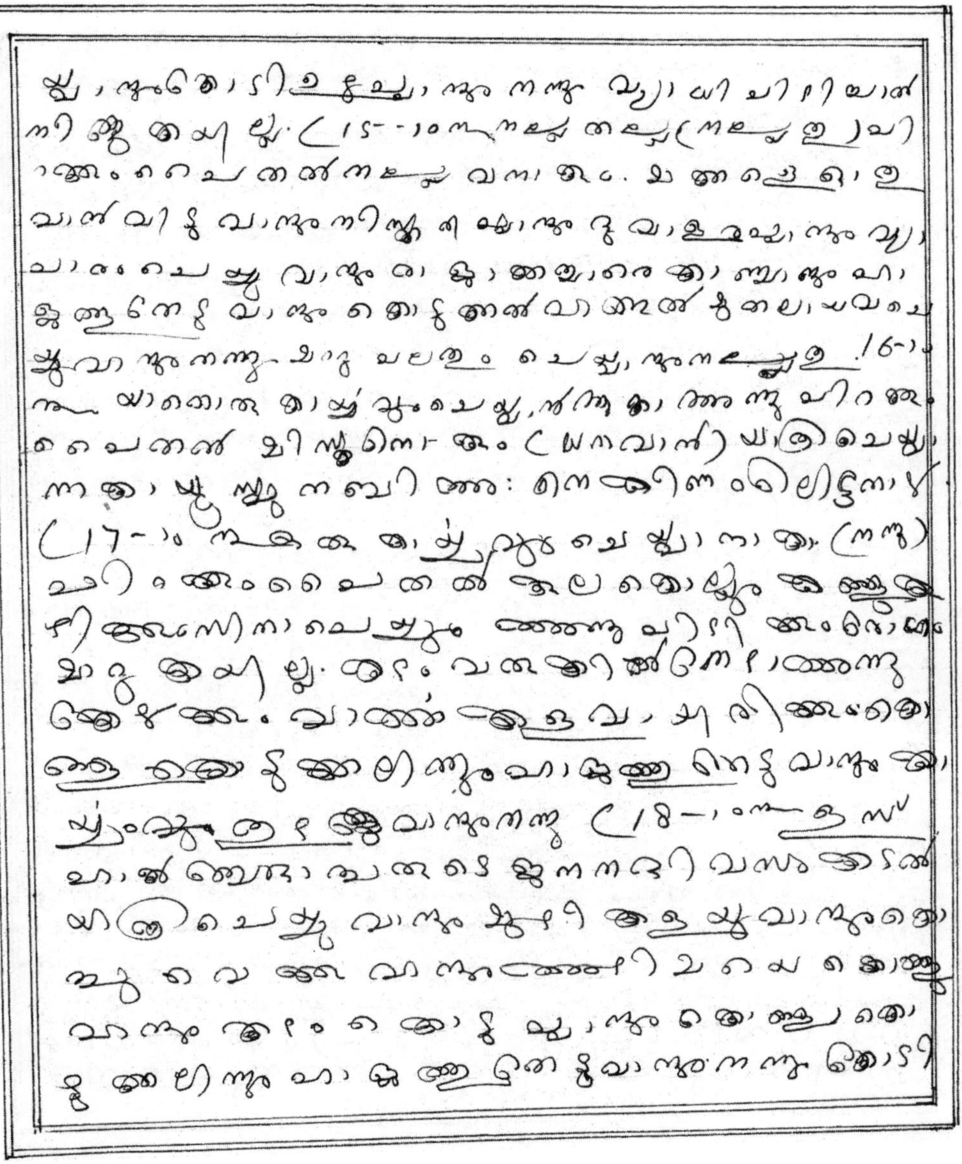

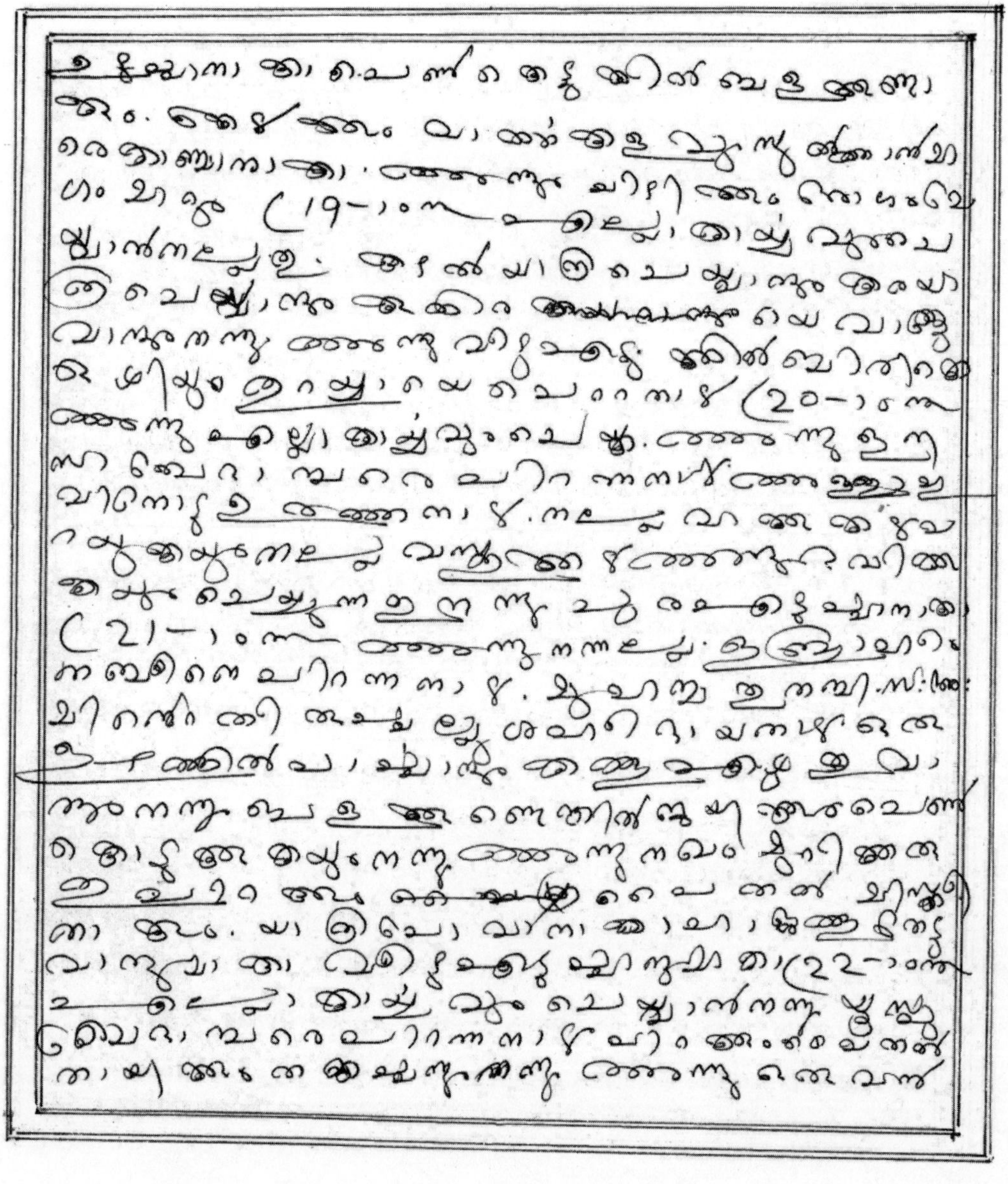

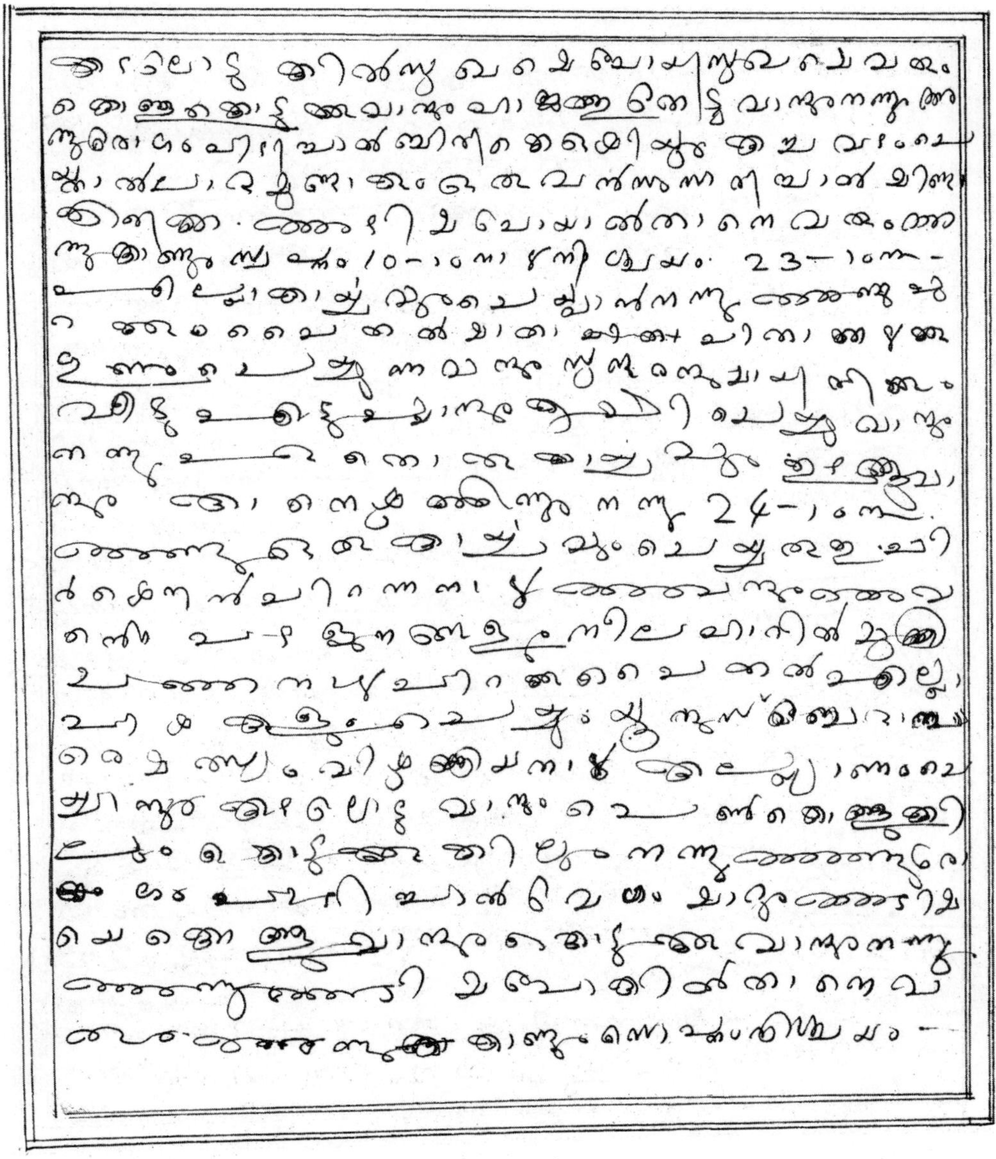

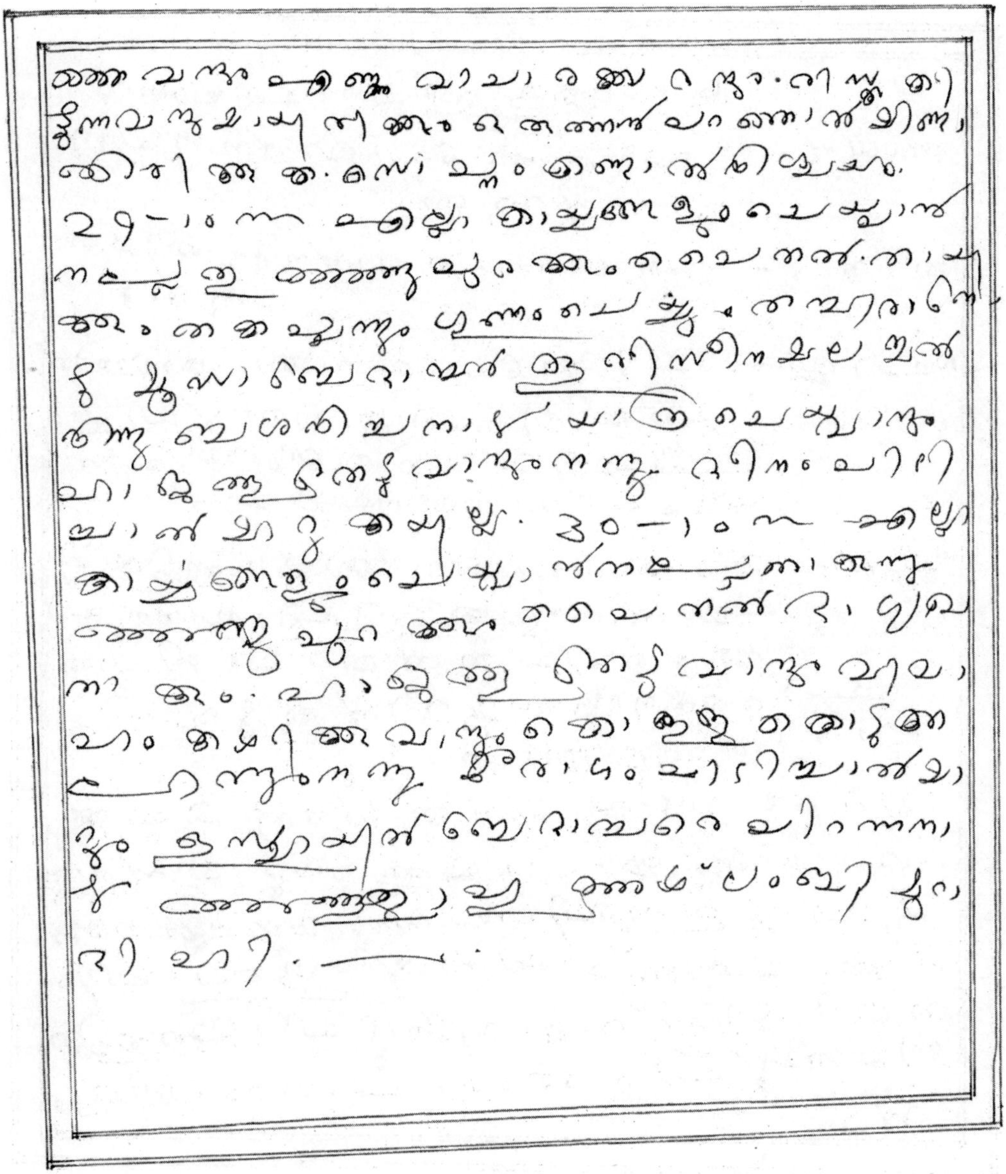

(90)

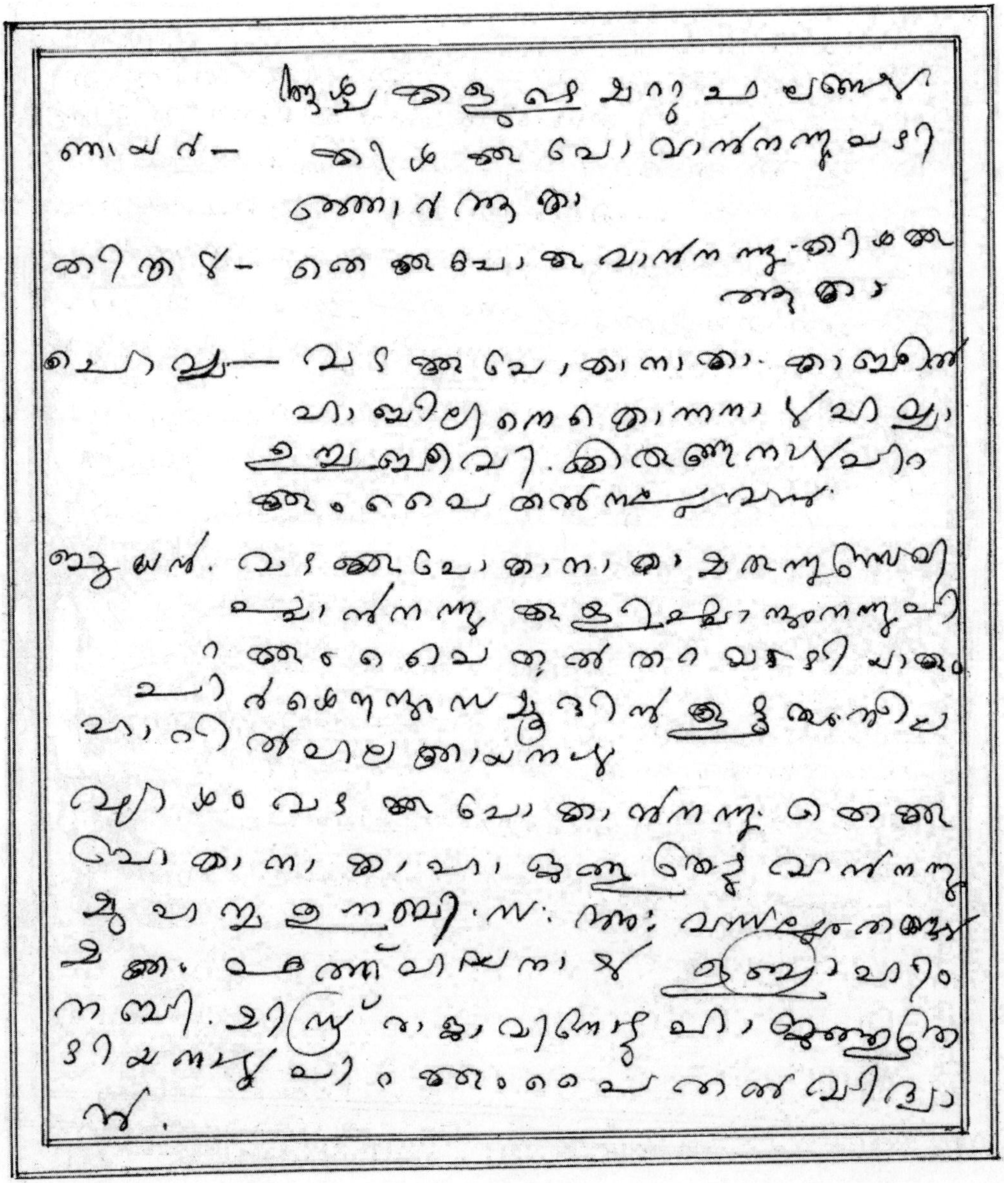

(91)

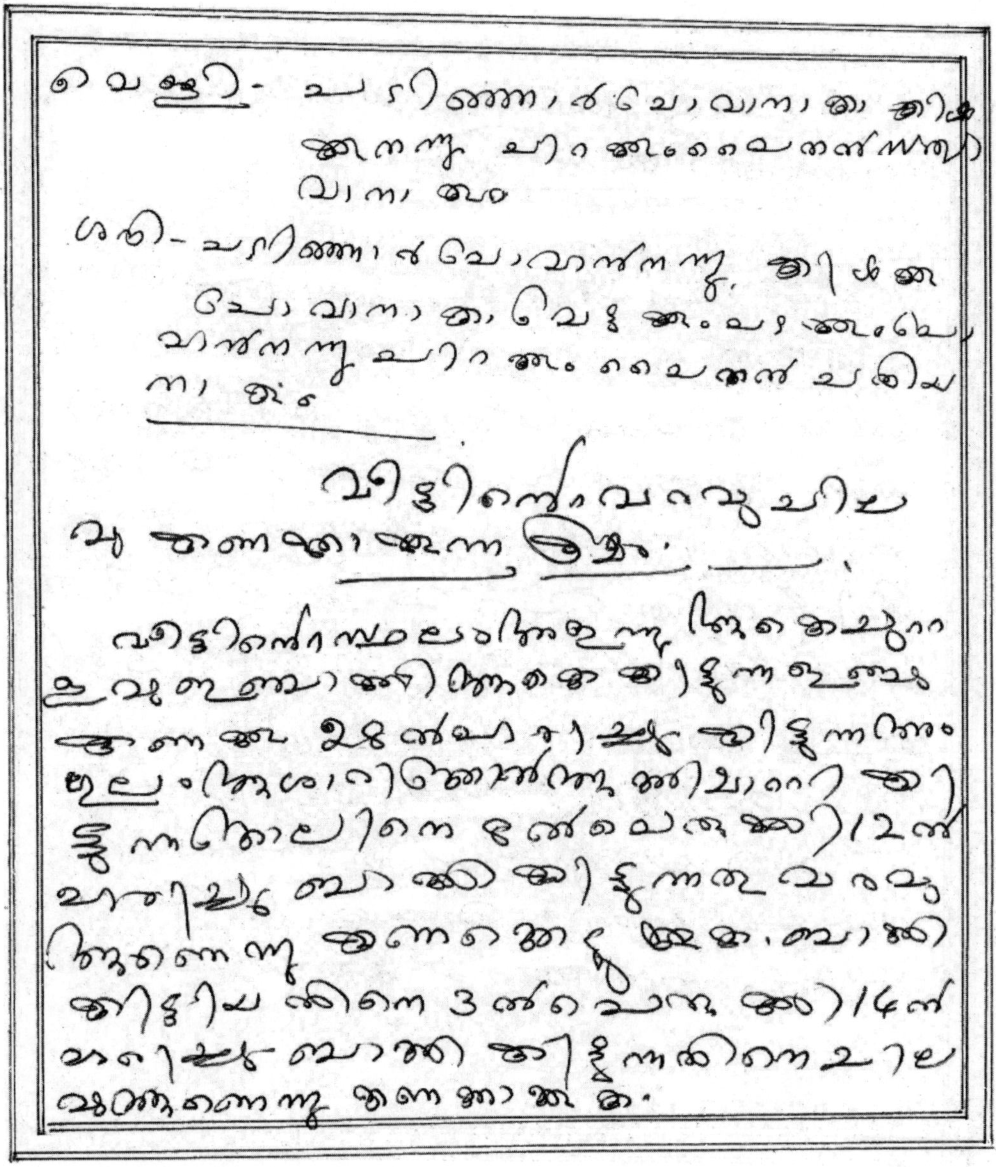

(92) [illegible] / [illegible]

[illegible]

[illegible]

[illegible] 28

ൽ ഹരിച്ചു [illegible]

[illegible] 8 ൽ [illegible]

[illegible] 12 ൽ [illegible]

[illegible] 28 ൽ

[illegible] 3 ൽ

[illegible] 14 ൽ ഹരിച്ചു

[illegible]

[illegible] 6 ൽ [illegible]

[illegible] 12 [illegible]

[illegible] 8 ൽ [illegible] വരാം

PART II

ANNOTATED ENGLISH TRANSLATION

CALICUT		SUHELI		KALPENI		KAVARATTI		ANDROTT		PITTI (BIRD ISLAND)		AGATTI		BANGARAM	
210															
72	253														
143		76													
62	242	271	11												
187		29		67											
78	258	218	38	115	295										
123		89		88		64									
70	282	241	81	182	2	256	76								
195		41		78		14		67							
82	262	199	19	121	301	155	335	87	267						
207		41		96		31		85		21					
84	264	171	351	118	298	121	301	91	271	104	284				
207		48		94		30		82		17		7			
85	265	178	358	123	303	136	316	95	275	122	302	226	46		
175		62		81		35		58		24		33		29	
87	267	203	23	138	318	189	9	106	286	210	30	245	45	248	68
220		62		111		48		95		39		19		18	
89	269	168	348	123	303	134	214	101	281	128	308	154	334	133	313
180		70		84		37		57		29		42		34	
90	270	202	22	43	323	192	12	144	324	208	29	236	56	238	58
160		91		95		62		55		51		60		54	
94	274	206	26	156	336	201	21	135	315	212	32	233	53	231	51
207		82		121		62		98		49		38		34	
95	275	175	355	135	315	154	334	115	295	154	334	188	008	169	349
178		96		110		66		76		55		57		51	
98	278	194	14	150	530	183	3	132	312	190	10	211	31	208	28
243		106		150		88		125		78		63		61	
99	279	164	344	134	314	148	328	120	300	165	45	159	339	153	333
240		131		169		112		138		119		112		84	
106	285	169	349	142	322	157	337	130	310	145	325	169	249	165	345

(1) (TRUE BEARINGS AND DISTANCES OF PORTS IN NAUTICAL MILES)[1]

[1] *Each unit comprises a sub-heading giving distances between two ports in nautical miles. The two columns immediately below provide the true bearings and the reciprocal in degrees. For example, in the first sub-heading, 210 is the distance in nautical miles between Calicut and Suheli. In the first column true bearings in degrees from the first point to the second point are given and in the second column the bearings from the second point to the first point are provided. For the reciprocal bearing, 180° is always added to the true bearing. If the result exceeds 360°, 360° are subtracted to obtain reciprocal bearings for performing the return journey (AKB). In the* ***Composite Circular Compass*** *reciprocal bearings may be found diagonally opposite to the true bearings (ATK).* ***The Revised Table and Compass Chart, Section 2a****, which had been framed by Kunhikunhi Malmi at a later date, bears corrections of errors found in* ***Section 1*** *above. For ports after Cheriyapanniyam, refer to* ***Section 2a.***

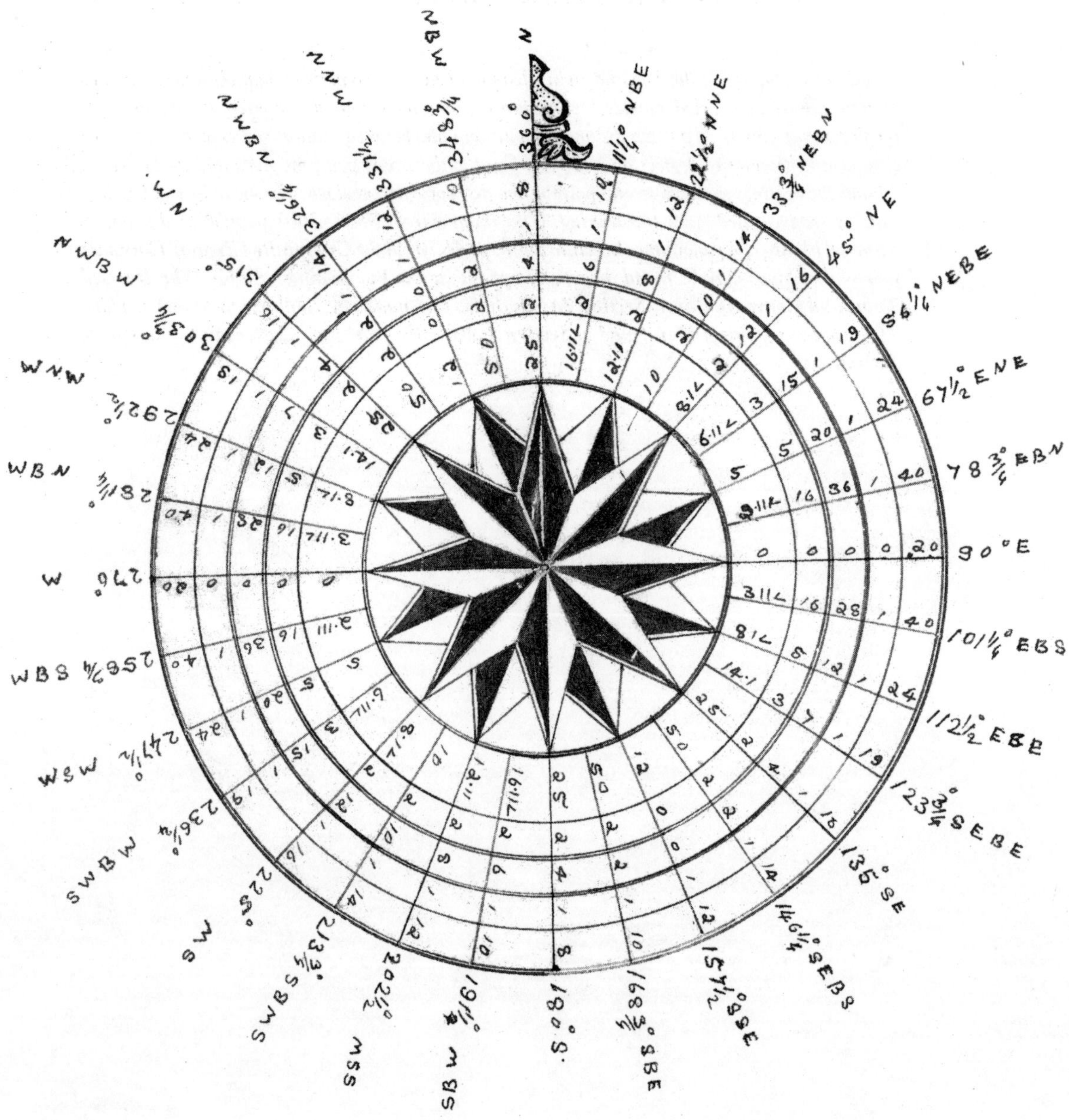
N
360°
11¼° NBE
22½° NNE
33¾° NEBN
45° NE
56¼ NEBE
67½° ENE
78¾° EBN
90°E
101¼° EBS
112½° EBE
123¾° SEBE
135° SE
146¼° SEBS
157½° SSE
168¾° SBE
180°S
191¼ SBW
202½° SSW
213¾° SWBS
225° SW
236¼° SWBW
247½° WSW
258¾ WBS
270° W
281¼° WBN
292½° WNW
303¾° NWBW
315° NW
326¼° NWBN
337½ NNW
348¾ NBW

(2) (COMPOSITE CIRCULAR COMPASS)[2]

[2] *In the **Composite Circular Compass**, there are six sets of numbers in six concentric circles. In each set the starting point is from the north, the direction of the Pole Star.*

On the outermost circle true bearings are given. The North is set at zero degree and the counting is done in clockwise direction. East is 090°, South is 180°, West is 270° and the North is 360°/000°.

*The second, third and fourth circles constitute an illustration of the portion of the Rahmani entitled, **Kanakku of Progression, Section 10**. For example, if a vessel is to sail north, that is the direction of the Pole Star, for a period of eight **chaamams** (3 × 8=24 hours) speed unstated (Col.2), the height of the Pole Star will increase by one (Col.3), and the vessel will go closer to mainland by 4 **chaamams** (4 × 12=48 miles) (Col.4).*

*On circle five, we find a presentation of the contents of **Kanakku of Distances Between Two Points in Chaamams, Section 9**. The starting point is NNW, point-31. If a vessel sails in between the directions of **Nashi Asthamanam** (the setting point of the star, **Nashi**, point 31), and **Farakaden Asthamanam** (the setting point of the star, **Farakaden,** point 32) the vessel will come closer to the mainland by two **chaamams** (2 × 12=24 miles).*

*Between the 32nd point and the first point, it is also two **chaamams** (2 × 12=24 miles). This will make a total of four **chaamams** (2+2), i.e. 48 miles.*

*On the sixth column, the speed in respect to one **chaamam** is given in different directions. If a vessel travels for a period of one **chaamam** (3 hours) in the first direction the distance covered is 25 miles and so on. (AKT, MM)*

(2A) (REVISED TABLE AND COMPASS CHART)[3]

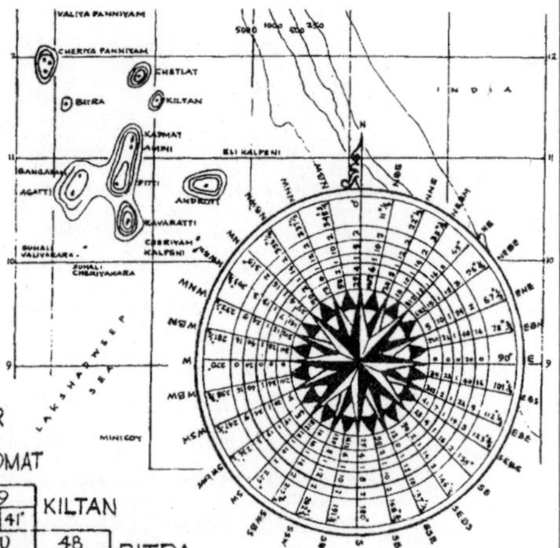

	ALICUT	SUHELI	KALPENI	KAVARATTI	ANDROTT	PITTI	AGATTI	BANGARAM	AMINI	PERUMALPAR	KADMAT	KILTAN	BITRA	CHETLAT	CHERIYAPANNIYAM	VALIYAPANNIYAM	ELI KALPENI
SUHELI	210 NM 72° 252°																
KALPENI	143 62° 242	76 271° 91°															
KAVARATTI	187 78° 258°	29 218° 38°	67 115° 295°														
ANDROTT	123 79° 259°	89 241° 61°	38 182° 2°	64 256° 76°													
PITTI	195 82° 262°	41 199° 19°	78 121° 301°	14 155° 335°	67 87° 267°												
AGATTI	207 84° 264°	41 171° 351°	96 118° 298°	31 121° 301°	85 91° 271°	21 104° 248°											
BANGARAM	207 85° 265°	48 178° 358°	94 123° 303°	30 135° 316°	82 95° 275°	17 122° 302°	7 226° 46°										
AMINI	175 87° 267°	62 203° 23°	81 138° 318°	35 189° 9°	58 106° 286°	24 210° 30°	33 245° 65°	29 248° 68°									
PERUMALPAR	220 89° 269°	62 168° 348°	111 123° 303°	42 134° 314°	97 101° 281°	35 128° 308°	16 154° 334°	21 133° 313°	39 83° 263°								
KADMAT	180 90° 270°	70 202° 22°	84 143° 323°	37 192° 12°	57 114° 294°	29 208° 28°	42 236° 56°	34 238° 58°	6 200° 20°	41 265° 85°							
KILTAN	160 94° 274°	91 206° 26°	95 156° 336°	62 201° 21°	55 135° 315°	51 212° 32°	60 233° 53°	54 231° 51°	32 215° 35°	56 252° 72°	19 221° 41°						
BITRA	207 95° 275°	82 175° 355°	121 135° 315°	62 154° 334°	98 115° 295°	49 154° 334°	38 188° 8°	34 169° 349°	43 126° 306°	17 197° 17°	40 116° 296°	48 92° 272°					
CHETLAT	178 98° 278°	96 194° 14°	110 150° 330°	66 183° 3°	76 132° 312°	55 190° 10°	57 211° 31°	51 208° 28°	35 176° 356°	45 231° 51°	27 170° 350°	20 126° 306°	30 255° 75°				
CHERIYAPANNIYAM	243 99° 279°	106 164° 344°	150 134° 314°	88 148° 328°	125 120° 300°	78 147° 327°	63 159° 339°	61 153° 335°	70 130° 310°	42 161° 341°	68 124° 304°	74 110° 290°	25 135° 315°	53 101° 281°			
VALIYAPANNIYAM	240 06° 286°	131 169° 349°	169 142° 322°	112 157° 337°	138 130° 310°	119 145° 325°	112 169° 349°	84 165° 345°	86 146° 326°	66 172° 352°	82 142° 322°	81 129° 309°	45 162° 342°	60 130° 310°	23 194° 14°		
ELI KALPENI	104 88° 268°	123 234° 54°	59 289° 19°	84 247° 67°	28 220° 40°	85 253° 73°	105 260° 80°	98 261° 81°	71 268° 88°	110 269° 89°	68 274° 94°	56 291° 111°	107 282° 102°	76 287° 107°	130 285° 105°	138 296° 116°	
MINICO	234 44° 224°	115 340° 160°	118 70° 250°	133 350° 170°	154 16° 196°	150 350° 170°	160 340° 160°	162 338° 158°	167 355° 175°	176 340° 160°	170 353° 173°	188 18° 198°	198 345° 165°	200 355° 175°	218 341° 161°	246 345° 165°	180 18° 198°

HAJI; M.P. KUNNI KUNNI MALMI

[3] *This sheet was prepared by Janab K.N.K. Mulla Koya under the guidance of Kunhikunhi Malmi. It is hand written. It bears corrections to inaccuracies found in the Chart, Section 1. Such charts were framed and kept on all sailing vessels (AKT).*

(3) (QUADRENNIAL TABLES OF DECLINATION OF THE SUN)[4]

[4] *Kunhikunhi Malmi has taken this table from the notebook of his teacher Syed Mohammed Koya Thangal of Kavaratti. This table provided the declination of the sun for each day of the month. In this chart each unit is made up of the date of the month in the topmost segment. Month names of the Gregorian Calendar starting with January are inserted in serial order. The first column on the left has the heading* ***Thi*** *from Malayalam* ***Thiyathi*** *meaning date. The second column has* ***dara****. This can be taken as* ***darja*** *for degree. The third column has the letters* ***da*** *indicative of* ***daqiq****, for minutes. In this way all the 365 days of a year are covered. This chart has been taken from European sources in which tables of declination of the sun are given in four-year cycles inclusive of the leap year. Cf.* ***Section 86****. In the Quadrennial Tables of Declination of the Sun year 2 has been taken as the leap year. The month of February, year 3 also shows 29 days but the figure in degrees and minutes appears to have been crossed out.*

Year 1

January			February			March			April			May			June		
Thi	dara	da															
1	23	2	1	17	10	1	7	40	1	4	27	1	15	.	1	22	2
2	22	57	2	16	53	2	7	17	2	4	50	2	15	18	2	22	10
3	22	51	3	16	35	3	6	54	3	5	13	3	15	36	3	22	18
4	22	45	4	16	14	4	6	31	4	5	36	4	15	54	4	22	25
5	22	39	5	15	59	5	6	8	5	5	59	5	16	11	5	22	32
6	22	32	6	15	41	6	5	54	6	6	22	6	16	28	6	22	36
7	22	25	7	15	22	7	5	22	7	6	44	7	16	45	7	22	44
8	22	17	8	15	3	8	4	58	8	7	7	8	17	1	8	22	50
9	22	9	9	14	44	9	4	35	9	7	29	9	17	13	9	22	55
10	22	..	10	14	25	10	4	11	10	7	52	10	17	33	10	23	..
11	21	51	11	14	5	11	3	48	11	8	44	11	17	46	11	23	5
12	21	41	12	13	46	12	3	24	12	8	36	12	18	4	12	23	9
13	21	31	13	13	26	13	3	1	13	8	58	13	18	19	13	23	13
14	21	21	14	13	5	14	2	37	14	9	19	14	18	34	14	23	16
15	21	10	15	12	45	15	2	13	15	9	41	15	18	49	15	23	19
16	20	59	16	12	24	16	1	50	16	10	2	16	19	3	16	23	21
17	20	47	17	12	3	17	1	26	17	10	23	17	19	16	17	23	23
18	20	35	18	11	42	18	1	2	18	10	44	18	19	30	18	23	25
19	20	23	19	11	21	19	..	39	19	11	5	19	19	43	19	23	26
20	20	10	20	11	.	20	S	15	20	11	26	20	19	56	20	23	27
21	19	57	21	10	38	21	N	9	21	11	46	21	20	8	21	23	28
22	19	44	22	10	16	22	..	32	22	12	7	22	20	20	22	23	28
23	19	30	23	9	54	23	..	56	23	12	27	23	20	32	23	23	27
24	18	19	24	9	32	24	1	20	24	12	47	24	20	44	24	23	26
25	18	1	25	9	10	25	1	43	25	13	7	25	20	55	25	23	25
26	18	49	26	8	48	26	2	7	26	13	28	26	21	5	26	23	23
27	18	31	27	8	25	27	2	30	27	13	45	27	21	15	27	23	21
28	18	16	28	8	3	28	2	54	28	14	4	28	21	26	28	23	19
29	17	51				29	3	17	29	14	23	29	21	35	29	23	16
[illegible]	17	43				30	3	41	30	14	42	30	21	44	30	23	13
31	17	27				31	4	4				31	21	53			

July			August			September			October			November			December		
දි	පැ	වි	දි	පැ	වි	දි	පැ	වි	දි	පැ	වි	දි	පැ	වි	දි	පැ	වි
1	23	9	1	18	7	1	8	24	1	3	5	1	14	22	1	21	47
2	23	5	2	17	52	2	8	2	2	3	28	2	14	41	2	21	57
3	23	"	3	17	36	3	7	40	3	3	42	3	15	..	3	22	5
4	22	55	4	17	20	4	7	18	4	4	15	4	15	19	4	22	14
5	22	50	5	17	4	5	6	56	5	4	38	5	15	37	5	22	22
6	22	44	6	16	48	6	6	33	6	5	1	6	15	55	6	22	29
7	22	39	7	16	31	7	6	11	7	5	24	7	16	13	7	22	36
8	22	25	8	16	15	8	5	48	8	5	47	8	16	31	8	22	43
9	22	25	9	15	57	9	5	26	9	6	10	9	16	48	9	22	49
10	22	18	10	15	40	10	5	3	10	6	33	10	17	5	10	22	55
11	22	10	11	15	22	11	4	40	11	6	56	11	17	22	11	23	..
12	22	2	12	15	5	12	4	18	12	7	18	12	17	39	12	23	5
13	21	54	13	14	47	13	3	55	13	7	41	13	17	55	13	23	9
14	21	45	14	14	28	14	3	32	14	8	3	14	18	11	14	23	13
15	21	36	15	14	10	15	3	9	15	8	26	15	18	26	15	23	17
16	21	26	16	13	51	16	2	45	16	8	48	16	18	42	16	23	20
17	21	16	17	13	32	17	2	22	17	9	10	17	18	57	17	23	22
18	21	6	18	13	13	18	1	59	18	9	38	18	19	11	18	23	24
19	20	55	19	12	53	19	1	36	19	9	45	19	19	25	19	23	26
20	20	44	20	12	34	20	1	12	20	10	15	20	19	39	20	23	27
21	20	33	21	12	14	21	..	49	21	10	37	21	19	53	21	23	27
22	20	21	22	11	54	22	..	26	22	10	58	22	20	6	22	23	28
23	20	9	23	11	33	23	N	2	23	11	19	23	20	19	23	23	27
24	19	57	24	11	13	24	S	21	24	11	40	24	20	31	24	23	26
25	19	44	25	10	52	25	..	45	25	12	1	25	20	43	25	23	25
26	19	31	26	10	32	26	1	8	26	12	22	26	20	55	26	23	23
27	19	18	27	10	11	27	1	13	27	12	43	27	21	6	27	23	21
28	19	4	28	9	50	28	1	55	28	13	3	28	21	17	28	23	19
29	18	50	29	9	28	29	2	18	29	13	22	29	21	28	29	23	15
30	18	36	30	9	7	30	2	41	30	13	43	30	21	38	30	23	12
31	18	22	31	8	45				31	14	2				31	23	8

Year 2

ജനുവരി			ഫെബ്രുവ			മാർച്ച്			ഏപ്രിൽ			മെയ്.			ജൂൺ.		
ദി	ഡി	മി	ദി	ഡി	മി	ദി	ഡി	മി	ദി	ഡി	മി	ദി	ഡി	മി	ദി	ഡി	മി
1	23	3	1	17	14	1	7	23	1	4	45	1	15	14	1	22	8
2	22	58	2	16	57	2	7	..	2	5	8	2	15	32	2	22	16
3	22	53	3	16	39	3	6	37	3	5	31	3	15	49	3	22	23
4	22	47	4	16	22	4	6	14	4	5	53	4	16	7	4	22	30
5	22	41	5	16	4	5	5	51	5	6	16	5	16	24	5	22	37
6	22	34	6	15	45	6	5	27	6	6	39	6	16	41	6	22	43
7	22	27	7	15	27	7	5	4	7	7	1	7	16	57	7	22	49
8	22	19	8	15	8	8	4	41	8	7	24	8	17	14	8	22	54
9	22	11	9	14	49	9	4	17	9	7	46	9	17	30	9	22	59
10	22	2	10	14	30	10	3	51	10	8	8	10	17	45	10	23	4
11	21	53	11	14	10	11	3	30	11	8	30	11	18	1	11	23	8
12	21	44	12	13	51	12	3	6	12	8	52	12	18	16	12	23	12
13	21	34	13	13	31	13	2	43	13	9	14	13	18	31	13	23	15
14	21	24	14	13	10	14	2	19	14	9	36	14	18	45	14	23	18
15	21	13	15	12	50	15	1	56	15	9	57	15	18	59	15	23	21
16	21	2	16	12	29	16	1	32	16	10	18	16	19	13	16	23	23
17	20	50	17	12	8	17	1	8	17	10	39	17	19	27	17	23	25
18	20	38	18	11	47	18	..	44	18	11	..	18	19	40	18	23	26
19	20	26	19	11	26	19	S	21	19	11	21	19	19	53	19	23	27
20	20	14	20	11	5	20	N	3	20	11	42	20	20	5	20	23	27
21	20	..	21	10	43	21	..	27	21	12	2	21	20	17	21	23	28
22	19	47	22	10	22	22	..	50	22	12	22	22	20	29	22	23	27
23	19	33	23	10	..	23	1	14	23	12	42	23	20	41	23	23	26
24	19	19	24	9	38	24	1	38	24	13	2	24	20	52	24	23	25
25	19	5	25	9	15	25	2	1	25	13	21	25	21	3	25	23	24
26	18	50	26	8	53	26	2	25	26	13	41	26	21	13	26	23	22
27	18	35	27	8	31	27	2	48	27	14	..	27	21	23	27	23	19
28	18	19	28	8	8	28	3	12	28	14	19	28	21	33	28	23	17
29	18	3	29	7	45	29	3	35	29	14	37	29	21	42	29	23	13
30	17	47				30	3	58	30	14	56	30	21	51	30	23	10
31	17	31				31	4	21				31	22	..			

ജൂലായി			ആഗസ്റ്റ്			സപ്തമ്പർ			ഒക്ടോബർ			നവമ്പർ			ഡിസമ്പർ		
ദി	നാ	വി	ദി	നാ	വി	ദി	നാ	വി	ദി	നാ	വി	ദി	നാ	വി	ദി	നാ	വി
1	23	6	1	17	55	1	8	7	1	3	23	1	14	30	1	21	54
2	23	1	2	17	40	2	7	45	2	3	46	2	14	58	2	22	3
3	22	57	3	17	24	3	7	23	3	4	9	3	16	14	3	22	12
4	22	51	4	17	8	4	7	1	4	4	22	4	16	33	4	22	20
5	22	46	5	16	52	5	6	39	5	4	55	5	15	54	5	22	27
6	22	40	6	16	35	6	6	16	6	5	19	6	16	9	6	22	35
7	22	33	7	16	19	7	5	54	7	5	24	7	16	27	7	22	41
8	22	27	8	16	2	8	5	39	8	6	4	8	16	44	8	22	48
9	22	19	9	15	44	9	5	9	9	6	27	9	17	1	9	22	53
10	22	12	10	15	27	10	4	46	10	6	50	10	17	18	10	22	56
11	22	4	11	15	9	11	4	23	11	7	13	11	17	35	11	23	4
12	21	56	12	14	51	12	4	..	12	7	35	12	17	51	12	23	8
13	21	47	13	14	33	13	3	37	13	7	58	13	18	7	13	23	12
14	21	38	14	14	14	14	3	14	14	8	20	14	18	21	14	23	16
15	21	29	15	13	55	15	2	51	15	8	42	15	18	38	15	23	19
16	21	19	16	13	36	16	2	28	16	9	5	16	18	53	16	23	21
17	21	8	17	13	17	17	2	5	17	9	27	17	19	8	17	23	24
18	20	58	18	12	58	18	1	41	18	9	48	18	19	22	18	23	25
19	20	47	19	12	38	19	1	18	19	10	10	19	19	36	19	23	26
20	20	36	20	12	18	20	..	55	20	10	32	20	19	50	20	23	27
21	20	24	21	11	58	21	..	31	21	10	53	21	20	3	21	23	27
22	20	12	22	11	38	22	N	8	22	11	14	22	20	16	22	23	27
23	20	..	23	11	18	23	S	16	23	11	25	23	20	28	23	23	27
24	19	47	24	10	57	24	..	39	24	11	56	24	20	40	24	23	25
25	19	35	25	10	37	25	1	2	25	12	17	25	20	52	25	23	24
26	19	21	26	10	16	26	1	26	26	12	38	26	21	4	26	23	22
27	19	8	27	9	55	27	1	49	27	12	58	27	21	14	27	23	19
28	18	54	28	9	34	28	2	13	28	13	18	28	21	25	28	23	16
29	18	40	29	9	12	29	2	36	29	13	38	29	21	36	29	23	13
30	18	25	30	8	51	30	2	59	30	13	58	30	21	45	30	23	9
31	18	10	31	8	29				31	14	18				31	23	4

Year 3

ജനുവരി			ഫെബ്രുവ			മാർച്ച്			ഏപ്രിൽ			മെയ്.			ജൂൺ		
ദി	ഡി	മ	ദി	ഡി	മ	ദി	ഡി	മ	ദി	ഡി	മ	ദി	ഡി	മ	ദി	ഡി	മ
1	22	59	1	17	1	1	7	28	1	4	39	1	15	9	1	22	6
2	22	54	2	16	43	2	7	5	2	5	2	2	15	27	2	22	14
3	22	48	3	16	26	3	6	42	3	5	25	3	15	45	3	22	21
4	22	42	4	16	8	4	6	19	4	5	48	4	16	3	4	22	28
5	22	35	5	15	50	5	5	56	5	6	11	5	16	20	5	22	35
6	22	28	6	15	31	6	5	33	6	6	33	6	16	37	6	22	41
7	22	21	7	15	13	7	5	10	7	6	56	7	16	53	7	22	47
8	22	13	8	14	50	8	4	46	8	7	18	8	17	10	8	22	53
9	22	4	9	14	30	9	4	23	9	7	41	9	17	26	9	22	58
10	21	55	10	14	15	10	3	59	10	8	3	10	17	41	10	23	3
11	21	46	11	13	55	11	3	36	11	8	25	11	17	57	11	23	7
12	21	36	12	13	35	12	3	12	12	8	47	12	18	12	12	23	11
13	21	26	13	13	15	13	2	48	13	9	9	13	18	27	13	23	14
14	21	15	14	12	55	14	2	25	14	9	30	14	18	42	14	23	17
15	21	4	15	12	34	15	2	1	15	9	52	15	18	56	15	23	20
16	20	53	16	12	13	16	1	37	16	10	13	16	19	10	16	23	22
17	20	41	17	11	52	17	1	14	17	10	34	17	19	23	17	23	24
18	20	29	18	11	31	18	..	50	18	10	55	18	19	37	18	23	26
19	20	16	19	11	10	19	..	26	19	11	16	19	19	50	19	23	27
20	20	4	20	10	48	20	S	3	20	11	37	20	20	2	20	23	27
21	19	50	21	10	17	21	N	21	21	11	57	21	20	14	21	23	27
22	19	37	22	10	5	22		45	22	12	17	22	20	26	22	23	27
23	19	22	23	9	43	23	1	8	23	12	37	23	20	38	23	23	27
24	19	8	24	9	21	24	1	32	24	12	57	24	20	49	24	23	26
25	18	53	25	8	59	25	1	56	25	13	17	25	21	..	25	23	24
26	18	38	26	8	36	26	2	19	26	13	36	26	21	11	26	23	22
27	18	23	27	8	14	27	2	43	27	13	55	27	21	21	27	23	20
28	18	7	28	7	51	28	3	5	28	14	14	28	21	30	28	23	17
29	17	51	29	7	28	29	3	29	29	14	33	29	21	40	29	23	14
30	17	35				30	3	53	30	14	51	30	21	49	30	23	11
31	17	18				31	4	16				31	21	58			

ജൂലായി			ആഗസ്റ്റ്			സെപ്റ്റംബർ			ഒക്ടോബർ			നവംബർ			ഡിസംബർ		
തീ	നാ	വി	തീ	നാ	വി	തീ	നാ	വി	തീ	നാ	വി	തീ	നാ	വി	തീ	നാ	വി
1	23	7	1	17	59	1	8	13	1	3	17	1	14	32	1	21	52
2	23	3	2	17	44	2	7	51	2	3	40	2	14	51	2	22	1
3	22	58	3	17	28	3	7	29	3	4	4	3	15	10	3	22	10
4	22	53	4	17	12	4	7	7	4	4	27	4	15	28	4	22	18
5	22	47	5	16	56	5	6	44	5	4	50	5	15	47	5	22	25
6	22	41	6	16	39	6	6	22	6	5	17	6	16	5	6	22	33
7	22	35	7	16	23	7	5	58	7	5	36	7	16	22	7	22	40
8	22	28	8	16	6	8	5	39	8	5	59	8	16	40	8	22	46
9	22	21	9	15	49	9	5	14	9	6	22	9	16	57	9	22	52
10	22	14	10	15	31	10	4	51	10	6	45	10	17	14	10	22	57
11	22	6	11	15	14	11	4	29	11	7	7	11	17	31	11	23	2
12	21	58	12	14	55	12	4	6	12	7	30	12	17	47	12	23	7
13	21	49	13	14	37	13	3	43	13	7	52	13	18	3	13	23	11
14	21	40	14	14	14	14	3	20	14	8	15	14	18	19	14	23	15
15	21	31	15	14	..	15	2	57	15	8	37	15	18	34	15	23	18
16	21	21	16	13	41	16	2	33	16	8	59	16	18	48	16	23	21
17	21	11	17	13	22	17	2	10	17	9	21	17	19	4	17	23	23
18	21	..	18	13	3	18	1	47	18	9	43	18	19	19	18	23	25
19	20	50	19	12	43	19	1	24	19	10	5	19	19	33	19	23	26
20	20	39	20	12	23	20	1	..	20	10	26	20	19	40	20	23	27
21	20	27	21	12	3	21	..	37	21	10	48	21	20	..	21	23	27
22	20	15	22	11	43	22	N	14	22	11	9	22	20	13	22	23	27
23	20	3	23	11	23	23	S	10	23	11	30	23	20	25	23	23	27
24	19	51	24	11	2	24	..	33	24	11	51	24	20	37	24	23	26
25	19	38	25	10	42	25	..	57	25	12	12	25	20	49	25	23	24
26	19	25	26	10	21	26	1	20	26	12	33	26	21	1	26	23	22
27	19	11	27	10	--	27	1	43	27	12	53	27	21	12	27	23	20
28	18	57	28	9	39	28	2	7	28	13	13	28	21	22	28	23	17
29	18	43	29	9	17	29	2	30	29	13	33	29	21	33	29	28	14
30	18	27	30	8	56	30	2	54	30	13	53	30	21	43	30	23	10
31	18	14	31	8	34				31	14	12				31	23	5

Year 4

ജനുവരി			ഫെബ്രുവ			മാർച്ച്			ഏപ്രിൽ			മെയ്			ജൂൺ.		
ദി	മ	മി	ദി	മ	മി	ദി	മ	മി	ദി	മ	മി	ദി	മ	മി	ദി	മ	മി
1	23	1	1	17	5	1	7	34	1	4	33	1	15	5	1	22	4
2	22	55	2	16	48	2	7	11	2	4	50	2	15	23	2	22	12
3	22	50	3	16	30	3	6	48	3	5	19	3	15	41	3	22	19
4	22	44	4	16	12	4	6	25	4	5	42	4	15	58	4	22	27
5	22	37	5	15	54	5	6	2	5	6	5	5	16	16	5	22	33
6	22	30	6	15	36	6	5	38	6	6	28	6	16	33	6	22	40
7	22	22	7	15	19	7	5	15	7	6	50	7	16	49	7	22	46
8	22	15	8	14	58	8	4	52	8	7	13	8	17	6	8	22	51
9	22	6	9	14	39	9	4	28	9	7	35	9	17	22	9	22	54
10	21	57	10	14	20	10	4	5	10	7	58	10	17	39	10	23	1
11	21	48	11	14	..	11	3	41	11	8	20	11	17	53	11	23	6
12	21	38	12	13	40	12	3	28	12	8	42	12	18	8	12	23	10
13	21	28	13	13	20	13	2	45	13	9	3	13	18	23	13	23	13
14	21	18	14	13	..	14	2	31	14	9	25	14	18	38	14	23	17
15	21	7	15	12	39	15	2	7	15	9	47	15	18	52	15	23	18
16	20	56	16	12	19	16	1	43	16	10	8	16	19	6	16	23	22
17	20	44	17	11	58	17	1	20	17	10	29	17	19	20	17	23	24
18	20	32	18	11	36	18	..	56	18	10	50	18	19	33	18	23	25
19	20	20	19	11	16	19	..	32	19	11		19	19	46	19	23	26
20	20	7	20	10	54	20		9	20	11	32	20	19	59	20	23	27
21	19	54	21	10	32	21		15	21	11	52	21	20	11	21	23	27
22	19	40	22	10	10	22	..	39	22	12	12	22	20	24	22	23	27
23	19	26	23	9	40	23	1	3	23	12	32	23	20	35	23	23	27
24	19	12	24	9	26	24	1	26	24	12	52	24	20	46	24	23	26
25	18	57	25	9	4	25	1	50	25	13	12	25	20	57	25	23	24
26	18	42	26	8	42	26	2	13	26	13	31	26	21	8	26	23	23
27	18	27	27	8	19	27	2	37	27	13	50	27	21	18	27	23	21
28	18	11	28	7	56	28	3	..	28	14	9	28	21	29	28	23	18
29	17	55	2			29	3	24	29	14	23	29	21	38	29	23	15
30	17	39				30	3	49	30	14	47	30	21	47	30	23	12
31	17	22				31	4	10				31	21	55			

ജൂലായി.			ആഗസ്റ്റ്			സെപ്റ്റംബ്ര			ഒക്ടോബർ			നവംബർ			ഡിസംബർ.		
ദി	നാ	വി	ദി	നാ	വി	ദി	നാ	വി	ദി	നാ	വി	ദി	നാ	വി	ദി	നാ	വി
1	23	8	1	18	2	1	8	18	1	3	11	1	14	27	1	21	50
2	23	3	2	17	47	2	7	56	2	3	35	2	14	46	2	21	59
3	22	59	3	17	32	3	7	34	3	3	58	3	15	5	3	22	8
4	22	54	4	17	16	4	7	12	4	4	21	4	15	24	4	22	16
5	22	48	5	17		5	6	49	5	4	44	5	15	42	5	22	24
6	22	43	6	16	43	6	6	27	6	5	7	6	16	..	6	22	31
7	22	36	7	16	27	7	6	5	7	5	30	7	16	18	7	22	38
8	22	30	8	16	10	8	5	45	8	5	53	8	16	36	8	22	44
9	22	23	9	15	53	9	5	20	9	6	16	9	16	53	9	22	50
10	22	15	10	15	35	10	4	57	10	6	39	10	17	10	10	22	56
11	22	8	11	15	19	11	4	33	11	7	2	11	17	28	11	23	1
12	22	..	12	15	..	12	4	11	12	7	24	12	17	43	12	23	6
13	21	51	13	14	44	13	3	48	13	7	47	13	17	59	13	23	10
14	21	42	14	14	23	14	3	25	14	8	9	14	18	15	14	23	14
15	21	33	15	14	4	15	3	2	15	8	32	15	18	31	15	23	17
16	21	23	16	13	46	16	2	39	16	8	54	16	18	46	16	23	20
17	21	13	17	13	26	17	2	16	17	9	16	17	19	1	17	23	22
18	21	3	18	13	7	18	1	52	18	9	38	18	19	15	18	23	24
19	20	52	19	12	47	19	1	25	19	10	..	19	19	29	19	23	26
20	20	40	20	12	28	20	1	6	20	10	21	20	19	43	20	23	27
21	20	29	21	12	8	21	.	42	21	10	43	21	19	56	21	23	27
22	20	18	22	11	48	22	..	19	22	11	4	22	20	10	22	23	27
23	20	6	23	11	28	23	N	4	23	11	25	23	20	22	23	23	27
24	19	53	24	11	7	24	S	28	24	11	45	24	20	35	24	23	26
25	19	41	25	10	47	25	..	51	25	12	7	25	20	46	25	23	25
26	19	28	26	10	26	26	1	15	26	12	28	26	20	58	26	23	23
27	19	14	27	10	5	27	1	38	27	12	48	27	21	9	27	23	20
28	19	..	28	9	44	28	2	1	28	13	8	28	21	20	28	23	18
29	18	46	29	9	22	29	2	25	29	13	28	29	21	30	29	23	14
30	18	32	30	9	1	30	2	48	30	13	48	30	21	40	30	23	11
31	18	17	31	8	39				31	14	8				31	23	8

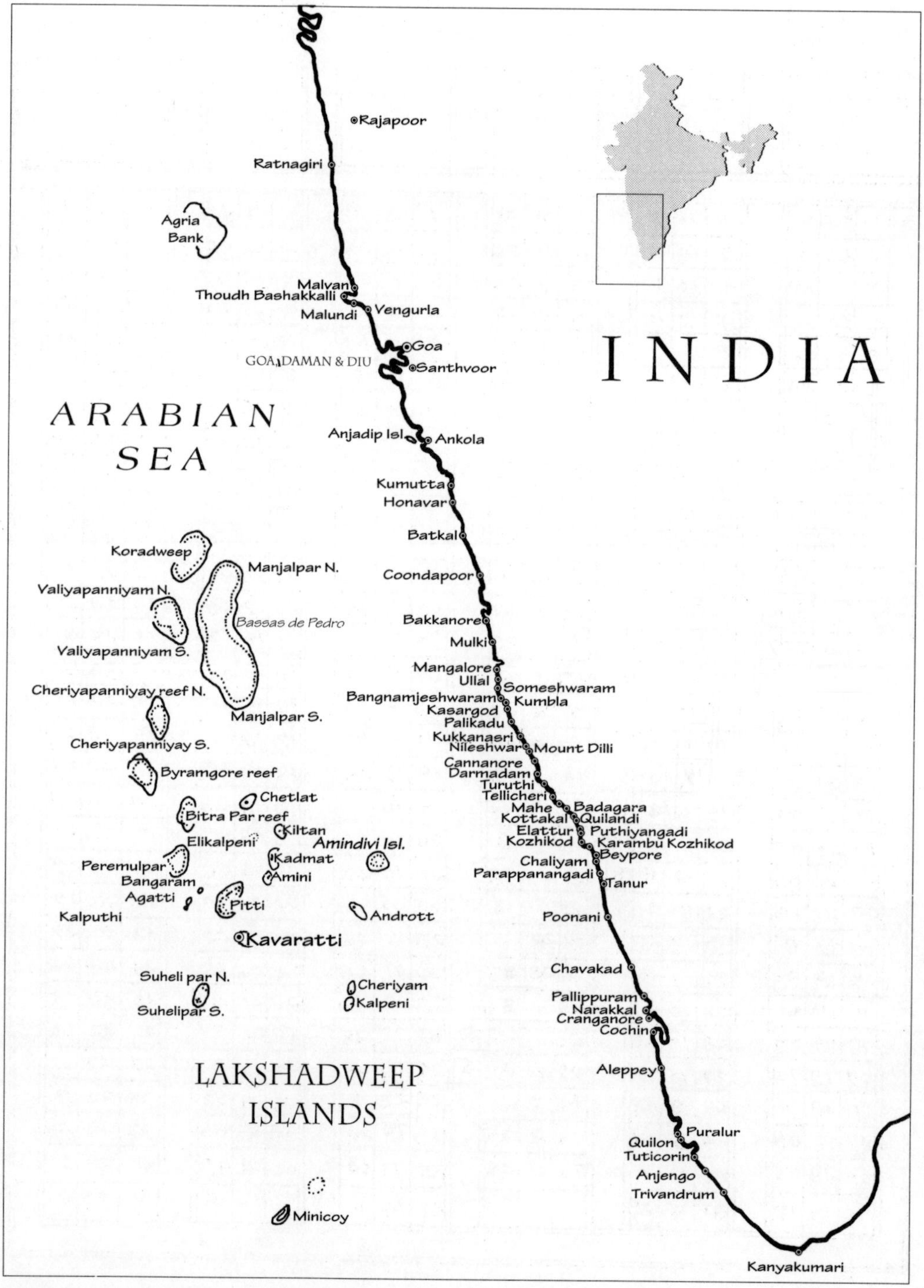

Fig. 20. West Coast of India in relation to text.
(International boundry of India is neither correct nor authentic)

(4) PORT LOCATION - *BUNDAR DARJA*[5]

Port	Latitude		Longitude	
	Degrees	Minutes	Degrees	Minutes
Minicoy	8	17	73	18
Suheli Southern tip	10	-	72	15
Suheli Northern tip	10	6	72	15
Kalpeni	10	7	73	35
Cheriyam	10	10	73	33
Kavaratti	10	32	72	57
Andrott	10	47	73	33
Pitti (near Kavaratti)	10	45	73	31
Agatti	10	51	72	11
Bangaram	10	55	72	35
Amini	11	6	72	42
Elikalpeni (a submerged reef)	11	15	73	57
Kadmat	11	14	72	44
Kiltan	11	28	72	58
Perumulpar (reef)	11	9	72	-
Bitra Par reef[6]	11	35	72	9
Chetlat	11	42	72	42
Cheriyapanniyam north end	11	58	71	46
Cheriyapanniyam south end	11	48	71	43
Valiyapanniyam north	12	23	72	5
Valiyapanniyam south	12	17	71	53
Manjalpar north	13	37	72	32
Manjalpar south	12	31	72	42
Koradweep	13	51	72	13
Kanyakumari	8	5	77	32
Trivandrum	8	31	76	57
Tuticorin	8	48	78	10
Anjanki (Anjengo)	8	40	76	46

Port	Latitude		Longitude	
	Degrees	Minutes	Degrees	Minutes
Quilon	8	53	76	35
Purakad (Puralur)	9	12	76	26
Aleppey	9	30	76	18
Cochin	8	58	76	14
Cranganore (Kodangallur)	10	8	76	18
Narakkal	10	10	76	8
Pallippuram	10	12	76	5
Chettuvazhi (not located)	10	28	76	2
Chavakkad	10	33	76	3
Ponnani	10	48	75	53
Tanur	10	58	75	52
Parappanangadi	10	50	75	47
Chaliyam	11	-	75	45
Beypore	11	10	75	47
Karambu Kozhikod[7]	11	12	75	46
Kozhikod	11	15	75	45
Puthiyangadi (Pudiyyadar)	11	18	75	44
Elathur (Elattur)	11	21	75	42
Quilandi	11	28	75	40
Kottakal	11	29	75	36
Vellimankal (not located)	11	30	75	31
Badakara (Badagara)	11	37	75	33
Mayyazhi (Mahe)	11	40	75	32
Tellicheri	11	44	75	28
Turuthi	11	46	75	27
Darmadam	11	45	75	27
Cannanore	11	52	75	21
Kazhikode (not located)	11	54	75	19
Ezhimala	12	1	75	15
Neershuram (Neechuram)	12	10	75	9
Kattukacheri (Kukkanasri)	12	11	75	7

Port	Latitude		Longitude	
	Degrees	Minutes	Degrees	Minutes
Padanakadu[8] (Palikadu)	12	15	75	6
Visha Kollam / (Visha Quilon)(not located)	12	23	75	2
Kanchirode (Kasargod)	12	28	75	-
Kumbala (Kumbla)	12	35	74	50
Maishuram (Bangnamjeshwaram)	12	42	74(75)	49(12)
Somasuram (Someshwaram)	12	45	74	48
Ullal	12	48	74	47
Mangalore	12	52	74	50
Kuthiravalli (not located)	13	-	74	48
Kaaranadu (not located)	13	6	74	40
Pattiya (not located)	13	12	74	30
Kottapatiya (not located)	13	15	74	28
Mulki	13	30	75	4
Bakkanore	13	20	74	55
Kuntapuram (Coondapoor)	13	37	74	33
Ganguli (Gangoli)	13	45	74	-
Byndoor (not located)	13	52	74	36
Saravallore (not located)	13	55	74	34
Battakal (Bhatkal)	13	57	74	33
Nithiriya (not located)	14	6	74	30
Anuvar (Honavar)	14	20	74	23
Kumutta	14	25	74	23
Ponnapuram (not located)	14	17	74	25
Jaseera Nithiriyam (not located)	14	15	74	24
Angola (Ankola)	14	35	74	17
Banthakod (not located)	14	56	74	14
Goa	15	28	73	55
Thykkore (not located)	15	35	73	50
Vinkorla (Vengurla)	15	53(50)	73	27(38)
Jazeera Thandavasi / (Thoudh Bashakkalli)	15	55	73	24

Port	**Latitude**		**Longitude**	
	Degrees	Minutes	Degrees	Minutes
Thanda Vasikkalu (not located)	15	58	73	10
Mathwa (Malvan)	16	10(03)	73	12(27)
Banthiv Thanan (not located)	16	23	73	2
Chanthavoor (not located)	16	37	73	-
Argriakara (Agria Bank)	16	39	71	58
Chavoor (not located)	16	47	73	28
Kadichur (not located)	16	38	73	27
Valaynthakalav (not located)	18	4	73	20
Ratnagiri	16	59	73	16
Rajapur	18	18	72	57
Canara Dweep (not located)	18	42	72	48
Bombay	19	54	72	48
Mayambi (Mahim)	19	10	72	40
Jidda	21	29	39	15
Mecca	21	-	40	-
Madeena	24	50	39	51

5 ***Bundar** means port. **Darja** is Arabic for degree. This list appears to be wholly derived from western maritime tradition. The terms used as headings in the original text were **tul** (longitude), **arlu** (latitude), **darja** (degree), **daqiq** (minute). All ports with the exception of the last three, are located on the sub-continent. Nomenclature is that which was prevalent in Lakshadweep at the time of the preparation of the manuscript. In the above table places which have not been identified have been noted as "not located" in parentheses. Modern names have been indicated in the same manner.*

6 *The reference to Bitra Island as **Par**/reef provides an important indicator for dating the text. Bitra was settled in 1928. The term **Bitra Par** may be indicative of the fact that these **Bundar Darja** tables were derived from a pre-1928 source. According to locations given under **The Position of Kou, Section 6, # 35**, Manjalpar (North), Manjalpar (South) and Koradweep are to be found on the Bassas de Pedro Bank.*

7 *According AKT the term **Karaabu** means clove. This port was situated between Calicut and Beypore.*

8 *Padana is a place name while **kadu** indicated forest (AKT).*

(5) (STAR TABLE)[9]

Name of Star	Degrees	Minutes
	dara	*daqiq*
Ayyook south leg	34	24
Thiruvonam south leg	24	–
Thiruvonam north leg	13	8
Farakaden	13	6
Kaarthika	15	11
Rohini	13	16
Ayyook north leg	52	45
Punatham	29	28
Kinalpees	36	52
Seer	31	16
Kasal	11	32
Naasi north leg	19	22
Naasi south leg	38	58
Maham	21	15
Aqrab	8	26
Artham	24	28
Thiruvonam	17	1
Himaren	11	20
Uththiraadam	15	45
Chothi	44	19
Chilli	15	22

[9] *Cf.* ***Names of Mujiras Section 8****. From early Vedic times astronomers in India identified twenty-eight or twenty-seven stars to mark the path of the sun and moon in the sky (AKB). These were called* ***Nakshatras****. Among the stars on this list* ***Thiruvonam, Kaarthika, Rohini, Punatham, Maham, Artham, Thiruvonam, Uththiraadam*** *and* ***Chothi*** *are* ***nakshatras****.* ***Ayyook*** *(south leg, north leg),* ***Seer, Kasal, Naasi*** *(north leg and south leg),* ***Aqrab, Himaren*** *and* ***Chilli*** *are directional stars (see* ***Section 8****).*

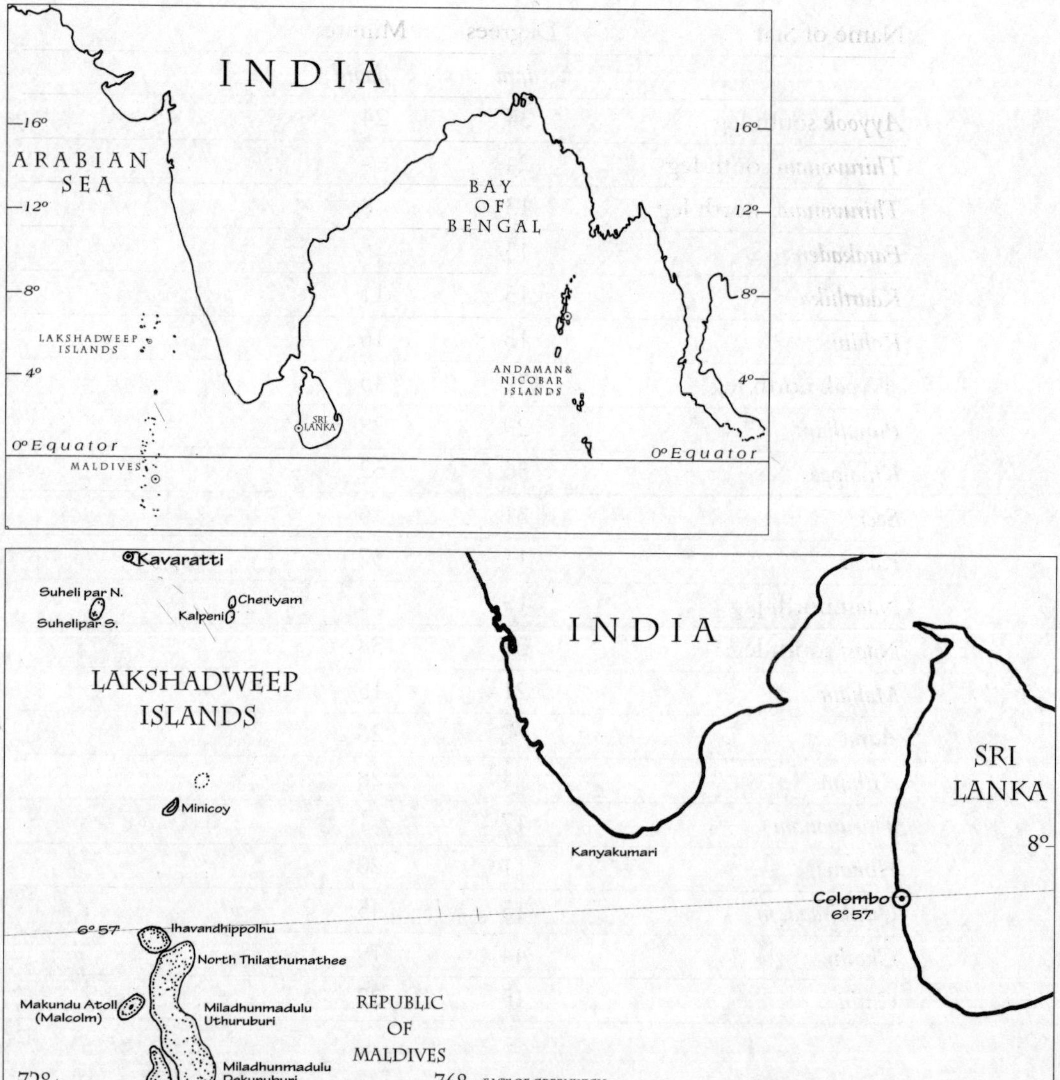

Fig. 21. Maldives and Sri Lanka in relation to the textual tables.
(International boundries of India, Sri Lanka and the Maldives are neither correct nor authentic.)

(6) POSITION OF POLE STAR[10]

1 If the Pole Star is seen as a Lotus flower above the sea level, it would be a place straight to Periya Ballikamam in Sri Lanka.[11] It is also suited to the north of Mahal Bada Thalam (Maldives). The distance between the two is 30 *chaamams.*[12]

2 If the Pole Star is half a finger,[13] it would be straight to Ballika. It is also suited to Pathiport. The distance between the two is 28 *chaamams* [**Tenakara in Sri Lanka and Padipork in Mahl**].

3 If the Pole Star is 3/4 finger it would be straight to Kali. It is also suited to Thippitti, Maideep, Shaik-Dweep and Marosmandalam. The distance between each of them is 27 *chaamams* [**Kali Chottamala** (**in Ceylon**), **Tippati, Maideep, Shaikdwiv, Marosmandalatinnamokum**].

4 If the Pole Star is one,[14] it would be straight to Thottakamam. It is also suited to Kenthikallu. The distance between the two is 26 *chaamams.*

5 If the Pole Star is 1 1/4, it would be straight to Nilanthur Beevak. It is also suited to Bahuraaskandy. The distance between the two is 25 *chaamams* [**Nillandurpuvakka and Kendikal**].

6 If the Pole Star is 1 1/2, it would be straight to Kumari (Kanyakumari). It is also suited to Kolathala Dweep [**Keladeladina**]. The distance between the two is 24 *chaamams.*

7 If the Pole Star is 1 3/4, it would be straight to Bilinchiyath Kodi [**Villinchiyakorna**].

8 If the Pole Star is 2, it would be straight to South Kollam (in Kerala). It is also suited to Maliku (Minicoy in Lakshadweep). The distance between the two is 20 *chaamams.*

9 If the Pole Star is 2 1/4, it would be straight to Kayamkulam (in Kerala).

10 If the Pole Star is 2 3/8, it would be straight to Kander.

11 If the Pole Star is 2 1/2, it would be straight to Ambalaaveliyam.

12 If the Pole Star is 2 5/8 , it would be straight to Porokadu.

13 If the Pole Star is 2 3/4, it would be straight to Kaattoor Kadav [**Kochiar**] (Kochi).

14 If the Pole Star is 2 7/8 , it would be straight to Kochi Azhi (entrance to Kochi).

15 If the Pole Star is 3, it would be straight to Kodungallur (the old port of Cranganore). It is also suited to Kalpeni Island. The distance between the two is 12 *chaamams.* It is also suited to Suhelipar. The distance between the

two is 8 *chaamams* [**between Kalpeni and Suhelipar**].

16 If the Pole Star is 3 1/8, it would be straight to Biliyankode.

17 If the Pole Star is 3 1/4, it would be straight to Ponnani. It is also suited to Kavaratti Island. The distance between the two is 17 *chaamams*.

18 If the Pole Star is 3 3/8, it would be straight to Thanore Kadav.

19 If the Pole Star is 3 1/2, it would be straight to the tip of Challiyath (tip of Challiyath is on the right side of the entrance to Beypore). It is also suited to Andrott Island. The distance between the two is 10 *chaamams*. It is also suited to Kavaratti Pitti (Bird island of Pitti near Kavaratti).[15] The distance between the two is 8 *chaamams* (between Kavaratti and Pitti). It is also suited to Agatti Island. The distance between the two is 2 *chaamams* (between Agatti and Pitti).

20 If the Pole Star is 3 5/8, it would be straight to Korapuzha (a river in Elathur in district Calicut). It is also suited to Bangaram. The distance between the two is 19 *chaamams* (between Bangaram and Korapuzha) [**Korepera**].

21 If the Pole Star is 3 3/4, it would be straight to Kurichikadav. It is also suited to Vellimankallu (Vellimankallu is a silvery rock shaped like a deer. A lighthouse is indicative of this point). The distance between the two is one *chaamam*. It is also suited to the submerged reef of Ezhikalpeni. The distance between the two is 6 *chaamams*. It is also suited to the tip of Pallicheri in Amini. The distance between the two is 8 *chaamams*. It is also suited to Peremulpar. The distance between the two is 5 *chaamams* [**Kurachikadave near Bellivangal close to Mahe**].

22 If the Pole Star is 3 7/8, it would be straight to Pampan Thuruthi. It is also suited to Annakkandam in Kadunga Mangalam (Kadmat Island). The distance between the two is 14 *chaamams*.

23 If the Pole Star is 4, it would be straight to Nayaka Madam. It is also suited to Kiltan Island. The distance between the two is 12 *chaamams*. It is also suited to Bitra Par. The distance between the two is 6 *chaamams* [**Nayakmadam** (in Vallapatanam), **from Kiltan to Bitrapar is 8 chaamams**].

24 If the Pole Star is 4 1/8, it would be straight to Ezhimala. It is also suited to Chetlat island. The distance between the two is 14 *chaamams*. It is also suited to the north end of Cheriya Panniyam Par. The distance between the two is 6 *chaamams*.

25 If the Pole Star is 4 1/4, it would be straight to Neechuram Nidiya Maram.[16]

26 If the Pole Star is 4 3/8, it would be straight to Kaanchirakode (Kasargod).

Fig. 22.

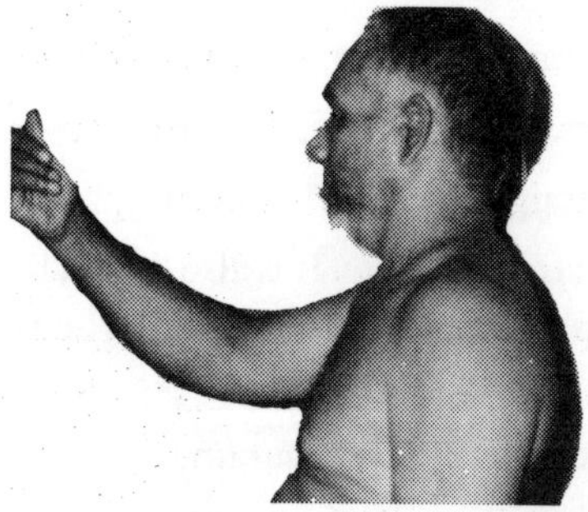

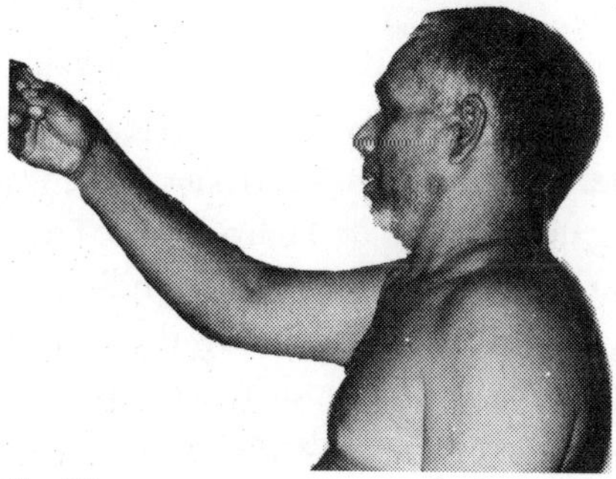

Fig. 23.

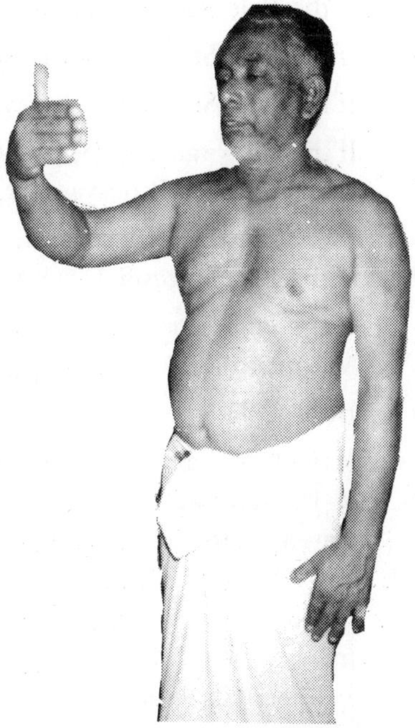

Fig. 24.

Figs. 22-24 illustrate the method of finger measurment which is also called *viral kanakku*. According to Kunhikunhi Malmi, the central point of body alignment is mid-chest. The arm is stretched out 2 1/2 spans from this point. The measurement starts with the little finger which is aligned against the horizon. Such finger measurements are also used in boat carpentry. See Figs. 25, 26.

Fig. 25. In the sewn-plank boat building tradition of Lakshadweep, after the keel has been laid, the lines along which holes for sewing will be drilled follow a two-finger width alignment from each edge of the keel plank.

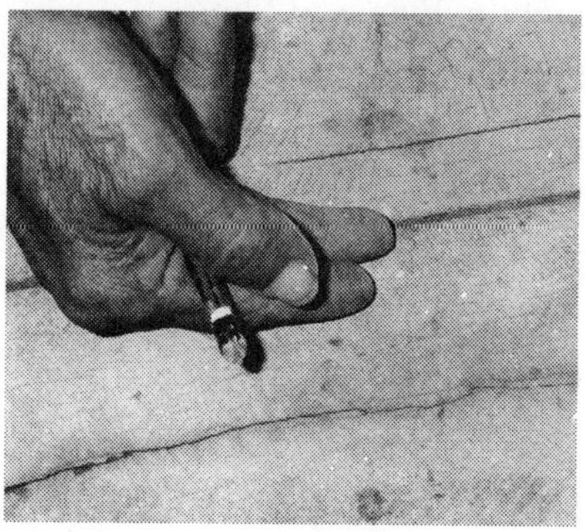

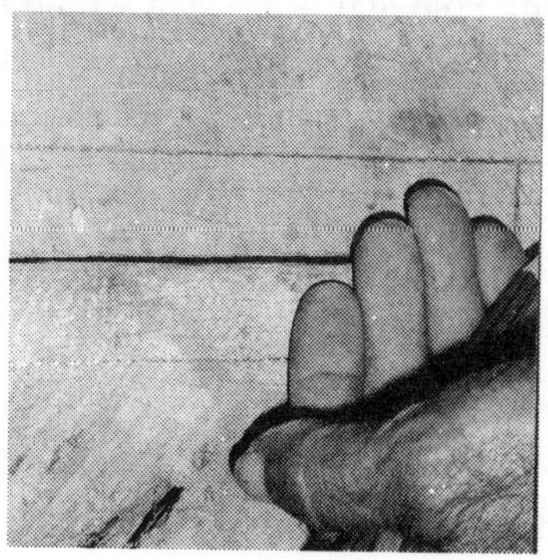

Fig. 26. In sewn boat carpentry the stitching is spaced by a four-finger unit.

27 If the Pole Star is 4 1/2, it would be straight to Kumbala Maishuram.[17]

28 If the Pole Star is 4 5/8, it would be straight to Mangalore Bundar.

29 If the Pole Star is 4 3/4, it would be straight to Alamaanpatty.

30 If the Pole Star is 4 7/8, it would be straight to south of Kattippadi.

31 If the Pole Star is 5, it would be straight to Bakanore. It is also suited to the north ofValiya Panniyampar [**Balliyapaiyampar**]. The distance between the two is 20 *chaamams*.

32 If the Pole Star is 5 1/8, it would be straight to Bairapuram.

33 If the Pole Star is 5 1/4, it would be straight to Byndoor Mala (Byndoor Mountain).

34 If the Pole Star is 5 3/8, it would be stright to Battakulam (Bhatkal).

35 If the Pole Star is 5 1/2, it would be straight to Kayakkanni. It is also suited to Baliyanithiriya. The distance between the two is 2 *chaamams*. It is also suited to the northern tip of Manjalpar (Bassas de Pedro Bank). The distance between the two is 16 *chaamams* (18 ***chaamams***). An indication of this place is its yellow colour. Many sea snakes including the Valamalisa (may be seen). The area which is 12 *pagam* in depth is seen as white.[18] White birds, reddish fish and sharks, assorted birds including kites and other tiny creatures (may be noticed). If all these things are found (the area must be) Kora Dweep otherwise known as the hazardous Manjalpar. From this point steer the boat more towards the right. It is well known that if the wooden craft is steered more to the left from this point it will be run into the reef[19] [**From Manjalpar you must sail to the northern side. If you sail to the southern side you will be wrecked as there are heavy rocks there**].

36 If the Pole Star is 5 5/8, it would be straight to the business centre of Ponnapuram Pandishai.

37 If the Pole Star is 5 3/4, it would be straight to Kumutta (Kumta).

38 If the Pole Star is 5 7/8, it would be straight to the tip of Uppala.

39 If the Pole Star is 6, it would be straight to the tip of Ancham Dweep (Anjediv).

40 If the Pole Star is 6 1/8, it would be straight to the tip of Panikada.

41 if the Pole Star is 6 3/8, it would be straight to Chadibala.

42 If the Pole Star is 6 1/2, it would be straight to Santhavoor in Goa.

43 If the Pole Star is 6 5/8, it would be straight to Maniyarapetta.

44 If the Pole Star is 6 3/4, it would be straight to the entrance of Bandey.

45 If the Pole Star is 7, it would be straight to Thonda Bashakkallu.

46 If the Pole Star is 7 1/4, it would be straight to Mallundi (Malvan).

47 If Pole Star is 7 3/8, it would be straight to Ashra.

48 If the Pole Star is 7 1/2, it would be straight to Karapattanachi (Kharapatan).

49 If the Pole Star is 7 5/8, it would be straight to Chaithavoor (Jaitapur).

50 If the Pole Star is 7 3/4, it would be straight to Ibrahim Pattanashi (Ibrahimpatan).

51 If the Pole Star is 7 7/8, it would be straight to Chankapuram.

52 If the Pole Star is 8, it would be straight to Mirya (Ratnagiri).

53 If the Pole Star is 8 1/4, it would be straight to Davool (Dabhol).

54 If the Pole Star is 8 3/8, it would be straight to Kelashi.

55 If the Pole Star is 8 1/2, it would be straight to Thandavallam (Janjira).

56 If the Pole Star is 8 5/8, it would be straight to the entrance to Chovvil (Chaul).

57 If the Pole Star is 8 3/4, it would be straight to Kandaer (Khanderi).

58 If the Pole Star is 9, it would be straight to Mayambi (Mahim).

59 If the Pole Star is 9 1/8, it would be straight to Bashai (Vasai).

60 If the Pole Star is 9 1/2, fingers it would be straight to Ulakkamala (Ulakka mountain, Pyramid Hill, Dangs).

61 If the Pole Star is 10, it would be straight to Daphani (Dahanu). It is also suited to Baharadiya. The distance between the two is 2 *chaamams*. It is also suited to Madamatti. The distance between the two is 6 *chaamams*.

62 If the Pole Star is 10 1/4, it would be straight to the island of Balashadikeni.

63 If the Pole Star is 10 1/2, it would be straight to the port of Surat.

64 If the Pole Star is 10 3/4, it would be straight to Kobari.

65 If the Pole Star is 11, it would be straight to Kampayath (Khambat).

66 If the Pole Star is 11 1/4, it would be straight to the port of Karachi.[20]

67 If the Pole Star is 10 1/2, it would be straight to Mambaai.

68 If the Pole Star is 10 1/4, it would be straight to Samathapattanam (Somnath Patan).

69 If the Pole Star is 10 1/8, it would be straight to the minaret of Dweepsha Munaram.

70 If the Pole Star is 10 1/4, it would be straight to Choratti Mangalore Pattanam.

71 If the Pole Star is 10 1/2, it would be straight to Koormiya.

72 If the Pole Star is 11, it would be straight to Jiham. It is suited to Sir Andamala (a mountain). The distance between the two is 40 *chaamams*.

It is also suited to Kaaba (Mecca). The distance between the two is 92 *chaamams.*[21]

73 If the Pole Star is 12, it would be straight to Sindu.

74 If the Pole Star is 12 1/2, it would be straight to Baja (Chach Bahar, Iran).

75 If the Pole Star is 13, it would be straight to Sharshasha (Sharjah).

76 If the Pole Star is 13 1/2, it would be straight to Komubaraa.

77 If the Pole Star is 14, it would be straight to the Port of Urmoos. It is also suited to Katheeb Bahrain. There is a small island in the centre of the two places.

Ameen

[10] *This table relates the altitude of the Pole Star to the latitude of ports mentioned. While navigating at sea and observing the altitude of the Pole Star using the technique of finger measurement, the contents of this table provided the mariner the latitudinal component of the position of his vessel. The position was related to other known sites and landmarks lying directly east and west in respect to the vessel. Distances between these positions was given in terms of* ***chaamams*** *(RBJ). The Pole Star is referred to as* ***Kou****. Prinsep (1836, 793) noted that the Maldivian term for Pole Star was* ***ghao****. The late Sayyid Sheikh Koya, a student of Kunnankalam Muthu Koya Thangal of Andrott, recited his version of* ***kou kanakku*** *to the Editor on 7 February 1989. His rendering has been indicated in "bold script" and has been placed within brackets in the above text. N. Muthukoya (Muthukoya, 1986, 38-42), quotes a similar table used by Lakshadweep sailors. Variations exist but are of a minor nature. This table of Pole Star altitude is called* ***Kou Kannaku*** *in Lakshadweep. The term which is used for finger is* ***viral****.* ***Viral*** *is a Tamil word. The equivalent term in Northern India would be* ***anguli****, a term used by Gujarati mariners. According to H.M. Grosset-Grange, the initial finger measurement was to be accorded a value of 2° 54', subsequent units being provided an equivalence of 1° 35'(Grosset-Grange, 1993, 22).*

[11] *Due to its low brilliance, the Pole Star was not visible to the mariner at sea when its altitude above the horizon was less than 6° to 7°. When it does become barely visible above the horizon, for which the synonym of the lotus flower has been used, the true altitude of the Pole Star is approximately 6° to 7°. According to # 1,* ***Section 6****, Periya Ballikamam in Sri Lanka and the point, north Mahal Bada Thalam (Maldives) are located within these latitudes. In modern times places which can be located within these latitudes are Colombo (6° 57' N) in Sri Lanka and North Thilathumathee in the Maldives. It is, therefore, proposed that the latitudes of the two positions given in # 1 is 6° 57' N. This latitudinal line is, therefore, taken as the zero line for measuring Pole Star altitudes and thus finding the latitude of the vessel at sea. This table is then used to relate the vessel's position to the nearest coast along the latitude and obtaining the linear distance to that part of the coastline (RBJ). In actual sailings a number of stars, other than the Pole Star, in rising or setting positions, were also used. These are listed in* ***Sections 7****,* ***8****,* ***9*** *and* ***10****.*

[12] *The* ***chaamam*** *may be taken as the Lakshadweep variant of the Arabic* ***zam****, taken as a unit in linear distance and accorded an equivalence of twelve miles. Cf. n. 2 above.*

[13] *For a description of finger measurements see de Saussure, 1928(b), 156-158; de Morais, 1960, 8-9; Luciano Pereira da Silva, 1946, 39; Fatimi, 1996, 283-284;* ***Grosset-Grange****, 27-78.*

These texts do not, however, demonstrate the process of measuring star altitude in terms of finger widths. (See illustrations, Saussure in Ferrand 1928, Fig. 22, 162; Grosset-Grange, in ***Grosset-Grange****, 6th part, Fig. 16) Figures 11-13 show how the fingers are aligned against the horizon to reach the level of the star being measured. The tip of the nose, taken as the central indicator of the face, constitutes the nodal point of measurement. The thumb is placed on the nose while the fore finger is stretched out. The star level is taken with the laterally placed finger/fingers positioned above the fore finger. The three points of reference are thus the nose, the horizon and the Pole Star. The* ***kamal*** *evolved as a refinement of this finger method of measuring star altitude.*

14 *For* ***viral*** *measurement demonstrated by Kunhikunhi Malmi see Figs. 22-24. In this text the word* ***viral****, denoting finger, is absent after the measurement of three-quarter of a finger is reached. Atta Koya Thangal is of the view that the absence of the word,* ***viral****, in the remaining portion of the text follows a literary convention by which undue repetition is avoided. The Editor, however, would like to propose that after the three-quarter finger unit, recourse was possibly taken to the instrument, the* ***kamal****. Measurements, however, could have been still taken by hand. Cf. Almeida, 1995, Fig. 32.*

15 *Pitti, near Kavaratti, is also called Bird Island, because its sole inhabitants are birds, the terns and noddies. Another island, also called Pitti, is located near Kalpeni.*

16 *Nidiya Maram refers to a tree which serves as a location marker (AKT).*

17 *Kumbala is the name of a village in Maishuram (AKT).*

18 *1* ***pagam*** *= 5 ft. The fathom has an equivalence of 6 ft. The light-coloured sandy seabed imparts its colour to the sea above it providing it with a whitish appearance. These waters are shallow.*

19 *It is because of the presence of such reefs and shoals that day-time sailing is preferred in the indigenous tradition. Europeans found it difficult to comprehend this factor.*

20 *After Karachi there would be a dip southwards in the route since the southern coast of Arabia had to be traversed if the destination were to be Mecca.*

21 *There is a steady progression in terms of finger measurements upto # 66. Between numbers 67 to 71 there is a fall to the 10 finger range. Number 72, at eleven fingers is followed by number 73 at twelve fingers. Moreover, both Surat, # 63, and Mambaai, # 67, are accorded the same Pole Star elevation. Since shoreline silhouettes and specific landmarks were also known, the experienced navigator could fashion his own adjustments to reach the port of his choice. It would appear that the vessel made a detour on reaching Karachi prior to proceeding to Hormuz and then to Bahrain.*

(7) LIE OF THE LAND
(Position of Places on the Coastline)

Sri Lanka to Kanyakumari:
From Elanadu (Sri Lanka)[22] to Kumari (Kanya Kumari) the measurement is 1 1/2 *nilam*[23] and it (Kanya Kumari) lies (in a) north-westerly direction.

Kanyakumari to South Kollam:
From Kumari to South Kollam the measurement is 1/2 *nilam* (which is) one *chaamam* above the setting point of *Kasal.*[24]

South Kollam to Mayambi:
From South Kollam to Mayambi (Mahim) the measurement is 7 *nilam* which (Mayambi) lies in the direction of the setting point of *Naasi.*

Mayambi to Jiham:
From Mayambi to Jiham the measurement is 2 *nilam* which (Jiham) lies at the setting point of *Ayyook.*

Jiham to Sindu:
From Jiham to Sindu the measurement is 1 *nilam*, which (Sindu) lies in the direction of the setting point of *Chothi.*

Sindu to Sharshasha:
From Sindu to Sharshasha the measurement is 1 *nilam* which (Sharshasa) lies in the direction of the setting point of *Kaarthika.*

Shershasha to Komubaaraa:
From Sharshasa to Komubaaraa the measurement is 1/2 *nilam* which lies in the direction of the setting point of *Kasal.*

Komubaaraa to Urmoos Bundar:
From Komubaaraa to Urmoos port the measurement is 1/2 *nilam* which (Urmoos) lies in the direction of the setting point of *Naasi.*

Ameen

[22] *The term used for* ***lie of the land*** *is* ***Karavasala****. The point of reference is Periya Ballikamam in Sri Lanka. According to Atta Koya Thangal Periya Ballikamam could perhaps be associated with Kandy, 7° 18' N. Cf.* ***Section 6****, n.11. Captain R.B. Jayaram notes that this table gives the difference in latitude in terms of* ***nilam (1 nilam*** *= 1° 36'), as well as the direction between different places.*

[23] *This table, involving North-South / South-North corrections,* ***tirfa****, in Arabic texts, is called* ***Kou Nila*** *in Lakshadweep.* ***Section 6*** *gives tables for east-west, west-east sailings in terms of longitudinal arc distances,* ***chaamams****. In such straight courses along the same latitude there is no difference in the height of* ***Kou****. In* ***Section 7*** *the longitudinal run is not in terms running down the latitude but in north-south or south-north directional shifts. These are marked in terms of changes in Pole Star altitude noted in* ***nilam****. This becomes evident in the correlations between* ***Section 7*** *and relevant portions of* ***Section 6****. In* ***Section 6*** *(1) at Periya Ballikamam in Sri Lanka Pole Star elevation is taken as zero. From this in (6) it rises to1 1/2 fingers at Kumari. In* ***Section 7****, Sri Lanka to Kanyakumari, the rise in elevation,* ***nilam****, in a north-westerly direction, is 1 1/2 . Here* ***nilam*** *takes the place of* ***viral****. In the section, Kanyakumari to South Kollam in* ***Section 7****, the difference is 1/2* ***nilam****. In* ***Section 6****, the difference in finger measurement elevation of the Pole Star between (6) and (8) is 1/2 finger. In* ***Section 7*** *direction is given in* ***chaamam*** *at the setting point of* ***Kasal.*** *Here* ***chaamam****, synonymous with the Arabic,* ***zam****, is taken in the sense of longitudinal alignement. In this way all the places in* ***Section 7*** *may be found listed in* ***Section 6****.*

[24] *The setting position of the star mentioned is referred to as* ***asthamanam*** *in the Malayalam text.*

(8) NAMES OF *MUJIRAS*[25]

Kou, Farakaden, Naasi, Nakha, Ayyook, Kasal, Chimak, Thurayya, Murug, Jousa, Seer, Aqrab, Khalb, Himaren, Chilli, Sullavar and *Suhail*[26]

[25] *The equivalent term in Arab navigation was* ***majra***. ***Majra*** *was taken in the sense of the course of sailing or the bearings taken. Refer to* **Section 10**, *note 30.*

[26] *Cf.* **Section 5**, *n.9, and* **Section 10**. *See also Tolmacheva, 1977, 1-43. The list of* ***mujiras*** *may be compared with that compiled by Custádio de Morais based on G. Ferrand and other sources (see de Morais, 1960, 25). The stars listed by de Morais comprise:*

Star	*Name*	*Constellation*
Farkad	*Guards*	β γ *Ursae Minoris*
Nach		β δ *Ursae Majoris*
Nakaht		*Cassiopia*
Aiiuk	*Capela*	α *Aurigae*
Vaki	*Vega*	α *Lyrae*
Simak	*Arcturus*	α *Bootis*
Suraia	*Pleiades*	η *Tauri*
Tair	*Altair*	α *Aquilae*
Djuza	*Riegel*	β *Orionis*
Tir	*Sirius*	α *Canis Majoris*
Iklil		β ∂ *Scorpionis*
Akrab	*Antares*	α *Scorpionis*
Himarin	*Dois Burros*	α β *Gruis*
Suhail	*Canopus*	α *Argus*
Salabar	*Achernar*	α *Eridani*

This comprises a total of fifteen stars.

Wind directions are linked with ***mujira*** *stars despite occasional deviations caused by temporary disturbances. Thus:*

Medam *and* ***Edavam*** *(half)*	*Wind remains at the setting point of* ***Chothi***
Edavam *(half) and* ***Mithunam,***	
Karkidakam *and* ***Chingam***	*Wind remains at the setting point of* ***Aqrab***
Kanni *and* ***Thulaam***	*Wind is at the setting point of* ***Naasi.***
Vrischikam	*Wind is at the rising point of* ***Ayook***

During the months of ***Dhanu****,* ***Makaram****,* ***Kumbam****, and* ***Meenam****, the wind blows from a northerly direction (AKT and MM). Cf. Tolmacheva, 1977, Figs.1, 2. According to A. Haji Kidave, Agatti, the following rising positions are taken in sailing: from Agatti to Calicut, star* ***Seer****; from Calicut to Agatti, star* ***Murug****; from Agatti to Chetlat, star* ***Eravathi****; Agatti to Kilton, star* ***Kasal****. On the return journey the setting points of the same group of stars are used. Positions can also be calculated on the basis of points at which the sun rises.*

(9) *KANAKKU* OF DISTANCES BETWEEN TWO POINTS IN *CHAAMAMS*[27]

(Table Showing Advance Made towards Mainland in *Chaamams*)

		(*Chaamam*)
(Downwards from *Naasi*)		
(Islands to Mainland)		
	Naasi to *Farakaden*	2
	Farakaden to *Kou*	2
	Kou to *Naasi*	2
	Naasi to *Nakha*	2
	Nakha to *Ayyook*	2
	Ayyook to *Kasal*	3
	Kasal to *Chimak*	5
	Chimak to *Thurayya*	16
	The middle of *Thurayya*	
	(to the middle of) *Murug*	32
	3/4th of the distance between	
	Thurayya and *Murug*	64
	7/8th the distance between	
	Thurayya and *Murug*	128
	15/16th of the distance between	
	Thurayya and *Murug*	256
	1/16th nearer to *Murug*	512
(Upwards from *Naasi*)		
(Mainland to Islands)		
	Naasi to *Nakha*	2
	Nakha to *Ayyook*	2
	Ayyook to *Kasal*	3
	Kasal to *Chimak*	5
	Chimak to *Thurayya*	16
	The middle of	

Thurayya (to the middle of)	
Murug	32,64,128,256,512
(Upwards from *Chilli*)	
(Mainland to Islands)	
Chilli to *Sullavar*	2
Sullavar to *Suhail*	2
Suhail to *Sullavar*	2
Sullavar to *Chilli*	2
Chilli to *Himaren*	2
Himaren to *Khalb*	2
Khalb to *Aqrab*	3
Aqrab to *Seer*	5
Seer to *Jousa*	16
The middle of *Jousa*	
(to the middle of)	
Murug	32,64,128,256,512

(Downwards from *Chilli*)	
(Islands to Mainland)	
Chilli to *Himaren*	2
Himaren to *Khalb*	2
Khalb to *Aqrab*	3
Aqrab to *Seer*	5
Seer to *Jousa*	16
The middle of *Jousa*	
(to the middle of)	
Murug	32,64,128,256,512[28]

Ameen

27 *This* ***chaamam*** *is to be taken as linear distance in terms of longitude deviation. Cf.* ***masafat****, the course between the meridian and distances east or west, Grosset-Grange, 1996, 218. The progression in all these tables up to the point at which the number 16 is reached are visually represented in the fourth segment of* ***Section 2, Composite Circular Compass****, counting inwards*

*from the outer segment (ATK). In the above table, (**Downwards from Naasi**), the counting, in terms of the **Composite Circular Compass** is taken from North to East. The term (**Downward**) is indicative of a sailing from the islands to the mainland. Since the alignment in sailing is in terms of the Western Indian coastline, the table starts, not from **Kou** but from the setting point of **Naasi**, equal to point 337 in the circular chart. **Murug** refers directly to the East. According to Captain R.B. Jayaram, this table shows the advance made in **chaamam** for a change of Pole Star altitude of one finger (see **Section 10**), equal to 100 miles, when sailings are undertaken in various directions as tabulated. The total advance is obtained by summing up all the values tabulated in **chaamam** from the top (**Naasi** to **Farakden**) up to the actual direction in which sailing was being undertaken.*

[28] *The numbers 32, 64, 128, 256, 512 are indicative of the graduated distance starting from the middle and moving through 3/4, 7/8, 15/16 and 1/6 between **Thurayya** and **Murug**, and the same gradation starting from the middle point between **Jousa** and **Murug** in the tables. Grosset-Grange has noted that with a good breeze, if there is a change in latitude by 8 **zam**, star elevation will change by one finger, equal to about four knots in speed. In 24 hours, 100 nautical miles on the route will equal the difference of one finger and a distance-time of 8 **zam**, each **zam** having a unit value of three hours (Grosset-Grange, 1993, 19). The table given by de Saussure reads: 1 **Isba** = 1° 37' = 97 nautical miles = 1 **tirfa** = 8 **zam** (unit of space) = 24 hours. (Saussure, 1928b, 153 and note 1). According to Kunhikunhi Malmi, 1 **darja** = 60 miles, 1 **daqiq** = 1 mile, 60 **daqiq** = 1 **darja**.*

(10) *KANAKKU* OF PROGRESSION[29]

1 If a journey is in the direction of *Kou* (Pole Star), for eight *chaamams*, *Kou* (the height of the Pole Star) is increased by one, and (the vessel) goes closer to the mainland by 4 *chaamams*.

2 If a journey is in the direction of *Farakaden* (east) for 10 *chaamams*, *Kou* is increased by one and (the vessel) goes closer to the mainland by 6 *chaamams*.

3 If a journey is in the direction of *Naasi* (east) for 12 *chaamams*, *Kou* is increased by one and the vessel goes closer to the mainland by 8 *chaamams*.

4 If a journey is in the direction of *Nakha* (east) for 14 *chaamams*, *Kou* is increased by one and the vessel goes closer to the mainland by 12 *chaamams*.

5 If a journey is in the direction of *Ayyook* (east) for 16 *chaamams*, *Kou* is increased by one and the vessel goes closer to the mainland by 12 *chaamams*.

6 If a journey is in the direction of *Kasal* (east) for 19 *chaamams*, *Kou* is increased by one and the vessal goes closer to the mainland by 15 *chaamams*.

7 If a journey is in the direction of *Chimak* (east) for 24 *chaamams*, *Kou* is increased by one and the vessel goes closer to the mainland by 20 *chaamams*.

8 If a journey is in the direction of *Thurayya* (east) for 40 *chaamams*, *Kou* is increased by one and the vessel goes closer to the mainland by 36 *chaamams*.

9 If a journey is in the direction of *Murug* (east) for 20 *chaamams*, *Kou* will not increase or decrease and (there is no gain) in the distance travelled.

10 If a journey is in the direction of *Jousa* (east) for 40 *chaamams*, *Kou* is reduced by one and the vessel goes closer to the mainland by 28 *chaamams*.

11 If a journey is in the direction of *Seer* (east) for 24 *chaamams*, *Kou* is reduced by one and the vessel goes closer to the mainland by 12 *chaamams*.

12 If a journey is in the direction of *Aqrab* (east) for 19 *chaamams*, *Kou* is reduced by one and the vessel goes closer to the mainland by 7 *chaamams*.

13 If a journey is in the direction of *Khalb* (east) for 16 *chaamams*, *Kou* is reduced by one and the vessel goes closer to the mainland by 4 *chaamams*.

14 If a journey is in the direction of *Himaren* (east) for 14 *chaamams*, *Kou* is reduced by one and the vessel goes closer to the mainland by 2 *chaamams*.

15 If a journey is in the direction of *Chilli* (east) for 12 *chaamams*, *Kou* is not reduced. The mainland neither comes closer nor recedes. (There is no gain) in the distance travelled.

16 If a journey is in the direction of *Sullavar* (east) for ten *chaamams*, *Kou* is reduced by one and the vessel goes away from the mainland by two *chaamams*.

17 If a journey is in thedirection of *Suhail* (east) for 8 *chaamams*, *Kou* is reduced by one and the vessel goes away from the mainland by 4 *chaamams*.

18 If a journey is in the direction of *Sullavar* (west) for 10 *chaamams*, *Kou* is reduced by one and the vessel goes away from the mainland by 6 *chaamams*.

19 If a journey is in the direction of *Chilli* (west) for 12 *chaamams*, *Kou* is reduced by one and the vessel goes away from the mainland by 8 *chaamams*.

20 If a journey is in the direction of *Himaren* (west) for 14 *chaamams*, *Kou* is reduced by one and the vessel goes away from the mainland by 10 *chaamams*.

21 If a journey is in the direction of *Khalb* (west) for 16 *chaamams*, *Kou* is reduced by one and the vessel goes away from the mainland by 12 *chaamams*.

22 If a journey is in the direction of *Aqrab* (west) for 19 *chaamams*, *Kou* is reduced by one and the vessel goes away from the mainland by 15 *chaamams*.

23 If a journey is in the direction of *Seer* (west) for 24 *chaamams*, *Kou* is reduced by one and the vessel goes away from the mainland by 20 *chaamams*.

24 If a journey is in the direction of *Jousa* (west) for 40 *chaamams*, *Kou* is reduced by one and the vessel goes away from the mainland by 36 *chaamams*.

25 If a journey is in the direction of *Murug* (west) for 20 *chaamams*, *Kou* neither increases nor decreases. (There is no gain) in the distance travelled.

26 If a journey is in the direction of *Thurayya* (west) for 40 *chaamams*, *Kou* is increased by one and the vessel goes away from the mainland by 28 *chaamams*.

27 If a journey is in the direction of *Chimak* (west) for 24 *chaamams*, *Kou* is increased by one and the vessel goes away from the mainland by 12 *chaamams*.

28 If a journey is in the direction of *Kasal* (west) for 19 *chaamams*, *Kou* is increased by one and the vessel goes away from the mainland by 7 *chaamams*.

29 If a journey is in the direction of *Ayyook* (west) for 16 *chaamams*, *Kou* is increased by one and the vessel goes away from the mainland by 4 *chaamams*.

30 If a journey is in the direction of *Nakha* (west) for 14 *chaamams*, *Kou* is increased by one and the vessel goes away from the mainland by 2 *chaamams*.

31 If a journey is in the direction of *Naasi* (west) for 12 *chaamams*, *Kou* will not increase.The mainland neither comes closer nor recedes. (There is no gain) in the distance travelled.

32 If journey is in the direction of *Farakaden* (west) for 10 *chaamams*, *Kou* is increased by one and the vessel goes closer to the mainland by 2 *chaamams*.[30]

Ameen

[29] *The Malayalam heading reads* ***Anavetti Kanakku****. According to Kunhikunhi Malmi the term,* ***Anavetti Kanakku****, included both longitudinal adjustments* ***(tirfat)*** *as well as corrections through dead reckoning. The decreasing dimensions in circles of latitude gave rise to these calculations of* ***tirfat*** *(see de Saussure, 1928b, 173; Tibbetts, 1971, 301). Kunhikunhi Malmi gives an equivalance of 100 miles for 1* ***Kou****. Cf.* ***Section 9****, n.28. If the sailing is oblique rather than directly latitudinal, sailing distance to the mainland is proportionately reduced. The west coast of India from Kollam/ Quilon in Kerala to Bombay is found to lie in the direction of the rising point of* ***Chilli****, and the setting point of* ***Naasi*** *respectively. Any journey performed in the direction of the setting point of* ***Naasi*** *is taken as zero point for purposes of undertaking a voyage from the islands towards India (see* ***Section 2****,* ***Composite Circular Compass****, point 31, and # 31 in* ***Section 10****. See also Fig. 27. If the sailing is from* ***Farakaden*** *(point 32 in the* ***Composite Circular Compass****), the vessel would approach closer to the mainland by two* ***chaamams****, 2 × 12 = 24 miles. This is also the meaning to be assigned to # 32 in* ***Section 10****. The meaning to be given to # 8 of* ***Section 10*** *is that if the vessel is proceeding in the direction of* ***Thurayya****, almost directly to the east, it will advance by 2+2+2+2+2+2+3+5+16 (36)* ***chaamams*** *(AKT, MM). Captain R.B. Jayaram has clarified that the table shows the distance required to be covered at an average vessel speed of four knots along various directions as shown, to achieve change of Pole Star altitude (i.e. latitude) by one finger. The total advance towards the destination is also shown. Cf.* ***Section 9****, n. 27.*

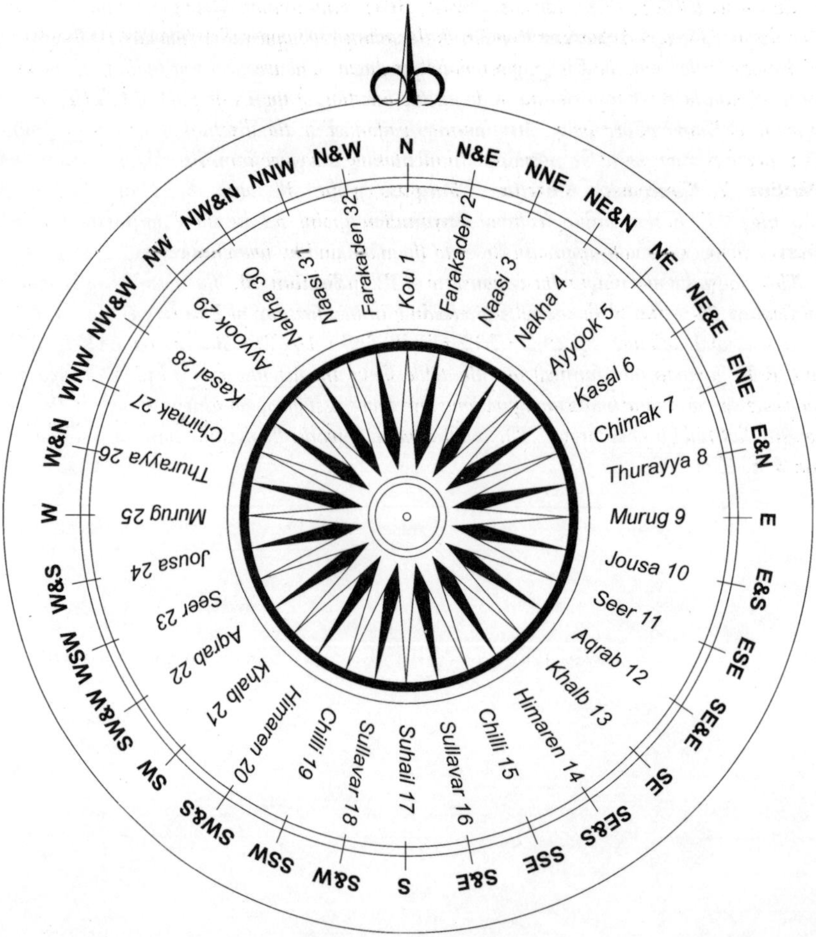

Fig. 27. Compass directions of 16 star clusters starting from the North, indicated by the Pole Star (*Kou*) (AKB).

30 *Figure 27 gives the compass directions of 16 star clusters from the North indicated by the Pole Star (**Kou**). The use of star rhumbs is mentioned in Arabic texts starting as early as the 10th century (Saussure, 1928a, 119-122; Tibbetts, 1971, 296). The complete set contains 32 rhumbs of which the north and south pole rhumbs are named after **Kou** and **Suhail** (Canopus) respectively. Apart from these two points, the rising and setting positions of an additional 15 directional stars are indicated, thus making up a total of 32 stellar derived rhumbs. (AKB)*

(11) THE CIRCULAR MOTION[31] OF THE SUN

The sun sojourns in the northern hemisphere for six months and then in the southern hemisphere for the next six months every year. He stays in the northern hemisphere in April, May, June, July, August and September, and in the southern hemisphere in October, November, December, January, February and March. The sun rises and sets exactly on the equator twice in a year. This happens on the twenty-first day of March and the twenty-first day of September.[32]

The journey towards the north (from the equator) starts every year on the twenty-first day of March and that journey continues up to the twenty-first day of June, when the sun would be at a place 23 1/2° north of the equator. Then he turns towards the south. On the twenty-first day of September, the sun reaches the equator and continues (the journey) to the south. He reaches the maximum distance in the south on the twenty-first day of December, when he will be at 23 1/2° south of the equator. He then turns towards the north and reaches the equator to further continue the above cycle of journey.

Ameen

[31] *The term used in the Malayalam text is **Vakragati**.*

[32] *Autumnal equinox actually occurs on 23 September.*

(12) MOTION[33] OF THE SUN

At the beginning of the month of *Hamal/ Medam*, the sun will be at the position of the star *Murug* (east point, when day and night are of equal duration). During the month of *Daur/ Edavam*, the sun will be at the position of the star *Kaarthika*. During the month of *Jousa/ Mithunam*, the sun would be at the position of the star *Chothi*. During the month of *Sharthan/ Karkidakam*, it returns to the position of *Chothi* (the longest day). During the month of *Asad/ Chingam*, it will be at the position of the star *Kaarthika*. During the month of *Sumbul/ Kanni*, it would be at the position of the star *Murug* (west point, day and night are of equal duration). During the month of *Meezaan/ Thulaam*, it will be at the position of *Makeram*. During the month of *Aqrab/ Vrischikam*, it will be at the position of *Seer*. During the month of *Qouz/ Dhanu*, it will be at the position of *Aqrab*. During the month *Jadin/ Makaram*, it returns to the position of *Aqrab*. During the month of *Dalb/ Kumbam*, it would be at the position of *Seer*. During the month of *Hooth/ Meenam*, it would be at the position of *Makeram*.[34]

Ameen

[33] *The term used in the Malayalam text is **Sooryagati**. It is to be noted that the fifth **Nakshatra** is spelt **Makeram** while the tenth sign of the zodiac is written as **Makaram**.*

[34] *See **Section 13**, n. 35.*

(13) (RATE OF CHANGE OF SUN'S DECLINATION)[35]

Month Name	*Daqiq* Minutes per day 1st 10 days	*Daqiq* Minutes per day 2nd 10 days	*Daqiq* Minutes per day 3rd 10 days	*Darja* Degree per month
	North	North	North	
Hamal	24	23	22	11 1/2
Daur	18	17	16	8 1/2
Jousa	8	7	6	3 1/2
	South	South	South	
Sharthan	6	4(7)	8	3 1/2
Asad	16	17	18	8 1/2
Sumbul	22	23	24	11 1/2
Meezaan	24	23	22	11 1/2
Aqrab	18	17	16	8 1/2
Qouz	8	7	6	3 1/2
	North	North	North	
Jadin	6	7	8	3 1/2
Dalb	16	17	18	8 1/2
Hooth	22	23	24	11 1/2

[35] ***Section 12*** *gives the motion of the sun on the ecliptic in its northward and southward journeys.* ***Section 13*** *has summarized this description in terms of declination deviations in degrees and minutes from the first point/day of each* ***raasi****/month. For the month of* ***Hamal/Medam****, the average movement of the sun 23' per day. The total change in declination of the sun in* ***Hamal*** *is 11° 30' and in the months of* ***Daur*** *and* ***Jousa*** *it is 8° 30' and 3° 30' respectively. Hence the maximum northerly declination is 23 1/2°, which is attained on 21 June. The sun then turns towards the south following the same sequence and reaches the equator at (W) on 23 September when the declination is 0°. It goes further south having the declination deviation 11 1/2°, 8 1/2° and 3 1/2° in the month of* ***Meezaan, Aqrab*** *and* ***Qouz****, the total being 23 1/2° towards the south from the west point (W) and reaches the south point (S) on 22 December. From (S), it takes a northward journey and reaches the equator (E) on 21 March, the declination being 0° again. Figure 28 illustrates the description given above.*

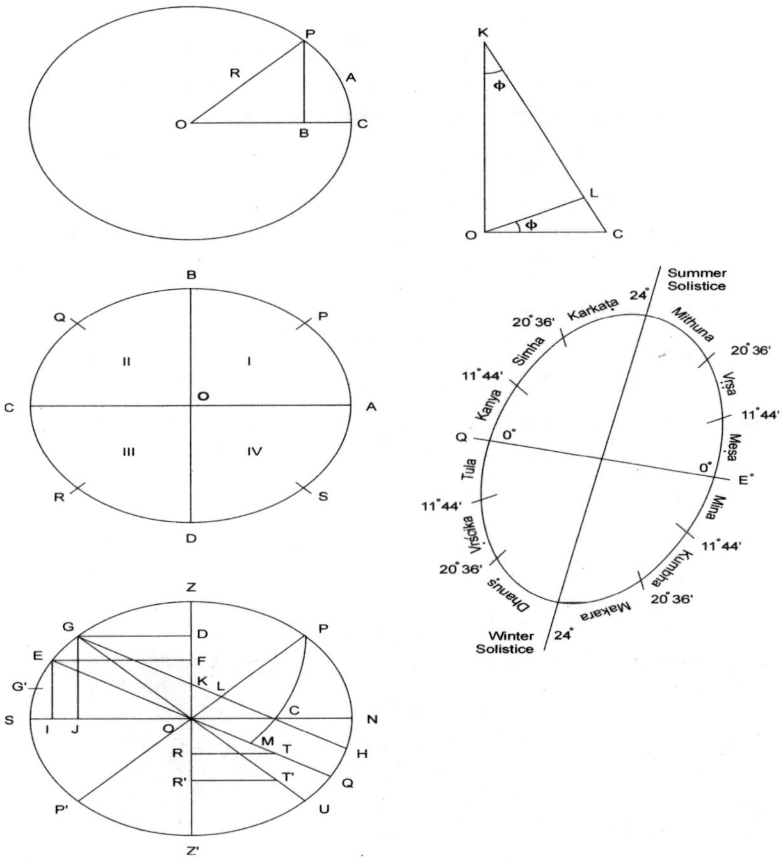

Fig. 28. Declination of the sun (AKB).
From *Hamal* (0°) to *Jousa* the Sun's declination increases from 0° to 23° 30' north (summer solstice). Between *Sharthan* and *Sumbul* the declination decreases from 23° 30' north to 0° (autumnal equinox). From *Meezan* to *Qouz* the declination increases from 0° to 23° 30' (winter solstice, *Makar Shankranti*). Between *Jadin* and *Hooth* the declination decreases from 23° 30' south to 0° (vernal equinox). Cf. Fig 7, Appendix 1.

(14) DEDUCTIONS FROM THE NOON MEASUREMENT[36]

1 If the sun is in the north of the equator and the person (in the vessel) is north to the sun, what is got as noon calculation is to be added to the calculation of the date to get the degree.

2 If the sun is in the north of the equator and the person (in the vessel) is south to the sun, what is got as noon calculation is to be subtracted from the date calculation to get the degree. This will be equal to the balance in the date calculation.

3 If the sun is above the equator and the person (in the vessel) is to the north of it, the date calculation is to be subtracted from the noon calculation to get the degree. This will be same as the noon calculation.

4 In case the sun is above the vessel, there would be no degree in the noon calculation and in case the sun is above the equator there would be no degree in the noon calculation.[37]

Ameen

29.

30.

31.

32.

33.

34.

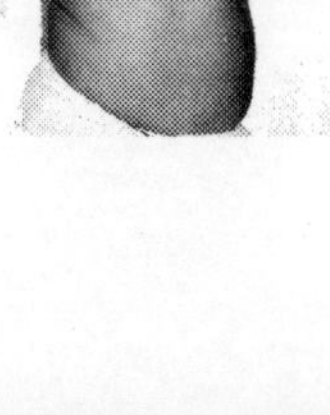

Figs. 29-34. Assessment of the altitude of the sun at noon. Kunhikunhi Malmi demonstrates how measurements are taken at sea to assess the exact moment of noon. The navigator is to take his position on the boat facing North. Fig. 29 shows the first position in body posture. Fig. 30 shows the first position of the lifted hand. In Fig. 31 care is taken to align the hand, mid torso to navel. Figs. 32, 33 show the movement of the hand reaching upwards towards the sun. Fig. 34 shows completion of this movement. If there has not been perfect body coordination the position of the sun will not coincide with the finger position in Fig. 34.

[36] *Prior to the introduction of the sextant, the* ***Kolpalagai*** *could have been used for taking these measurements.*

[37] ***Section 14*** *is difficult to comprehend. A scientific explanation is offered below.*

I. If the sun is north of the equator and the zenith of the sailing vessel lies north of the sun, what is found by adding the noon measurement (zenith distance) to the declination of the sun for the day is the latitude in degrees.

II. If the sun is north of the equator and the zenith of the sailing vessel lies south of the sun, what is found by subtracting the latitude in degrees from the declination of the sun for the day is the noon measurement (zenith distance).

III. If the sun is south of the equator and the sailing vessel lies north of the sun, the declination of the sun for the day is to be subtracted from the noon measurement (zenith distance) to get the latitude in degrees.

IV. In case, the noon sun is at zenith, the zenith distance equals zero, therefore, the latitude equals the declination of the sun. In case the noon sun is on the equator the declination is zero and, therefore, latitude equals meridian zenith distance. For details refer to Fig.35.

Let SN, EQ, Z and P be the Horizon, Equator, Zenith and Pole with reference to the observer at O. S', S", S"' are different positions of Sun. From this the following four rules emerge:

i. $ES' + S'Z = EZ = NP$
i.e. $\delta + z = \phi$, δ = *declination of sun*
z = *zenith distance, and* ϕ = *latitude of the place*

ii. *For position S"', ES" = EZ + ZS",* $\delta = \phi + z$

iii. *For position S"', ZS"'– ES"' = EZ ,* $z - \delta = \phi$

iv. *When te sun is at the zenith,* $z = 0$, $\delta = \phi$;
when the sun is at E , $\delta = 0$, *then* $z = \phi$

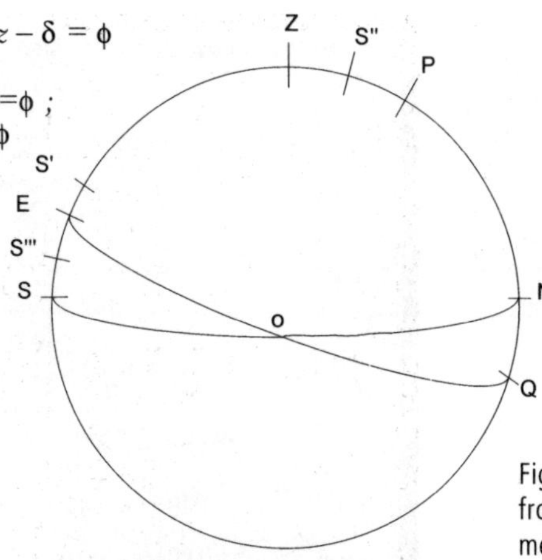

Fig. 35. Deductions from the noon measurement.

It may be noted that mid-day will be at zenith at places on 23 1/2° N latitude on 21 June, on 0° latitude on 21 March and 23 September, and on 23 1/2° S latitude on 22 December (AKB). Atta Koya Thangal has noted that whereas ***Section 14*** *is related to position finding at sea, the utility of* ***Section 78*** *below,* ***Knowing the date from the Noon Measurement****, is related to the fixation of* ***Muhurtham****, auspicious moment, for domestic activities.*

(15) NAMES OF THE *SAAYATH*

Shams, *Zuhra*, *Athaarid*, *Qamar*, *Suhal*, *Musthari* and *Mirreq*[38]

Ameen

[38] *See* ***Section 18**, n. 41.*

(16) NAMES OF THE *NAKSHATRAS*[39]

Aswathi, Bharani, Kaarthika, Rohini, Makeram, Thiruvaathira, Punatham, Pooyam, Aayilyam, Maham, Pooram, Uththiram, Artham, Chiththira, Chothi, Visaakam, Anizham, Tirkettam, Moolam, Pooraadam, Uththiraadam, Thiruvonam, Avittam, Chathayam, Poorapuraththaathiri, Uththiraththaathiri, Eravathi

Ameen

[39] *In view of the fact that there is a concordance between lunar mansions as recorded in SS VIII, 2-21, Arabic* ***manzil*** *(Saussure, 1928b, 145-146),* ***Jazira*** *Arabic equivalents in Lakshadweep, twenty-seven* ***nakshatras*** *in Malayalam usage (see also* ***Section 17*** *and note), and the twenty-seven asterisms in the Maldives-Minicoy* ***Nakaiy*** *calendar (Fig.36), the following table of concordance has been prepared:*

Fig. 36.
Nakaiy calendar.
Printed in Male,
Maldives.
Averhuge,
Community Hall.
Falessery, Minicoy.

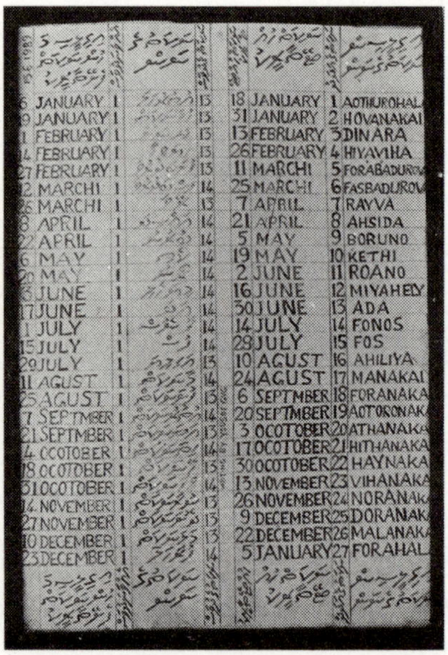

LUNAR MANSIONS

No.	**Sanskrit**	*Arabic*	***Jazira*** *Arabic*	**Nakaiy** *Maldives-Minicoy*
1	**Asvini**	**As-saratayn**	**Sharthan**	**Assidha**
2	**Bharani**	**Al-butayn**	**Batheen**	**Burunu**
3	**Krttika**	**At-turayya**	**Thuraya**	**Kethi**
4	**Rohini**	**Ad-dabaran**	**Dabran**	**Roanu**
5	**Mrgasira**	**Al-haka**	**Haqath**	**Miahelia**
6	**Ardra**	**Al-han[c]a**	**Hanyath**	**Adha**
7	**Punarvasu**	**Ad-dira**	**Diraay**	**Funoas**
8	**Pusya**	**An-natra**	**Nadrath**	**Fus**
9	**Aslesa**	**At-tarf**	**Tharfath**	**Ahuliha**
10	**Magha**	**Al-jabha**	**Jabath**	**Maa**
11	**Purva Phalguni**	**Az-zubra**	**Zabrath**	**Fura**
12	**Uttara Phalguni**	**As-sarfa**	**Sarfath**	**Uthura**
13	**Hasta**	**Al-awwa**	**Avva**	**Atha**
14	**Citra**	**As-simak al-a[c]zal**	**Simak**	**Hitha**
15	**Svati**	**Al-gafr**	**Ofar**	**Hei**
16	**Visakha**	**Az-zubanayn**	**Zayale**	**Vihaa**
17	**Anuradha**	**Al-iklil**	**Ikleel**	**Nora**
18	**Jyestha**	**Al-kalb**	**Kalb**	**Dhosha**
19	**Mula**	**As-sawla**	**Shoolath**	**Mula**
20	**Purva Asadha**	**An-na[c]im**	**Nayayim**	**Furahalha**
21	**Uttara Asadha**	**Al-balda**	**Baldath**	**Uthurahalha**
*	**Abhijit**	**Sa[c]ds ad-dabih**	**Saithdhabih**	**Avihi**
22	**Sravana**	**Sa[c]d bula**	**Saith Ballizh**	**Huvan**
23	**Dhanistha**	**Sa[c]d as-su[c]ud**	**Saith Suyooth**	**Dhinasha**
24	**Satabhisa**	**Sa[c]d al-ahbiya**	**Ahibiyath**	**Hiyavihaa**

25	***Purva Bhadrapada***	***Al-fargat al-awwal***	***Fary Muhadham***	***Furabadhuruva***
26	***Uttara Bhadrapada***	***Al-farg at-tani***	***Fary Muahar***	***Fasbadhuruva***
27	***Revathi***	***Batn al-hut***		***Reyva***

The ***Jazira*** *Arabic equivalents for the Arabic lunar mansions is based on material provided by ATK and MM. The* ***Nakaiy*** *calendar is followed both in the Maldives as well as in Minicoy. In Minicoy, such calendars, procured from and printed in the Maldives, are in usage. There appears to be some change in terms of equivalent Gregorian calendar dates from year to year. Information on the* ***Nakaiy*** *has been gathered from informants in Minicoy, Husain Marrakar, Valumagothi, and Ali Thakru, Edurukage. A Maldivian printed source (Maniku, 1987, 68-179), has also been utilised.*

The ***Nakaiy*** *calendar projects seasonal conditions for each calendrical unit as well as the activity appropriate to it. Among activities covered are planting, harvesting, fishing and sailing. In sailing a distinction is made between the Bay of Bengal and the Arabian Sea. Between the second week of May and the first week of September there are no sailings to Bengal. Sailings to the east coast of India was preferred with the Northeast monsoon winds in the fifth* ***Nakaiy*** *month* ***Dhinasha****, starting 1 February. According to Husain Marrakkar, each* ***Malmi*** *would maintain a book which would include the* ***Nakaiy*** *calendar and notings of all that had been learnt from the ustad. Such books were called* ***Nakai thery foiy****, translated as,* ***Book Concerning Nakaiy****. These would also provide details about auspicious directions for travel. The contents were similar to those of the Lakshadweep* ***Rahmani****. In present times 27 asterisms have been used in the* ***Nakaiy*** *calendar. Earlier there was a 28th one, the additional asterism being called* ***Avihi****. In each year of a three year cycle, three days were reduced. Every fourth year,* ***Avihi****, marked by an asterisk in the chart, comprising twelve days, was interposed between the third and fourth* ***Nakaiy*** *months,* ***Uthurahalha*** *and* ***Huvan*** *respectively.*

(17) SHAPE OF THE *NAKSHATRAS* [40]

1 The first day (*nakshatra*) *Aswathi* is to be known as Head of a Horse which is like the ring on the brow of the elephant.

2 *Bharani* is like three stones in a fireplace.

3 *Kaarthika* is like the fish, *pathi meen*.

4 *Rohini* is like a curve.

5 *Makeram*, three, is like the head of a deer or like three eyes of the coconut.

6 *Thiruvaathira* is also called *Athira* and is only a single star but as big as one and a half stars. It rises by 5.30 in the evening in *Chingam* (last month of the year in the island - Malayalam calendar).

7 *Punatham*, a group of six stars, like a local craft with six oars.

8 *Pooyam*, like a reaping knife

9 *Aayilyam* like the (local domestic) grinding stone

10 *Maham*, four, like a plough

11&12 *Pooram* and *Uththiram*, like a cot

13 *Artham* a group of five stars like a palm

14 *Chiththira* is like an ear of paddy. (A child learning to write makes the outlines of the first letter of the alphabet on such a bed of paddy.)

15&16 *Chothi* and *Visaakam* are like the holes of a net.

17 *Anizham*, five, like the canopy of an arecanut tree

18 *Tirkettam*, three, like a (drawn out) bow

19 *Moolam*, like a bugle

20 *Pooraadam*, like a closed door

21 *Uththiraadam*, without (clear) shape

22 *Thiruvonam,* like a bamboo stick

23 *Avittam* five, like a wheel

24 *Chathayam*, a winnow

25&26 *Poorampuraththaathiri* and *Uththiraththaathiri*, like the canopy of a cot

27 *Eravathi*, like a rocking cradle

Ameen

[40] *Cf. Tibbetts, 1971, 79-120. The forms of the* ***nakshatras*** *given above may be compared to those in the* ***Sakalya-Samhita*** *(cf. Sengupta, 1934, 150-151). An attempt is being made to tabulate this material as follows:*

	Sanskrit	*Malayalam*	*Sakalya*	*Rahmani*
1	***Asvini***	***Aswathi***	*Horse-head*	*Horse-head*
2	***Bharani***	***Bharani***	*Yoni*	*Fire-place*
3	***Krttika***	***Kaarthika***	*Razor*	
4	***Rohini***	***Rohini***	*Cart*	*Curve*
5	***Mrgasira***	***Makeram***	*Deer-head*	*Deer-head*
6	***Ardra***	***Thiruvaathira***	*Ruby*	
7	***Punarvasu***	***Punatham***	*House*	*Boat with Six Oars*
8	***Pusya***	***Pooyam***	*Arrow-head*	*Reaping Sickle*
9	***Aslesa***	***Aayilyam***	*Wheel*	*Grinder*
10	***Magha***	***Maham***		*Plough*
11	***P. Phalguni***	***Pooram***	*Cot*	*Cot*
12	***U. Phalguni***	***Uththiram***	*Cot*	*Cot*
13	***Hasta***	***Artham***		*Palm of Hand*
14	***Citra***	***Chiththira***	*Pearl*	
15	***Svati***	***Chothi***	*Coral*	*Holes of Net*
16	***Visakha***	***Visaakam***	*Gateway*	*Holes of Net*
17	***Anuradha***	***Anizham***	*Bali (Oblation)*	*Canopy of Arecanut Tree*
18	***Jyestha***	***Tirkettam***	*Ear-ring*	*Bow*
19	***Mula***	***Moolam***		*Lion-tail*
20	***P. Asadha***	***Pooraadam***	*Elephant-tusk*	*Closed Door*
21	***U. Asadha***	***Uththiraadam***	*Cot*	
*	***Abhijit***			
22	***Sravana***	***Thiruvonam***	*Drum*	*Bamboo Stick*
23	***Dhanistha***	***Avittam***	*Drum*	*Wheel*
24	***Satabhisaj***	***Chathayam***	*Circle*	*Winnow*
25	***P.Bhadrapada***	***Poorampuraththaathiri***	*Cot*	*Canopy of Cot*
26	***U.Bhadrapada***	***Uththiraththaathiri***	*Cot*	*Canopy of Cot*
27	***Revathi***	***Eravathi***	*Drum*	*RevolvingCradle*

(SRS)

(18) THE FIRST *SAAYATH*

Sunday	Daytime	*Shams*	Night	*Athaarid*
Monday	Daytime	*Qamar*	Night	*Musthari*
Tuesday	Daytime	*Mirreq*	Night	*Zuhra*
Wednesday	Daytime	*Athaarid*	Night	*Suhal*
Thursday	Daytime	*Musthari*	Night	*Shams*
Friday	Daytime	*Zuhra*	Night	*Qamar*
Saturday	Daytime	*Suhal*	Night	*Mirreq*[41]

41 This table contains the names of the lords of the first hours of the daytime and of the night for each weekday. In Hellenistic astrology, a planet is assigned as the lord or regent of each of the twenty-four hours, the nychthemeron, starting from the sunrise. The lord of the first hour is treated as the lord of the the whole weekday and the weekday is designated accordingly. Thus the Sun is the lord of the first hour of Sunday. Consequently the day is called Sun's day or Sunday. The sequence in which the planets are assigned to the successive hours is arranged according to the size of the orbits of the planets: Saturn, Jupiter, Mars, Sun, Venus, Mercury and Moon.

In Arabic, ***saayath*** *denotes the "hour of 60 minutes" and also its lord. The present table shows the lords of the first hours not only of the daytime but of the night as well. In the Islamic calendar the days of the week are reckoned from sunset to sunset. What is otherwise known as "Saturday night" is treated here as the night of Sunday. Cf. Saha, 1955, 169-170; Sachau, 1910, 213-214. For convenience, the table is rearranged in the following manner:*

Weekday	***Lord of the first hour of the daytime***		***Lord of the first hour of the night***	
Sunday	*Sun*	*(**Shams**)*	*Mercury*	*(**Athaarid**)*
Monday	*Moon*	*(**Qamar**)*	*Jupiter*	*(**Musthari**)*
Tuesday	*Mars*	*(**Mirreq**)*	*Venus*	*(**Zuhra**)*
Wednesday	*Mercury*	*(**Athaarid**)*	*Saturn*	*(**Suhal**)*
Thursday	*Jupiter*	*(**Musthari**)*	*Sun*	*(**Shams**)*
Friday	*Venus*	*(**Zuhra**)*	*Moon*	*(**Qamar**)*
Saturday	*Saturn*	*(**Suhal**)*	*Mars*	*(**Mirreq**)*

(SRS)

(19) *KANAKKU* OF INAUSPICIOUS PERIODS

On Saturday (the inauspicious) time begins at the moment when the shadow is 42 feet and extends up to (the moment when it is) 18 feet.

On Friday,	it is from 10 feet to 6 feet.
On Thursday,	3 1/2 feet to 2 feet
On Wednesday,	one foot before noon to noon.
On Tuesday,	1/2 foot to 2 feet.
On Monday,	3 1/2 feet to 6 feet.
On Sunday,	10 feet to 18 feet.

These are the inauspicious times, not good for anything except for digging and burying.[42]

42 *The Malayalam heading reads* ***Kuliyam Kanakku***. ***Sections 21*** *and* ***82*** *also deal with inauspicious periods. These periods are termed* ***Kuliyam***. *In this section, time is measured in shadow lengths. For this method, see* ***Section 20*** *below. This section employs archaic Tamil terms for some of the weekdays, which are not generally used in modern Malayalam.* ***Kari*** *= Saturn;* ***Tirumadi*** *= illustrious Moon;* ***Veyyavan*** *= Sun;* ***Pakkiran*** *= Mars ? (SRS) According to local beliefs these* ***Kuliyam*** *timings are, however, favourable for planting coconut seedlings (AKT).*

(20) *KANAKKU* OF FEET

(Shadow lengths in feet at hourly intervals) Just when you feel that the Sun has risen, it (the shadow) is 98 feet.

For 28 feet, *saayath* 1
For 14 feet, *saayath* 2
For 7 feet, *saayath* 3
For 3 1/2 feet, *saayath* 4
For 1 3/4 feet, *saayath* 5

For standing feet (i.e. when the shadow is congruent with one's feet), *saayath* 6 in the afternoon.

For 1 3/4 feet, *saayath* 7
For 3 1/2 feet, *saayath* 8
For 7 feet, *saayath* 9
For 14 feet, *saayath* 10
For 28 feet, *saayath* 11
For 98 feet, *saayath* 12[43]

Ameen

[43] *This section refers to a system of time measurement by means of a sundial, using one's own body as the gnomon or the shadow thrower. The height of the human body is supposed to be seven times the length of the foot. For clarity, the table is rearranged as follows:*

Hours since	*shadow length*
sunrise	*in feet*
0	*98*
1	*28*
2	*14*
3	*7*
4	*3*
5	*1*
6	*0*

Hours since	*shadow length*
sunrise	*in feet*
7	*1*
8	*3*
9	*7*
10	*14*
11	*28*
12	*98*

The table is obviously meant for regions on the equator, where 3 hours after sunrise and 3 hours before sunset, the length of the shadow equals the height of the gnomon, i.e. 7 feet (SRS).

(21) INAUSPICIOUS PERIODS AT NIGHT[44]

After the sunset on Wednesday, from 2 1/2 *naazhikas* for 2 1/2 *naazhikas* it is inauspicious.
After the sunset on Tuesday, from 6 *naazhikas* for 2 1/2 *naazhikas* it is inauspicious.
After the sunset on Monday, from 10 *naazhikas* for 2 1/2 *naazhikas* it is inauspicious.
After the sunset on Sunday, from 14 *naazhikas* for 2 1/2 *naazhikas* it is inauspicious.
After the sunset on Saturday, from 18 *naazhikas* for 2 1/2 *naazhikas* it is inauspicious.
After the sunset on Friday, from 24 *naazhikas* for 2 1/2 *naazhikas* it is inauspicious.
After the sunset on Thursday, from 26 *naazhikas* for 2 1/2 *naazhikas* it is inauspicious.
The above periods are certainly bad for commencing anything except digging and burying.

Ameen

[44] *This section provides the inauspicious periods known as* ***nahasus*** *which occur at night.* ***Section 19*** *above provides a table for the measurement of time during the day by the shadow lengths in feet. At night, on the other hand, time is measured by means of a water clock in units of 24 minutes, each called* ***naazhika****. The* ***nahasus*** *commence at different moments on different weekdays but always last 2 1/2* ***naazhikas****, equal to 1 hour. Assuming that the mean sunset occurs at 6:00 pm, the table is rearranged in modern time notation as follows:*

Wednesday	*07:00 pm - 08:00 pm*
Tuesday	*08:24 pm - 09:24 pm*
Monday	*10:00 pm - 11:00 pm*
Sunday	*11:36 pm - 00:36 am*
Saturday	*01:12 am - 02:12 am*
Friday	*03:36 am - 04:36 am*
Thursday	*04:24 am - 05:24 am*

This peculiar order of the weekdays is based on the initial moments of the ***nahasus****, which progressively move foreward each night. It will be seen that this table is nearly the same as the one given in* ***Section 82****, where the time units are in modern notation (SRS). The original malayalam title reads* ***Raatriyil ulla Nahasu****.* ***Nahasu*** *appears to be derived from Persian,* ***nahs****, sinister aspect of stars.*

(22) *KANAKKU* OF *CHARANAA*[45]
(Inauspicious Conjunctions between *Nakshatras* and Weekdays)

Bharani is not good on the day when the sun was created (Sunday).
Chiththira is not good, on the little Moon (Monday).
Uththiraadam is not good for Tuesday.
(Avittam)[46] is not good for the reddish Wednesday.
Pooraadam is not good for the well-known Friday.
Eravathi is not good on conch like (*sankha*) Saturday.

These stars are not good once in all the (2 × 7) fourteen days. A sailing vessel starting on these days will not come back. If a girl child attains puberty on that day, she would become barren. If a male child is born, he would become mad. If a woman delivers on that day, she would die. If any person goes on a journey that day he would be like a man whose hands are in the mouth of a snake.

Ameen

[45] *Thursday is not mentioned. Friday, normally is auspicious but if it is in conjunction with* ***Pooraadam*** *it is inauspicious (AKT).*

[46] ***Avittam*** *is written in the text as Akitam.*

(23) *NAKSHATRAS* FORBIDDEN FOR JOURNEY

The star next to the first one is not good. *Anizham* together with the next three are not good. *Chothi* together with *Visaakam* is not good. If you say *Chathayam*, it is not good either. Including *Thiruvonam*, all these nine stars not good for travel.[47]

[47] *The Malayalam text reads* ***Padavari Nakshatrangal*** *as the heading. According to AKT, the word* ***padavari*** *implies that anyone who goes on a journey under any of these of* ***nakshatras*** *will not come back in that season. The nine stars, or more correctly,* ***nakshatras****, are* ***Bharani****,* ***Anizham****,* ***Tirkettam****,* ***Moolam****,* ***Pooraadam****,* ***Chothi****,* ***Visaakam****,* ***Chathayam*** *and* ***Thiruvonam****.*

(24) NAMES OF THE *RAASIS*

Medam, Edavam, Mithunam, Karkidakam, Chingam, Kanni, Thulaam, Vrischikam, Dhanu, Makaram, Kumbam, Meenam.

(25) *KANAKKU* OF THE *RAASIS*

Aswathi at noon time is *Karkidakam Raasi.*
Kaarthika at noon time is *Chingam Raasi.*
Makeram at noon time is *Kanni Raasi.*
Punatham at noon time is *Thulaam Raasi.*
Maham at noon time is *Vrischikam Raasi.*
Artham at noon time is *Dhanu Raasi.*
Chothi at noon time is *Makaram Raasi.*
Aayilyam at noon time is *Kumbam Raasi.*
Pooraadam at noon time is *Meenam Raasi.*
Thiruvonam at noon time is *Medam Raasi.*
Chathayam at noon time is *Edavam Raasi.*
Mithunam Raasi is between *Poorampuraththaathiri* and *Uththiraththaathiri.*

Ameen

(26) POSITION OF THE *RAASIS*[48]

Medam Raasi stands at the rising point of *Chothi.*
Edavam Raasi stands at the east.
Mithunam Raasi stands at the rising point *of Seer.*
Karkidakam Raasi stands at the south-east.
Chingam Raasi stands towards the south.
Kanni Raasi stands at the south-west.
Thulaam Raasi stands at the setting point of *Seer.*
Vrischikam Raasi stands at the west.
Dhanu Raasi stands at the setting point of *Chothi.*
Makaram Raasi stands at the north-east direction.
Kumbam Raasi stands at the north direction
Meenam Raasi stands at the north-west direction.

Ameen

[48] *Cf. Filliozat, 1968, 89-94.* ***Kanakku of the Raasis, (Section 25)*** *above relates the position of the* ***Raasi*** *in terms of its relevant* ***nakshatra****. This is necessary for* ***muhuratham*** *fixation. It is also a useful mnemonic device for recalling the position of* ***raasi*** *in relation to* ***nakshatra****.* ***Section 26,*** *however is to be related to* ***Section 60*** *and to Fig. 39 below. AKT. For furthur details see n. 70.*

(27) GOOD AND EVIL EFFECTS OF ACTIONS UNDER *RAASIS*

Medam, good for spending, not good for marriage.
Edavam, good for keeping treasures, not good for wearing new clothes.
Mithunam, good for house construction, not good for travel.
Karkidakam, good for harvesting fruit, not good for sowing.
Chingam, good for construction of bridges, not good for meeting relatives.
Kanni, good for writing marriage contracts, entering a new house and for war; not good for house construction.
Thulaam, good for wearing new clothes, not good for circumcision.
Vrischikam, good for planting of trees, not good for harvesting.
Dhanu, good for the child to take the first step, not good for ritual bathing.
Makaram, good for circumcision, not good for ship construction.
Kumbam, good for ritual bathing, not good for ear boring.
Meenam, good for travelling and for all other things.[49]

Ameen

[49] *Seasonal changes are noted in conformity with this solar calendar. With* ***Kanni*** *the fair weather starts. The vessels are then hauled into the sea and put to service. The monsoon starts with the month of* ***Medam****. The vessels would stop their service, being hauled back to their shelters ashore. Cultivation and deep-sea fishing are also governed by this solar calendar, and indeed, a chapter on cultivation is included in this manuscript.*

(28) MALEFIC DATES

The third day after the commencement of the month is not good.
The fifth day is also not good.
The thirteenth day is also not good.
The sixteenth day is also not good.
Any day after the twentieth is also not good.
Especially, the twenty-first day is not good.
The twenty-fourth day, the twenty-fifth day and the last Wednesday are not good.

Ameen

(29) MALEFIC WEEKDAYS IN A MONTH

If the commencement of the month is on Sunday, every Monday of that month is not good.
If the commencement of the month is on Monday, every Friday of that month is not good.
If the commencement of the month is on Tuesday, every Tuesday of that month is not good.
If the commencement of the month is on Wednesday, every Saturday of that month is not good.
If the commencement of the month is on Thursday, every Wednesday of that month is not good.
If the commencement of the month is on Friday, every Sunday of that month is not good.
If the commencement of the month is on Saturday, every Thursday of that month is not good.

Ameen

(30) POSITION OF THE *RAASIS* (Zodiac Signs and their Corresponding *Nakshatras*)

Medam	=	*Aswathi* + *Bharani* + 1/4 *Kaarthika*
Edavam	=	3/4 *Kaarthika* + *Rohini* + 1/2 *Makeram*
Mithunam	=	1/2 *Makeram* + *Thiruvaathira* + 3/4 *Punatham*
Karkidakam	=	1/4 *Punatham* + *Pooyam* + *Aayilyam*
Chingam	=	*Maham* + *Pooram* + 1/4 *Uththiram*
Kanni	=	3/4 *Uththiram* + *Artham* + 1/2 *Chiththira*
Thulaam	=	1/2 *Chiththira* + *Chothi* + 3/4 *Visaakam*
Vrischikam	=	1/4 *Visaakam* + *Anizham* + *Tirkettam*
Dhanuvam	=	*Moolam* + *Pooraadam* + 1/4 *Uththiraadam*
Makeram	=	3/4 *Uththiraadam* + *Thiruvonam* + 1/2 *Avittam*
Kumbam	=	1/2 *Avittam* + *Chathayam* + 3/4 *Poorapuraththaathiri*
Meenam	=	1/4 *Poorapuraththaathiri* + *Uththiraththaathiri* + *Eravathi*[50]

Ameen

[50] *The section gives the relationship of 12* ***raasis*** *with 27* ***nakshatras****. The same correspondance is generally displayed graphically on the backs of Islamic astrolabes. See for example Kareghat, 1950, Fig. 1,2 (SRS).* ***Raasis*** *and* ***nakshatras*** *are markers on the ecliptic belt and appear to rise and set from east to west due to inner rotation of the earth, covering 360° in one complete rotation. Since there are 12* ***raasis*** *and 27* ***nakshatras*** *each* ***raasi*** *covers 360°÷12 = 30°, and each* ***nakshatra*** *covers 360 ÷27 = 13°20'. Again, 12* ***raasi*** *= 27* ***nakshatra*** *space. Therefore one* ***raasi*** *covers 27/12 = 2* ***nakshatra*** *space. The relationship may be seen from the following table:*

Raasi	***Nakshatras***	***Nakshatra*** *Space*
1. ***Medam*** *(0°-30°)*	*1.* ***Aswathi*** *(13°20')*	*1*
	2. ***Bharani*** *(13°20')*	*1*
	3. ***Kaarthika*** *(3°20')*	*1/4*
2. ***Edavam*** *(30°-60°)*	*3.* ***Kaarthika*** *(10°)*	*3/4*
	4. ***Rohini*** *(13°20')*	*1*
	5. ***Makeram*** *(6°40')*	*1/2*
3. ***Mithunam*** *(60°-90°)*	*5.* ***Makeram*** *(6°40')*	*1/2*
	6. ***Tiruvaathira*** *(13°20')*	*1*
	7. ***Punatham*** *(10°)*	*3/4*
4. ***Karkidakam*** *(90°-120°)*	*7.* ***Punatham*** *(3°20')*	*1/4*

Raasi		***Nakshatra***	***Nakshatra** Space*
	8.	***Pooyam** (13°20')*	1
	9.	***Aayilyam** (13°20')*	1
5. ***Chingam** (120°-150°)*	10.	***Maham** (13°20')*	1
	11.	***Pooram** (13°20')*	1
	12.	***Uththiram** (3°20')*	1/4
6. ***Kanni** (150°-180°)*	12.	***Uththiram** (10°)*	3/4
	13.	***Artham** (13°20')*	1
	14.	***Chiththra** (6°40')*	1/2
7. ***Thulaam** (180°-210°)*	14.	***Chiththra** (6°40')*	1/2
	15.	***Chothi** (13°20')*	1
	16.	***Visaakam** (10°)*	3/4
8. ***Vrischikam** (210°-240°)*	16.	***Visaakam** (3°20')*	1/4
	17.	***Anizham** (13°20')*	1
	18.	***Tirkettam** (13°20')*	1
9. ***Dhanu** (240°-270°)*	19.	***Moolam** (13°20')*	1
	20.	***Pooraadam** (13°20')*	1
	21.	***Uththiraadam** (3°20')*	1/4
10. ***Makaram** (270°-300°)*	21.	***Uththiraadam** (10°)*	3/4
	22.	***Thiruvonam** (13°20')*	1
	23.	***Avittam** (6°40')*	1/2
11. ***Kumbam** (300°-330°)*	23.	***Avittam** (6°40')*	1/2
	24.	***Chathayam** (13°20')*	1
	25.	***Poorapuraththathiri**(10°)*	3/4
12. ***Meenam** (330°-360°)*	25.	***Poorapuraththathiri** (3°20')*	1/4
	26.	***Uththiratthaathiri** (13°20')*	1
	27.	***Eravathi** (13°20')*	1

The relationship may also be seen in this following diagram:

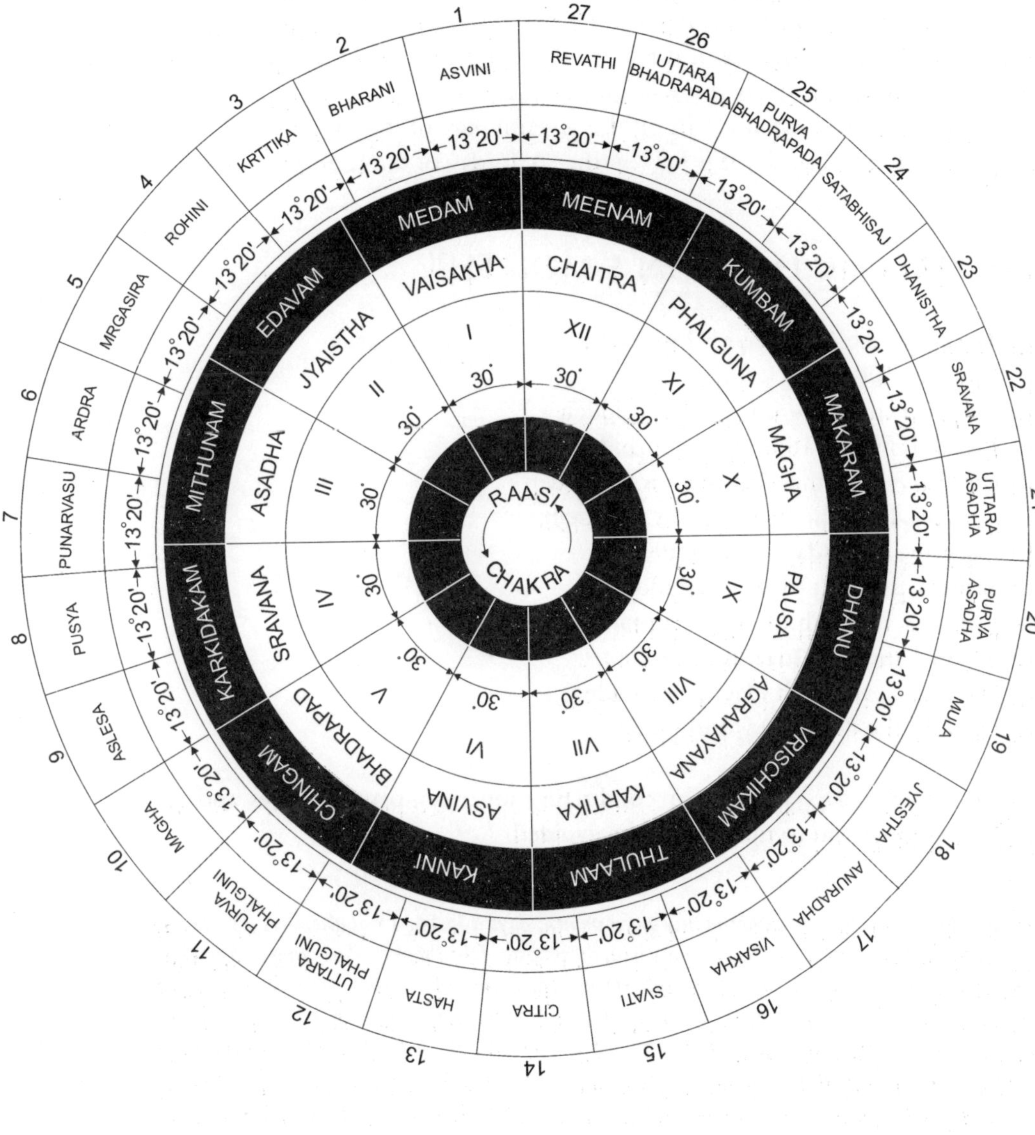

Fig. 37. *Raasis* (AKB)

(31) MALEFIC (COMBINATIONS OF) DATES AND WEEKDAYS

Sunday will be a bad day if it falls on the twelfth (day of the month).
Monday will be a bad day if it falls on the eleventh (day of the month).
Tuesday will be a bad day if it falls on the tenth (day of the month).
Wednesday will be a bad day if it falls on the ninth (day of the month).
Thursday will be a bad day if it falls on the eighth (day of the month).
Friday will be a bad day if it falls on the seventh (day of the month).
Saturday will be a bad day if it falls on the sixth (day of the month).

(32) MALEFIC DATES IN A MONTH[51]

In *Muharram*, the 12th (day) is forbidden.
In *Safar*, the 10th (day) is forbidden.
In *Rabiul Auwal*, the 4th (day) is forbidden.
In *Rabiul Akhir*, the 18th (day) is forbidden.
In *Jamathul Auwal*, the 28th (day) is forbidden.
In *Jamathul Akhir*, the 28th (day) is forbidden.
In *Rajab*, the 12th (day) is forbidden.
In *Saabaan*, the 26th (day) is forbidden.
In *Ramzaan*, the 27th (day) is forbidden.
In *Sawwaal*, the 30th (day) is forbidden.
In *Dul Kaaida*, the 18th (day) is forbidden.
In *Dul Hijj*, the 8th (day) is forbidden.

These specified days are bad for conducting journeys, planting trees and approaching kings and so they should be avoided.

Ameen

[51] *According to Islamic convention in any given month, days 13, 14, 15 as also days 28, 29, 30 are considered to be days of fast in conformity with the practice of the Prophet. According to Atta Koya Thangal, both on new as well as on full-moon nights, the tide reaches its maximum point. Simultaneously there is also a belief that at the final dissolution of the world all land will be covered by floods. This explains the timing of these fasts. Days 28, 29, 30 are the days when the new moon is likely to be sighted. If the new moon is sighted on either day 28 or 29, there will be no fasting on the day subsequent to the sighting. Another feature of the Islamic calendar is that it is lunar. Unlike the Gregorian calendar which has a set number of days for each month in a four-yearly cycle, in the Islamic lunar calendar a month can extend to 32 days. According to the Shariat if the new moon is sighted by two reliable witnesses, this marks day 1 of the new lunar cycle. According to one interpretation of the Shariat which is followed by some sects it is possible to adopt a mathematical*

calculation for calendrical purposes, but this is done only if the moon cannot be sighted even on day 30 of the lunar cycle. In this case the month is given a total of 32 days to cover any margin of error. There would be an automatic rectification on the next sighting of the new moon. An alternative method which is followed is that even if the new moon is not sighted, the particular month is given 30 days, rectification taking place on the next sighting of the new moon. Cf. comments of R. Morelon above page 5.

(33) *KANAKKU* OF TIME UNITS

In a day, there are 60 *naazhikas*, 30 in the day and 30 at night.
In a day, there are 12 *raasis*, 6 in the day and 6 at night.
In a day, there are 24 *saayaths*, 12 in the day and 12 at night.
In a day, there are 8 *chaamams*, 4 in the day and 4 at night.
In 1 *chaamam*, there are 1 1/2 *raasis*, 3 *saayaths*, 7 1/2 *naazhikas*.
In 1 *raasi*, there are 2 *saayaths*, 5 *naazhikas*.
In 1 *saayath*, there are 2 1/2 *naazhikas*.
In 1 *naazhika*, there are 60 *vinaazhikas*, 24 minutes[52] (24 minutes corresponds to 1 *naazhika)*
In 1 year, there are 360 days, or 365 1/4 days.
In 1 year, there are 12 months.
In 1 year, there are 52 weeks.
In 1 month, there are 30 days, or 31 days.
In 1 week, there are 7 days.
In 1 *Kou*, there are 100 miles.
In 1 *chaamam*, there are 12 miles.
In 1 mile, there are 4 seconds.[53]

52

1 ***chaamam***	*= 3 hours = 7 1/2* ***naazhikas***
5 ***naazhikas***	*= 2 hours= 1* ***raasi****.*
2 1/2 ***naazhikas***	*= 1 hour*
60 ***vinaazhika***	*= 1* ***naazhika*** *(AKT, MM)*

The ***naazhika*** *is clearly the* ***nadika*** *referred to by AKB in note 3 of Appendix 1.*

[53] *The last three lines have been added in the margin in the Malayalam text. The day is divided into eight* ***chaamams****, 4 during the day and 4 at night. These are easily observable. The first* ***chaamam*** *begins with the rising of the sun and ends when the sun is at an angle of 45°. The second* ***chaamam*** *ends at 90°, at noon. The third again is at 45° in the descending circle and the fourth at sunset (SRS). In* ***Section 33*** *the number $365^1/_4$in line 9 and the 31 days in line 12 are to be taken as rectifications added by Kunhikunhi Malmi to a more popular, and possibly a more ancient system of reckoning the length of the solar year and duration of a month at 360 and 30 days respectively.*

(34) POSITION OF THE MOON IN THE ZODIAC[54]

Count the days from the beginning of the month. Double this number and add 5 to it. Divide the sum by 5 and take the quotient.
Next, find out the zodiac sign in which the sun is situated on this day. From this sign onwards, count until you reach the number represented by the quotient. This will be the sign in which the moon is situated on this day.

If the (given) date is higher than 15, add 1 to the quotient.[55]

Ameen

[54] *Cf. lunar mansions in Tibbetts, 1971, 79-120.*

[55] *This process of computation will be clear from an example. 23 March 1998 is 23* ***Dil Kaaida****. Double 23 = 46. Add 5 = 51. Divide it by 5. The quotient is 10. Since the given date is higher than 15, add 1 to quotient. We get 11. The sun is in* ***Hamal****. So starting from* ***Hamal****, count up to 11. The eleventh is* ***Dalb****. So the moon is in* ***Dalb*** *(SRS).*

(35) ESTIMATING THE LONGITUDE FROM THE LATITUDE AND ALSO THE *CHAAMAM* FROM THE *KOU*[56]

(Estimating the Longitude from the distance run (*chaamams*) and from the Latitude observed through *Kou* or the noon measurement)

Find out the position of the vessel by looking at the sun. It may sometimes be beyond the sun (in the north) and sometimes in between the sun and the equator.
Whatever it may be, the above finding is to be multiplied with the distance to be gained in the direction in which the vessel is moving.
The above figure is to be divided by 15. The quotient is the *chaamam* (latitude) to the place of your destination.

[56] ***Section 35*** *demonstrates how the concept of traverse tables (****Nuri****) had been internalised by the Islanders. The method of Dead Reckoning has been adapted in this Section for journeys from the Islands to the mainland and vice versa. The method of calculation given below may be entitled,* ***Relating Difference in Latitude Measured from Kou to the Distance Covered Whilst Sailing Along a Course (045°)***

1. In a voyage from Kavaratti to Mangalore, the distance from Kavaratti to Mangalore = 17 ***chaamams*** *= 17× 8'.25 = 140.25 miles (1* ***chaamam*** *= 8'. 25 in terms of difference of latitude if the sailing is along a course of 045°,NE).*

2. The difference in latitude between Kavaratti (10° 32') and Mangalore (12° 52') is 2° 20' = 140' = 140 miles.

3. We know from **Section 10** *that 1 finger* ***(kou)*** *= 100 miles along a meridian. (N-S).*

For example:

a) Let us say the vessal sails a distance of 10 chaamams (10 × 12 = 120 miles) along a course 045°(NE), at mid-latitude of 11°30'N.

b) Then the difference in latitude ***(arlu)*** *will be 83'.33 (i.e. 1° 22'.33) for a mid-latitude of 11°30'N.*

c) The difference in latitude between Kavaratti and Mangalore is, however, 2° 20'N.

d) Therefore, the vessel has yet to achieve another difference in latitude of 2° 20' –1° 22'.33 = 0° 58'N.

e) To achieve a difference in latitude of 58', the further distance required to be travelled by the vessal is (58 ÷ 83.33) × 10 = 7 chaamams (i.e. 7 × 12 =84 miles) along course 045° (NE) (RBJ, AKT).

(36) *NAKSHATRAS* IN CONJUNCTION WITH THE MOON

Count the months from *Medam* up to the current month. Double this figure. Similarly count from *Aswathi* until the doubled figure is reached. The last one is the star (*nakshatra*) under which the (current) month commenced. Then count one star each for each day of the current month, add one more to it.[57]

Ameen

[57] *Given a solar month and a date, the problem is to find the corrresponding* ***nakshatra****. Example. Find the* ***nakshatra*** *for 21* ***Makaram.*** *Counting from* ***Medam, Makaram*** *is the tenth month. Double 10. You get 20. Count from* ***Aswathi****; the twentieth* ***Nakshatra*** *is* ***Pooraadam****. Therefore the current month commenced under* ***Pooraadam****. Count again from* ***Pooraadam*** *up to (20 + 1 =) 21. You get* ***Chothi****. Therefore, the* ***Nakshatra*** *on 21* ***Makaram*** *is* ***Chothi*** *(SRS).*

(37) *KANAKKU* FOR DETERMINING THE DATE[58]

Count the days from *Medam* to a particular day. Add 18 to it. Count from *Hamal* to complete the sum. The last count would be the date of the particular day.

[58] *In earlier times the average Lakshadweep islander had little need for day to day calendrical reckoning. If at sea, recourse would be taken to the navigator. Dates were necessary for locating the position of the sun resulting from equinoctial changes in altitude. The Arabic calendar starting from* ***Hamal****, and the Malayalam calendar starting from* ***Medam*** *are solar calendars, and are therefore, comparable. The basic purpose of this calculation is to understand the declination of the sun (AKT). Cf. Figs. 29-34.*

(38) DATES IN A MONTH (ARABIC)

Hamal	31	*Meezaan*	30
Dour	31	*Aqrab*	30
Jousa	32	*Qouz*	29
Sarathan	31	*Jadeen*	29
Asad	31	*Dalb*	30
Sumbul	31	*Hooth*	30

(39) DATES IN A MONTH (MALAYALAM)[59]

Medam	31	*Thulaam*	30
Edavam	31	*Vrischikam*	29
Mithunam	31	*Dhanu*	30
Karkidakam	31	*Makaram*	29
Chingam	31	*Kumbam*	30
Kanni	31	*Meenam*	30[60]

[59] *This follows the solar calendar based on the Kollam era starting AD 824-825. In the calendar for AD 1997, published by* ***The Mathrubhumi****, the National Daily in Malayalam, published at Kozhikode, Kochi, Thiruvananthapuram, Thrissur, Kannur and Kottayam, the following correspondences have been found:*

Malayalam	*Number of days*	*Gregorian*
Dhanu	*29*	*16 December-13 January*
Makaram	*30*	*14 January -12 February*

Kumbam	*30*	*13 February-14 March*
Meenam	*30*	*15 March-13 April*
Medam	*31*	*14 April-14 May*
Edavam	*31*	*15 May-14 June*
Mithunam	*32*	*15 June-16 July*
Karkidakam	*31*	*17 July-16 August*
Chingam	*31*	*17 August-16 September*
Kanni	*31*	*17 September-17 October*
Thulaam	*30*	*18 October-16 November*
Vrischikam	*29*	*17 November-15 December*

60 *The months in the two tables correspond with each other, the only difference being the respective units to which 29 days are ascribed. In the month of* ***Hamal****, the sun is on the eastern point. During the course of the three months,* ***Hamal, Dour, Jousan****, the sun reaches the highest northern point, the Tropic of Cancer. During the next three months,* ***Sharathan****,* ***Asad*** *and* ***Sumbul****, the sun moves towards the equator, reaching its west point during the month of* ***Sumbul****. The month of* ***Meezaan*** *marks the movement of the sun from the west point. During the next three months,* ***Meezaan, Aqrab, Qouz,*** *the sun reaches the Tropic of Capricorn. This marks the shortest day of the year in the northern hemisphere. During the next three months,* ***Jadeen****,* ***Dalb*** *and* ***Hooth****, the sun starts its northward journey towards the equator. Both the sections provide the number of days the sun stays in each* ***raasi****, with the total number being 365 days. The sun's stay in* ***Jousa/ Mithunam*** *is the maximum, reaching 32 days in the Arabic calendar. This is because the velocity of the sun is minimum for its position in apogee, near 21 June. Likewise sun's velocity is maximum, i.e. its stay becomes minimum (29/30 days) when it is in its perigee on* ***Qouz/Dhanu raasi****, i.e. 22 December (AKB). The calendrical system which constitutes the basis of this Islamic solar calendar is not clear. Unlike the calendar cited by Ibn Majid, there is no reference to the* ***Nairuz*** *calendar. See Tibbetts, 1971, 361-364; Ferrand, 1924, 230-234; Grosset-Grange, 1996, 229-231.*

(40) *NAAZHIKAS* BETWEEN (THE RISINGS OF TWO SUCCESSIVE) *NAKSHATRAS*[61]

	Naazhikas
Between *Aswathi* and *Bharani*	3
Bharani and *Kaarthika*	1 1/8
Kaarthika and *Rohini*	2
Rohini and *Makeram*	2
Makeram and *Thiruvaathira*	1 1/8
Thiruvaathira and *Punatham*	2 1/8
Punatham and *Pooyam*	2
Pooyam and *Aayilyam*	1 1/8
Aayilyam and *Maham*	1 1/8
Maham and *Pooram*	1
Pooram and *Uththiram*	1/8
Uththiram and *Artham*	1/8
(Artham and *Chiththira)*	(2 1/8)
(Chiththira and *Chothi)*	(2 1/8)
Chothi and *Visaakam*	2 1/8
Visaakam and *Anizham*	1/8
Anizham and *Tirkettam*	2
Tirkettam and *Moolam*	2
Moolam and *Pooraadam*	1/8
Pooraadam and *Uththiraadam*	2
Uththiraadam and *Thiruvonam*	3 1/8
Thiruvonam and *Avittam*	2 1/8
Avittam and *Chathayam*	4
Chathayam and *Poorapuraththaathiri*	3
Poorapuraththaathiri and *Uththiraththaathiri*	7
(Uththiraththaathiri and *Eravathi*	(5)
Eravathi and *Aswathi)*	(6 2/8)

Ameen

[61] *There is a lacuna towards the close of this table in the original manuscript: the distances between* ***Uththiraththaathiri*** *and* ***Eravathi****; and between* ***Eravathi*** *and* ***Aswathi*** *are wanting. Line 13 reads: "****Artham, Chiththira*** *and* ***Chothi*** *2 1/8". Actually there should be two lines giving the distances first between "****Artham*** *and* ***Chiththira****" and then between "****Chiththira*** *and* ***Chothi****". Upon enquiry, Kunhikunhi Malmi provided the data which is placed in parentheses. Even so there is still a minor lacuna. The total distance from* ***Aswathi*** *back to* ***Aswathi*** *should be 60* ***naazhikas****, but the number we get here is 58* ***naazhikas*** *(SRS).*

(41) *KANAKKU* FOR THE COMMENCEMENT OF *MUHARRAM*

If Sunday comes on *Muharram* six, food material will be less in that year, men and wild animals will increase.

If Monday comes on *Muharram* six, it would be a peaceful year. Plenty of rain and good crop of tubers. More kings will die.

If Tuesday comes on *Muharram* six, there will be increase in disease, plentiful rains, more death among women and babes, more people will lose eye (sight).

If Wednesday comes on *Muharram* six, it would be peaceful, prosperous and free of riots and other complications. Increase in food, no scarcity of water.

If Thursday comes on *Muharram* six, it would be a peaceful year. (However) there would be war somewhere.

If Friday comes on *Muharram* six, all wild animals and human beings will be more satisfied.

If Saturday comes on *Muharram* six, more rain, more wealthy people will die, *fakirs* (mendicants) will receive welcome.

(42) *KANAKKU* OF CHILDBIRTH

Pooram, the child will die soon
Uththiram and Artham, the child may become an administrator
Chiththira, he will be wealthy
Chothi, he will be a beggar
Visaakam, a debtor
Child born at *Aayilyam* noon, will be liked by kings
Tirkettam, a slave
Moolam, a leader
Uththiraadam, a great man
Child born at *Thiruvonam* noon, will be respected by people
Avittam, a successful child
A child born at *Chathayam* noon, will respect the people.
Poorapuratthaathiri, a *khatib* (a person who leads the Friday prayer)
Uththiratthaathiri, a leader

Ameen

(43) *KANAKKU* OF THE TILTING OF THE MOON (Position of the Lunar Cusps)

In the months of *Meenam* and *Medam*, the southern tip of the moon (the lunar crescent) is elevated. In the months of *Edavam* and *Mithunam*, both tips are at the same level. In the months of *Karkidakam, Chingam, Kanni, Thulaam, Vrischikam, Dhanuvam, Makaram,* the northern tip is elevated.[62]

[62] *Sanskrit classical astronomy teaches how to calculate and draw the elevation of lunar cusps. A special chapter is devoted to the computation of* ***Candra-srnga-unnati*** *or the "elevation of the horns of the moon" in nearly every Siddhanta text.* ***SS****, ch.10; or* ***SSi. Ganitadhyaya****, ch.14. The present section gives only an approximate idea of the elevation of the lunar cusps in the Lakshadweep Islands. Here, during the solar months of* ***Meenam*** *and* ***Medam*** *(roughly from 18 February to 19 April) the southern tip is elevated; in the months of* ***Edavam*** *and* ***Mithunam*** *(20 April - 20 June) both the tips are level and in the remaining months, the northern tip is elevated (SRS). (See Fig. 38).*

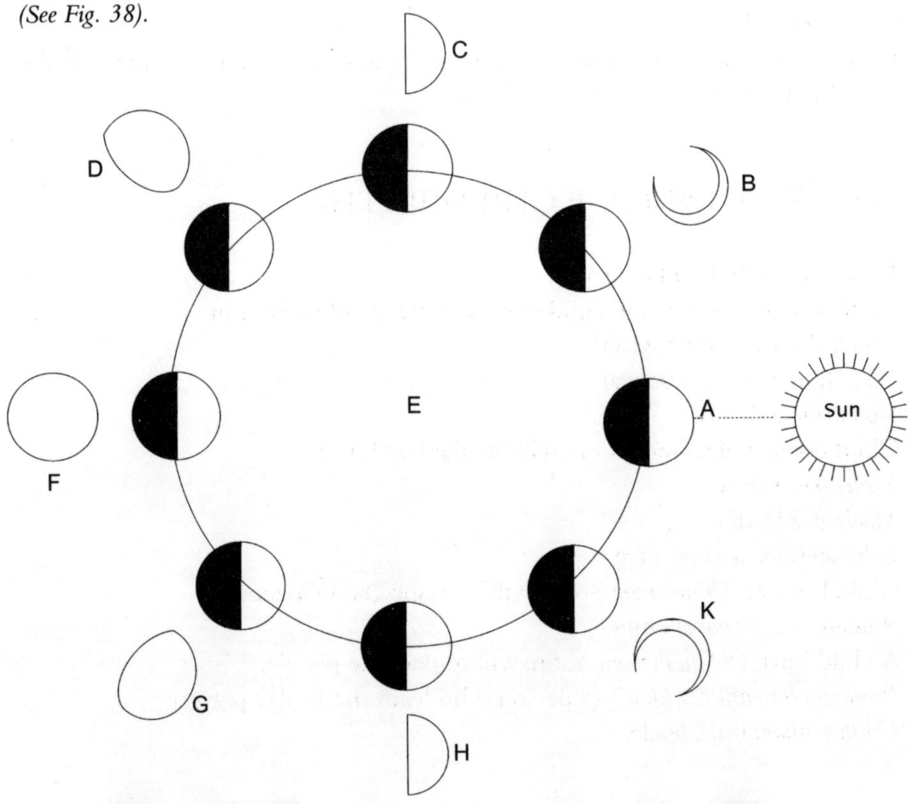

Fig. 38. Phases of the Moon. The position of the Lunar Cusps. The positions of the moon a,b,c,d,f,g,h,k, correspond to the A,B,C,D,F,G,H,K as seen from the earth (E).

(44) GOOD AND EVIL EFFECTS OF THE LUNAR ECLIPSE

A lunar eclipse in *Muharram* will result in great increase in population; in *Safar* less rain; in *Rabiul Awwal*, more production in crops, major disease; in *Rabiul Akhir*, deaths will increase, kingdoms will fall; in *Jamathul Awwal*, prosperity and fall in price (of commodities); in *Jamat ul Akhir*, employment will be more; in *Shaban*, increase in rain; in *Rajab*, unity among people; in *Ramzaan*, more deaths; in *Shawwaal*, more rumours; in *Dul Kaida*, faithfulness; in *Dul Hijj*, prosperity and mutual help.

Ameen

(45) *KANAKKU* FOR THE COMMENCEMENT OF *MUHARRAM*

(Finding the Weekday Corresponding to First of *Muharram*)[63]

Note down the year according to the *Hijra* calendar. Subtract 930. Multiply the remainder by 4. Keep this aside. Now multiply 930 by 11 and divide the result by 30. If the balance is 19 or more it should be taken as a unit of 30. If it is less than 19, it may be left out. This result is to be multiplied by four and added with the original number. Divide the sum by 7. Then count from Sunday upto the completion of the remainder. The last count in which it falls will be the day *Muharram* started.

Ameen

63 *The problem is to find out the weekday on which the lunar month* **Muharram** *commences in any given year. However, there seems to be a lacuna after the fifth sentence, for 930 ×11 ÷ 30 will always be 341. If the word "balance" means remainder, it is always zero. If it means quotient, it is always more than 19 (SRS). To this query, AKT has offered the following clarification:*

The commencement of **Muharram** *as calculated by this method need not be the same as the day determined by the sighting of the moon. There may be a month(s) when there was no sighting of the moon. Then one should continue to count the days up to 30 and, when a month is thus completed, begin again from the first day of the next month. It is not known why 930 has to be multiplied by 11 and then divided by 30 when we know that the figure is always 341. However, an example is worked out below:*

Current ***Hijra*** *is*	=	*1419*
Deduction	=	*930*
	=	*489*
Multiply 489 by 4	=	*1956 ...... (1)*
Multiply 930 by 11	=	*10230*
Divide 10230 by 30	=	*341*
Multiply 341 by 4	=	*1364 ...... (2)*
Add (1) and (2)	=	*1956 +1364*
	=	*3320*
Divide 3320 by 7	=	*474 -- 2*

Counting from Sunday, the second day is Monday. According to the ***Mathrubhumi*** *Calendar, 1* ***Muharram*** *was on Monday 27 April 1998 (AKT).*

(46) *KANAKKU* FOR THE COMMENCEMENT OF A MONTH[64]

Count the months from *Muharram* to a particular month, in which the calculation is to be made. Add two more months to it. Subtract three.
Subtract a day from the months which have an odd number of days. This is to be divided by seven.
The balance is to be taken as *Muharram* one and the last day of the week, thus counted is the day on which the particular month started.

Ameen

[64] *The problem is to find the weekday in which the month of* ***Rabiul Akhir*** *had commenced. We write below the number of days in each month from* ***Muharram*** *to* ***Rabiul Akhir****:*

Muharram	*31*
Safar	*31*
Rabiul Awwal	*30*
Rabiul Akhir	*28*
Total	*120 --(a)*

Add 2 more months, i.e.,	
Jamathul Awwal	*30*
Jamathul Akhir	*29*
Total	*59 --(b)*
Subtract 3 from (b)	*56 --(c)*

*Count the number of months having an odd number of days in (a). There are two (**Muharram** and **Safar**). Add (a) and (c) to get the sum 176. Then from this subtract 2 to get 174. Divide 174 by 7 . The remainder will be 6. Then start counting the days from Sunday. The sixth day is Friday. According to the **Mathrubhumi** calendar, the month, **Rabiul Akhir,** commenced on Friday, 24 July 1998. (AKT)*

(47) (ASCERTAINING) WHICH WEEKDAY (FALLS ON) THE FIRST OF *KANNI*[65]

Count the days from *Kanni* to a particular day when you are ascertaining the day. This is to be divided by seven. Note down the remainder.

The above remainder is to be counted with that particular day in the descending order. The day you get last is the day when the month of *Kanni* commenced.[66]

Ameen

*[65] **Kanni** is a significant month as it marks the opening of the fair weather. It also initiates the long distance sailing season. Cf. n.49.above.*

*[66] Example: On 5 **Chingam** (falling on Friday 21 August 1998, according to the **Mathrubhumi** calendar), we want to ascertain when the month of **Kanni** commenced in the previous year. List the days of the months from **Kanni** up to 5 **Chingam**.*

Kanni	*31*
Thulaam	*30*
Vrischikam	*29*
Dhanu	*30*
Makaram	*29*
Kumbam	*30*
Meenam	*30*

Medam	*31*
Edavam	*31*
Mithunam	*32*
Karkidakam	*31*
Chingam	*5*
Total	*339*

*Divide 339 by 7. The quotient is 48 and the remainder 3. Count 3 days backwards begining from the weekday on which 5 **Chingam** falls : Friday, Thursday, Wednesday. This means the month **Kanni** commenced on a Wednesday. This is confirmed by the **Mathrubhumi** calendar of 1997, according to which **1 Kanni** occurred on Wednesday, 17 September 1997 (AKT).*

(48) *NAKSHATRA* AT THE COMMENCEMENT OF A MONTH

Take the month of *Vrischikam* followed with subsequent months upto a particular day. Add 15 to it. The sum is to be counted starting from *Anizham*. The last *Nakshatra* thus received is the *Nakshatra* with which the month began.[67]

Ameen

[67] *The problem is that of corroborating the date of the commencement of a month with its corresponding* ***nakshatra****. For example, we could take a particular date, 8* ***Chingam*** *of the current year. The calculation would then take the following form for adding the number of days in each month, starting with* ***Vrischikam.***

Vrischikam	*29*
Dhanu	*30*
Makaram	*29*
Kumbam	*30*
Meenam	*30*
Medam	*31*
Idavam	*31*

Mithunam	*32*
Karkidakam	*31*
Chingam	*8*
Total	*281*
Add	*15*
	296

This figure of 296 is divided by 27 (number of ***nakshatras*** *). The remainder, 26, is to be counted from the* ***nakshatra Anizham****. If we start counting the* ***nakshatras*** *from* ***Anizham*** *the concluding* ***nakshatra*** *would be* ***Chothi****. This would correspond to 8* ***Chingam****. From this the* ***nakshatra*** *prevailing at the time of the commencement of the month could be identified (AKT, Mohan). The Calendar used is the* ***Mathrubhumi*** *for 1998.*

(49) *KANAKKU* FOR FINDING THE *MAYYAM*

The distance between Siraj Hidh and Mekka is 92 *chaamams*. Subtract 1/3 from it. Divide it by 5 and then subtract 13 *darja* from it. A journey from this point in the southward direction for (such) a time until the five stars of *Farakaden* are in alignement (would lead to), the place where Mekka is situated. 22 2/3 *chaamams* (from this place) know that this is the *Mayyam* of the world (*meyan*, Persian, centre) *Baithul Mukhaddis* (Mosque in Jerusalem), the place of the last judgement.

Ameen

(50) *NAKSHATRAS*, GOOD, BAD OR NEUTRAL

Rohini, Makeram, Punatham, Pooram, Uththiram, Artham, Avittam, Uththiraadam, Uththiraththaathiri, these nine stars are good.
Aswathi, Kaarthika, Chothi, Visaakam, are not good for travel.
The one closer to the first one (i.e *Bharani*) is not good. The three beginning with *Anizham* are not good. *Chothi* and *Visaakam* are not good. *Chathayam* is not good. All these nine *nakshatras* which have been read are *paadavary* (no return within the same season is possible).
Neutral *nakshatras* : *Kaarthika, Thiruvaathira, Aayilyam, Maham, Pooram, Chiththira, Pooraadam, Poorapuraththaathiri, Eravathi.* These nine *nakshatras* which have been read are like fish playing in the water (neutral).

(51) MALEFIC *NAKSHATRAS* IN A WEEK

The respected *Bharani*, and the other that is *Aayilyam, Pooram, Tirkettam, Visaakam, Chothi, Maham* and the twelfth star. If somebody proceeds on a journey while these stars are rising, he is like a man destined to die. He is like a man whose hands are inside the mouth of a snake.

(52) (FAVOURABLE *NAKSHATRAS* IN A WEEK)

Sunday	*Aswathi, Rohini, Makeram, Punatham, Pooyam, Artham, Moolam, Uththiram* and *Revathi.*
Monday	*Makeram, Pooyam, Aayilyam, Pooram, Uththiram, Anizham, Thiruvonam, Chathayam* and *Rohini.*
Tuesday	*Aayilyam, Uththiram, Artham, Chothi, Visaakam, Uththiraadam, Uththiraththaathiri, Aswathi* and *Pooyam.*
Wednesday	*Artham, Visaakam, Anizham, Moolam, Pooradam, Chathayam, Kaarthika, Makeram* and *Uththiram.*
Thursday	*Anizham, Pooradam, Uththiraadam, Thiruvonam, Avittam, Aswathi, Punatham, Aayiliam* and *Visaakam.*
Friday	*Uththiraadam, Avittam, Chathayam, Uththirathaathiri, Eravathi, Makeram, Pooram, Artham* and *Pooraadam.*
Saturday	*Revathi, Aswathi, Kaarthika, Rohini, Aayilyam, Chothi, Anizham* and *Avittam.*

(53) GOOD AND BAD *NAKSHATRAS* IN A WEEK

Name of the Day	Good *nakshatras*	Bad *nakshatras*
Sunday	*Moolam*	*Visaakam*
Monday	*Tirkettam*	*Kaarthika*
Tuesday	*Maham*	*Avittam*
Wednesday	*Uththiram*	*Chothi*
Thursday	*Pooradam*	*Uththiraadam*
Friday	*Pooyam*	*Pooram*
Saturday	*Makaram*	*Revathi*[68]

If the *nakshatra* and week-day coincide, then it is good for doing all things. (Such action) will be fruitful.

68 *Compare the above with* ***Section 52****. The stars listed in column one for Monday, and Tuesday in* ***Section 52*** *are absent in* ***Section 53****. For Thursday, Friday and Saturday in* ***Section 52 Uththiraadam****,* ***Pooram*** *and* ***Revathi*** *respectively are taken as favourable while the opposite is the case in* ***Section 53****.*

(54) *NAKSHATRAS* ASSOCIATED WITH WINDS

Rohini, Pooyam, Uththiram, Visaakam, Chothi, Pooraadam, Chathayam - these seven *nakshatras* bring strong winds.

Revathi, Kaarthika, Tirkettam, Moolam, Chothi, Visaakam, Chathayam, Thiruvonam. These seven bring cyclonic winds. These will intensify further if the *nakshatras* coincide with *Shams.*[69]

69 *The meaning of the last sentence in Section 54 is that if the* ***nakshatras*** *rise along with the sun the intensity of the wind will increase. Winds are associated both with* ***raasi*** *as well as* ***nakshatra****. Cf.* ***Section 8****, n.26.*

(55) *KANAKKU* FOR WEARING NEW CLOTHES (ON WEEKDAYS)

Friday, increase in love towards people
Saturday, diseases and misery
Sunday, misery

Monday, increase in wealth and children
Tuesday, fire, prostitution, humiliation and similar calamities
Wednesday, good for everything, blessings
Thursday, wisdom and knowledge

Ameen

(56) *KANAKKU* FOR LAYING THE FOUNDATON OF A HOUSE

Lay the foundation stone in *Edavam raasi*. The roofing can be done in *Mithunam raasi*. The face of the saints called *Aouliyas* should always fall on the front part of the house. There should not be any hindrance to it such as a coconut tree, arecanut tree and so on. Nor should there be cattle sheds in the direction through which the *Aouliyas* are supposed to look into the house.

(57) *NAKSHATRAS* FOR SOWING SEEDS

Aswathi, sow all seeds.
Bharani, (good) for all seeds
Kaarthika, arecanut can be planted.
Rohini, sow all seeds.
Makeran, if seeds are sown, they will have fungus and be affected by insects.
Tiruvaathira, Punatham, Pooyam, Anizham, Maham, sow the seeds.
Pooram, if seeds are sown, they will be destroyed by rats.
Chiththiram, Artham, sow all the seeds.
Chithira, watering
Chothi, cultivation of horse gram (*muthira*)
Visaakam, Aayilyam, Tirkettam, Moolam, Pooraadam, Uththiraadam, Thiruvonam, Avittam, Chathayam, Poorapuratthaathiri, Uththirattaathiri, Revathi, sow all seeds.

(58) *KANAKKU* FOR WEARING NEW CLOTHES (UNDER DIFFERENT *NAKSHATRAS*)

If new clothes are worn in *Aswathi,* there will be more attachment (within the family).
If new clothes are worn in *Bharani,* there will be mourning (within the family).

If new clothes are worn in *Kaarthika* and *Rohini,* there will be *artham* (wealth).
If new clothes are worn in *Makeram,* there will be rat bite.
If new clothes are worn in *Thiruvaathira,* (the person wearing it) will lie.
If new clothes are worn in *Punatham,* marriage to a woman of one's choice.
If new clothes are worn in *Pooyam,* decrease in longevity.
If new clothes are worn in *Aayilyam,* snake bite.
If new clothes are worn in *Maham and Pooram,* there will be mourning (in the family).
If new clothes are worn in *Uththiram,* prosperity will ensue.
If new clothes are worn in *Artham,* more profit; *chennivayadhi* (reddish skin).
If new clothes are worn in *Chiththra, chenniviyadhi* (reddish skin).
If new clothes are worn in *Visaakam,* what is desired will be obtained.
If new clothes are worn in *Anizham,* ornaments will be worn.
If new clothes are worn in *Tirkettam,* vacillation.
If new clothes are worn in *Moolam,* mourning (in the family).
If new clothes are worn in *Pooradam,* knowledge will be attained.
If new clothes are worn in *Uththiraadam,* contagious disease.
If new clothes are worn in *Thiruvonam,* clear vision will be attained.
If new clothes are worn in *Avittam,* there will be sorrowful thoughts.
If new clothes are worn in *Chathayam,* knowledge will be attained.
If new clothes are worn in *Poorapurattathiri,* clear vision.
If new clothes are worn in *Uththiraththathiri,* there will be disease.
If new clothes are worn in *Revathi,* there will be blessings from God.

(59) *KANAKKU* FOR FORECASTING THE DESTINY OF A WOMAN AT BIRTH

Hamlu (Hamal) raasi and *Mirreq saayath*:
Good face, a marking on the head, beauty spot on the face, a spot above the whiteness of the eye; straight and speedy; good among the ladies; relatives die before her; shows anger towards whomsoever she wants; diseases; husband dies and she gets his property; father dies before mother; few children

Dour raasi and *Zuhra saayath*:
Speaks with a smile; good relations with relatives; fond of delicious meals; good memory; angry towards the family, does not do good for them, yet prosperous; increased cheating; sells away properties; less children, father dies before the mother; fear of evil spirit like *Jinnu*

Jousa raasi and *Athaarid saayath*:
Bright face; spot on the chest; does not cheat; earns property; good children; will be good; more than three husbands; live to middle age

Sharthan raasi and *Qamar saayath*:
Tall; understands whatever she sees; deceives with a smiling face; good intelligence; abundance of hair; greedy; husband will be wealthy; he dies and she gets the property

Asad raasi and *Shams saayath*:
Talks less; speaks whatever comes into the mouth; spot on the left hand; disturbs her husband; many brothers and sisters; children will be good to her; fat body; great age

Sumbul raasi and *Athaarid saayath*:
Short; pleasant face; long hair; likes actors and dramas; loves her husband and relatives

Sumbul raasi and *Zuhra saayath*:
Good habits, thoughtful nature; earns property; makes no distinction between good and bad; loves her husband; less fame.

Aqrab raasi and *Mirreq saayath*:
Good character; less interest in husband and children; bad behaviour; asks for many things; never-ending poverty; serious disease after sixty

Qouz raasi and *Musthari saayath*:
Clever; short; reddish eye of a cat; reddish hair; deceitful; interest in business

Jadin raasi and *Suhal saayath*:
Angry; deceitful; spot on the forehead; likes much bad language

Dalb raasi and *Suhal saayath*:
Speaks like a man; large eyes; deceitful; truthful; proud; looks at the body while walking

Hooth raasi and *Musthari saayath*:
Good manners; likes flowers and other beautiful things; good faith; short; dies before father, mother and children; many children; blessed

Ameen

(60) *KANAKKU* FOR HOUSE CONSTRUCTION

Take the centre of a house. Erect fencing, (*padipura*) at a distance of 40 feet. Construct the following portions in the following directions:

Kitchen, *Edavam*
Treasure, *Mithunam*
Cattle shed, *Karkidakam*
Mortar and pestle, *Chingam*
Bathing tank, *Kanni*
Shop, *Thulaam*
Mosque, *Vrischikam*
Blacksmith's hut, *Dhanu*
Temple, *Makaram*
Death rites, *Kumbam*
Well, *Meenam*[70]

Ameen

[70] *Fig. 39 below provides the directions of the twelve* ***raasis****. Since raasis* ***are*** *associated with a variety of baneful effects, certain directions are to be avoided in planning the location of different elements of a house. For example the well for drinking water may be located in the direction of* ***Karkidakam raasi*** *but trees and gardens are to be avoided here (AKT). It is to be noted that* ***Medam raasi*** *is missing. Mention of temple location suggests that* ***Kanakku for House Construction*** *is either of mainland origen or is a vestige of the pre-Islamic culture of Lakshadweep.*

(61) GOOD AND EVIL EFFECTS OF HOUSE CONSTRUCTION ON DIFFERENT WEEKDAYS

Sunday, sorrow; (effects of) Shaitan
Monday, prosperity; children will multiply
Tuesday, shame and sorrow
Wednesday, good for everything; residents will be good people
Thursday, an intelligent person will be born
Friday, prosperity and wealth
Saturday, increase in wealth

(62) GOOD AND EVIL EFFECTS OF HOUSE CONSTRUCTION IN DIFFERENT MONTHS

Muharram, if a house is constructed residents will face poverty
Safar, victory; many children; fear from snakes
Rabiul Awwal, victory; many children
Rabiul Akhir, residents will not be happy
Jamathul Awwal, increase in prosperity
Jamathul Akhir, gold, prosperity, fame
Rajab, health, happiness and increase in prosperity
Saabaan, leprosy and destruction
Ramzaan, destruction by fire
Shawwaal, prosperity and good health
Dul Kaaida, lying and quarrelling
Dul Hijj, pleasure and happiness

Ameen

(63) GOOD AND EVIL EFFECTS OF HOUSE CONSTRUCTION UNDER DIFFERENT *NAKSHATRAS*[71]

If a house has been constructed in *Rohini*, he will inevitably become a debtor.
In *Makeram*, the person who had the house constructed will benefit along with his relatives.
In *Thiruvaathira*, residents will have stomach diseases.
In *Punatham*, ladies will increase.
In *Pooyam*, residents will leave because of destruction.
In *Aayilyam*, more deaths; there will be death every six months.
In *Maham*, residents will have contagious diseases.
In *Pooram*, disturbances from rats
In *Uththiram*, prosperity in many ways (*artham*)
In *Artham*, goodness in many ways
In *Chiththira*, perpetual mourning
In *Chothi*, persons will leave the house.
In *Visaakam*, good for many things
In *Anizham*, owner and residents will not prosper

In *Tirkettam*, good for every thing
In *Moolam*, help from the people; sons will be born
In *Pooraadam*, bad day
In *Uththiraadam*, good for some things
In *Thiruvonam*, vacation of house due to death
In *Avittam*, there will be death
In *Chathayam*, house will be vacated
In *Poorapuratthaathiri*, no prosperity
In *Uththiratthaathiri*, treasure will be found within the area of the house
In *Eravathi*, disturbances
In *Aswathi*, bitter quarrel and violence
In *Bharani*, disturbances from thieves
In *Kaarthika*, fire will be afraid of the house

[71] *The subject headings of Section 61, 62, 63, read as simple sentences of Section 60, in the original text. These sentences have been used as subject headings to provide greater coherence to the translation.*

(64) GOOD AND EVIL EFFECTS OF THE *SAAYATH* (GENERAL EFFECTS)

Qamar, Zuhra and *Musthari* are good *saayaths. Suhal* and *Mirreq* are bad *saayaths. Athaarid* and *Shams* are neither good nor bad.

Ameen

(65) MALE AND FEMALE *SAAYATHS*

Athaarid, Shams and *Mirreq* are male. *Qamar, Zuhra* and *Musthari* are female. *Suhal* can be both male and female.

Ameen

(66) FRIENDSHIP AND ENMITY BETWEEN *RAASIS* AND *SAAYATHS*

Hamal and *Mirreq*, male *raasi*, friends, *Shams* and *Zuhra*.
Dour and *Zuhra*, female *raasi*, colour, yellow, friends, *Shams* and *Zuhra*, enemy *Mirreq*.
Jousa and *Athaarid*, female *raasi*, colour, green, friends, *Shams* and *Mirreq*, enemy *Musthari*.
Sharthan and *Qamar*, female *raasi*, colour, black, friends, *Zuhra* and *Athaarid*, enemy, *Shams*.
Asad and *Shams*, male *raasi*, friends, *Musthari* and *Mirreq*, enemy, *Qamar*.
Suhal and *Athaarid*, female *raasi*, colour, white, friends, *Zuhra* and *Musthari*, enemy, *Mirreq*.
Meezan and *Zuhra*, male *raasi*, friends, *Athaarid* and *Suhal*, enemy.
Musthari Aqrab and *Mirreq*, female *raasi*, colour, black, friends, *Shams* and *Musthari*, enemy, *Suhal*.
Qouz and *Musthari*, male *raasi*, friends, *Qamar* and *Suhal*, enemy, *Athaarid*.
Jadeen and *Suhal*, female *raasi*, colour, black, friends, *Shams* and *Musthari*, enemy, *Mirreq*.
Dalb and *Suhal*, female *raasi*, colour, black, friends, *Athaarid* and *Musthari*, enemy, *Shams*.
Hooth and *Shams*, female *raasi*, friends, *Musthari* and *Zuhra*, enemy, *Qamar*.

Ameen

(67) GOOD AND EVIL EFFECTS OF THE *SAAYATHS*

Shams	It is good for meeting kings, nobility; bad for journeys and giving loans.
Zuhra	Good for giving women in marriage; establishing friendship and for similar actions
Athaarid	Good for marriage
Qamar	Good for everything but a cause of misery may come in the way.
Musthari	Good for meeting kings, ministers and friends
Mirreq	Enmity will develop in one matter.
Suhal	Enmity; bad circumstances; attachment and coveting

Ameen

(68) *KANAKKU* OF MARRIAGES IN (DIFFERENT) MONTHS

Muharram	-	If there is marriage there will be quick separation
Safar	-	Prosperity declines; becomes poor; fear from snake
Rabiul Auwal	-	Good; many children will be born
Rabiul Akhir	-	Anxiety will increase; disease and increase of life
Jamathul Auwal	-	Women will receive many blows
Jamathul Akhir	-	Affection and love
Rajab	-	Healthy and happy children
Saaban	-	Will become *fakir*
Ramzaan	-	Quarrels will increase
Shawwaal	-	Will live well but spend much
Dul Kaaida	-	Many children and more expenditure
Dul Hijj	-	Best living with great blessing

Ameen

(69) *KANAKKU* FOR APPLYING THE HORN

(This is a system of bloodletting by making an incision on the head and sucking the blood out through a horn. If it is done on a particular date in the month it may have the following effects:)

On the first day application of the horn will lead to contagious diseases.
On the second day application of the horn will lead to (feeling of) severe cold.
On the third day application of the horn will lead to leucoderma.
On the fourth day application of the horn will lead to body turning yellow.
On the fifth day application of the horn will lead to fever.
On the sixth day application of the horn will lead to infection, sores.
On the seventh day application of the horn will lead to fear.
On the eighth day application of the horn will lead to diseases affecting the brain.
On the ninth day application of the horn will lead to headache.
On the tenth day application of the horn will lead to phobia.
On the eleventh day application of the horn will lead to giddiness.
On the twelfth day application of the horn will lead to skin infection.
On the thirteenth day application of the horn will lead to leucoderma.
On the fourteenth day application of the horn will lead to decline of eyesight.

On the fifteenth day application of the horn will lead to forgetfulness.
On the sixteenth day application of the horn will lead to leucoderma.
On the seventeenth day application of the horn will lead to the disappearance of body pain and tiredness will disappear.
On the eighteenth day application of the horn will lead to improvement of vision.
On the ninteenth day application of the horn will lead to increase in strength.
On the twentieth day application of the horn will lead to disease from poisoning.
On the twenty-first day application of the horn will lead to increase in strength.
On the twenty-second day application of the horn will lead to good strength.
On the twenty-third day application of the horn will lead to increase in strength.
On the twenty-fourth day application of the horn will lead to pain, variable body temperature.
On the twenty-fifth day application of the horn will lead to increase in strength.
On the twenty-sixth day application of the horn will lead to sorrow.
On the twenty-seventh day application of the horn will lead to friendship with Satan.
On the twenty-eighth day application of the horn will lead to respect from the people.
On the twenty-ninth day application of the horn will lead to increased help from the public.
On the thirtieth day application of the horn will lead to the disappearance of pain and disease.

Ameen

(70) MALE AND FEMALE *RAASIS*

Medam, Mithunam, Chingam, Thulaam, Dhanu and *Kumbam* are male *raasis*. The rest are female *raasis*. Male and females *raasis* occur one after the other (i.e. alternately).[72]

Ameen

[72] *Cf. BrJ, I, II (SRS)*

(71) GOOD AND EVIL EFFECTS OF *RAASIS*

Medam, Karkidakam, Thulaam, Makaram, these four *raasis* are good for sailing and also for visiting desired places.
Meenam, Kanni, Dhanu, Mithunam, these four are good for all things.
Edavam, Chingam, Vrischikam, Kumbam, these are not good for anything.

Ameen

(72) LIGHT AND DARKNESS OF *RAASIS*

Medam, Edavam, Mithunam, Karkidakam, Dhanu, Makaram. These are blind in the daytime. They have light in the night time.
Chingam, Kanni, Thulaam, Vrischikam, Kumbam, Meenam. These are blind in the night time. They have light in the daytime.

Ameen

(73) *KANAKKU* FOR PUBERTY ON WEEKDAYS

(If a girl attains puberty on a particular day of the week the effects will be as follows:)
Sunday, beautiful
Monday, husband will always be with her
Tuesday, sorrowful
Wednesday, speedy conception
Thursday, misery and sorrow
Friday, will be beautiful and enjoy more wealth
Saturday, destruction in the house.

Ameen

(74) KANAKKU FOR PUBERTY UNDER *RAASIS*

(If a girl attains puberty under a particular *raasi*, the effects will be as follows:)

Medam, God knows what will happen to her.
Edavam, milking the cow (family will prosper through cattle rearing).

Mithunam, prosperity and love.[73]
Karkidakam, prosperity.
Chingam, more children.
Kanni, destruction in the house.
Thulaam, property from unknown source will accrue.
Vrischikam, she will be affected by disease and sorrow.
Dhanu, cause sorrow immediately.
Makaram, (she will be) lucky.
Kumbam, (she will be) beautiful.
Meenam, she will love others.

[73] *The Malayalam term used is* ***Kama.***

(75) *RAASIS* AND MATCHING *SAAYATHS*

(The union of the following *raasis* and *saayaths* is auspicious:)

Medam (with) *Mirreq*, *Shams* and *Zuhra*.
Edavam (with) *Zuhra*, *Shams* and *Suhal*.
Mithunam (with) *Athaarid*, *Shams* and *Mirreq*.
Karkidakam (with) *Qamar*, *Zuhra* and *Athaarid*.
Chingam (with) *Shams*, *Musthari* and *Mirreq*.[74]

Ameen

[74] *The same will continue for the remaining* ***raasis*** *beginning with* ***Kanni****, that is to say:*

Kanni *(with)* ***Mirreq, Shams*** *and* ***Zuhra***.
Thulaam *(with)* ***Zuhra, Shams*** *and* ***Suhal***.
Vrischikam *(with)* ***Athaarid, Shams*** *and* ***Mirreq***.
Dhanu *(with)* ***Qamar, Zuhra*** *and* ***Athaarid***.
Makaram *(with)* ***Shams, Musthari*** *and* ***Mirreq***.
Kumbam *(with)* ***Mirreq, Shams*** *and* ***Zuhra***.
Meenam *(with)* ***Zuhra, Shams*** *and* ***Suhal***.

(76) EFFECTS OF RAT-BITE IN THE DAYTIME

Saturday, danger, leprosy
Sunday, dangerous disease
Monday, happiness
Tuesday, happiness and profit
Wednesday, disease and loss
Thursday, beginning with sorrow, ending in happiness
Friday, sorrow and afterwards happiness

Ameen

(77) POSITION OF THE *AOULIYAS*[75]

(The saints, called *Aouliyas*, are expected to be found in the following directions and places on different dates of the month:)

(DATES OF THE MONTH)

1	11	21	stands on elephant in the direction of east
2	12	22	stands on horse in the direction of south-east
3	13	23	stands on frog in the direction of south
4	14	24	stands on wolf in the direction of south-west
5	15	25	stands on cow in the direction of west
6	16	26	stands on donkey in the direction of north-west
7	17	27	north
8	18	28	stands on horse in the direction of north-east
9	19	29	on the earth
10	20	30	on the sky

Ameen

[75] *AKT explains the local belief system in the following words: "**Aouliyas** are those who have attained the stage **fana**, purification and renunciation of the material world for the attainment of eternity. In this stage they will be able to hear and see things which are not audible or visible to the ordinary person. Their actions will be guided by God." For the directions occupied by the **Aouliyas**, see Fig.39.*

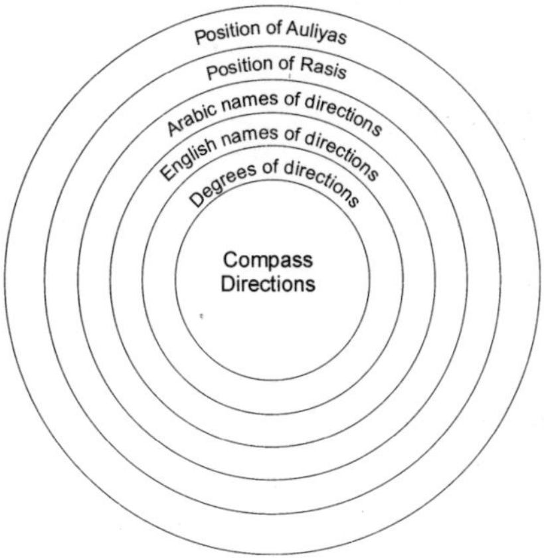

Fig. 39. Position of the *Aouliyas* (AKT)

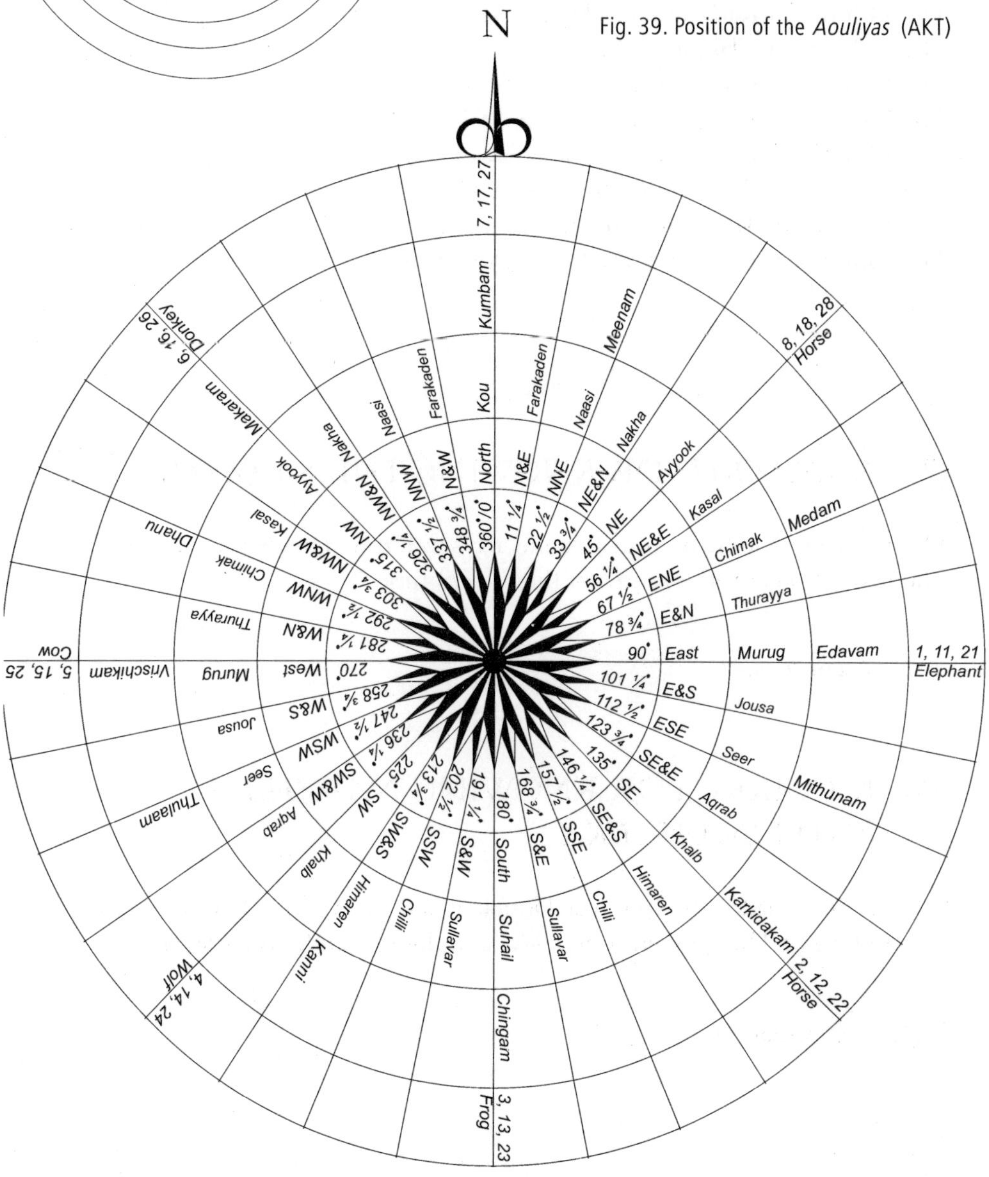

(78) KNOWING THE DATE FROM THE NOON MEASUREMENT

The 13th day of *Meenam* is the first day of *Medam*.
The 14th day of *Medam* is the first day of *Edavam*.
The 14th day of *Edavam* is the first day of *Mithunam*.
The 15th day of *Mithunam* is the first day of *Karkidakam*.
The 14th day of *Karkidakam* is the first day of *Chingam*.
The 14th day of *Chingam* is the first day of *Kanni*.
The 14th day of *Kanni* is the first day of *Thulaam*.
The 13th day of *Thulaam* is the first day of *Vrischikam*.
The 12th day of *Vrischikam* is the first day of *Dhanu*.
The 14th day of *Dhanu* is the first day of *Makaram*.
The 12th day of *Makaram* is the first day of *Kumbam*.
The 13th day of *Kumbam* is the first day of *Meenam*.

Ameen

(79) *KANAKKU* FOR KNOWING THE *SAAYATH*

Measure your shadow by your feet and add seven to it. Divide this sum by 105. The share you get is the *saayath* of the present time.[76]

[76] *Cf.* ***Section 20****, n.41.*

(80) *KANAKKU* FOR KNOWING *NAAZHIKA* AND *VINAAZHIKA*[77]

Measure your shadow by your feet. Double it and add 11 to it. This sum is to be divided by 210. The quotient is *naazhika* and the remainder is *vinaazhika*.

[77] *Cf. above,* ***Section 33****.*

(81) *KANAKKU* FOR MEASUREMENT OF THE HOUSE

If a disease is not cured in the house this *kanakku* should be seen (applied) in the first *saayath* of Thursday.

Measure the length and breadth of the house with a coir rope. The sick person should hold one end of the rope and the other will be held by the measurer.[78] The length of the coir rope should be folded into three equal parts. Leave out one part. Stretch out the remaining two parts. The sick person measures the two parts in *muzham*.[79] Measure eight units in each occasion until the length (of the coir rope) is exhausted.[80] If there is no remainder the sick person has to leave the house. If the balance is 7 *muzham*, the house is good. If it is fire, the owner's *raasi* is of the calf. That house is always good. If it is six the owner's *raasi* is of a donkey. If it is four, the owner's *raasi* is of granite stone. In that house there will be many and serious diseases. Soon the house has to be demolished. If the quotient is three, the owner's *raasi* is of a fish. In that house there would be prosperity, blessing and goodness. If the quotient comes two, go out of the house, immediately. If the quotient is one, the owner's *raasi* is of a horse. That is very good. God alone knows the rest.

Ameen

[78] *In Lakshadweep such measurements are usually taken by a **Malmi** or Navigator.*

[79] *In this case the owner, the patient, measures the rope in units of **muzham**, one **muzham** comprising the length from elbow to tip of little finger (see Fig. 43).*

[80] *What is meant here is that the remaining length of the coir is being measured in multiples of 8 **muzham**, the initial **muzham** being personally measured out by the patient.*

(82) INAUSPICIOUS PERIODS IN THE NIGHT[81]

Wednesday night after sunset from 6:48 for one hour
Tuesday night after sunset from 8:24 for one hour
Monday night after sunset from 10:00 for one hour
Sunday night after sunset from 11:36 for one hour
Saturday night after sunset from 1:12 for one hour
Friday night after sunset from 3:38 for one hour

Thursday night after sunset from 4:24 for one hour
This inauspicious time is bad for everything except for digging and burial.

Ameen

[81] *The heading in Malayalam reads* ***Rathriyil ulla Kuliyam****. Cf.* ***Sections 19, 21****. The present system is nearly identical with what is presented in Section 21 above, with slight differences in the case of Wednesday and Friday (SRS). It is not clear why the word* ***nahasu*** *was used in* ***Section 21*** *while the word* ***kuliyam*** *is found in* ***Section 82****.*

(83) METHOD OF FRAMING THE *KANAKKU* OF PLACES BEYOND SOUTH KOLLAM

Go towards the south till the longitude of the place of destination is reached. Go in the south direction till the latitude of the place of destination is reached.
Find the remaining *chaamam* (distance in longitude). It is to be distributed among *Kou* (the distance) covered in the journey.
The result is to be counted beginning from the south direction and the place where the *chaamam* (i.e. the result) ends is the direction of the place of your destination.
Similarly the direction of a place beyond boundary can be obtained by counting from the north direction.[82]

Ameen

[82] *Cf.* ***Sections 7, 9,*** *and* ***10*** *above.*

(84) *KANAKKU* FOR *MARMA*[83]

Sunday	evening	4:30	to	6:00
Monday	morning	7:30	to	9:00
Tuesday	evening	3:00	to	4:30
Wednesday	noon	12:00	to	1:30
Thursday	noon	1:30	to	3:00
Friday	morning	10:30	to	12:00
Saturday	morning	9:00	to	10:30

[83] *This system is identical to what is known as **Raahukalam** in South India, especially in Tamil Nadu and Kerala. All the almanacs and vernacular calenders indicate the times of occurance of **Raahukalam** when the planet **Raahu** is said to exercise its baneful influence in each weekday. No important work is undertaken during such a period.*

*The **Rahmani** contains four different notations of inauspicious periods in weekdays in **sections 19, 21, 82** and **84**. **Section 19** gives the inauspicious periods in the daytime in terms of shadow lengths as time units. **Section 21** enumerates the inauspicious periods in terms of **naazhikas** equal to twenty-four minutes. **Sections 82** and **84** on the other hand give inauspicious periods in terms of modern time units (i.e. hours and minutes, counted from midnight). **Sections 19** and **20** hence appear to be survivals of an obsolete system (SRS).*

*The identification of time units provided in **section 84** with periods of **Raahukalam** as proposed by Professor S R Sharma is supported by Professor V S Sharma of Tiruvanantapuram. However this explanation does not throw light on why this section should be called **Kanakku of Marma**. It is also of intrest that neither Kunhikunhi Malmi nor Atta Koya Thangal could explain the meaning of the word **Marma**. **Marma** may be derived from **Marman**, a particular concept of Ayurvedic anatomy, in which vulnerable points of the human body are taken into account. The application of this concept was manifold in yoga, massage and the martial arts. In Kerala its therapeutic angle was greatly stressed apart from its linkage with the martial arts. In the reference above, the times indicated could possibly also refer to the periods when these points were at their most sensitive levels (Mohan). See Rosu, 1981. In veiw of the importance given to the martial arts in Kerala, the connection, if any, between **marman, marma** and **raahukalam** needs much further investigation.*

(85) IDENTICAL WITH SECTION (49)

(86) *KANAKKU* FOR FINDING OUT *HAMAL*[84]

Subtract 430 from *Hijra* year. Divide (this) by 4. If the remainder is one then (take) in first *Hamal*; for two, the second *Hamal*, for three the third *Hamal*. For four (zero, take) the fourth *Hamal*. If there is no remainder then also (take) the fourth *Hamal*.

[84] *The word **hamal** in this section is to be taken in the sense of the appropriate table in the set of four tables given in **Section 3**. In the Lakshadweep context it was important to have concordance between the Gregorian and the Hijra calender for purposes of navigation and **muhurtham** fixation.*

(87) IDENTICAL WITH SECTION (53)

(88) IDENTICAL WITH SECTION (72)

(89) EFFECTS OF EACH DATE IN A MONTH

1 The first day of the commencement of the month is good for doing everything. Suitable day for approaching kings and requesting them for favours; for buying and selling; for cultivation, travel, marriage contracts. Anything lost on this day may be found. A disease contracted on this day will soon be cured.

2 On this day Havva Umma (Eve) was created. A child born on this day will be good. People will not pay attention to what is said to them. Hair cutting, bloodletting with the horn, horse riding should not be undertaken. Good for marriage contract, travelling, requesting for favours. Slave lost will not be found. Anything heard on this day is a lie. Any dream on this day is certain to come true.

3 Not good. Adam, may protection be on him, was thrown out of Paradise on this day. On this day Haabeel and Khaabeel quarrelled. On this day blood and water fell on the earth. A child born on this day will not be good. (The child) will be a drunkard, murderer, adulterer and debtor. Any disease contracted will not be cured. Any dream on that day is certain to materialise on the next day. Not good for travelling. Give alms and read the Quran.

4 Good for all things. A child born will be unlucky. A disease contracted on this day will be cured. Good for sailing, hunting, laying of pillars for a house. Any dream on this day, the day when the sons of the prophet were murdered, is certain to happen.

5 It is not good for doing anything. Any child born on this day will have the fortunes of a king. If a disease is contracted on this day it will be cured. This is the day on which Sulaiman, may protection be on him, left the kingdom; (the day on which) the children of the prophet were murdered; (when) Noah, may protection be on him, left for the dense forest; when Khabeel was born. Any dream on this day will certainly materialise on the tenth day.

6 Good for doing all things. A child born on this day will be tall and fat, will be respected by the public, will be a learned person. Good day for contracting marriage, going on travel and requesting favours. Bloodletting with horn should not be undertaken. A good day to buy a house and a slave. A slave lost will return by himself.

7 The day may be good or bad. On this day do not do anything, but (if you do) do good things. If a birth takes place this day the child will be stillborn. If he survives, he will be a murderer, a drunkard and adulterer, indulge in drink and so on. A slave lost will be found. Good for travelling, contracting marriage, hunting, approaching kings, debating and quarrelling.

8 A good day for doing everything. Good for ritual bathing for women, for giving (by bride) of first drink to groom (after marriage ceremony) and for first intercourse. Not good for business, travelling, cultivating, and house construction. Good for approaching king. If there is a difference of opinion with anybody, the friendship will be broken. A disease contracted will be cured.

9 Not good and do not do anything. After noon is good. A child born on this day will have good fortune. Will be a good boy to parents. He will be murdered. He will be treated badly. Good for pilgrimage and requesting for favours. The lost, will be found.

10 A good day to start doing everything. Child born on this day will be good to parents, will live long. Good for cultivation, writing letters, sailing, for buying and selling, for asking favours. That which is lost will be found. No hair cutting. If it is done medicine will have to be used. Not good for meeting kings. Marriage contract (entered into) will be broken. Any disease contracted on that day will be cured after prolonged treatment. Slave lost will not be found. Animals purchased on that day will multiply. Good day for taking medicine.

11 Giving and taking a woman will be good. Child born on this day will bring wealth to the parents. He will live long. He will get property. Good day for requesting favours. Disease contacted on this day will be later cured. Bad for meeting kings. Do four *rakayats* (in *namaaz*, the process of shifting from standing to prostrate position and reverting to original standing

posture is taken as one *rakayat*) in the place chosen for *namaaz*. While engaged in prayer, in each *rakayat* recite *al fathiha* three times, followed by a recital of *surath ul iklaas* three times and in the last prostration recite the *surath* "*Iyyaka Naibudu Vaiyyaka Nasthaeten*" eighteen times, keeping in your heart the favour you desire. Complete the course of *namaaz*. Then your desire will be fulfilled.[85]

12. A good day to start doing all things. Good to give and take women. Child born on this day will do good to his parents. The boy will do service like a slave and maintain the mosque. He will not commit sin. A good day for asking favour. Prophet Mohammed (may peace and blessings be on Him) was born on this day.

13. A bad day. Do not start doing anything. Still birth. However, if the child survives it will commit all sins. It is good for fasting, (preparing to give) *zakat* and for reading the Quran. Prophet Ibrahim was placed in wild fire by Nimrod on this day. Marriage contracted will end in divorce. Disease will not be immediately cured.

14. Start doing everything. Child born on this day would wish to study. Will earn property (when he is) closer to death. Good for sailing and wearing of new clothes. Contagious disease will not be cured.

15. Neutral day. Child born on this day would be a good child. Good to send children to learn the Quran, for prayer, to meet the King, request favours for buying and selling and so on.

16. Not good for doing anything. Do not do anything but good. A child born on this day will be poverty stricken (but will aquire) wealth. Not good for journey. Prophet Joseph, may protection be upon him, was put in the well on this day.

17. Not good for doing anything. Do not do anything but good on this day. A child born on this day will kill somebody, become a drunkard and commit adultery. Disease will not be cured. Loan given on this day cannot be recovered. News heard on this day will be false. A good day to return property if stolen, and to ask for favours.

18. Prophet Ishaq, may peace be on him, was born on this day. Good for sailing, hair cutting, bloodletting with horn, buying a slave, giving loans, to give and to take, asking favours, wearing new clothes. Marriage contracts will lead to bad relations. Anything heard will be a lie. Not good for audience with Sultan. Diseases contracted will be immediately cured.

19. Good for doing everything. Good for sailing and travelling and buying a horse. A house constructed on this day will be vacated. Thuryya was born on this day.

20. A good day. Do everything on this day. Prophet Isa (Jesus Christ, peace be upon him) was born on this day. On this day Isa spoke to Allah. Speak good thing and have good food. Not good for house construction.

21. Not a good day. Prophet Ibrahim, peace be on him, was born on this day. The tooth of Prophet Mohammed (peace and blessings be upon him) was lost on this day in a war. Good for staying somewhere and also for writing letters. If there is a dispute it will end in success. Good for giving women. Do not cut nails on this day. If a child is born he would become a very poor man. Not good for journey and also not good for asking favours. Not good for house construction.

22. Good for all things. Prophet Yousuf was born on this day. A child born on this day will be a good child for his father. On this day anyone sailing will reach destination without difficulty and return. Good for taking and giving and asking favours. If a disease occurs on this day it would get cured later. If business is undertaken it will be profitable. If anybody speaks up keep your mouth shut and ignore him. A slave lost will come back by himself. A dream on this day will certainly materialise on the tenth day.

23. Good for doing everything. A child born on this day will do good to his parents and will be charming. Good for house construction, cultivation, marriage contract, for starting any new thing.

24. Do not do anything. Pharoah was born on this day. He and his soldiers were drowned in the river Nile on this day. A child born on this day will commit sins. Prophet Yunus, peace be upon him, was swallowed by a mighty fish on this day. This day is good for sealing the marriage contract, giving and taking women, buying and selling a slave. A disease contracted on this

day will be cured soon. A slave lost on this day will return by himself. A dream on that day will be certain to materialise.

25. Not good for doing anything. A child born on this day will prosper. The people of Egypt had misfortunes on this day. Not good for journey. News heard will be false.

26. Good for doing everything. A child born on this day will do good to his parents. Marriage contracts on this day will end in bad relations. A disease occurring on this day will get cured in course of time. A slave lost will return. Not good for journey and marriage contracts. Good for asking favours.

27. Good day for doing everything. A child born on this day will be a good child. Prophet Mohammed (peace and blessings be upon him) got a male child on this day. It is good for construction of houses, writing of letters, sailing and for asking favours. Do not cut hair this day. Do not let blood with horn of cow. News heard this day will be false. A dream on this day will certainly materialise on this twentieth day.

28. Good for doing everything. A child born on this day will commit sin and not live long. If somebody says ill of you, keep silent. A dream on this day is sure to materialise.

29. Good for doing everything. It was on this day that the Prophet Moosa, (peace be upon him), spoke to God from Mount Sinai. A child born on this day would do good to his parents. It is also good for journeys and for asking a favour. A disease contracted on this day will not be cured.

30. Good day for doing everything. Prophet Ismail peace be upon him, was born on this day. A child born on this day will be lucky. This day is good for marriage contracts, returning stolen property and asking favours. A disease contracted on this day will be cured. Allah knows best the desires of all.

[85] *It is prohibited that an activity for which there is no authorisation should be solicited in this manner. This prayer could only be performed if permission and direct guidance of the spiritual leader was available (AKT).*

(90) OTHER EFFECTS OF WEEKDAYS

Sunday	Good for a journey towards the east, and not towards the west.
Monday	Good for a journey towards the south and not towards the east.
Tuesday	Bad for a journey towards the north. Khabeel killed Habeel on this day. Havva Umma attained puberty. A child born on this day will be a good one.
Wednesday	Bad for a journey towards the north. Good for taking medicines. Good for special bathing. A child born on this day will be the best behaved. Pharoah and his people, also the people of the Talmud, lost their lives in the blue waters of the sea on this day.
Thursday	Good for a journey towards the north, and bad for the south. Good for trying to get a desired thing. Prophet Mohammed (peace and blessings be upon Him) and his companions got the illustrious victory of Mekka on this day. Prophet Ibrahim (peace be upon him) obtained his desire from the king of Egypt, this day. A child born on this day will be a scholar.
Friday	Good for a journey towards the east and not to the west. A child born on this day will be truthful.
Saturday	Good for a journey towards the west and not towards the east. Good for hunting and war. Child born on this day will be a liar.

(91) ASSESSMENT OF INCOME AND EXPENDITURE OF A HOUSE

Take the perimeter of a house in inches. Divide it by 28. Convert the result into the unit of scale used by the carpenter (x).

Multiply this (x) by eight and divide the product by 12 ($8x \div 12$). The remainder (r) is treated as the income of a family. On the other hand, if it (x) is multiplied by 3 and divided by 14, the remainder will be the expenditure. The income should always be higher than the expenditure.

(92) METHOD OF ASSESSMENT OF INCOME AND EXPENDITURE WHILE CONSTRUCTING A HOUSE

Take the perimeter of the house and convert it into inches. Divide this by 28 and again convert it (perimeter) into *kole* (a local unit of length measuring from mid-chest to outstretched middle finger of hand, equal to 2 1/2 ft.). Then multiply it (measurement in *kole)* by eight and divide the product by 12. The remainder is the income.

The result of division by 28 is to be multiplied by 3 and then divided by 14. The remainder is the expenditure.

Arrange the perimeter of the house in such a way that the expenditure does not exceed 6 and the income ranges between 12 and 8.

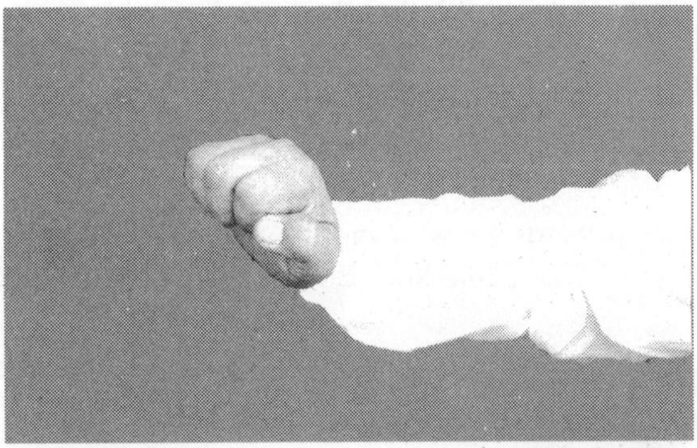

Fig. 40.

Fig. 41.

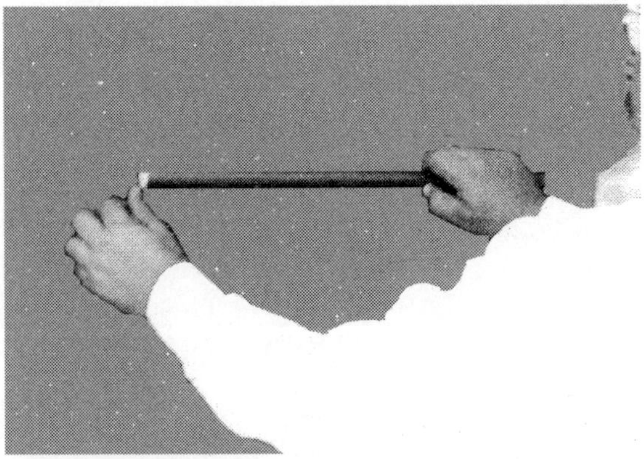

Fig. 42.

Fig. 43.

Figs. 40-43. Carpentry measurements also having a bearing on earlier methods of appraising star altitude.

E.P. Atta Koya Thangal could not recollect the carpentry measurement shown in Fig.40. This is the unit called *dhubban* by Arab navigators. Fig.10 above illustrates one *mushti* equal to six inches. When a tree trunk is hewn into planks, a single *mushti* is used to assess if the log in the round would suit the purpose. Fig.41 shows a double *mushti* equal to one foot. The experienced carpenter would cut a two *mushti* segment from the spine of a coconut leaf and use this as a measure. Cf. Fig. 42. Fig. 43 shows E.P. Atta Koya Thangal demonstrating the length of one *ashari* (carpenter) *kole.* The measurement is taken from mid-section of the collar bone to the outstretched middle finger. The scale is as follows:

1 *mushti* = 6 inches
1 double *mushti* = 1 foot
5 single *mushti* = 1 *kole*
1 *kole* = 2 1/2 feet

APPENDIX I

ASTRONOMICAL HERITAGE *VIS-À-VIS* NAVIGATIONAL TRADITIONS IN INDIA

Sea and river voyages were common activities in Indian life from early times. The vast coast-line and the network of river systems in India constituted natural advantages. There is ample evidence that peoples of this subcontinent made journeys across the rivers or oceans to far-off places for business. Such a journey was considered to be the harbinger of good fortune. Descriptions from Vedic, post-Vedic, Buddhist and Jaina literature as also foreign travel accounts have confirmed such voyages and their purpose (Moti Chandra, 1977, 102-103; Sidebotham, 1986, 20-27). D.D. Kosambi thinks that with the consolidation of Mauryan Empire in the westcoast, Indian Buddhist monasteries played a significant role in commercial intercourse with the countries of the west through the ports such as Śuppāraka (Sopra), Kalliena (Kalyan) among others. About one hundred Indian Buddhist monasteries were excavated which were established between the first and the eighth centuries AD. These are located near the inter-connecting routes covering difficult terrain in western India. The Buddhist text, *Jātakamālā* of Āryasūra (1st century AD), contemporary with the *Periplus*, refers to the Bodhisattva as a perfect pilot and relates that "Knowing the course of celestial luminaries, he was never at a loss with respect to regions of the ship, being perfectly acquainted with the different prognostics, the permanent, the occasional and the miraculous ones, he was skilled in the establishment of a given time as proper or improper, by means of manifold marks, observing the fishes, the colour of the water, the species of the ground, birds, rocks etc., he knew how to ascertain rightly the parts of the sea, further he was vigilant, not subject to drowsiness and sleep, capable of enduring the fatigue of cold, heat, rain and the like, careful and patient. So being skilled in the art of taking a ship out and bringing her home, he exercised the profession of one who conducts the merchants by sea to their destination." (Speyer, 1895, 124-125; Tibbetts, 1971, 1-2).

1. Early Astronomical Knowledge

What is meant by the "course of celestial luminaries" is not known. However there is no denying the fact that various types of relationship between the cycle of human activities and the regularity of heavenly phenomena including movement of the sun, moon, planets, the sun's path (ecliptic) and positions of *nakṣatras* and the constellations with reference to diurnal and annual motion were already known. By the eighth century AD Indians had more or less a clear idea of the following aspects:

1.1 All heavenly bodies appear to move from east to west because of the earth's rotation. The earth's axis is tilted and, when produced, meets the celestial sphere at two points. The star (Ursa Minor) lies close to the northern celestial point. This star is treated as the Pole Star for all practical purposes.

1.2 The celestial equator is coplaner (lies in the same plane) to the earth's equator and is at right angles to the direction of the celestial axis.

1.3 The sun travels not in the plane of the equator, but in that of the ecliptic with a motion which varies every day. Therefore the duration of the daylight is not always the same except on the equator. The diurnal motion of the sun is parallel to the equator. According to Indian tradition, the earth's equator passes over a hypothetical city called Laṅkā.[1] The prime meridian passes over Ujjain and Laṅkā. Thus Laṅkā is situated on the intersection of the equator and the prime meridian.

1.4 The observer's horizon has four cardinal points, viz. the north point (where the celestial meridian passing through the zenith of the observer and the celestial pole meets the horizon below the pole), the south point (the opposite of north point on the horizon), the east and the west points (the two points of intersection of the celestial equator and the horizon), east being the point met by moving in clockwise direction from the north point, and west the opposite of east point. The rising and setting points of the sun vary. This variation is due to the declination deviation of the sun towards north or south. The north celestial pole is only seen since it is above the horizon. The great circle passing through north, zenith and the south points is known as the celestial meridian, and the great circle passing through east, zenith and the west points is known as the prime meridian.

1.5 The path of the sun (ecliptic) or of the moon was supposed to be circular one of 360° and was marked by 27 or 28 *nakṣatras* (lunar mansions). The *Taittirīya Saṃhitā* (IV.4.10) and the *Vedāṅga Jyotiṣa* (verse 29) and all the later Siddhāntas give the name of 27 *nakṣatras* in the sky. These are (1) *Aśvinī*, (2) *Bharaṇī*, (3) *Kṛttikā*, (4) *Rohiṇī*, (5) *Mṛgaśīrṣa*, (6) *Ārdrā*, (7) *Punarvasu*, (8) *Puṣya*, (9) *Āślesā*, (10) *Maghā*, (11) *Pūrvaphālgunī*, (12) *Uttaraphālgunī*, (13) *Hasta*, (14) *Citrā*, (15) *Svātī*, (16) *Vīśākhe*, (17) *Anūrādhā*, (18) *Jyeṣṭhā*, (19) *Mūlā*, (20) *Pūrvāṣāȳhā*, (21) *Uttarāsāȳhā*, (22) *Śravaṇa*, (23) *Dhaniṣtha*, (24) *Śatabhiṣaj*, (25) *Purva Bhādrapadā*, (26) *Uttara Bhādrapadā*, and (27) *Revatī*. The *Vedāṅga Jyotiṣa* (BC 500) took *Bharaṇī* as the starting point of its *nakṣatra* list. Siddhāntic texts from the first century onwards placed the starting point at *Aśvinī*, probably because of the precision of the equinoxes. The moon makes one revolution among stars in about 27 days. This may be the reason why the number of *nakṣatras* was limited to 27. The *nakṣatras* were conceived as 27 *nakṣatra* spaces in the *Vedāṅga-Jyotiṣa*, each covering a space of 13° 20', for 13° 20' × 27 = 360°. The *nakṣatra* space was further subdivided into 124 parts (*parvas*) on the basis of a five year cycle when the sun, moon and the beginning of *Dhaniṣṭha* (winter solstice) were in conjunction.

The use of *Dhaniṣṭha* also indicates that the path of the sun was marked by the twelve zodiac signs viz. (1) *Meṣa* (Aries), (2) *Vṛṣa* (Taurus), (3) *Mithuna* (Gemini), (4) *Karkaṭa* (Cancer), (5) *Siṃha* (Leo), (6) *Kanyā*, (Virgo), (7) *Tulā*, (Libra), (8) *Vṛścika* (Scorpio), (9) *Dhanuṣ* (Sagittarius), (10) *Makara* (Capricorn), (11) *Kumbha* (Aquarius), and (12) *Mīna* (Pisces), each covering a space 30°, known as *rāśi*, for 30° x 12 = 360°. Sankara Balakrishna Dikshit believes that the zodiacal sign names starting with *Meṣa* began to be used in India between BC 700 and 300 (Sewell and Dikshit, 1995, 10). These zodiac signs are quite common in the *Yavanajātaka* (Yur.I.14-25) and later Siddhāntic texts. The Siddhāntic texts report that the summer equinox, summer solstice, autumnal equinox and winter solstice start at the first point respectively of *Meṣa*, *Karkaṭa*, *Tulā*, and *Makara*.[2] The equinoxes and solstices were determined generally from the shadow of the gnomon. The *Vedāṅga Jyotiṣa* first gave a rule for determining the length of the day between the two solstices, the shortest day being 12 *muhūrtas* at the winter solstice and the longest day being 18 *muhūrtas* at the summer solstice.[3] On the summer and autumnal equinox the day and night are of equal duration.

1.6 The *Vedāṅga Jyotiṣa* gives a formula for calculating day lengths from shadow lengths. The *Arthaśāstra* (II.20.41-42) of Kautilya (1st century AD) gives the annual variation of gnomon shadow (*chāyāpuruṣa*) for a gnomon of 12 *angulas*. It also states that the diurnal variation of the gnomon midday shadow is zero. Obviously this data was meant for summer solstice day. Other texts of the same period like *Candraprajñapti*, *Ṣūryaprajñapti*, *Śārdūlakarṇāvadāna*, *Yavanajātaka*, *Atharvajyotiṣa* contain similar measures of shadow lengths which follow a linear zig-zag function. The *Mul Apin* of the Babylonian astronomy and some Greek shadow tables also mention noon shadow. While the Babylonian text gives a fixed noon shadow length of 5/6 rather than 1 cubit for the summer solstice, equinox and winter solstice, the Greek tables (about BC 200) report a value from 2 feet to 8 feet for summer to winter solstice with reference to a man's shadow. The difference between the maximum and minimum length of the shadow is 6 feet (equal to a man's height, though it may vary). However, in Indian tradition the height of the gnomon is fixed at 12 *aṅgulas*.

1.7 Trigonometric tables were formulated for conversion of *Jyā* (R Sine) and *Kojyā* (R Cosine) lengths in a quarter circle into arcual measure and vice versa.

1.8 Formulae to calculate declination of the sun, latitude and longitude of places, and so on were also available in these texts.

2. Knowledge of the Half Chord

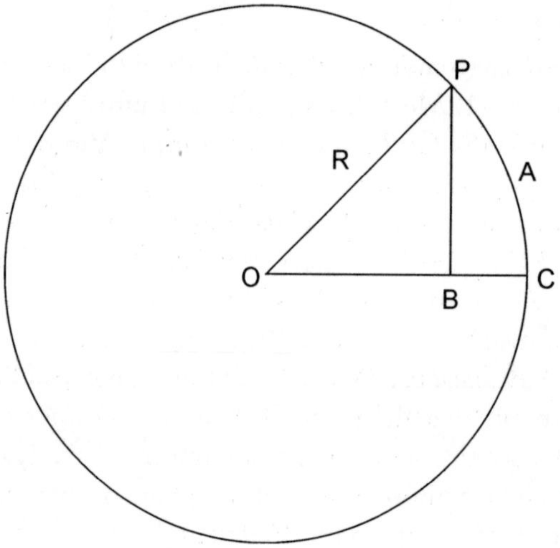

Fig. 1.

Before proceeding further, it is important to understand how Indians tried to convert linear *jyā* lengths into arcual measure.

In Fig. 1, for any arc A (= CP) in a circle of radius R (= OP=OC) and centre O, let PB be the perpendicular on OC. In *Siddhāntic* tradition it would follow that

PB = *Jyā* A, OB =*Kojyā* A , BC = *Utkramajyā* A = R – *Kojyā* A.

In modern notation,

PB = R sine POB = R sine A ; OB = R cosine POB = R cosine A,

when angle POB = A .

Obviously,

PB = *Jyā* A = R sine A,

OB = *Kojyā* A = R cosine A and

BC = *Utkramajyā* A = R– R cosine A.

No tan or cot function (tan A = PB/OB or cot A = OB/PB) was used in the ancient period. Possibly this was beyond the scope of definition.

The radius R of the circle is called *trijyā*. Varāhamihira has taken R = 120', Brahmagupta as 3270', *Sūryasiddhānta* as 3438'. Later scholars have refined the value further. When R = 1, the Indian and modern systems become identical.

2.1 Conversion table for changing *Jyā* length to arcual measure and vice versa

Indian texts took into consideration quarter of a circle (90°) and divided it into 24 divisions of 3°45' each. The *jyā* lengths drawn from points at an interval of 3° 45' were tabulated. Varāhamihira (AD 505) in his *Pañcasiddhāntikā* (IV. 6-11) gave this table for a circle of radius 120'. Such tables were very common in Indian tradition and were widely used for converting arcual (or angular) measure into R sine (*jyā*) lengths and vice versa. Twenty-four *jyā* tables are available for R = 3438' (*Āryabhaṭīya*, *Paitāmahasiddhānta*, *Sūryasiddhānta*, *Siddhānta Śiromaṇi* and others); 3237' (Brahmagupta, AD 627), 3437' 44" 19"' (Govindāsvamī, 9th century), 3437' 44" 48"' (Mādhava 15th century) and others. It may also be noted in this connection that the linear R sine (*jyā*) length has also been expressed in sexagesimal units like minutes (*aṅgula*) and parts (*vyāṅgula*). The methods for calculating these tables are also given by all astronomical works. The table as given by Varāhamihira is reproduced below together with the explanation provided by him.

Table I

***Jyā* or R sine table for calculating arcual measure at an interval of 3° 45'**

S No	Arc/Angle	Rsine (*jyā*)	S No	Arc/Angle	Rsine(*jyā*)
1	3° 45'	7' 51"	13	48° 45'	90' 13"
2	7° 30'	15' 40"	14	52° 30'	95' 12"
3	11° 15'	23' 25"	15	56° 15'	99' 46"
4	15° 0'	31' 4"	16	60° 0'	103' 55"
5	18° 15'	38' 34"	17	63° 45'	107' 37"
6	22° 30'	45' 56"	18	67° 30'	110' 52"
7	26° 15'	53' 5"	19	71° 15'	113' 37"
8	30° 0'	60' 0"	20	75° 0'	115' 55"
9	33° 45'	66' 40"	21	78° 45'	117' 42"
10	37° 30'	73' 3"	22	82° 30'	118' 59"
11	41° 15'	79' 7"	23	86° 15'	119' 44"
12	45° 0'	84' 51"	24	90° 0'	120'

The values were calculated from the four basic formulae (*PS*.IV.2), viz. *Jyā* 90° = R, *Jyā* 60° = $\sqrt{3/2}$ R, *Jyā* 30° = 1/2 Rwhich could be obtained from the radius, an equilateral triangle, a square and an equilateral hexagon respectively. The other values (*PS*.IV.3-5) were obtained by the formulae:

$$Jy\bar{a}\,(90^\circ - A) = \sqrt{(R^2 - Jy\bar{a}^2 A)},$$

$$Jy\bar{a}\,A/2 = 1/2\sqrt{[R - Jy\bar{a}\,(90^\circ - A)]^2 + (Jy\bar{a}A)^2}$$

$$Jy\bar{a}\,A = \sqrt{R/2\,[R - Jy\bar{a}\,(90^\circ - 2A)]} \qquad \text{(Bag, 1979, 234-236).}$$

For planetary positions exceeding 90°, a circle was divided into four quadrants (*SS*, II.30). The first and the third quadrants were designated as odd (*viṣama*) and the second and the fourth as even (*sama*). In Fig. 2, quadrants AOB and COD are odd, and BOC and AOD are even. If P, Q, R, S be the positions of planets in the first, second, third and fourth quadrants respectively, then for quadrants AOB and COD, AP and CR are *bhujas*, BP and DR are *koṭis*. For quadrants BOC and AOD, BQ and DS are *koṭis*, CQ and AS are *bhujas*. These relations are expressed in the following formulae:

R sine (90° + A) = R cosine A

R sine (180°– A) = R sine A

R sine (180°+ A)= –R sine A

R sine (270°– A) = –R cosine A

R sine (270°+ A) = –R cosine A

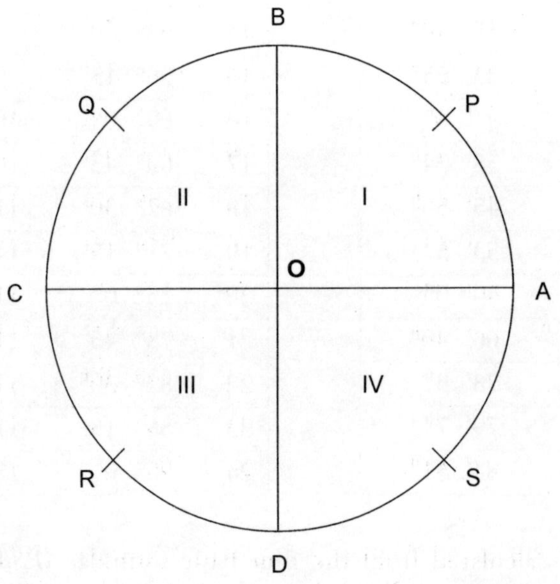

Fig. 2.

3. Celestial Pole

Since early times, constellations like the Great Bear and Orion have attracted the attention of many civilizations because of their distinctive appearance. In India, the Great Bear is known as *Sapta-ṛṣis*. Each of the seven constituent stars were named after the *ṛṣis* - *Marīci, Vaśiṣṭha, Aṅgira, Atri, Pulastya, Pulaha* (b) and *Kratu* (a). The line joining the two stars, *Pulaha* and *Kratu*, when produced, passes through a star half as bright at some distance. This star is the Pole Star or Polaris. It is called *Dhruva* in Sanskrit which means fixed (Fig. 3). The line joining *Pulaha* and *Kratu* is circumpolar. It makes one full rotation in about 24 hours around the Pole Star.

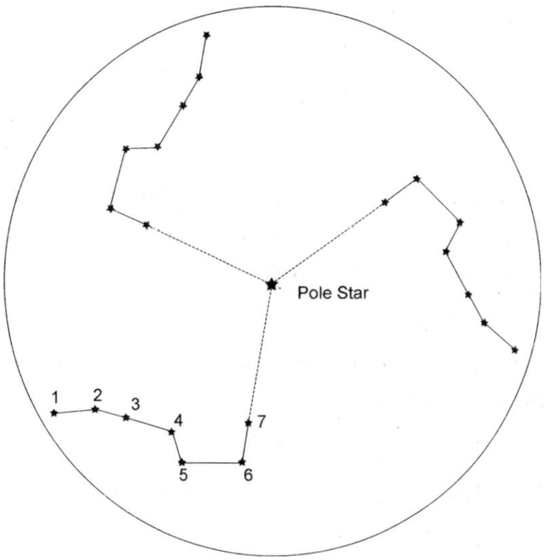

Fig. 3. *Saptarsi* (Great Bear)

1. *Marīci*
2. *Vaśiṣṭha*
3. *Aṅgira*
4. *Atri*
5. *Pulasta*
6. *Pulaha* (β)
7. *Kratu* (α)

4. Altitude and Zenith Distance of the Sun

In Fig. 4, let O be the observer, NZSZ' the celestial meridian (*yāmyottara-vṛtta*) passing through the north, zenith, south and nadir points. Let SON be the orthogonal projection of the celestial horizon (*kṣitija*), EOQ that of the celestial equator (*viṣuva-maṇÿala*), ZZ' (through E and W, the east and west points) of the prime vertical (*sama-maṇÿala*), GH of the diurnal circle, POP' of the six o'clock circle on the plane of the meridian. When the sun is at G in the northern hemisphere,

GS = meridian altitude (*unnatāṃśa*) = GE + ES = declination + co-latitude,

GZ = meridian zenith distance (*natāṃśa*) = complement of GS = 90°– GS.

When the sun is at G' in the southern hemisphere,

G'S = meridian altitude = ES – G'E = co-latitude – declination,

and G'Z = meridian zenith distance = 90° – G'S.

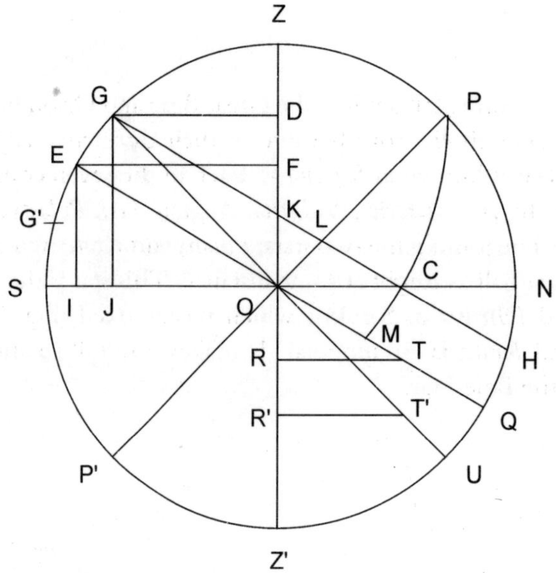

Fig. 4.

There were several formulae known for calculating the altitude of the sun (*STV.* IV.20). For this purpose, properties of similar, right-angled triangles were used as well as the properties of spherical triangles:

$$a \div \text{sine } A = b \div \text{sine } B = c \div \text{sine } C.$$

There were many methods for finding the altitude of the sun. A few are given below for different positions of the sun.

4.1 The sun is at the equinoctial point E (Fig. 4).

The arc EZ = arc PN = latitude of the observer = zenith distance of the sun, arc ES = arc Z P = co-latitude.

This fact was known in ancient India. The sides of the right-angled triangle EIO were known respectively as R sine co-latitude (*lambajyā*, EI), R sine latitude (*akṣajyā*, IO) and radius (*trijyā*, EO). Likewise in the right-angled triangle ORT, OR is the gnomon, RT the shadow and OT the hypotenuse. Then from the two similar triangles EIO and ORT, we deduce EI/EO = OR/OT or, R sine (equinoctial midday altitude) ÷ radius = 12 ÷ hypotenuse of the equinoctial shadow, or, R sine (equinoctial midday altitude) = 12 × R ÷ hypotenuse of the equinoctial shadow or, R sine(co-latitude) = 12 × R÷ hypotenuse of the equinoctial shadow (*MBh.* III.5)

4.2 The sun is on the meridian at G on any other day (Fig. 4).

Then from the similar triangles GDO and OR' T', OD / OG =OR' / OT' ,

or, R sine (midday altitude) radius = 12 ÷ hypotenuse of the shadow or, R sine (midday altitude) = 12 × R ÷ hypotenuse of the shadow. This formula is found in *MBh.* III.5; *BSS.* III.28ab and 29ab; *SŚe.* IV.45; *SS.* III.21; *SŚi.* III. 40ab.

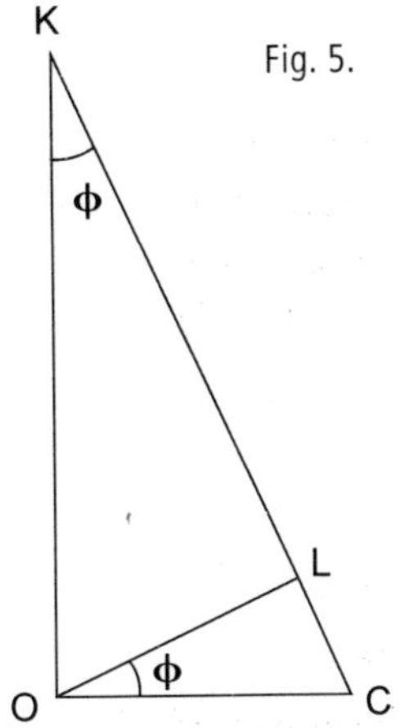

Fig. 5.

4.3 The sun is on the prime meridian at K (Fig. 5).

Let KO and KC be the perpendiculars from K on the east-west line and on the rising-setting line (line of intersection of the planes of the celestial horizon and of the diurnal circle). Then,

OK = R sine a (a being prime meridian altitude),

OC = R sine (the sun's *agrā*),

OL= R sine (declination),

KOC = right angle.

OK ÷ R sine angle KCO = OC ÷ R sine angle OKC or,

R sine a ÷ R sine (90°– latitude)= R sine (the sun's *agrā*) ÷ R sine (latitude) or,

R sine a = R cosine (latitude) × R sine (the sun's *agrā*) ÷ R sine (latitude).

When R sine (the sun's *agrā*) = R sine (declination) × R ÷ R cosine (latitude) or, R sine a = R sine (declination) × R÷ R sine (latitude) — (*MBh*.III.37-38)

= R sine (longitude) × R sine 24°÷ R sine (latitude) —— (*PS*.IV.35)

The prime vertical altitude of the sun is possible only when the sun is in the northern hemisphere and its declination is less than the latitude of the place. Brahmagupta was aware of this limitation and rectified this in his *BSS* (III.22).

4.4 When the sun is at any other position S (Fig. 6).

Let SA be the perpendicular from S on the horizon, SC the perpendicular from S on the rising-setting line. Then from the triangle SAC, SA = SC × R cosine (latitude) ÷ R Or, R sine (altitude) = *cheda* × R cosine (latitude) ÷ R, where *cheda* SC = day radius ± earth-sine, and day-radius = R cosine (declination), earth-sine = R sine (latitude) × R sine (declination) ÷ R sine (co-latitude). The plus or minus sign is applicable depending on whether as the sun is to the north or south side of the equator. This formula is found in *ABh*. IV.28 (see also Gupta 1977)*MBh*.III.20;*SS*.III.34cd-35ab;*SŚe*.IV.34ab.

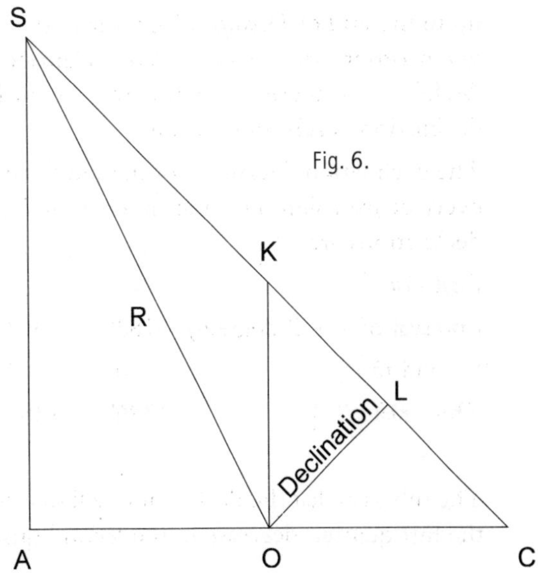

Fig. 6.

5. Declination of the Sun

The declination of the sun is measured by its deviation towards north or south from the celestial equator. Obviously the declination becomes zero when it is on the equator, and it is maximum when the sun is in 3 signs or 9 signs i.e. when it is on the summer solstice or winter solstice. Varāhamihira (*PS.* IV.16) says that

R sine (declination) = R sine (*sāyana* longitude) × 61÷150

or, R sine (declination) = R sine (longitude) × 61÷150

Again, maximum declination (in linear distance) = 120' × 61÷150 = 48' 48"

The maximum declination (in arcual measure) = arc of 48' 48" = 24°

It may also be noted that when the longitude reckoned from the point of intersection of equator and ecliptic is within 6 signs, the declination is north, when it is more than 6 signs, it is south. Bhāskara I replaced the fraction 61/150 by 1397/3438 and its convergents (*MBh.*III.6-7; IV.25; *LBh.* II.16). Later scholars changed this formula into:

R sine (declination) = R sine (longitude) × R sine 24° ÷ R (*TS.*II.17-19).

Varāhamihira (*PS.*IV.17-18) says: "The intervals of declinations in minutes for interval of quarter-signs are, in *Sāyana Meṣa*: 183, 180, 175, 166; in *Sāyana Vṛṣabha* 156, 144, 128,104, and *Sāyana Mithuna*: 90, 63, 40, 11. These are to be added successively to get the declinations from *Meṣa* (Aries) to *Mithuna* (Gemini). Then from *Karkaṭa* (Cancer) to *Kanyā* (Virgo), these should be deducted in the reverse order, until at the end of *Kanyā*, the declination is zero. These declinations from *Meṣa* to the end of *Kanyā* are north. Then from *Tulā* (Libra) up to the end of *Dhanus* (Sagittarius), the southern declinations increase in the given order, and from *Makara* (Capricorn) to *Mīna* (Pisces) the southern declinations decrease in the reverse order, until at the end of *Mīna* the declination is zero once again."

The declination deviations of the sun from the ecliptic in minutes are given for every quarter sign, i.e. at an interval of 7 1/2 degrees of longitude. Hence the declinations are:

First *rāśi*					
(interval of 7 1/2 degrees):	183',	363',	538',	704',	(11°44'),
Second *rāśi* (") :	860',	1004',	1132',	1236',	(20°36'),
Third *rāśi* (") :	1326',	1389',	1429',	1440',	(24°).

The rule says that the declination will start from the equinox and will increase in the first quarter, decrease in the second quarter of the year, again increase, then decrease following the same order. This may be seen in Fig. 7. For the moon, the above method gives the mean declination. Its true declination is the mean declination plus (or minus) latitude, according as it is in the same or different direction.

Fig. 7.

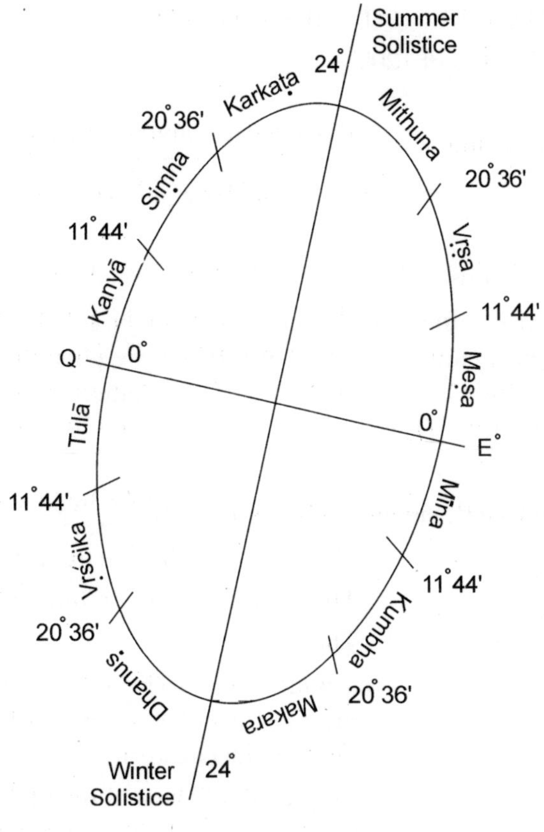

6. Terrestrial Latitude

No formal definition of latitude (*akṣa*) is available, but it is clear from the earlier texts that the distance of a place from the equator towards the pole was considered as latitude and measured by *jyā* lengths in *aṅgulas* or arcs in degrees. This was determined from the measurement of zenith distance of the sun at midday or by the altitude of the Pole. Since the altitude and the zenith distance are complementary to each other, zenith distance was also calculated from the altitude and vice versa. The shadows cast by a gnomon (*śanku*) of 12 *aṅgulas* on a circle of radius 120' at midday on different occasions were used for determining the terrestrial latitudes of different places (*PS*, IV.20-21). There were several other methods as shown below:

6.1 In Fig. 4, let E be the position of the midday sun on an equinoctial day. Let OR be the gnomon of 12 *aṅgulas*, RT the midday shadow and OM the corresponding hypotenuse. Then EF = R sine (latitude), since PN = EZ.

From similar triangles EFO and ORT,

$$EF = OE \times RT \div OT = R \times RT \div OT,$$

or, for a radius of 120',

$$\text{R sine (latitude)} = \frac{120' \times \text{midday equinoctial shadow}}{\sqrt{12^2 + (\text{midday equinoctial shadow})^2}}$$

The arc of this is the latitude. This rule is valid for all places.

6.2 On any other day, let the midday sun be at the point G (Fig. 4). Then GD = R sine (zenith distance). Let OR' be the gnomon of 12 *aṅgulas*, R'T' the shadow, and OT' the hypotenuse. Then from the similar triangles GDO and O R' T', we get GD =R × R' T' ÷ OT', or in other words

$$\text{R sine (zenith distance of the sun)} = \frac{120' \text{ x midday shadow}}{\sqrt{12^2 + (\text{midday shadow})^2}}$$

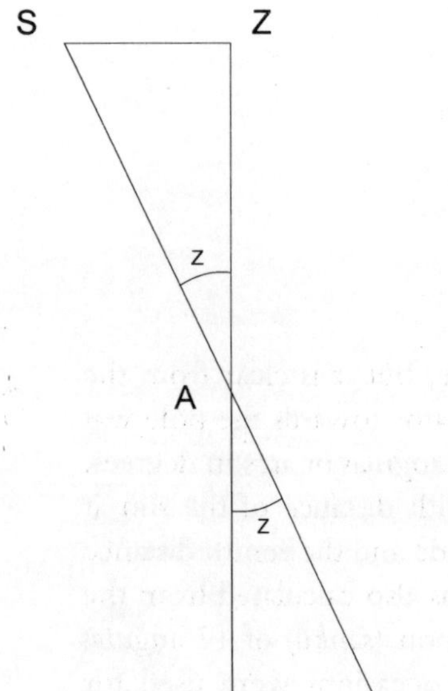

Fig. 8.

The arc of this, is the zenith distance z.

Then,

latitude = z + declination (if the declination is north of the equator), or = z - declination (if the declination is south of the equator).

The zenith distance of the midday sun was possibly determined by the following method (Fig. 8). If OA be the gnomon of 12 *aṅgulas* pointing to Z as zenith, OB the midday shadow, BA the hypotenuse pointing to S as the direction of the sun, then angle SAZ = zenith distance = angle OAB, and R sine angle OAB = R × OB÷BA = $120' \times \text{midday shadow} \div \sqrt{(\text{midday shadow})^2 + (12)^2}$

When the shadow is known, zenith distance can be determined. When the zenith distance and the declination are known, the latitude and the altitude can be determined. Varāhamihira also gives a method for finding the declination of the sun.

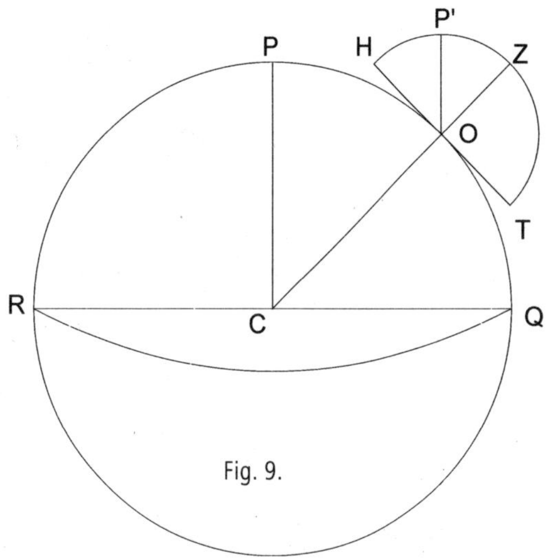

Fig. 9.

6.3 Latitude from the Altitude of the Pole.

In Fig. 9, let O = observer, QOR = observer's meridian cutting the equator at Q and R, Arc QO = latitude of the place, HT = observer's horizon, OP' the direction of the pole, and Z the observer's zenith direction. Then

Altitude of the pole = HP' = 90° – P'Z = 90° – PO = OQ = latitude of the place of the observer.

This fact was known from early times since latitude and co-latitude have also been made proportional to zenith distance and altitude, as shown under sections 4.1- 4.4.

6.4 Example 1. To find the latitude of the place, if the equinoctial shadow length is 5 *aṅgulas*, gnomon 12 *aṅgulas* and R = 120'.

By the rule given in section 6.1,

$$\text{R sine (latitude)} = \frac{5 \times 120'}{\sqrt{12^2 + 5^2}} = \frac{600}{13} = 46'9''$$

Now, to find the arc of R sine 46' 9"

From Table I, for R sine 53' 5" – arc is 26° 15'

for R sine 45' 5" – arc is 22° 30'——**a**

for difference 7' 9" – arc is 3°45'

For difference (46' 9" – 45' 56") or 13", the arc is 7' (by the Rule of Three)—**b**

Adding **a** and **b**, we get arc of 46' 9" = 22° 30' + 7' = 22° 37'.

Hence the latitude of the place is 22°37'. It may be noted that the shadow lengths were given in terms of *aṅgula*, *prati-aṅgula* (or *vyāṅgula*), and *prati-pratyaṅgula* in sexagesimal system.

7. Terrestrial Longitudes

The distance of a place from the prime meridian measured along the *sphuṭa-paridhi* through the place in *yojanas* is called the longitude (*deśāntara*) of the place. *Sphuṭa-paridhi* is a small circle running parallel to the equator. The prime meridian passes through Lanka, Ujjain, Rohitaka and Meru. The list of place names situated on the prime meridian differs from text to text. The following is the method for finding out the longitude as given in *SS*, I.60 and *MBh*, II.3-4.

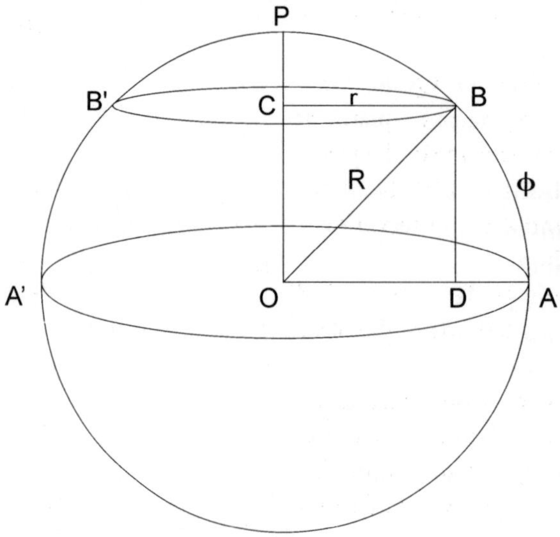

Fig. 10.

In Fig. 10, let P be the pole, AA' the terrestrial equator and BB' the *sphuṭa-paridhi* drawn parallel to the equator through a place B having latitude AB. Let OA and CB be the radii of the equator and *sphuṭa-paridhi*, and BD the perpendicular to OA. Then from the proportion,

circumference of the equator ÷ R = *sphuṭa-paridhi* ÷ R cosine AB, we get

sphuṭa-paridhi = R cosine AB x circumference of the equator ÷ R= R cosine (latitude) x circumference of the equator ÷ R.

And, BC = longitude of B = OD = R cosine AB = R cosine (latitude).

The circumference of the terrestrial equator was taken as 3299 *yojanas* by Bhāskara I and 3300 *yojanas* by Bhāskara II and others.[4]

The *Sūryasiddhānta* (I.63-65) also suggests a method for finding the longitude from the time difference in *nāḍīs* (*nāḍīkās* or *ghaṭikās* or *ghaṭīs*) of lunar eclipse between the meridian of Ujjain and the local meridian. For this purpose, the time of the total lunar eclipse or of the emergence of the moon was usually taken, because these can be observed more distinctly than the first contact. The time at Ujjain was obtained by computation. If the place is to the east of Ujjain, local time will exceed the computed time, otherwise the place will be to the west of Ujjain. Time was measured by a water clock and a sidereal day was noted as 60 *nāḍīkās* (*VJ* 37; *SS*, I.63-65; *MBh*, II.8-10). The longitude would then be calculated from the following proportion:

circumference of the equator ÷ 60 *nāḍīs* = longitude ÷ time difference,

longitude in *yojanas* = time difference × circumference of the equator ÷ 60.

8. Instruments in Use

A large number of instruments are described by earlier writers. Āryabhaṭa I (b. AD 476) describes nine, Varāhamihira (AD 505) thirteen, Brahmagupta (b. AD 598) seventeen, Lalla (9th century) twelve, Śrīpati (11th century) sixteen, Bhāskara II (b. AD 1114) ten, and so on (Ohashi, 1994, 158-671). Some selected instruments are described below.

8.1 Gnomon *(Śaṅku-yantra)*: In sections 4.1-4.4, the gnomon was vertical and the shadow was at the base on a horizontal circular plane. The types of gnomon and its shadows in the forenoon and afternoon and also the corrections due to the declination are given by all the Siddhāntas (*SS*.III.1-4; *PS*.XIV.14-16; *SŚe*.IV.2-3). The gnomon played a very important role in Indian tradition for measurement of time, determination of solstices, equinoxes and of terrestrial latitude. From the height of the gnomon and the length of the shadow, one can calculate the meridian zenith distance of the sun. This zenith distance at the time of equinoxes equals the latitude of the place of observation. In the Indian tradition the gnomon has a standard height of 12 *aṅgulas*. Each *aṅgula* was further sub-divided into 60 *pratyaṅgulas*. Al-Bīrunī reports that in the Arabic tradition the gnomon was divided into 7 divisions. Each unit was called foot which was further sub-divided into 60 parts. There were other types of L-shaped or triangular vertical gnomons used in India by other astronomers including Jai Singh which are not discussed here.

Apart from the vertical gnomons, horizontal gnomons were also used in India. In the case of the former, the shadow is measured on a horizontal plane, whereas in the case of the horizontal gnomon, the shadow is measured on a vertical plane. In Fig. 11, let OA be the gnomon. The shadow AB falls on a vertical

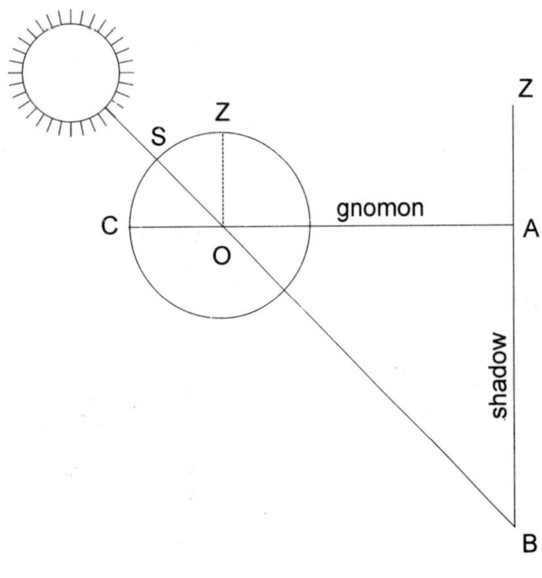

Fig. 11.

column ZB. This column is graduated in *ghaṭikās* for time as well as in *angulas* for noting arcual measure. OB is the hypotenuse which points to the sun, OZ the zenith direction at O on COA. The arc CS represents the altitude and the arc SZ the zenith distance.

Then CS : SZ = shadow : gnomon,

or R sine (altitude) : R sine (zenith distance) = shadow : gnomon.

The *Vṛddha-Vaśiṣṭha-Siddhānta* (III.61-62) describes this horizontal gnomon.[5]

8.2 Double Quadrant (*Dhanur-yantra*) and Quadrant (*Turya-golaka-yantra*):

Both Āryabhaṭa I and Brahmagupta have described these instruments. The *Dhanur-yantra* is semi-circular while the *Turya-golaka-yantra* is a quarter circle. Their function is almost the same. In Fig. 12, let ADB be the

Fig. 12.

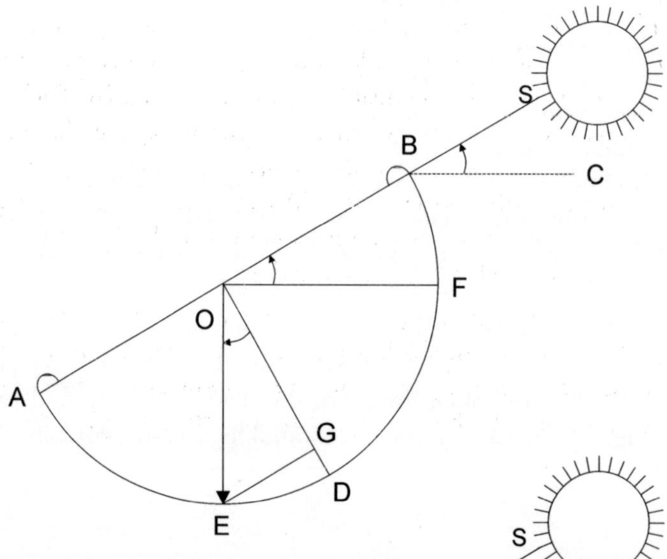

Fig. 13.

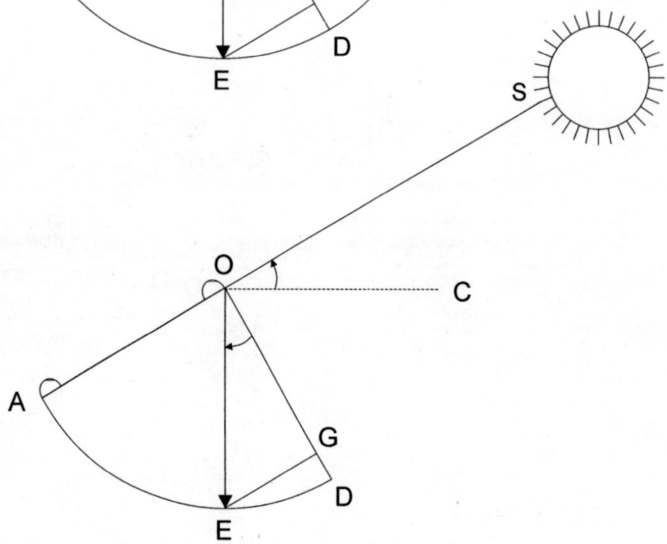

semi-circular instrument with sighting vents at A and B. O is the centre and OD the radius. The circumference AD is graduated with degrees and also with *ghaṭikās*. When the chord AB is directed towards the sun S (or the pole), the arc DE (between OD and the plumb line OE) gives the altitude. This is obvious since angle SBC = angle BOF = 90° – angle DOF = angle DOE.

The *Turya-golaka-yantra* (Fig. 13) has been described by Brahmagupta (*BSS*.XXII.17) and others (*VVS*.III.53-58; *SŚi*.Gola. XI.15). Here AD is the quarter circle having sighting vents at A and O. ED represents the altitude the remaining portion being the same as that of *Dhanur-yantra*.

8.3 *Yaṣṭi* and *Nalaka-yantra* (staff and tube instruments).

The staff (*yaṣṭi*) and tube (*nalaka*) instruments represented the radius of the celestial sphere and were used for determination of the position of heavenly bodies and also for terrestrial surveying. Descriptions of these instruments are available in most of the Siddhāntas (Ohashi, 1994, 216-226). *Nalaka* is a sighting tube which is usually hinged at a plane for seeing the pole and other bodies. For sighting the pole, Varāhamihira has explained (*PS*. XIII.30-33) that a (wooden) plank has to be fixed above the ground at eye-level. After due leveling, upon this plank, a sighting instrument is installed in south-north orientation. It is then so adjusted that the pole may be seen through the tube (see Fig. 14). When so sighting, the perpendicular AN from the end of the instrument to the plank will be equal to R sine of the raised angle ASN, which is the latitude of the place. The base SN is R cosine of the raised angle, where R =120'. The R sine (latitude) can easily be converted to arcual measure from Table I in section 2.1. For a circle of 360°, the radius is roughly 57° since pi is 3.1416. It is plausible that a circle of radius 120' might have been constructed for measurement of altitude.

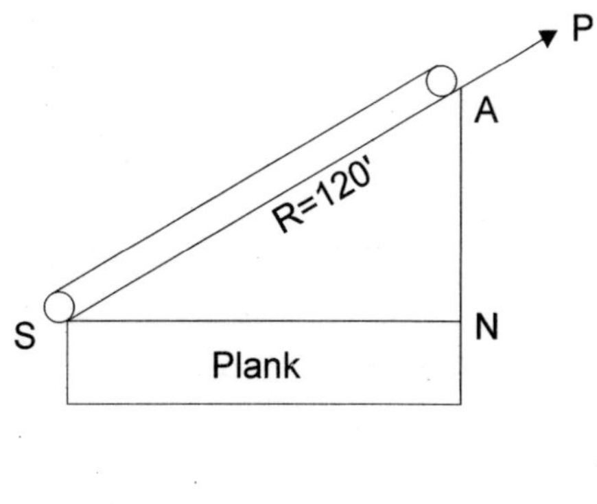

Fig. 14.

8.4 *Śakata-yaṇtra* (V-shaped staffs)

The *Śakata-yaṇtra* (cart instrument) is mentioned by Varāhamihira and Brahmagupta as a variation of *Yaṣṭi-yantra*, though the name is given by Lalla and Śrīpati. Brahmagupta describes it as follows: "A circle with a radius equal to the length of the staff should be drawn on the ground, and the circumference be graduated in degrees. The two staffs AB and AC are joined at one end, A. The other ends point towards the moon and the sun respectively. The distance between the two ends is measured by a string BC. The degrees of the angular distance which is known by the chord BC should be divided by 12. The quotient gives the number of the elapsed *tithis.*" Alternatively, one may multiply half the length of the string by the radius and divide by the length of the staff, then convert the result into degrees with the help of the sine table. This is then doubled. This is the angular distance between the moon and sun. This angular distance can also be obtained from the graduated circle by placing upon it the staffs aligned as before (see Fig. 15).

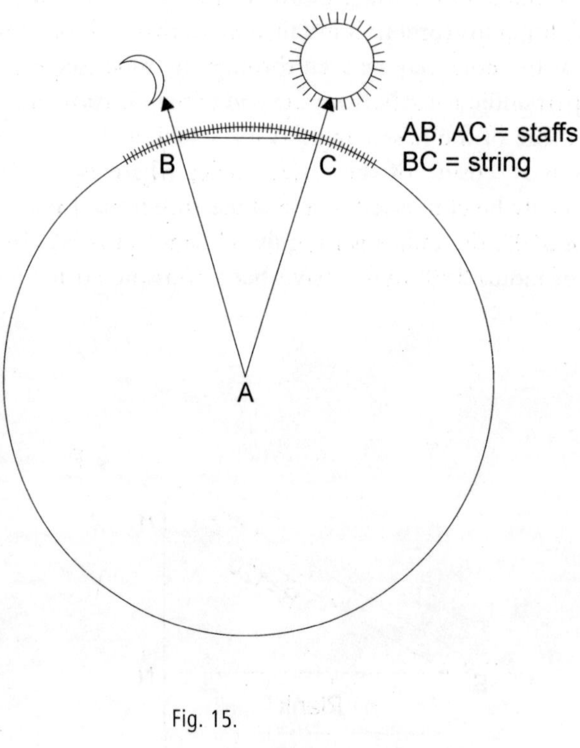

Fig. 15.

9. India and Central Asian Interaction

The Caliphs of Baghdad, al-Mansūr (AD 754-775) and al-Māmūn (AD 813-833) took great interest in the achievements of Indian scientists. Sirazhdinov quotes a legend which says that when the Indian Embassy arrived at the court of al-Manṣūr, among them there was a man who was familiar with the Indian astronomical works, *Siddhāntas*. He acquainted the Baghdad scientists with the methods of Indian astronomers. The methods were called in Arabic *Sindhind* calculus (Sirazhdinov,1990, 173-174). During this period, the *Sindhind* (the Arabic version of the *Brāhmasphuṭasiddhānta* of Brahmagupta), *Arkand* (the Arabic version of the *Khaṇḍakhādyaka* of Brahmagupta) and *Arjabar* (Arabic version of the *Āryabhaṭīya* of Āryabhaṭa) were available to Central Asian scholars through the efforts of the Caliphs (Khan,1997, 237-238). About the same time Pahlevi astronomical tables of pre-Islamic Persia were also translated into Arabic. These were named *Zīj al- Shahriyār.* Then came the translation of *Almagest* of Ptolemy. By the first half of the 9th century Ptolemy's *Geography* (*al-Jughrāᶜfīya*) had also been translated. These adaptations and translations laid the basis of the Arabic literature on astronomy, mathematics and geography. The first writer was al-Khwārizmī (died c. AD 850). Others who followed him are al-Kindī (died AD 873-874), Ḥabash al-Ḥāsib (died c. AD 864-874), al-Farghanī (flourished AD 861), Abū Mashar (died AD 886), Thābit bin Qurra (died AD 901), al-Battānī (died AD 929), al-Bīrūnī (AD 973-1048) and others (Fatimi, 1960, 86). Al-Khwārizmī's *Zīj* mentioned by al-Qiftī (the well-known Arabic historian who lived in the second half of the 13th century), belonged to the earliest *Zījes.* These were very important in medieval astronomical literature. They contain detailed astronomical and trigonometric tables. *Zījes* composed in the 8-10th centuries were influenced on the one hand by Indian works and on the other by the *Almagest* of Ptolemy. The results obtained by the astronomers of pre-Islamic Iran were also of great importance.

Al-Bīrūnī (AD 973-1048), an outstanding mathematical geographer of Central Asia, stayed in north and north-western India, mainly in the Punjab and the borders of Kashmir for nearly thirteen years, from AD 1017 to 1030. He was able to collect the values of latitudes for a few places from Sanskrit astronomical works or Arabic translations, such as Ujjain (*Arīn* in Arabic) 24° (according to Hindu canon), 22° 29' (accord*ing to the Composition of Spheres* by Yaᶜqūb ibn Ṭāriq, based on *al-Arkand*, i.e. *Khaṇḍakhādyakā* ; Kanoj 26° 35', Taneshar 30° 12' (Balabhadra), 27° (Abū-Ahmed); Kashmir 34° 9', and the straight shadow there being 8 7/60 digits (*aṅgulas*). Bīrūnī has quoted the latitude of Ujjain as 4 3/5 from Yaᶜqūb ibn Ṭāriq's *Composition of Spheres*, which he however rejected as being too low (Sachau,1910, I. 316-317). Actually 4 3/5 *aṅgulas* is the value of the equinoctial midday shadow. This, when converted, gives a latitude of 20° 58', whereas the correct latitude of Ujjain is 23° 11'.

During Al-Bīrūnī's time there was a good deal of confusion about the identification of prime meridian line which was considered as the reference line for measuring longitude. Bīrūnī believed that the confusion had really started with the Greeks who sometimes calculated longitude from the Fortunate Islands and sometimes from the most distant point on the Atlantic coast (see also Varadarajan, 1997, 60). Al-Bīrūnī had his own preference for the meridian passing through Susul-Aqsa, the farthest point in Africa (Barainy, 1957, 173). As regards methods of determining longitude, Bīrūnī says that the Hindus express longitude differences in *yojanas*, that is in linear measure, unlike Muslim astronomers who express them by equatorial times corresponding to the distance between the two meridians. Such differences are immaterial because longitude differences can be expressed in time, degrees and distances, since equinoctial time is reckoned as the 360th part of a circle and difference in 1h = 360° ÷ 24 = 15 degrees of the circumference. Hindu astronomers also gave longitude differences in time with reference to the lunar eclipse.

10. Astrolabe, a Versatile Instrument of the Medieval Period and its Impact

By the 14th century, India had become aware of the astrolabe. A few astrolabes are available in different museums of north India.[6] Muḥammad Muqim's astrolabe (Archaeological Museum, Red Fort, Delhi, Regd. No. 40.420) contains three circular columns for place names (*al-bilād*), their latitudes (*al-'arūḍ*) and longitudes (*al-ṭūl*) so that it could be used as a gazetteer (Sen, 1990, 115-122). The back (*zahr*) contains a zodiacal calendar, altitude scales, a square for measuring shadows, sine graphs, declination graphs of the sun, and so on. The back is divided into four quadrants by vertical and horizontal diameters. The rim of each of the two upper quadrants is divided into 90 degrees for altitude measurements and both the rims of the two lower quadrants were used for shadow cotangent scales. The upper left quadrant is engraved with equally spaced parallel horizontal and vertical lines containing sine graph for calculating sines and cosines of the altitude. The upper right quadrant is engraved with stereographic projections of the sun's declination circles.

The two lower quadrants also contain two squares with a common side. The side of the right hand square is divided into 7 equal parts, each called a foot (*aqdām*) and the left hand square is divided into 12 equal parts, each called a finger (*isb*^{c}*ā*). This is perhaps a compromise between the Indian gnomon of 12 *aṅgulas*, and the Arabic gnomon of 7 feet which follows from the Greek tradition. The shadow lengths were also known in feet and fingers respectively.

From this the altitude was calculated by using the cot function[7] (Cot A = s/g, where s = shadow, g = gnomon height, and A = altitude) or sometimes in tan function. A gnomon may cast a horizontal or vertical shadow according as the gnomon is placed vertically and horizontally.

The rete or spider (*'ankabūt*), the ornamental part of the instrument, contains a star map showing stereographic projections of the ecliptic and the positions of some prominent stars. The ecliptic is divided into 12 signs. Six signs engraved below the central horizontal line from left to right are: *al-ḥamal* (Aries), *al-thụr* (Taurus), *al-jawzā* (Gemini), *al-sāraṭān* (Cancer), *al-asad* (Leo), *al-sunbulah* (Virgo). The other six, marked above the horizontal line from right to left are: *al-mīzān* (Libra), *al-aqrab* (Scorpio), *al-qaws* (Sagittarius), *al-jaddī* (Capricorn), *al-delv* (Aquarius) and *al-hut* (Pisces). The impact of this instru-ment is found in later Sanskrit texts. Latitudes of 75 cities appear in degrees and minutes in the *Yantrarāja* of Mahendra Suri (AD 1370) while latitudes (*akṣāṃśā)* and longitudes (*tūlāṃśa*) of twenty places are found in the *Siddhāntatattvaviveka* of Kamalākara (AD 1658) (*STV. Madhyamādhikāra*, vs. 174), and in some other texts.

11. Indigenous Medieval Tradition for Measuring Latitude and Longitude

Pingree (1996) has identified five tables of equinoctial midday shadow lengths from the Sanskrit collections of the Pennsylvania University, Pennsylvania, Bodleian Library, Oxford and Wellcome Institute, London. The manuscripts give lists respectively of 175, 92, 75, 120, and 52 names of towns together with their equinoctial midday shadow lengths in *aṅgulas* and *vyāṅgulas.* The terrestrial latitudes in degrees and minutes are not supplied in the tables. Pingree has supplied them in parentheses. However, the latitude can be calculated easily with the help of the rules explained in Sections 2.1 and 6.1. Pingree believes that these manuscripts belong to the seventeenth, eighteenth or nineteenth century and that these lists are all compilations from earlier sources. As regards the purpose he says, "These coordinates were used for calculating the local time, for prepa-ration of local *pañcāṅgas* and for computing planetary longitudes or the times and magnitudes of eclipses for the locality."

A select list of shadow lengths for a gnomon of 12 *aṅgulas* is given below. Column 3 (correct shadow) and column 4 (latitude in degrees and minutes) were absent in the original but were added by Pingree.

Table II

Place names with midday shadow lengths for measuring terrestrial latitude

Place Name	Shadow	Correct Shadow	Latitude
	(*ang.; vyāṅ.*)	(*ang.; vyāṅ.*)	(*deg.; min.*)
1. Gopa (Goa)	3; 0	3; 20	(14; 0)
2. Bījapura	3; 30	3; 38	(16; 16)
3. Golakunda	3; 45	3; 46	(17; 21)
4. Col (Chaul)	4; 0	4; 02	(18; 26)
5. Nāsika	4; 24	4; 22	(20; 08)
6. Gangāsāgara (Sagar Island)	4; 56	4; 48	(22; 21)
7. Ujjaina (Ujjain)	5; 0	5; 09	(22; 37)
8. Yodhapura (Jodhpur)	5; 28	5; 56	(24; 30)
9. Ajmera	5; 52	5; 59	(26; 04)
10. Dillī (Delhi)	6; 0	6; 34	(26; 34)
11. Kanaujja (Kanauj)	6; 10	6; 08	(27; 10)
12. Sonapatha (Sonepat)	6; 40	6; 39	(29; 04)
13. Jalaṃdhara (Jullundur)	7; 0	7; 18	(30; 15)
14. Lahora (Lahore)	7; 30	7; 22	(32; 0)

12. Navigational Tradition

The *Rahmani* of Kunhikunhi Malmi is a navigational manual. It contains data like compass distances between various ports of Lakshadweep and Calicut (the mainland Indian port) and their angular distances in degrees, declination tables of the sun at the end of each day and solar months for four consecutive years, latitudes of ports in finger measurements and longitudes in *chaamams* and also in degrees, a list of altitudes of the Pole Star for more than 77 places in fingers and their relative distances in *chaamams* (1 *chaamam* = 12 miles), declination deviation of the sun from the equator, names of the solar months in Malayalam and Arabic, names of the *nakṣatras* in Malayalam, noon and shadow measurements besides various other topics. There is also a tradition of the use of instruments like the Quadrant, *Kolpalagai* and *Rapalagai* (*Kamāl*) for altitude measurements. Lakshadweep is a melting point of several cultures. There have been close links with the traditions of the mainland through the ports of Malabar. Some of the parallels will be noted.

12.1 In the Sanskrit astronomical tradition, Ursa Major (*sapta-ṛṣis*) is used for the identification of the Pole Star. Kunhikunhi Malmi, the compiler of *Rahmani*, demonstrated personally to the author of this appendix how the Pole Star is located with the help of Ursa Major. He also stressed the importance of the Pole Star as the main guiding star for sailors.

12.2 The twenty-seven *nakṣatra* names of the Islands (Sections 16-17) are derived from Sanskrit through Malayalam.

12.3 The twelve *rāśi* names (Section 24) are also derived from Sanskrit through Malayalam. The Malayalam names appear in Kollam 252 (AD 1076-77). The relationship between *rāśi* and *nakṣatra* (Section 30) is the same in the Indian tradition. Besides these, the *Rahmani* also contains Arabic names of the zodiac signs for solar months (Section 38). The declination deviation of the sun at the first point of each *rāśi* being 11 1/2, 20, $23^1/2$ in degrees (Section 13) follows the Indo-Arabic tradition, though the values are not in complete agreement (cf. # 5 and # 10 above).

12.4 Names of units of time like *naazhika* and *vinaazhika*, and their relationship with *rāśi,* day, month and year (Section 33) are derived from the Sanskrit astronomical tradition. The time unit *chaamam*, which equals 7 1/2 *naazhikas* (= 3 hours), is derived from Sanskrit *yāma*, through Prakrit *jāma*, which carries the same sense.

12.5 The altitude of the Pole was recognized in Indian tradition as equivalent to the latitude of the place of the observer. The latitude table of Lakshadweep (Section 6) gives the latitudes of major ports of the west coast and of Lakshadweep Islands in *viral* or finger measurements. The distances in *chaamams* between two ports on the same parallel (Section 6) imply longitudinal measurement. This method of measuring longitude in terms of distance is analogous to that described in # 7 above. In the *Rahmani*, Section 6 follows the traditional mode of expressing latitudes and longitudes, whereas Section 4 appears to be derived from European sources. The following table is based on both the sections. It may be noted that in the last column the longitudes are relative, that is to say, these are distances between two places situated on the same parallel. For example, the first row shows that Kumari and Kelathala Dveepa are both situated on the same parallel but are 20 *chaamams* apart from one another. However, the significant feature is that there is a continuity in tradition of expressing the latitude in *viral* and the longitude in *chaamam.*

Table III

Place Names with the altitude of the Pole in Fingers and Longitude in degrees and *Chaamams* and also in degrees

Place Name	Altitude of pole in *Viral*	Latitude in Degrees	Longitude in Degrees	Relative Longitude in *Chaamam*
Kumari	1 1/2	8° 5'	77° 32'	
Kelathala Dweepa	1 1/2	8° 5'		24
Kodungallur	3	10° 8'	76° 18'	
Kalpeni Island	3	10° 7'	73° 35'	12
Suhelipar (north tip)	3	10° 6'	72° 15'	8
Ponnani	3 1/4	10° 48'	75° 53'	
Kavaratti	3 1/4	10° 32'	72° 57'	17
Chaliyam Mulla	3 1/2	11° 0'	75° 45'	
Andrott	3 1/2	10° 47'	73° 33'	10
Kavaratti Pitti	3 1/2	10° 45'	73° 31'	8
Agatti	3 1/2	10° 51'	72° 11'	2
Nayaka Madam	4			
Kiltan Island	4	11° 28'	72° 58'	12
Bitrapar	4	11° 35'	72° 09'	6
Ezhimala	4 1/8	11° 15'	73° 57'	
Chetlat	4 1/8	11° 42'	72° 42'	14
Cheriyapanniyam Par	4 1/8	12° 23'	72° 05'	6

The altitude of the Pole is given here in finger measurement. This method is based on similar triangles to those of the Indian noon-shadow measurement with a gnomon of 12 *aṅgulas*. However, the methodology of measurement in the two cases is different. In the former, the altitude of the Pole was directly measured by an instrument, whereas in the latter, the latitude was calculated by applying a rule on the basis of noon-shadow lengths. In the noon-shadow measurement the gnomon as well as the noon-shadow were in fingers, but the net result was expressed in a ratio, a pure number, when the question of altitude was concerned. The method of direct measurement of the Pole was also attempted by Varāhamihira (cf. # 8.3 above).

It has been suggested that the instrument used in Lakshadweep for measuring the altitude directly was the *Kamāl* (cf. #12.6 below). There is no doubt that the measuring of latitude and longitude was done by specialised groups. The ordinary sailors in Lakshadweep, as locally reported, commited to memory the values of latitude in *viral* (finger) and longitude in *chaamams* to identify their positions at sea.

12.6 Instruments in Lakshadweep

Four instruments are found in Lakshadweep. These are the Quadrant, Hourglass, *Kolpalagai* and *Rapalagai* (*Kamāl*). Of these, the Quadrant and the Hourglass are known elsewhere also. These are used both in the daytime and at night. The *Kolpalagai* and the *Rapalagai*, on the other hand, are of Indian Ocean origin. The former is used in the daytime while the latter is employed at night and they thus form a complementary pair. The *Rapalagai* is the same as the *Kamāl* of Arabic texts (Cf. Fatimi, 1996, 283). It is reported by E.P. Attakoya Thangal that the astrolabe and a few other instruments were also known though no sample has been brought to the notice of the author of this appendix.

Quadrant

The wooden quadrant found in Lakshadweep (Fig. 16) was used for finding the altitude of the sun. It has one cut out slit instead of two raised sighting vents found in Indian traditional quadrant (Fig. 13). It contains parallel lines as found in the astrolabe with graduation in degrees at the rim. It has also a plumb line to measure the altitude similar to Indian quadrant.

Fig. 16.

Kolpalagai

This is an improved version of the gnomon. This wooden instrument consists of two long straight bars and two quadrants of different radii but with a common centre. Both the quadrants are graduated in degrees. The larger one has also markings for hours. There are three wooden plugs. One plug is permanently fixed at B. The other two plugs A, and C, can be moved respectively along the smaller and the larger quadrants as required. Plug B has a horizontal slit and plug C has a round hole in the middle Fig. 17a.

The instrument is so held that the shadow of plug A falls on the slit in plug B. Then the observer moves the plug C so that it is in alignment with plug B. This produces two similar triangles ADB and BFC. Arc GA is the altitude of the sun which is the equivalent of arc HC. On the larger quadrant, the arc HC can be measured in degrees and the time elapsed since sunrise in hours.

Two specimens of this instrument have been examined. The first, presently in the Central Library at Kavaratti, is originally from Bitra Island. The second one is in Kiltan Island.

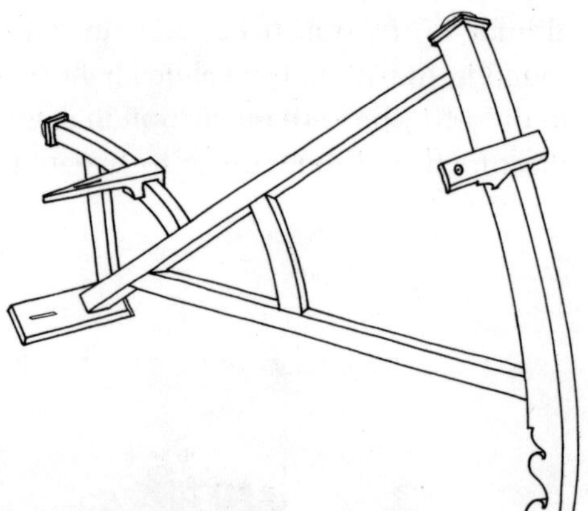

Fig. 17 a.

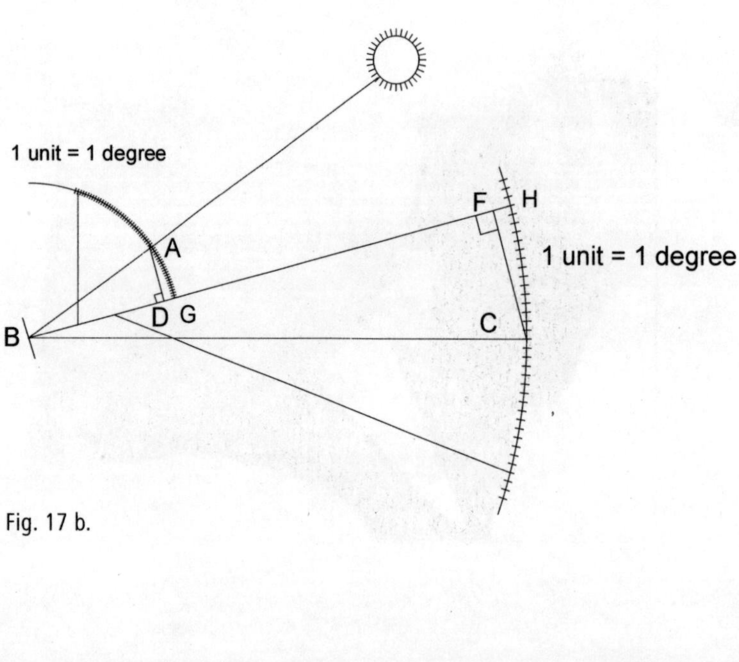

Fig. 17 b.

Rapalagai (Kamāl)

It is a simple rectangular board with a cord fixed at the centre, having knots at irregular intervals (Fig. 18a.). One of the knots is held by the teeth and the board is held with the extended hand in such a way that the Pole Star is seen just above the board and the lower edge of the board is aligned with the horizon. In this position, the altitude would be measured from the knots while the knot in the teeth represents a particular port or island. This instrument was not known to the west prior to the voyage of Vasco da Gama. Arabic texts, however, refer to this instrument (Fatimi, 1996, 288). There are several references to *Kamāl* in Portuguese literature (cf. Pereira de Silva, 1946, 34-35). In Lakshadweep, its use has continued into the early decades of the 20th century.[8]

As to the construction of the *Kamāl*, the description by James Prinsep (1836, 784-794), who had verified a few cases, will be of interest. To obtain the altitude of a star, the board was held close to the eye of the observer with the central cord stretched between the teeth or closer to the nose or eye, and so fixed that the star could be seen at its upper edge and the horizon at its lower edge. Obviously the altitude depends on the size of the board and its distance from the teeth.

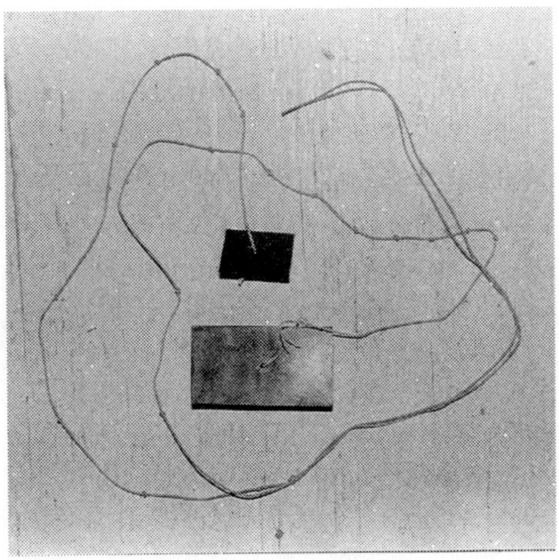

Fig. 18 a. *Rapalagai*

In fig.18b, let CD (= a) be the side of the board and OB (= b) the length of the cord, (b = 5 a), then possibly the knots were fixed at 6 b ÷[12 – (n–1)], the knot n (= 1, 2,......12) being at a distance from the point of attachment of the string to the board. The markings may be understood from the following:

Let O be the observer, OC the direction of the star and OD the direction of the horizon. OC and OD makes an angle A with the string OB. Then cot A = OB ÷ CB (where CB is the half board), but angle 2A is required which is the angle of altitude. Since the board is of fixed height, and the distances of the knots identifying the ports vary, the reconstructed fig.18 c may be seen where the half of the total angle 2A is readjusted to get the point S, then cot A = SB ÷ CB. If the angle is different, it will be S'B ÷ CB. The same figure may be rearranged as fig. 18 d, keeping the distance fixed with varying heights, though this is beyond the scope of this appendix. Now the successive knots and the corresponding altitudes may be calculated as follows:

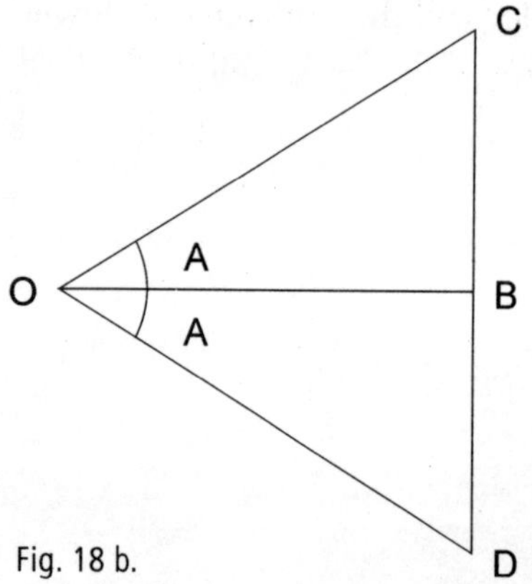

Fig. 18 b.

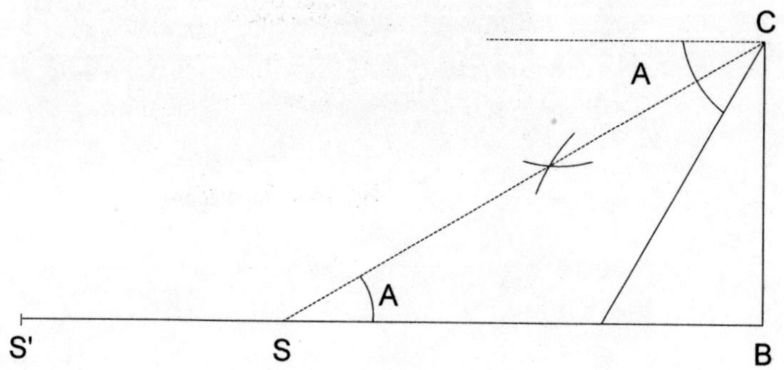

Fig. 18 c.

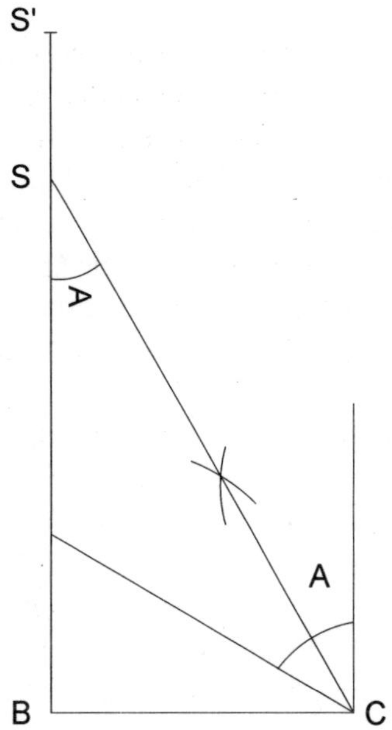

Fig. 18 d.

1. 1st knot (n=1), SB = 6 b ÷ 12 = 5 a ÷ 2, CB = a ÷ 2, cot A = SB ÷CB = 5 = cot 11° 9', altitude A_1 = 2A =22° 18'
2. 2nd knot (n=2), SB = 6 b ÷ 11 =30 a ÷ 11, CB = a ÷ 2, cot A =SB ÷ CB = cot 10° 23', altitude A_2 = 2A = 20° 46'
3. 3rd knot (n=3), SB = 6 b ÷ 10 = 3 a, CB = a ÷ 2, cot A = SB ÷ CB = cot 9° 27', altitude A_3 = 2A = 18° 54'
4. 4th knot (n=4), SB = 6 b ÷ 9 =10 a ÷ 3, CB = a ÷ 2, cot A = SB CB = cot 8° 32', altitude A_4= 2A = 17° 4'
5. 5th knot (n=5), SB = 6 b ÷ 8 = 15 a ÷ 4, CB = a ÷ 2, cot A = cot 7° 36', altitude A_5 = 15° 12'
6. 6th knot (n=6), SB = 6 b ÷ 7 = 30 a ÷ 7, CB = a ÷ 2, cot A = cot 6° 39', altitude A_6 =13° 18'
7. 7th knot (n=7), SB = 6 b ÷ 6 = 5 a , CB = a ÷ 2, cot A = cot 5° 42', altitude = A_7 = 11° 24'
8. 8th knot (n=8), SB = 6 b ÷ 5 = 6 a , CB = a ÷ 2, cot A =cot 4° 46', altitude = A_8 = 9° 32'
9. 9th knot (n=9), SB = 6 b ÷ 4 = 15 a ÷ 2, CB = a ÷ 2, cot A = cot 3° 48', altitude = A_9 = 7° 36' and so on. So the 9th knot in the cord determines the angle A as 3° 48', 8th knot 4° 46', 7th, 5° 42' and so on. Differences of approximately 1° in altitude may be seen as one goes from the 9th knot to a knot closer to the board.

The methodology for the use of *the Kamāl* is very simple. When a *Kamāl* has nine knots and the board is held by the extended hand with the last knot (knot 9) between the teeth and with thePole Star being focussed above the board and the horizon below, the angle A is taken as 5°. This angle varies depending on the size of the board. If the angle is greater, then hold the second last knot by the teeth, leaving the last knot hanging below. The angle will be 6° (= 5° + 1°). If the four knots are hanging from the teeth, then the angle will be 9° (= 5° + 4°) and so on. If the height of the board is known in fingers, the distances of the knots will also be known in fingers without affecting the cot A which is a ratio. To what extent the value of one finger = 100 miles in linear distance (Section 33) reflects actuality is yet to be tested. The set of values will be different if the length of cord b is taken as b = 6 a, where a is the height of the board. The *Kamāl* could be held steadily and was considered more consistent than the finger measurements. It is meaningful if the position of the viewer changes horizontally. According to Varadarajan (1998b, 691), the progressive refinement of *Kamāl* as a tool may be seen in *Balestilha* or *Balistī*, another novel instrument of the Indian Ocean area for measurement of altitude.

13. Concluding Remarks

The Indian navigational tradition is still largely unexplored. Apart from the *Rahmani* of Kunhikunhi Malmi, several other *Rahmanis* exist in Laksha-aweep. These need to be studied as well. In ancient India, one can find a systematic approach in developing the relationship between arc-lengths (R sine, R cosine) and its arc within a specified quarter circle, gnomon of 12 fingers and its noon-shadow lengths, and their various applications for measuring altitude, zenith distance, declination of heavenly bodies including latitude and longitude of places. From Indian sine and cosine functions and the gnomon of 12 fingers, the Arabs developed cot and tan functions. All these functions are graphically represented on the astrolabes. In India, determination of the latitude was defined in terms of both fingers and degrees, but the determination of longitude had not yet reached the same degree of accuracy. The knowledge of longitude was perfected only in the first half of the nineteenth century when the trigonometrical survey was introduced. In conclusion, we may say that the *Rahmanis* of Lakshadweep such as the present one, preserve a valuable, though little known, facet of the interface between the theoretical knowledge as available in Sanskrit astronomical writings on the one hand, and the practical application of astronomical elements in navigation on the other.

AKB

NOTES

1. *Lankā* is described in the SS.XII.37-39 as a great city (*mahāpurī*) situated on an island (*dvīpa*) to the south of India (*Bhārata-Varṣa*). The island of Ceylon which bears the name Laṅkā, is not the astronomical Lankā, as the former is about six degrees to the north of the equator. According to Lalla, the prime meridian line passes through Lankā Kumārī, Kāñcī, Kṛṣṇa (the river), Śvetaśaila (the white mountain), Ujjayinī, Gargarāta, Malavanagara, Rohitaka (Rohtak), Kuruksetra (the battle field of Bharata war), Himavān (the Himalayas), and Meru (Mbh, 47-49).

2. The dates are 21 March, 21 June, 23 September and 22 December respectively.

3. One day (civil day) = 30 *muhūrtas*; 1 *muhūrta* =2 *nāḍikās*, 366 (civil) days = 12 solar months = 6 ṛtus = 2 ayanas = 1 solar year (VJ, text11, note 1).

4. According to Āryabhaṭa I, 1 *yojana* = 8000 ṇr (height of a man with raised arms, *ABh* I. 7). Taking the length of a cubit as 1 1/2 ft, 1 *yojanā* would equal 9 miles.

5. According to Ohashi (1994, 195-196), the horizontal gnomon was also used in the Delhi Sultanate and Mughal periods.

6. National Museum, New Delhi; Archaeological Museum, Red Fort, Delhi; Salar Jung Museum, Hyderabad; Jantar Mantar Observatory, Jaipur; Khuda Bakhsh Oriental Public Library, Patna; Rampur Raza Library, Rampur, all have important collections of astrolabes and other astronomical instruments. See S.R. Sarma (1994). A number of Sanskrit works deal with the construction and use of the astrolabe, such as Mahendra Suri, *Yantrarāja* (A 1470), *Padmanābha*, *Yantrarāj-adhikāra* (15th century AD), ed. and tr. Ohashi, 1997; *Yantraprakāra* of Sawai Jai Singh (18th century AD), ed. and tr. S.R. Sarma, 1986.

7. In the 7 ft. gnomon, the shadow-lengths were 36, 30, 24, 18, 12 and 6 feet, whereas in 12 finger gnomon, the shadow-lengths were 60, 54, 48, 42, 36, 30, 24, 18, 12 and 6 fingers (*aṅgulas*). In the former the altitude varies from 11° to 49° whereas in the latter it varies from 11° to 64° (Khareghat, 1950, 9).

8. Details of two *kamāls* are published. (Pereira de Silva, 1946, 31-41). The first specimen measured 6.65 cm x 4.8 cm. It has 16 knots in the cord, which represent the height of the Pole Star at 16 ports situated between the point of Cale on the island of Ceylon, stretching along the Coromandal coast extending up to the mouth of the Ganges. The smaller side of the board gives six heights of the Pole Star (from 16° to 21°) corresponding to six ports, and the larger side gives six heights of the Pole Star (from 6° to 15°) corresponding to 10 other ports. The greater the angle, the closer will be the board. Some of the knots are further demarcated by interlacing with small cords, indicating possibly the principal ports. This specimen was formerly in the Museum fuer Kunstgewebe, Hamburg, but it is no longer there. The second specimen was described by James Prinsep (1836). Its size: 5 x 2 cm.; no. of knots = 9, height of the Pole Star from 9 ports varies from 5° to 14° approximately. Prinsep got it from a Maldivian sailor. This was used to measure polar altitudes over an area extending from the middle of the Maldives or the southern tip of Ceylon up to Calcutta.

AKB

APPENDIX II

THE SOLAR CALENDAR

In West Asia, there have been several systems of the solar calendar. The oldest was the Egyptian calendar circa BC 1200. This envisaged a year of 365 days, consisting of 12 months of 30 days each followed by 5 extra days called *Epagomenai* (12 × 30 + 5). About 520 BC the Achaemenid Emperor Darius (reigned 521-496 BC) adopted the Egyptian calendar, but added an intercalary month of 30 days in a cycle of 120 years. The next system in chronological order is the Rumi era or Syro-Macedonian era starting from 1 October, 312 BC. Ulugh Beg (born AD1394, died AD1449), however, treated it as a Christian calendar, and assigned to the various months the same number of days as in the existing Christian calendar. In AD 632, the Yazdijird calendar was introduced in Iran. The twelve months were named *Farvardīn, Ardibahisht, Khordād, Tīr, Mordān, Sharṭvār, Mehr, Ābān, Āzar, Dāi, Bahman* and *Esfand.*

In AD 1079, Sultan Jalāluddin Mālik Shah Seljuki established the *Jalālī* or *Mālikī* era with the help of [c]Umar Khayyām. The length of the year was 365.24242 days. There were probably 8 intercalary days in a cycle of 33 years. The month names are the same as in the Yazdijird calendar. The months are true solar months, in the sense that they correspond to the sun's passage through the signs of the zodiac.

However, no solar calendrical system of the Middle East seems to use names of the zodiac signs for solar months. In fact, even the current names for the lunar months, such as *Muḥarram* and others etc., are originally names of solar months in pre-Islamic times.

In various regions of India, solar months are employed in addition to the lunar months. Often the names of the solar months are similiar to those of the lunar months, e.g. *Caitra, Vaiśākha,* and so on, but in Orissa and Kerala, the names of the zodiac signs are used to designate the solar months. In Kerala, the Sanskrit names of the zodiac signs/ solar months undergo certain phonetic changes and read as follows: *Medam, Edavam* and others found in Section 39.

Again, the beginning of the year varies from region to region. In Kerala, the new year begins when the sun enters the zodiac sign, Virgo or *Kanni.* Thus the first day of the solar month, *Kanni,* is the New Year's day (cf. Saha, 1955, 164-167, 241-242; Swamikannu Pillai, 1982, 7-8, and Table II). Therefore, it is important to know on which weekday the first of *Kanni* falls (cf. Section 47).

The same system appears to have been adopted in Lakshadweep. In Section 39, the terms *Medam, Edavam* and others in serial order refer both to the zodiac signs as well as to the solar months. The corresponding Arabic terms, in Section 38, *Ḥamal, Dour* and so on are also used in the same way to denote the zodiac signs and also the solar months.

This double nomenclature, i.e. calling the solar months by the Sanskrit and Arabic names of the zodiac signs, has spread further to Madagascar as well (cf. E.J. Brill's *First Encyclopaedia of Islam,* 1913-1936, Reprint: 1987, V, s.v. Madagascar, by Gabriel Ferrand). However, neither the date nor the place of introduction of this system is known.

SRS

APPENDIX III

THE HOURGLASS

Rāmacandra Vājapeyin's *Yantraprakāśa* (AD 1428) contains a detailed and unambiguous description of the sand clock (*kācayantra*) which measures the Indian time unit of a *ghaṭī* of 24 minutes. European sand clocks, on the other hand, are made to measure the hour of 60 minutes along with its multiples or fractions. (See Fig. 2 in the Introduction above.) Therefore, if the sand clock was transmitted from Europe to India, where it was adapted to the Indian system of reckoning time in *ghaṭīs*, such a transmission ought to have taken place before AD 1429.

In Europe itself the first undisputed mention of the sand clock occurs in the English naval records of 1345/46. Its pictorial representation, in a fresco at Siena in Italy, pertains to about the same period. If Europe had been the source of the sand clock which was described by Ramachandra in 1428, the only possible route of transmission, say between 1350 and 1400, should have been through the Islamic world. However, the Islamic world did not know of the sand clock until the late sixteenth century when it was imported from Europe.

Therefore, one must conclude, at least tentatively, that the sand clock developed independently in India and in Europe. Again, Jñānarāja, in his *Siddhāntasundara* (AD 1503) mentions the water clock and sand clock together as though the two were equally popular at his time.

At the end of the sixteenth century, Europeans brought to India sand clocks that measured the hour or its fractions, and these were accepted at the Mughal court. Since then it appears that European sand clocks were used in India side by side with the indigenous ones. In 1668-72, John Marshall noticed such indigenous sand clocks at Patna "Made like our houre-glasses in England, which are exact *gurry*". Here Marshall makes a clear distinction between the English sand clock that measured the hour and the Indian device that measured the *ghaṭī* (cf. Sarma, 1992, 235-276, esp. 243-246).

SRS

APPENDIX IV

THE QUADRANT

The quadrant (Sanskrit, *tūriya-yantra*; Arabic: *rub^ca*), has been known since the time of Ptolemy in the second century AD. It is made in the form of a quarter circle. The arc is graduated in degrees from 1 to 90. One of the radial edges is equipped with two sights. An index or a plumb-line is suspended from the apex of the right angle. When the sun or a star is viewed through the sights, the index shows on the arc the angle of elevation or altitude of the heavenly body. If the arc is graduated in hours of *ghaṭīs*, one can also directly read the time elapsed since sunrise. However, because of the seasonal variation of the altitude, separate hour/*ghaṭī* scales are reqired for each season/solar month. Such a quadrant is called a horary quadrant. Quadrants produced in India, with Sanskrit legends, belong to this category (cf. Appendix I, 8.2).

A variant was developed at Baghdad in the ninth century. The radial edges were divided sexagesimally, and from these divisions, parallels were drawn to produce a grid of sines and cosines of the angles marked on the arc. This variant is called sine quadrant (Arabic *rub^ca al-mujayyab)*. With this quadrant many trigonometrical problems can be solved, apart from its utility in measuring the altitude of a heavenly body.

Fig.1. Quadrant

Fig.2. Detail of the Quadrant

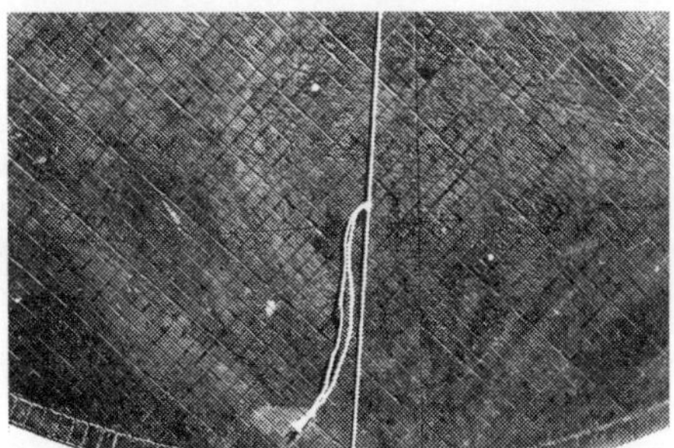

Another variant is the astrolabic quadrant. It is not quite clear when and where it was developed, but it was very popular in Ottoman Turkey, where it was made of wood. One radial edge is cut in a such way that it contains two upright struts through which fine holes are bored. These two struts function as the sights.The quadrant found in Lakshadweep is made of wood and has the outer form of the Turkish quadrant. It is, however, calibrated as a sine quadrant, and is, indeed, called *rub^{c}a al-mujayyab*. From both the edges, sixty parallel lines are engraved to form a sine-cosine graph. Each fifth of the parallel lines is highlighted by carving it deeper than the others. See Fig. 1. However neither the degrees on the arc, nor the divisions of the radii are numbered. A plumbline is suspended from the centre. It is to be noted that a detailed study of the Lakshadweep quadrant is still awaited.

SRS

APPENDIX V

SECTION HEADINGS ARRANGED ACCORDING TO TOPIC

NAVIGATION

(1) (True Bearings and Distances of Ports in Nautical Miles)
(2) (Composite Circular Compass)
(2a) (Revised Table and Compass Chart)
(3) (Quadrennial *Hamal* Tables)
(4) (*Bundar Darja* / Port Location)
(5) (Star Table)
(6) Position of the *Kou*
(7) Position of Places on the Coastline
(8) Names of *Mujiras*
(9) *Kanakku* of Distances between Two Points in *Chaamams*
(10) *Kanakku* of Progression
(14) Deductions from the Noon Measurement
(35) Estimating the Longitude from the Latitude and also the *Chaamam* from the *Kou*
(40) *Naazhikas* between (the Risings of Two Successive) *Nakshatras*
(49) *Kanakku* for Finding the *Mayyam* (Centre of the World)
(54) *Nakshatras* associated with Winds
(78) Knowing the Date from the Noon Measurement
(83) Method of Framing the *Kanakku* of Places beyond South Kollam
(86) *Kanakku* for Finding out *Hamal*

ASTRONOMY

TIME MEASUREMENT

(20) *Kanakku* of Feet
(33) *Kanakku* of Time Units
(79) *Kanakku* for Knowing the *Saayath*
(80) *Kanakku* for Knowing the *Naazhika* and *Vinaazhika*

ZODIAC AND LUNAR MANSIONS

(17) Shape of the *Nakshatras*
(25) *Kanakku* of *Raasis*
(26) Position of *Raasis*
(30) Position of *Raasis* (Zodiac Signs and their Corresponding *Nakshatras*)
(40) *Naazhikas* between (the Risings of Two Successive) *Nakshatras*

PLANETARY MOTION

(11) Circular Motion of the Sun
(12) Motion of the Sun
(13) (Rate of Change of Sun's Declination)
(43) *Kanakku* of the Tilting of the Moon

CALENDRICAL ELEMENTS

(15) Names of the *Saayaths*
(16) Names of the *Nakshatras*
(18) The First *Saayaths*
(24) Names of the *Raasis*
(38) Dates in a Month (Arabic)
(39) Dates in a Month (Malayalam)

CALENDAR COMPUTATIONS

(34) Position of the Moon in the Zodiac
(36) *Nakshatras* in Conjunction with the Moon
(37) *Kanakku* for Determining the Date
(41) *Kanakku* for the Commencement of *Muharram*
(45) *Kanakku* for the Commencement of *Muharram* (Finding the Weekday Corresponding to First of *Muharram*)
(46) *Kanakku* for the Commencement of a Month
(47) (Ascertaining) which Weekday (falls on) the First of *Kanni*
(48) *Nakshatra* at the Commencement of a Month

ASTROLOGY

WEEKDAYS

(90) Other Effects of Weekdays, General Effects

SAAYATHS

(64) Good and Evil Effects of the *Saayaths*
(65) Male and Female *Saayaths*

(66) Friendship and Enmity between *Raasis* and *Saayath*
(67) Good and Evil Effects of the *Saayaths*

RAASIS
(27) Good and Evil Effects of Actions under *Raasis*
(70) Male and Female *Raasis*
(71) Good and Evil Effects of *Raasis*
(72) Light and Darkness of *Raasis*
(75) *Raasis* and Matching *Saayaths*

NAKSHATRAS
(22) *Kanakku* of *Charanaa* (Inauspicious Conjunctions between *Nakshatras* and Weekdays)
(36) *Nakshatras* in Conjunction with the Moon
(50) *Nakshatras*, Good, Bad or Neutral
(51) Malefic *Nakshatras* in a Week
(52) Favourable *Nakshatras* in a Week
(53) (Good and Bad *Nakshatras* in a Week)
(54) *Nakshatras* Associated with Winds

MONTHS & DATES
(28) Malefic Dates
(29) Malefic Weekdays in a Month
(31) Malefic (Combinations of) Dates and Weekdays
(32) Malefic Dates in a Month
(86) *Kannaku* for finding out *Hamal*
(89) Effects of Each Date in a Month

INAUSPICIOUS PERIODS IN DAYTIME & NIGHT
(19) *Kanakku* of Inauspicious Periods
(21) Inauspicious Periods at Night
(82) Inauspicious Periods in the Night
(84) *Kanakku* for *Marma*

LUNAR ECLIPSE
(44) Good and Evil Effects of the Lunar Eclipse
(57) *Nakshatras* for Sowing Seeds

HOUSE CONSTRUCTION
(56) *Kanakku* for Laying the Foundation of a House
(60) *Kanakku* for House Construction

(61) Good and Evil Effects of House Construction on DifferentWeekdays
(62) Good and Evil Effects of House Construction in Different Months
(63) Good and Evil Effects of House Construction under Different *Nakshatras*
(81) *Kanakku* for the Measurement of the House
(91) Assessment of Income and Expenditure of a House
(92) Method of Assessment of Income and Expenditure while Constructing a House

PUBERTY
(73) *Kanakku* for Puberty on Weekdays
(74) *Kanakku* for Puberty under *Raasis*

MARRIAGE
(68) *Kanakku* of Marriages in Different Months

NEW CLOTHES
(55) *Kanakku* for Wearing New Clothes (on Weekdays)
(58) *Kanakku* for Wearing New Clothes (under Different *Nakshatras*)

CHILDBIRTH
(42) *Kanakku* of Childbirth
(59) *Kanakku* for Forecasting the Destiny of a Woman at Birth

JOURNEY
(23) *Nakshatras* Forbidden for Journey

BLOODLETTING
(69) *Kanakku* for Applying the Horn

RAT-BITE
(76) Effects of Rat-bite in the Daytime

AOULIYAS
(77) Position of the *Aouliya*

SRS

ABBREVIATIONS

Note: For Sanskrit texts, if two numbers are quoted, the first denotes the chapter and the second the verse. Where there is only one number this is to be taken as the page number.

ABh	*Āryabhaṭīya of Āryabhaṭa,* ed. & tr., K.S. Shukla, New Delhi, 1976.
BrJ	*Bṛhajjātaka of Varāhamihira,* Bombay 1863.
BSS	*Brāhmasphuṭa-Siddhānta,* ed., Sudhakara Dvivedi, Benaras, 1902.
Grosset-Grange	H.M. Grosset-Grange, *La Navigation Arabe en Océan Indien au moment des Grandes Découvertes,* collection of articles published in *Jeune Marine* (Le Havre), between 1977 and 1979, compiled with hand written pagination in holdings of library of Musée de Marine, Paris.
LBh	*Laghubhāskarīya of Bhāskara I,* ed. & tr., K.S. Shukla, Lucknow, 1963.
MBh	*Mahābhāskarīya of Bhāskara I,* ed. & tr., K.S. Shukla, Lucknow, 1960.
PS	*Pañcasiddhāntikā of Varāhamihira,* ed. & tr., T.S. Kuppanna Sastry and K.V. Sarma, Madras, 1993.
SDV	*Śiṣyadhīvṛddhidatantra of Lalla with the commentary of Mallikārjuna Sūri,* ed. & tr., Bina Chatterjee, New Delhi, 1981.
SSe	*Siddhāntaśekhara of Śrīpati,* Parts I & II, Calcutta, 1936, 1947.

SSi	*Siddhāntaśiromaṇi of Bhāskara II*, ed., Bapudeva Sastri, Benares, 1866.
SS	*Sūryasiddhānta*, tr. E. Burgess, *Journal of the American Oriental Society*, 6, 141-500, 1859-60; reprint, ed., P.C. Sengupta, Calcutta, 1935.
STV	*Siddhāntatattvaviveka of Kamalākara*, ed., Sudhakara Dvivedi, Benaras, 1885.
Tamil Lexicon	*Tamil Lexicon,* II, University of Madras, 1982.
TS	*Tantrasaṃgraha of Nīlakaṇṭha Somayājī*, ed. K.V. Sarma, Hoshiyarpur, 1977.
VJ	*Vedāṅga Jyotiṣa in its Rk and Yājus Recensions,* ed., & tr. T.S. Kupanna Sastry, and K.V. Sarma, New Delhi.
VVS	*Vrddha Vaśīṣta Siddhānta* in *Jyotiṣa-Siddhānta-Saṃgraha,* ed.,Vindhyesvari Prasad Dvivedi, Benaras, 1917.
YVJ	*Yavanajātaka of Sphujidhvaja*, ed. & tr. D. Pingree, Cambridge, Mass, 1978

BIBLIOGRAPHY

Albuquerque, L. de, et al. 1969 — *Arte de Navegar de Manuel Pimentel*, Lisboa.

Albuquerque, L. de 1988 — *Instruments of Navigation*, Lisbon.

Almeida, G. de 1995 — *Roteiro do Céu,* Lisboa.

Andrewskutty, A.P. 1973 — *Language of the Laccadive Islands*, Ph.D. thesis, University of Kerala.

Bag, A.K 1979 — *Mathematics in Ancient and Medieval India*, Delhi.

Bag, A.K., et al. 1990 — *Interaction between Indian and Central Asian Science and Technology in Medieval Times*, I, New Delhi.

Barainy, S.H. 1957 — Kitāb al-Taḥdīd of Al-Bīrūnī, *Islamic Culture*, 31,165-177.

Braz, C.A. Moura 1962 — Das Marinharias Oreintal e Ocidental o Encontro, *Boletim de Sociedade da Geografia de Lisboa,* 23-79.

Chandra, Moti 1977 — *Trade and Trade Routes in Ancient India,* New Delhi.

Clos-Arceduc, M.A. 1960 — La Genèse de la Projection de Mercator, in: M. Mollat, ed., *Le Navire et l'Economice Maritime du Nord de l'Europe du Moyen-Age au XVIII*[e] *Siècle*, Paris, 143-153.

Cortesão, J. 1975 — *Obras Completas,Os Descobrimentos Portugueses*, I, Lisbon.

Fatimi, S.Q. 1960 — In Quest of Kalah, *Journal of Southeast Asian History,* 1,2, 62-101.

Fatimi, S.Q. 1996 — History of Development of the *Kamal,* in: Ray, Salles, 1996 283-292.

Ferrand, G. 1924 — L'element Persan dans Textes Nautiques Arabes des XV et XVI Siècles, *Journal Asiatique*, 193-257.

Ferrand, G. 1928 — *Introduction à l' Astronomie Nautique Arabe*, Paris.

Filliozat, J. 1968 — La Determination des Positions de Soleil en Astronomie Indienne Ancienne, *Archives Internationales d'Histoire des Sciences,* Nos 82-83, Janvier - Juillet, 89-94.

Grosset-Grange, H. and Rouaud, A. 1993 — *Glossaire Nautique Arabe Ancien et Moderne de l'Océan Indien*, Paris, 1975, reprint.

Grosset-Grange, H. 1996 — Arabic Nautical Science, in: Roshdi Rashed, 1996, 202-242.

Gundert, Hermann 1872 — *A Malayalam and English Dictionary*, 1st ed., 1992, reprint, Kottayam.

Gupta, R.C. 1977 — On Some Mathematical Rules from Āryabhaṭīya, *Indian Journal of History of Science, 1977* 12 (2), 200-206.

Hammer-Purgstall, J. von 1835, 1836 — Tr., Extracts from the Mohit, that is the Ocean, A Turkish Work on Navigation in the Indian Seas, *Journal of the Royal Asiatic Society of Bengal,* III, 545-553; V, 441-481.

Kunju, A.P. Ibrahim 1979 — The Mappilas: Their History and Culture, *Journal of Kerala Studies*, March-June.

Khan, M.S.
1977
Āryabhaṭa I and Al-Bīrūnī, *Indian Journal of History of Science*, 12 (2), 237-244.

Khareghat, M.P.
1950
Astrolabes, Bombay.

Maddison, F.
1979
Medieval Scientific Instruments and the Development of Navigational Instruments in the XVth and XVIth Centuries, *Agrupamento de Estudos de Cartografia Antiga*, XXX, Coimbra.

Maniku, Hasan Ahmed
1987
Seasons of the Maldives, *Rasain*, 7, 168-179.

Morais, Custádio de
1960
Determinação das coordenadas geográficas no Oceano Índico pelos Portugueses e Àrabes no princípio do seculo XVI, *Boletim do Centro de Estudos Geográficos*, II, 18, 3-49.

Mota, A. Teixeira da
1966
Méthodes de Navigation et Cartographie Nautique dans l'Océan Indien avant le XVIe Siècle, *Studia*, II, 49-91.

Muthukoya, N.
1986
Lakshadweep Noottandukaliloode, Androth.

Norie, J.W.
1864
A Complete Epitome of Practical Navigation Containing All Necessary Instruction for keeping Ship's Reckoning at Sea: With the most Approved Methods of Ascertaining the Latitude by Meridian, Single or Double Altitudes and the Longitude by Chronometers, or Lunar Observations; A Journal of a Voyage from London to Madeira, and Every Other Requisite to Form the Complete Navigator; the Whole Being Rendered Perfectly Easy, and Illustrated by Several Engravings to which is Added A

Correct and Extensive Set of Tables, Preceded by a Copious Explanation of Each Table, Eighteenth Edition, Navigation Warehouse and Naval Academy, No. 157 Leadenhall Street, London.

Ohashi, Y. 1994 — Astronomical Instruments in Classical Siddhantas, *Indian Journal of History of Science*, 29 (2), 155-314.

Ohashi, Y. 1997 — Early History of Astrolabe in India, *Indian Journal of History of Science*, 32 (3) 199-295.

Pereira, J.M. Malhão 1994 — Experiencias com Instrumentos de Navegaçao da Epoca dos Descobrimentos, *Mare Liberum*, 7, 165-183.

Pillai, C. Madhavan 1985 — *The NBS Malayalam English Dictionary*, 1st ed. 1976, reprint, Kottayam.

Pingree, D. 1996 — Sanskrit Geographical Tables, *Indian Journal of History of Science*, 31 (2), 173-220.

Prinsep, J. 1836 — Note on Nautical Instruments of the Arabs, *Journal of the Royal Asiatic Society of Bengal*, V, 784-794.

Prinsep, J. 1928 — Note on Nautical Instruments of the Arabs, in: Ferrand, 1928, 1-24.

Rashed, Roshdi 1996 — *Encyclopedia of the History of Arabic Science*, I, London, New York.

Ray, H.P. and Salles, J.F. 1996 — *Tradition and Archaeology, Early Maritime Contacts in the Indian Ocean*, New Delhi.

Reis, A.E. dos 1989 — O Quadrante Náutico, *VI Reunião da Náuticae Hidrografia*, Lisboa, 243-247.

Reis, A.E. dos and Machado, R. Sousa 1992 — Nautical Instruments at the time of the Discoveries, *Oceanos*, 87-93.

Robinson 1846 — *Report on the Amindivi Islands*, Revenue Department, Government of Madras.

Rosu, A. 1981 — Les Marman et les Arts Martiaux Indiens, *Journal Asiatique,* 417-451.

Sachau, E. 1910 — Tr., *Alberuni's India*, London.

Saha, M.N. 1955 — *Report of the Calendar Reform Committee*, Government of India, New Delhi.

Sarma, S.R. 1986 — Ed. and tr., *Yantraprakāśa of Sawai Jai Singh*, Supplement to *Studies in History of Science and Medicine*, 10-11.

Sarma, S.R. 1992 — Astronomical Instruments in Mughal Miniatures, *Studien zur Indologie und Iranistik*, 16-17, 235-276.

Sarma, S.R. 1994 — Indian Astronomical and Time-Measuring Instruments - A Catalogue in Preparation, *Indian Journal of History of Science*, 29 (4), 507-528.

Saussure, Leopold de 1928 a — L'origine de la Rose des Vents et l'Invention de la Boussole, in: G. Ferrand, 1928, 31-127.

Saussure, Leopold de 1928 b — Commentaire des Instructions Nautiques de Ibn Majid et Sulayman al Mahri, in: G. Ferrand, 1928, 129-175.

Sen, S.N. 1990 — The Astrolabe - A Case of Transmission of Technique of Astronomical Instrument in Medieval India, in: A.K. Bag et al, 1990, 111-131.

Sengupta, P.C. 1934 — *The Khaṇḍakhādyaka: An Astronomical Teatiseof Brahmagupta*, Calcutta.

Sewell, R. and Dikshit, S.B. 1995 — *The Indian Calendar*, 1897, reprint, Delhi.

Sidebotham, S.E. 1986 — *Roman Economic Policy in the Erythra Thalassa (30 BC-217 AD)*, Leiden.

Speyer 1895 — Tr., *Jātakamālā*, London.

Sirazhdinov, S. Kh. 1990 — Scientific Contacts with special reference to Mathematics andAstronomy of Central Asia and India during 9-15 Centuries, in: Bag, et al, 1990, 172-183.

Silva, Luciano Pereira da 1943 — *Obras Completas,* I, Lisboa A Astronomia dos Lusiadas, 199-521.

Silva, Luciano Pereira da 1946 — *Obras Completas,* III, Kamal, tábuas da Indía e tavoletas nauticos, 31-41.

Swamikannu Pillai, L.D. 1982 — *Indian Choronology, Solar, Lunar and Planetary, BC 1 to AD 1000*, New Delhi.

Taylor, E.G.R. 1971 — *The Haven Finding Art*, London.

Tibbetts, G.R. 1969 — *The Navigational Theory of the Arabs in the Fifteenth and Sixteenth Centuries,* Agrupamento de Estudos de Cartografia Antiga, XXXVI, Coimbra.

Tibbetts, G.R. 1971 — *Arab Navigation in the Indian Ocean before the Coming of the Portuguese*, London.

Tolmacheva, M. 1977 — An Analysis of the Arab Wind Rose, Paper presented at 1997 Convention of the Middle East Studies Association, NewYork, Nov. 9-12.

Turstig, H.G. 1980 — *"Jyotiṣa" das System der Indischen Astrologie*, Wiesbaden.

Varadarajan, Lotika 1980 — Traditions of Indigenous Navigation in Gujarat,*South Asia*, Indian Ocean Issue, III, 28-35.

Varadarajan, Lotika 1983 a — Indian Textiles and Early Trade Routes of the Orient, in B. Datta, et. al, eds., *Aruna Bharati, Professor A.N. Jani Felicitation Volume*, Baroda, 343-355.

Varadarajan, Lotika 1983 b — Indian Seafaring: The Precept and Reality of Kalivarjya, *The Great Circle*, 5, 1-12.

Varadarajan, Lotika 1987 — Indian Participation in the Trade of the Southern Seas, in: Satish Chandra, ed., *The Indian Ocean,* New Delhi, 90-108.

Varadarajan, Lotika 1991 — Perspectives on Maritime Activity in Gujarat, in:Aniruddha Gupta, ed., *Minorities on India's West Coast*, Delhi, 1-16.

Varadarajan, Lotika 1997 — Parallel and Meridian - Contours of the Discoveries, *Portugal Newsletter,* 4 (9), 58-64, New Delhi.

Varadarajan, Lotika 1998 — *Sewn Boats of Lakshadweep*, Panjim.

Waters, D.D. 1958 — *The Art of Navigation in England in Elizabethen and Early Stuart Times*, London.

Zarelli, P.B. 1994 — Kalarippayatt in Medieval Kerala, in M.G.S. Narayanan et al. eds. *Malabar*, Malabar Mahotsav 1993 Souvenir, Madras.

INDEX

N
North
East
South
West
1, 11, 21 Elephant
2, 12, 22 Horse
3, 13, 23 Frog
4, 14, 24 Wolf
6, 16, 26 Donkey
8, 18, 28 Horse